INVISIBLE
WEAPONS

INVISIBLE WEAPONS

*Liturgy and the Making
of Crusade Ideology*

M. Cecilia Gaposchkin

Cornell University Press

ITHACA AND LONDON

First published 2017 by Cornell University Press

Printed in the United States of America

Library of Congress Cataloging-in-Publication Data

Names: Gaposchkin, M. Cecilia (Marianne Cecilia), 1970– author.
Title: Invisible weapons : liturgy and the making of crusade ideology / M. Cecilia Gaposchkin.
Description: Ithaca : Cornell University Press, 2017. | Includes bibliographical references and index.
Identifiers: LCCN 2016031349 (print) | LCCN 2016032343 (ebook) | ISBN 9781501705151 (cloth : alk. paper) | ISBN 9781501707971 (epub/mobi) | ISBN 9781501707988 (pdf)
Subjects: LCSH: Catholic Church—Liturgy—History—Middle Ages, 600–1500. | Catholic Church—Liturgy—Texts—History and criticism. | Crusades. | War—Religious aspects—Catholic Church—History of doctrines.
Classification: LCC BX1973 .G37 2017 (print) | LCC BX1973 (ebook) | DDC 264/.0200902—dc23
LC record available at https://lccn.loc.gov/2016031349

For Mum and Dad

Contents

Illustrations and Maps

Illustrations

Maps

Acknowledgments

The debts accrued in writing this book are wholly disproportionate to its value, and I can only begin to repay them by acknowledging them here and thanking those who made them for the support that was given to me throughout. In the earliest stages William Chester Jordan, Teofilo Ruiz, and Thomas Madden wrote in support of grant applications that in turn gave me the time to write this book. These resulted in a semester as Shelby Cullom Davis fellow in the History Department at Princeton that allowed for the early stages of research and writing, and then a fellowship from the National Endowment for the Humanities that gave me a year off to finish drafting the manuscript. I thus owe these foundations and my recommenders for the extraordinary and enriching opportunities of time and environs to nourish this project. At Princeton, I owe particular thanks to William Chester Jordan, chair of the History Department, and Dan Rogers, who was at the time director of the Davis Center and who provided the warm and collegial atmosphere in which I began to sketch out my ideas for this book. I am also grateful to the Nelson A. Rockefeller Center for Public Policy and the Social Sciences and the Leslie Center for the Humanities at Dartmouth College for travel grants allowing research in European collections in 2011 and 2012, and to Dartmouth for supporting my research and permitting me leave time.

In the process of research and writing I have collected countless debts. Among scholars who read and commented on individual chapters are Amnon Linder, Iris Shagrir, Sebastián Salvadó, Christoph Maier, Norman Housley, Nicholas Paul, Jessalynn Bird, David Perry, Megan Cassidy-Welch, Alexa Sand, Carl Estabrook, Katherine Allen-Smith, Stan Metheny, and John Wickstrom. Amnon Linder, Christoph Maier, Sebastián Salvadó, Iris Shagrir, Philippe Buc, and Jessalynn Bird have all also shared with me their own unpublished research, digital reproductions of critical manuscripts, or unpublished writings. I owe a special debt to Stan Metheny, one of my greatest intellectual resources, who has for years been willing to discuss the medieval liturgy with me and has offered no end of help. At an intermediary stage, having finished a full draft, a number of colleagues and friends read and commented on the entire manuscript, including Tom Madden, whose enthusiasm for the project from the very beginning gave me the confidence to take it on, and Sebastián Salvadó, whom I came to know in the course of this project and who has been a generous interlocutor at every stage. Both read the manuscript in draft and helped me identify areas of strength and weakness. The manuscript was substantially revised after the manuscript review, sponsored by the John Sloan Dickey Center for International Understanding at Dartmouth. To those who participated in the review, including Paul Cobb, Andrea Tarnowski, Kevin Reinhart, Christopher MacEvitt, Sean Field, George Dameron, and especially Christoph Maier and Louis Hamilton, who both came from some distance to do so, I offer particular thanks. It is an act of no little intellectual generosity to spend time reading someone else's unpolished, unfinished work with a view to helping her improve it. I also thank Peter Potter, my editor at Cornell University Press, for his interest in the book and his willingness to see it through with me. To Jay Rubenstein and William Purkis I also owe great thanks for insights into a late draft. Throughout, Jay Rubenstein has generously and patiently engaged with me on large and small points of interpretation. Aurora McClain helped me finalize a penultimate draft. I am grateful to all. The remaining mistakes are of course all of my own making.

I want in particular to recognize the extent to which I have benefited from the work of several younger scholars, both graduate students and recent Ph.D.s, who were generous enough to share their important discoveries with me while their own work was still in progress. Sebastian Salvadó shared with me his own invaluable research on the ordinal tradition before it was published. Cara Aspesi, who at the time was working on her doctorate at Notre Dame, informed me of the importance of Lucca Biblioteca Arcivescovile ms. 5, which I had until then neglected. This saved me from several misinterpretations. Thomas Lecaque, recently finished from the University of Tennessee, told me of the eleventh-century Sacramentary of LePuy which had just come to light and pointed me to the digital files of the entire manuscript. This discovery came at a late stage, but the reader will find many references to it in the early chapters of the book.

Among that special category of colleagues who have grown into true and lifelong friends, and whose friendship I have repeatedly exploited as interlocutors and readers, I am particular indebted to and grateful for Sean Field,

Christopher MacEvitt, Thomas Madden, Alexa Sand, and Anne Lester. I also have the special luck to have, at Dartmouth, an extraordinary group of colleagues who are also dear friends, and who have enriched my life in endless ways as an historian and a teacher: Lisa Baldez, Robert Bonner, Leslie Butler, Jane Carroll, Phyllis Katz, Rich Kremer, Christopher MacEvitt (again), Edward Miller, Kevin Reinhart, Walter Simons, Andrea Tarnowski, Anne Sa'adah, and Barbara Will. At Dartmouth, I also thank Margo White, Bay Lauris Byrne-Sim, and Natasha Maldi for careful and competent work at various stages of research and writing, and Britney Tappen, Hilary McNamee, and Faith Sylvia, for generous and cheerful support.

Earlier versions of chapters 2 and 5 were published previously in *Speculum* (vol. 88) and the *Journal of Medieval History* (vol. 40). Ideas for chapter 4 were substantially worked out in a preliminary article published in *Mediaeval Studies* (2015).

It will doubtless be unsurprising to many readers that the single greatest debt of gratitude goes to my family. I will not even try to express what I owe to Paul, who has always been unfailing in his practical and moral support of both my professional goals and my personal happiness; to my children, Michael and Donald (Danny), who give me unbounded joy; and to my parents, Anne and Mike, without whose lifelong example of intellectual passion and true vocation I certainly would not have had the courage to become a historian. In more recent years, I am indebted to my parents for the many practical and significant ways they have cheerfully helped me as I sought to establish a place in my profession while raising young children. They have always been equally committed to and interested in both. Though paltry as recompense, I offer this book to them in heartfelt and loving thanks.

Abbreviations and Citation Conventions

General

Andrea *Sources*	Alfred J. Andrea. *Contemporary Sources for the Fourth Crusade.* The Medieval Mediterranean. vol. 29. Leiden: 2000.
Annales Ecclesiastici	Raynaldi Oderici, et al., eds. 37 vol. Barri-Ducis: 1864–1883.
BHL	*Bibliotheca Hagiographica Latina antiquæ et mediæ ætatis.* Brussels: 1898. *Novum supplementum,* 1986.
C&C	Jessalynn Bird, Edward Peters, and James M. Powell, eds. *Crusade and Christendom: Annotated Documents in Translation from Innocent III to the Fall of Acre, 1187–1291.* Philadelphia: 2013.
CCSL	*Corpus Christianorum series latina.* Turnhout: 1954–.
CCCM	*Corpus Christianorum continuatio mediaeualis.* Turnhout: 1971–.
Letters	Malcolm Barber and Keith Bate, eds. *Letters from the East: Crusaders, Pilgrims and Settlers in the 12th–13th Centuries.* Farnham, UK: 2010.
Mansi	Giovanni Domenico Mansi. *Sacrorum conciliorum nova et amplissima collectio.* 53 vols. Paris: 1901–1927.
MGH	*Monumenta Germaniae Historica.* Berlin: 1826–, including the *Scriptores* series.
PL	J.-P Migne, ed. *Patrologia cursus completes.* Series latina. Paris: 1844–1891.
RHF	Martin Bouquet, et al., eds. *Recueil des historiens des Gaules et de la France.* 24 vols. Paris: 1738–1904. Reprint, Farnborough, UK: 1967.

RHC Occ. | *Recueil des Historiens des Croisades.* Series Occidentales. 5 vols. Paris: 1841–1906.

RS | Roll Series. Otherwise known as the *Rerum Britannicarum medii aevi scriptores.* London: 1858–1965.

Liturgical

AH | Guido Maria Dreves and Clemens Blume, eds. *Analecta hymnica medii aevi.* 55 vols. Leipzig: 1886–1922. Reprint, New York: 1961.

Angoulême Scr. | Patrick Saint-Roch, ed. *Liber Sacramentorum Engolismensis: manuscrits B.N. Lat 816, Le sacramentaire gélasien d'Angoulême.* Turnhout: 1987. Cited by item number.

Autun Scr. | O. Heiming, O.S.B., ed. *Liber Sacramentorum Augustodunensis,* CCSL 49B. Turnhout: 1984. Also known as the Phillipps Sacramentary. Cited by item number.

Cantus | http://cantusdatabase.org/. Cited by item number.

Cantus Index | http://cantusindex.org/. Cited by item number. Note that numbering systems in the Cantus database and the Cantus index originate with and are consistent with Hesbert's CAO. Identifiers not found the CAO (especially for nonoffice items) are in addition to and augment the material known from Hesbert. I only cite the Cantus or Cantus ID identifying number when it is not found in the CAO. Otherwise, all CAO citations can also be identified in the Cantus and Cantus Index Databases.

CAO | René Jean Hesbert and Renatus Prévost. *Corpus Antiphonalium Officii. Rerum ecclesiasticarum documenta.* Series maior, Fontes 7–12. Rome: 1963. Cited by item number.

CBP | Edmond Eugène Moeller, ed. *Corpus benedictionum pontificalium. Édité avec une étude, un index scripturaire et liturgique et un index verborum.* Turnhout: 1971–. Cited by item number.

CO | Edmond Moeller and Joanne Maria Clément, eds. *Corpus Orationum.* 14 vols. CCSL 160. Turnhout: 1992–. Cited by item number.

Dondi | Cristina Dondi. *The Liturgy of the Canons Regular of the Holy Sepulchre of Jerusalem: A Study and Catalogue of the Manuscript Sources.* Bibliotheca Victorina XVI. Turnhout: 2004. Cited either by page number, or by the manuscript sigla (H^1–H^{18}) that are identified on page 13 and fully catalogued at pp. 146–252.

DWM | Dedicated War Mass. See entry for Linder RA.

Gelasian Scr. | Leo Cunibert Mohlberg, ed. *Liber Sacramentorum Romanae Aeclesiae Ordinis anni circuli (Cod. Vat. Reg. lat 316/Paris*

Bibl. Nat. 7193, 41/65 (Sacramentarium Gelasianum). Rerum Ecclesiasticarum Documenta, Fontes IV. Rome: 1960. Cited by Item number.

Gellone Scr. — Antoine Dumas, ed. *Liber Sacramentorum Gellonensis*. 2 vols. CCSL, 159–159A. Turnhout: 1981. Cited by item number.

Gregorian Scr. — Gregorian Sacramentary. Deshusses, Jean. *Le Sacramentaire Grégorien: ses principales formes d'après les plus anciens manuscrits*. 3 vols. Spicilegium Friburgense 16 (3rd ed.), 24 (2nd ed.), 28 (2nd ed.). Fribourg: 1988–1992. Cited by item number.

Leofric Scr. — F. E. Warren, ed. *The Leofric Missal*. Oxford: 1883. Reprint, Farnborough, UK: 1968. Cited by page number.

Leroquais *Brév.* — Victor Leroquais. *Les bréviaires manuscrits de bibliothèques publiques de France*. 5 vols. Paris: 1934.

Leroquais *Sacr.* — Victor Leroquais. *Les sacramentaires et les missels manuscrits des bibliothèques publiques de France*. 3 vols. Paris 1924.

Linder RA — Amnon Linder. *Raising Arms: Liturgy in the Struggle to Liberate Jerusalem in the Late Middle Ages*. Turnhout: 2003. When followed by "DWM," citation refers to one of the thirty-nine Dedicated War Masses that Linder edited and published in chapter 3, from pp. 195–273.

Liber Ordinum — Marius Férotin. *Le liber ordinum: en usage dans l'église wisigothique et mozarabe d'Espagne du cinquième au onzième siècle*. Monumenta Ecclesiae liturgica 5. Paris: 1904.

Missale Franc. — Leo Cunibert Mohlberg, Leo Eizenhöfer, and Petrus Siffrin, eds. *Missale Francorum*. Rerum Ecclesiarum Documenta. Series Maior, Fontes II. Rome: 1957.

M¹ — The mass for the "festivitas sancte hierusalem" represented in London BL Add. 8927. See chapter 4.

M² — The mass for the commemoration of the capture of Jerusalem represented in Rome, Biblioteca Apostolica Vaticana, Barb. Lat. Ms. 659 and Barletta, Archivio della Chiesa del Santo Sepolcro, ms. s.n. See chapter 4.

O¹ — The office for the "festivitas sancte hierusalem" represented in London BL Add. 8927. See chapter 4.

O² — The office for the 15 July commemoration of the capture of Jerusalem represented in Barletta, Archivio della Chiesa del Santo Sepolcro, ms. s.n ("In liberatione sancte civitatis ierusalem"), Rome, Biblioteca Apostolica Vaticana, Barb. Lat. Ms. 659 ("In liberatione sancti civitatis iheruslaem de manibus turchorum"), and Lucca Biblioteca Arcivescovile ms. 5. See chapter 4.

LePuy Scr. — The LePuy Sacramentary, late eleventh century. In private hands. Digital images of the entire manuscript (as of January 4, 2016)

	available at http://www.uni-regensburg.de/Fakultaeten/phil_Fak_I/Musikwissenschaft/cantus/. Cited by folio.
Missale Romanum	Robert Lippe, ed. *Missale Romanum Mediolani, 1474.* London: 1899.
Nevers Scr.	A. J. Crosnier, M. Fouché, R. de Lespinasse, and C. Morizot, eds. *Sacramentarium Ad Usum Aecclesiae Nivernensis.* Nevers: 1873.
RGP	Cyrille Vogel and Reinhard Elze, eds. *Le Pontifical romano-germanique du dixième siècle.* 2 vols. Studi e testi 226–227. Vatican City: 1963.
RP12	Michel Andrieu, ed. *Le Pontifical Romain au Moyen-Age: Tome I: Le Pontifical Romain du XIIe siècle.* Studi e testi 86. Vatican City: Biblioteca apostolica vaticana, 1938.
RP13	Michel Andrieu, ed. *Le Pontifical Romain au Moyen-Age: Tome II: Le Pontifical de la Curie Romaine au XIIIe siècle.* Studi e testi 87. Vatican City: 1940.
PWD	Michel Andrieu, ed. *Le Pontifical Romain au Moyen-Age: Tome III: Le Pontifical de Guillaume Durand.* Studi e testi 88. Vatican City: 1940.
Roda Pnt.	J. R. Barriga Planas. *El sacramentari, ritual i pontifical de Roda: cod. 16 de l'arxiu de la catedral de Lleida, c. 1000.* Barcelona: 1975. Cited by item number.
Saint Amand Scr.	C. Coebergh and Pierre de Puniet. *Liber sacramentorum Romanae ecclesiae ordine exscarpsus.* 1977. Cited by item number.
SMRL	Stephen Joseph Peter Van Dijk. *Sources of the Modern Roman liturgy: The Ordinals by Haymo of Faversham and Related Documents (1243–1307).* Studia et documenta Franciscana 1–2. Leiden: 1963.
Verona Scr.	Leo Cunibert Mohlberg, ed. Sacramentarium Veronese (Leonianum) (Cod. Bibl. Capit. Veron. LXXXV[80]). Rerum ecclesiasticarum documenta. Series maior, Fontes, 1. Rome: 1956. Cited by item number.
Vich Scr.	Alejandro Olivar, ed. *El Sacramentario de Vich.* Monumenta Hispaniae Sacra. Serie liturgica 4. Barcelona: 1953. Cited by item number.
Ripoll Scr.	Alejandro Olivar. *Sacramentarium Rivipullense.* Monumenta Hispaniae Sacra. Series litúrgica 7. Barcelona 1954. Cited by item number.

References to liturgical items within offices are indicated by service (first vespers, matins, and so forth), genre item (antiphon, responsory, and so forth), and when necessary, number. For service: V=vespers, C=compline, M=matins, L=lauds. For genre: A=antiphon, R=responsory, V=verse,

H=hymn, L=lection, and so forth. Thus VA2 stands for the second antiphon of first vespers. MR3 stands for the third matins responsory, and so forth.

Narrative Sources

AA

Albert of Aachen

Facing-page (Latin and English) edition and translation: Albert of Aachen. *Historia Ierosolimitana: History of the Journey to Jerusalem*. Translated and edited by Susan B. Edgington. Oxford: 2007.

BB

Baldric (Baudry) of Bourgeuil (of Dol)

Latin edition: *The Historia Ierosolimitana of Baldric of Bourgueil*, edited by Steven Biddlecombe. Woodbridge, UK: 2014.

Caffaro

Caffaro

Latin edition: Caffaro. *De Liberatione Civitatvm Orientis*, in *Annali genvesi di Caffaro e de' suoi continuatori*. Rome: 1890–1929, 97–124.

English translation: "The Liberation of the Cities of the East" in *Caffaro. Genoa and the Twelfth-Century Crusades*. Translated by Martin Hall and Jonathan Phillips. Farnham: 2013, 107–125.

EA *Chr.*

Ekkehard of Aura.

Latin edition: Franz Josef Schmale, ed. *Frutolfs und Ekkehards Chroniken und die anonyme Kaiserchronik*. Darmstadt: 1972, 125–162.

EA *Hierosolymita*

Ekkehard of Aura.

RHC Occ. 5:7–40.

Epistulae

Heinrich Hagenmeyer. *Epistulae et chartae ad historiam primi belli sacri spectantes. Die Kreuzzugsbriefe aus den Jahren 1088–1100: Eine Quellensammlung zur Geschichte des ersten Kreuzzuges mit Erläuterungen*. Innsbruck: 1901.

FC

Fulcher of Chartres

Latin edition: Fulcher of Chartres, ed. *Historia Hierosolymitana*. Edited by Heinrich Hagemeyer. Heidelberg, 1913.

English translation: Fulcher of Chartres. *A History of the Expedition to Jerusalem 1095–1127*. Translated by Frances Rita Ryan. Knoxville: 1969.

GF

Gesta Francorum

Facing-page (Latin and English) edition and translation: *Gesta Francorum et aliorum Hierosolimitanorum*. Edited and translated by Rosalind Hill. London: 1962.

GN   Guibert of Nogent

Latin edition: R. B. C Huygens, ed. *Dei Gesta per Francos et cinq autres texts*. CCCM 127A. Turnhout 1996.

English translation: *The Deeds of God through the Franks: A Translation of Guibert de Nogent's Gesta Dei Per Francos*. Edited by Robert Levine. Woodbridge: 1997.

HdE   *Historia de Expeditione Friderici imperatoris*

Latin edition: Anton Chroust. *Historia de expeditione Friderici imperatoris et quidam alii rerum gestarum fontes eiusdem expeditionis*. MGH SS rerum Germanicarum, NS 5. Berlin: 1928.

English translation: G. A. Loud. *The Crusade of Frederick Barbarossa: The History of the Expedition of the Emperor Frederick and Related Texts*. Farnham, UK: 2010.

HdV   *Hystoria de via et recuperatione Antiochiae atque Ierusolymarum (olim Tudebodus imitatus et continuatus)*. Edited by Edoardo d'Angelo. Florence: 2009. Sometimes referred to as the *Historia de via*.

Latin edition: *Historia peregrinorum euntium Jerusolymam*, the Montecassino Chronicle, and Tudebodus imitatus et continuatus).

Cited by chapter/sentence number provided in d'Angelo edition, along with page number.

Joinville   Jean de Joinville

French edition and modern French translation: Jean de Joinville. *Vie de Saint Louis*. Edited by Jacques Monfrin. Paris: 1995.

English translation: Joinville and Villehardouin. *Chronicles of the Crusades*. Translated by Caroline Smith. London: 2008.

Cited by paragraph numbers (§) used in both the edition and English translation.

JV   Jacques de Vitry

Latin edition: Jacques de Vitry. "Epistolae." In *Serta Mediaevalia: Textus varii saeculorum X–XIII, in Unum Collecti*. Edited by R. B. C. Huygens. CCCM 171. Turnhout: 2000.

JW   John of Würzburg

Latin edition: John of Würzburg. "Peregrinatio." In *Peregrinationes Tres: Saewulf, John of Würzburg, Theodericus*, edited by Robert Huygens. CCCM 139, 79–141. Turnhout: 1994.

MP   Matthew Paris

Latin edition: Matthew Paris, ed. *Matthæi Parisiensis, monachi Sancti Albani, Chronica majora*. Edited by Henry Richards Luard. RS 57. London: 1872.

English translation: Matthew Paris. *Matthew Paris's English History: From the Year 1235 to 1273.* 3 vols. London: 1852.

OP   Oliver of Paderborn

Latin edition: Oliver of Paderborn, ed. *Die Schriften des Kölner Domscholasters, Späteren Bischofs von Paderborn und Kardinal-Bischofs von S. Sabina Oliverus.* Edited by Hermann Hoogeweg. Bibliothek des Litterarischen Vereins in Stuttgart 202. Tübingen: 1894.

English translation: C&C 158–225.

PT   Peter Tudebode

Latin edition: *Petrus Tudebodus: Historia de Hierosolymitano Itinere.* Edited by J. H. and L. L. Hill. Paris: 1977.

English translation: Peter Tudebode. *Historia De Hierosolymitano Itinere. Memoirs of the American Philosophical Society* 5:101. Philadelphia: 1974.

PVC   Peter of Les Vaux-de-Cernay

Latin edition: Peter of les Vaux-de-Cernay. *Petri Vallium Sarnaii monachi Hystoria albigensis.* 3 vols. Edited by Pascal Guébin and Ernest Lyon. Paris: 1926–1939.

English translation: Peter of les Vaux-de-Cernay. *The History of the Albigensian Crusade.* Edited and translated by W. A. Sibly and M. D. Sibly. Woodbridge, UK: 1998.

RA   Raymond of Aguilers

Latin edition: Raymond d'Aguilers. *Le "Liber" de Raymond d'Aguilers.* Documents relatifs à l'histoire des croisades 9. Paris: 1969.

English translation: Raymond d'Aguilers. *Historia Francorum qui ceperunt Iherusalem; Translated with Introduction and Notes by John Hugh Hill and Laurita L. Hill.* Philadelphia: 1968.

RC   Ralph of Caen

Latin edition: Radulphus Cadomensis. *Tancredus* CCCM 231. Edited by E. D'Angelo. Turnhout: 2011.

English translation: Bernard S. Bachrach and David S. Bachrach, eds. *The Gesta Trancredi of Ralph of Caen: A History of the Normans on the First Crusade.* Crusade Texts in Translation 12. Aldershot: 2005.

RClari   Robert of Clari

Old French edition: Robert of Clari. *La conquête de Constantinople: édition bilingue.* Champion classiques. Série "Moyen âge" 14. Edited by Jean Dufournet. Paris: 2004.

English translation: Robert of Clari. *The Conquest of Constantinople: Translated from the Old French of Robert of Clari by Edgar Holmes McNeal.* New York: 1936.

RH *Gesta*   Roger of Hoveden (formerly attributed to Benedict of Peterborough). *Gesta*.

Latin edition: *Gesta regis Henrici Secundi Benedicti abbatis: The Chronicle of the Reigns of Henry II and Richard I.A.D. 1169–1192: Known Commonly under the Name of Benedict of Peterborough*. RS 49. Edited by William Stubbs. 2 vols. London: 1867.

RH *Chron.*   Roger of Hoveden *Chronica*

Latin edition: *Chronica magistri Rogeri de Houedene*. Edited by William Stubbs. RS 51. Vol. 4. London: 1868–1871.

English translation: *The Annals of Roger of Hoveden: Comprising the History of England and of Other Countries of Europe from A.D. 732 to A.D. 1201. Tr. from the Latin, with Notes and Illustrations, by Henry T. Riley*. 2 vols. London: 1853.

RR   Robert of Reims

Latin edition: Robert of Reims. *The Historia Iherosolimitana of Robert the Monk*. Edited by Damien Kempf and Marcus Bull Woodbridge. Woodbridge, UK: 2013.

English translation: Robert of Reims. *Robert the Monk's History of the First Crusade = Historia Iherosolimitana*. Translated by Carol Sweetenham. Crusade texts in translation 11. Aldershot, UK: 2005.

QBS   Reinhold Röhricht. *Quinti Belli Sacri Scriptores Minores*. Geneva: 1879.

Salimbene   Salimbene *Chronica*

Latin edition: Salimbene de Adam. *Chronica*. Edited by G. Scalia. Turnhout: 1965. Reissued as CCCM 125–125A (1998–1999).

English translation: Salimbene. *The Chronicle of Salimbene de Adam*. Edited by Joseph L. Baird, Giuseppe Baglivi, and John Robert Kane. Binghamton, NY: 1986.

WC   Walter the Chancellor

Latin edition: Walter the Chancellor. *Galterii Cancellarii Bella Antiochena*. Edited by Heinrich Hagenmeyer. Innsbruck: 1896.

English translation: Thomas S. Asbridge and Susan B. Edgington. *Walter the Chancellor's the Antiochene Wars*. Brookfield, VT: 1999.

WP   William of Puylaurens

Latin edition: Guilelmus de Podio-Laurentii. *Chronique = Chronica magistri Guillelmi de Podio Laurentii: text édité, traduit et annoté par Jean Duvernoy*. Edited by Jean Duvernoy. Paris: 1976.

English translation: *The Chronicle of William of Puylaurens—The Albigensian Crusade and Its Aftermath*. Translated by W. A. Sibly and M. D. Sibly. Woodbridge, UK: 2003.

WT   William of Tyre

     Latin edition: *Chronicon*. CCCM 63, 63A. 2 vols. Edited by R. B. C. Huygens. Turnhout: 1986. (Reissued in single volume in 2013, retaining page numbers of original edition.)

     English translation: William of Tyre. *A History of Deeds Done beyond the Sea*. Edited by Emily Atwater Babcock and A. C. Krey. New York: 1943.

WT Cont The Continuator of William of Tyre

     Old French edition: Margaret Ruth Morgan. *La Continuation de Guillaume de Tyr (1184–1197)*. Paris: 1982.

     English translation: Peter W. Edbury, ed. *The Conquest of Jerusalem and the Third Crusade*, Crusade Texts in Translation. Aldershot: 1998.

Note that in general I have not included the Latin text when I am quoting from a translation except when the Latin itself is required to make a point. Translations of Scripture are mostly taken from the Douay Reims version of the Bible. I have taken the liberty of adapting translations.

INVISIBLE
WEAPONS

Introduction

In early June 1098, more than two years into the First Crusade and following a brutal eight-month siege, the Franks captured the ancient and venerable city of Antioch. Two days later Kerbogha, the atabeg of Mosul, arrived with a relief army and the victors became the besieged. Already weakened by the long journey and previous fighting, the Franks were now ravaged by illness and a scarcity of food and water. Outside the city walls, daily skirmishes fueled a rising panic. As things looked increasingly desperate, two visionaries began reporting instructions revealed to them from heaven.[1] On Thursday, 10 June, Peter Bartholomew, a layman (probably) in the Provençal contingent of the army, reported that Saint Andrew had told him to go and find the relic of the Holy Lance that had pierced Christ's side at the Crucifixion. The next morning, Friday, 11 June, a priest named Stephen of Valence reported to the military leaders that Christ himself had appeared to him. Christ, Stephen reported, said that although He had thus far accompanied and aided the Christians, permitting them to win all their battles, He was dismayed at the numerous evils committed within the camp, for which "a great stench arises to heaven."[2] On Monday, 14 June, following another vision, the crusaders gathered at the Church of Saint Peter to search for the Lance. Peter Bartholomew dug it out of the ground. But other signs were ominous. A meteor flamed in the sky. Men were dying of starvation and disease. Deserters fled over the walls at night. And Kerbogha's army loomed outside.

---

1. John France, "Two Types of Visions on the First Crusade: Stephen of Valence and Peter Bartholomew," *Crusades* 5 (2006): 1–20.

2. GF 57–58; PT 99 (tr. 74–75). See also RA 73 (tr. 56).

At this point the ecclesiastical authorities called on all the Franks to supplicate God.[3] Stephen of Valence claimed that Christ himself had instructed him:

> Tell my people to turn back to me and I shall return to them. . . . Christians must undertake penance [*accipiant poenitentias*]. They shall in bare feet make processions through the churches and give alms to the poor. The priests shall chant mass and perform communion with the body and blood of Christ. Then they shall begin battle, and I shall give them the help of Saint George, Saint Theodore, Saint Demetrius, and all the pilgrims who have died on the way to Jerusalem.[4]

For three days—25, 26, and 27 June; Friday, Saturday, and Sunday—the Franks performed a series of liturgical exercises, beseeching God through ritual prayer to forgive their sins and grant them victory. "And when this was done," the men from Lucca wrote home, "each army armed itself for war."[5]

The next day, 28 June, the crusaders marched out to meet Kerbogha's forces. This was to be the decisive battle for Antioch. Bishops and priests, dressed in their white vestments, reciting psalms and hymns to God, followed in procession alongside the men of arms into the field. And the crusaders won a resounding victory. It was an extraordinary, miraculous event. Later, it was said that saints George, Theodore, and Demetrius had indeed fought alongside the crusaders.[6] "And by God's help," recorded one account, "we defeated them."[7] It was certainly to God that the crusaders attributed their success.[8] To describe the extraordinary turn of events, four of the principal leaders of the First Crusade sent a letter to the "whole world who profess the Catholic faith." The "king of the Persians" (the sultan in Baghdad), they explained, had promised another battle four months hence, for the Feast of All Saints (1 November).[9] The crusade princes thus asked that Christians in the West supplicate God with alms, masses, and prayers in the three days just prior to the planned battle: "Hence we all fervently pray to you that you fast, give alms and say masses religiously and continually. In particular, help us with many prayers and alms on the third

3. For dates, see Heinrich Hagenmeyer, *Chronologie de la Première Croisade* (1094–1100) (Paris: 1902), 149–174.

4. PT 99–100 (tr. 75).

5. *Epistulae* XVIII (p. 167).

6. PT 112 (tr. 87–88). Mercurius replaces Theodore in GF 69.

7. GF 70. See also PT 112 (tr. 88).

8. GF 70.

9. Nothing else is known about such a letter from the sultan or any other such communication. *Epistulae* XII (p. 304).

day before the Feast [of All Saints], a Friday, on which, with Christ Triumphant, we will join battle fiercely."[10] As in late June, the crusaders appealed
to the liturgy in their crusading fight. That is, they were appealing to God
through liturgical supplication to request His aid in fighting war in
His name.

From the very beginning and throughout the history of the crusades, crusaders and their supporters made recourse to liturgical prayer, masses, and
alms in their fight. In one sense, the liturgy was one of their weapons of war,
likened often to temporal arms. Liturgical rites were performed both by
crusaders on the campaign and at home in support of the crusade. During
this long period, crusaders, their supporters in the Latin West, and settlers in
the East requested prayers and entreaties on behalf of their goals and in
memory of their victories. Shortly after the capture of Jerusalem on 15
July 1099, the archbishop of Reims wrote home instructing the bishop of
Arras to organize prayers in churches throughout the diocese so that Christ
"might bring victory to King Godfrey against the enemies of Christians."[11]
A generation after the creation of the crusader states, the Patriarch and the
Prior of Jerusalem wrote West and asked the archbishop of Santiago, also
engaged in warring against Muslims, to "protect us with your prayers and
your temporal arms," promising to pray constantly for him in return.[12] In
1189, as he headed off on the Third Crusade, Frederick Barbarossa, writing
from Philippopolis before reaching Constantinople, asked his son Henry to
"persuade religious persons of our empire to pray unceasingly to God for
us."[13] Honorius III, in instituting monthly processions in order to aid the
crusaders embarked on the Fifth Crusade, wrote of how visible enemies
could be fought with "invisible weapons, that is, prayers."[14]

This book is about those invisible weapons; about the prayers and liturgical rituals that were part of the battle for the faith. It tells the story of the
greatest collective religious undertaking of the Middle Ages, putting front
and center the ways in which Latin Christians communicated their ideas
and aspirations for crusade to God through liturgy, how liturgy was deployed in crusading, and how liturgy absorbed the ideals or priorities of
crusading. The hope is that, in bringing this material together as it relates to
crusading, in trying to connect the evidence of liturgy and prayer found in
medieval liturgical books with the larger narrative of crusading, in looking

10. *Epistulae* XII (pp. 154–155) (tr. *Letters* 26).
11. *Epistulae* XX (p. 176).
12. The letter dates to about 1120 (tr. *Letters* 42).
13. HdE 43 (tr. *Letters* 89).
14. Honorius III, RHF v. 19, 639: *Adversus hostes visibiles invisibilibus armis, id est, orationibus, dimicare.*

systematically and chronologically at the rites and texts that were deployed for the success of crusading and during the crusades themselves, we can understand something important about the culture of holy war in the Middle Ages. Together, the liturgy helped construct the devotional ideology of the crusading project, endowing war with religious meaning, placing crusading ideals at the heart of Christian identity, and embedding crusading warfare squarely into the eschatological economy.

Crusading and the Liturgy

It was the liturgy that made crusading a sacramental act. Although praying for success on the battlefield was hardly unique to the crusades,[15] it was a particularly important part of the devotional and ideological side of crusading, and one that has specific and heightened contours within that history. The devotional character of the First Crusade—for all intents and purposes the first mass lay religious movement—is now well established. It was strongly influenced by the culture and prestige of Benedictine monasticism (whose basis was the *opus dei*—the singing of the liturgy), which was in turn melded with the ideals of the knightly class.[16] Historians are perhaps less certain of the religious texture and content of later crusades, particularly after the institutionalization of crusading in the thirteenth century and even more so after the increasing professionalization of soldiering in the fourteenth and fifteenth centuries.[17] Yet the continued use of and appeal to liturgical intercession throughout its history is a mark of the practice of crusade spirituality and a measure of the religious threads woven into the fabric of medieval crusading that continued through to the end of the Middle Ages. It is also central to how religious ideas and practices influenced the evolving ideology of crusade.

15. David Bachrach, *Religion and the Conduct of War, c. 300–c. 1215* (Woodbridge, UK: 2003).

16. H. E. J. Cowdrey, *The Crusades and Latin Monasticism, 11th–12th Centuries* (Aldershot, UK: 1999); Marcus Bull, *Knightly Piety and the Lay Response to the First Crusade: The Limousin and Gascony, c. 970–c. 1130* (Oxford: 1993); Bernard Hamilton, "Ideals of Holiness: Crusaders, Contemplatives, and Mendicants," *International History Review* 17 (1995): 693–712; William J. Purkis, *Crusading Spirituality in the Holy Land and Iberia, c. 1095–c. 1187* (Woodbridge, UK: 2008).

17. For the later crusades, see Kenneth M. Setton, *The Papacy and the Levant, 1204–1571*, 4 vols. (Philadelphia: 1976–1984); Harry Hazard, ed. *A History of the Crusades, vol. 3, The Fourteenth and Fifteenth Centuries* (Madison, WI: 1975); Norman Housley, *The Later Crusades, 1274–1580: From Lyons to Alcazar* (Oxford: 1992); Norman Housley, *Religious Warfare in Europe, 1400–1536* (Oxford: 2002); Norman Housley, *Crusading and the Ottoman Threat, 1453–1505* (Oxford: 2012); Norman Housley, *Documents on the Later Crusades, 1274–1580* (New York: 1996); Christopher Tyerman, *God's War: A New History of the Crusades* (Cambridge, MA: 2006), 825–922.

By "liturgy," we mean the formal and ritualized prayer of the Church, which includes the Eucharistic service (the Mass), the Divine Office (the *opus dei*), and a host of other public rites, including processions, blessings, and other formal prayers performed during the Middle Ages (mostly) in Latin.[18] The term itself derived from the Greek (*leitourgia*), denoting a public service—that is something done for the benefit of the community—and in the early Christian context came to mean those ritual actions done by the Church on behalf of its members. The term was not much used in the Middle Ages. Instead, medieval authors tended to speak of the divine offices (*de divinis officiis*) or the ecclesiastical offices (*de ecclesiasticis officiis*). But since the medieval meaning of *officium* was duty or service, the terms connoted the same sense of work or tasks done as a social good or on behalf of public benefit. The idea was that prayer had a collective goal, and thus, as it bears on the history of the crusades, liturgical rites might comprise anything from a votive procession asking God for help in a forthcoming battle (like the ones performed on 25, 26 and 27 June 1098), to a commemorative feast celebrating a victory, to a votive mass in support of the army, all directed toward a common goal understood to benefit all of *christianitas*.

Liturgy was (and is) constituted of both texts (prayers, chants, readings) and symbolic actions (processions, prostrations, benedictions) and thus had both devotional and social functions. The ritual of liturgy was mostly corporate ritual, in that it was done either by the community, or by an individual or subset of the community on behalf of the entire community. The community might be defined as the members of the monastery and its patrons, as the crusaders on campaign, as Christianitas in general, or as "the church" (the Augustinian church, that is the whole collection of saved souls, past, present, and future) as a whole. The liturgy was at once commemorative ("do this in remembrance of me"), playing a central role in constructing sacred memory and interpreting the experience of sacred history, and it was supplicatory, constituting one part of the community's ongoing conversation with God. All liturgy was (is) in either praise and thanksgiving for the glory of God, or in supplication for the redemption of mankind, although in its individual instances the liturgy took on many different forms and had a variety of specifically intended functions. In the context of crusading, liturgy was used in praise of God's glory in delivering the miracle of victory (particularly after the First Crusade) or, more usually, in supplication requesting help in battle or in attaining further victory.

---

18. Aimé Georges Martimort et al., *The Church at Prayer: An Introduction to the Liturgy*, 4 vols. (Collegeville, MN: 1985–1988), 1:7–18.

The liturgy always operated on different registers, often linking the temporal, specific, and historic to the transcendent and eschatological. It was what bridged the mundane to the sublime—even what *made* it sublime. And it always assumed that men were acting within God's larger providential plan. So a prayer for the crusades was linked to individual, and ultimately communal, salvation. A prayer for success on the battlefield was linked to God's success in His eschatological battle against the devil. The feast day commemorating the Capture of Jerusalem celebrated the victory of 1099 but also placed that event within a broad vision of Christian history rooted in a biblical narrative that spanned from Creation to the Apocalypse. The incorporation of the aims and events of crusading into liturgical practice therefore placed these secular events, bounded by time and history, within an eschatological register that afforded the theory and practice of crusading even greater sacrality and endowed these with redemptive power and providential meaning.

This book examines the logic and history of this devotional language. It explores where and how the liturgy underwrote crusade, either directly, through those rituals, or ideologically, through language and ideas; and then further how and when liturgy absorbed or reflected the ideals of crusade and responded to events in the history of the crusades. It is, in this sense, a devotional history of the crusades. It traces, through the liturgy, the set of religious ideas and beliefs that gave meaning to crusading and connected crusading to the larger blueprint of salvation and Christian eschatology. Because the liturgy encompassed the rites of communion with and expression toward the God who oversaw Providence and effected the outcome of affairs on earth, the liturgy articulated the relationship between crusade on the one hand and personal and collective salvation on the other. The rites and their texts identified for the community the spiritual and eschatological place of the crusading project. They connected ideologically the Old Testament typologies of holy war to the crusader battlefield. And they demonstrate (for us) the ways in which crusaders and their supporters connected the experience and aspirations of crusading to the religious ideas that animated it.

Throughout this history, particular attention is given to devotional ideas transmitted through the liturgy. This is straightforward, since the liturgies themselves are preserved as texts, and these texts can be the subject of chronological and thematic analysis. A secondary goal is to explore ways in which the liturgy, with respect to crusading, could be formative, that is, could participate in the fighting, thinking about, recruiting for, celebrating, or repenting after, various "crusading" enterprises or endeavors. This is trickier, because the dots are often farther apart. To do this, we must connect the concrete texts that we find prescribed in liturgical books to events described in other, usually narrative, sources. There are certainly some gaps. But taken together, we can trace the role of the liturgy, and its development and performance, in the formation of a "crusading society" in the West.

In an important sense, the liturgy was what defined the way in which the crusades were understood as part of the eschatological economy. We cannot understand the history of crusading without paying attention to how Latin Christians communicated their ideals and aspirations to the God in whose name they were fighting. In what follows I argue that (1) The liturgy provided the building blocks of militant eschatology and penitential piety, both of which were essential to the formation of crusade ideology. How the First Crusade took shape, and what in its immediate aftermath it came to mean, was, I think, irrevocably inflected by this complex of ideas set out by the liturgy. (2) Throughout this history and at particular moments of need, the allegorical bellicism of the liturgy was deallegorized—or actualized—for the purposes of warfare. (3) After the (atypical) First Crusade, it was primarily the liturgy that did the work of sacralizing and resacralizing the military effort in the specific context of each new crusade. (4) Through the liturgy, the crusades were placed at the heart of the medieval eschatological economy. (5) In the early crusades Christian liturgy gave meaning to the crusading effort; over time, it was crusading that reshaped the Christian liturgy. (6) As crusading became a core concern of the liturgy in the high and later Middle Ages, it also became increasingly central to Christian identity and aspirations. In sum, the liturgy explicitly sacralized a mode of warfare that lasted more than four centuries, embedded the aspirations of crusade into the fabric of Western culture, and in the end, was instrumental in redefining Christianity itself along a bellicose axis that shaped over a long period of time deep and protracted cultural biases in European society.

Premises and Parameters

A history of these liturgical texts and their ritualized deployment reveals the ideologies of the West that underwrote holy war and formed the context of spirituality and idealism that constituted both motivations for crusades and the lens through which crusading was given meaning. In recent decades, as part of the cultural turn in the study of the crusades and medieval history in general, important work has been done on the liturgy of crusading, although no integrated analytical narrative has yet been undertaken.[19] A number of the liturgical forms associated with crusading have

---

19. I list here only the most important. Others will be cited throughout the text. James A. Brundage, "'Cruce signari': The Rite for Taking the Cross in England," *Traditio* 22 (1966): 289–310; Kenneth Pennington, "The Rite for Taking the Cross in the Twelfth Century,"

been discussed as forms of propaganda, as a way of inculcating the laity with ecclesiastical values.[20] This is an important feature of their history. But I prefer herein to think about them somewhat differently, to think about these texts and their rituals mostly as moments of sacred communication with God about the core ideals of the Christian community. First and foremost I have wanted to take seriously and to trace over time what was said in these prayers, both as a kind of history of ideas and as a history of devotion.

With the exception of chapter 3, which looks to the well-known narrative evidence for the crusade campaigns, the sources for this project are mostly the texts found in liturgical books—sacramentaries and missals (books containing prayers of the mass, designed for priests), breviaries (books containing the texts and chant of the office), pontificals (books with materials specifically for bishops), and ordinals (instruction for the rites for the entire liturgical year for a particular community). For those for whom these terms remain unclear, a short explanatory introduction to these types of sources is given in the following chapter, titled Preliminaries. In any event, these are mostly prescriptive, not descriptive, texts, and are surely limited for this. So, for instance, we have many, many surviving texts for masses "against pagans" (*contra paganos*), or masses "for the holy land" (*pro terra sancta*). Yet in many cases, we have little specific indication of when, or why, or even whether, any given mass was actually performed. Discussion of these texts can consequently seem somewhat disembodied. Likewise, we have dozens of requests for prayers and processions to be performed for a particular crusade (see chapter 6), but very few descriptions of processions ever *having been* performed.

Traditio 30 (1974): 429–435; Lucy Pick, "*Signaculum Caritatis et Fortitudinis:* Blessing the Crusader's Cross in France," *Revue bénédictine* 105 (1995): 381–416; Christoph T. Maier, "Crisis, Liturgy and the Crusade in the Twelfth and Thirteenth Centuries," *Journal of Ecclesiastical History* 48, no. 4 (1997): 628–657; Cristina Dondi, *The Liturgy of the Canons Regular of the Holy Sepulchre of Jerusalem: A Study and Catalogue of the Manuscript Sources,* Bibliotheca Victorina XVI (Turnhout: 2004); and the many works of Amnon Linder, most important of which are "The Liturgy of the Liberation of Jerusalem," *Mediaeval Studies* 52 (1990): 110–131; "'Like Purest Gold Resplendent': The Fiftieth Anniversary of the Liberation of Jerusalem," *Crusades* 8 (2009): 31–51; and especially the extraordinary *Raising Arms: Liturgy in the Struggle to Liberate Jerusalem in the Late Middle Ages,* Cultural Encounters in Late Antiquity and the Middle Ages 2 (Turnhout: 2003), which is hereafter cited as Linder RA.

20. Linder RA xv. Benjamin Weber, *Lutter contre les Turcs: les formes nouvelles de la croisade pontificale au XVe siècle,* Collection de l'École française de Rome 472 (Rome: 2013), 442–443; Constantinos Georgiou, "Propagating the Hospitallers' *Passagium:* Crusade Preaching and Liturgy in 1308–1309," in *Islands and Military Orders, c. 1291–c. 1798,* ed. Emanuel Buttigieg and Simon Phillips (Farnham, MD: 2013), 53–63; Janus Møller Jensen, *Denmark and the Crusades, 1400–1650* (Leiden: 2007), 104, 115–116; Maier, "Crisis," 638–641.

And yet in another sense the prayers speak for themselves. We can examine their themes, their evolution, their variety, and the geography of their dispersion. We can look at their transcription into liturgical volumes as measures of reception. We can use the texts of these formal prayers to reconstruct the ideological and devotional imagination within which the crusades took root. And we can examine the moments in which these prayers were deployed to effect a certain memorial or supplicatory end, and how and when they were adapted to particular contexts. In so doing, we trace the development of the ideas they contained and the ideologies they expressed.

Because of this, innovation through continuity and meaning in context are central themes of this book. Liturgy is an inherently conservative medium, and most new liturgical uses were variations on established forms.[21] Innovation was often derived from context. In this, the notion from intellectual history of serial contextualization is helpful. Speaking of ideas, or *an* idea, the intellectual historian David Armitage described serial contextualization as "the reconstruction of a sequence of distinct contexts in which identifiable agents strategically deployed existing languages to effect definable goals such as legitimation and delegitimation, persuasion and dissuasion, consensus-building and radical innovation."[22] Instead of the history of ideas, Armitage proposed the study of ideas *in* history. This book examines, instead of ideas, liturgical texts and rites (which, of course, contained ideas); how old liturgies (texts and rituals) were deployed to effect the definable goals of victory against the enemies of Christ; how those rites were used to legitimate crusading, to broaden the crusading base, to foster recommitment and support, and to reify the very goal at the heart of the crusading endeavor; and how rituals were used, in moments of crisis, to express cohesion, consensus, and piety. That is, instead of studying the history of the liturgy, we are looking at liturgy *in* history. The venerable study of liturgical history has been long and largely preoccupied with questions of origins and canon formation, an approach that, though fruitful and necessary to further inquiry, risks treating liturgical forms, once established, as static in meaning. The study of liturgy *in* history sees the liturgy, instead, as dynamic. It examines the ways in which liturgical rites and texts were deployed in specific historical moments, how their meaning was

---

21. Baumstark made the point almost a century ago that despite its apparent conservatism, liturgy was anything but static, responding to social and religious history. Anton Baumstark, *On the Historical Development of the Liturgy*, trans. Fritz West (Collegeville, MN: 2011), 43–52. Originally published in German in 1922.

22. David Armitage, "What's the Big Idea? Intellectual History and the Longue Durée," *History of European Ideas* 38, no. 4 (2012): 498.

shaped by those contexts, and how they in turn shaped history. New contexts appropriated old texts and gave them new meaning. And so, it has been, I hope, possible to nestle an analysis of these texts and the rituals they accompanied within the larger, well-studied history of crusading so as to give these prescriptions an interpretation that unfolds in their unfolding context.

One premise of this study is that liturgy and liturgical expression were fundamental aspects of clerical, and to a certain extent, larger medieval culture. The liturgy was an interpretive realm. The liturgy, much or most of which was known, innately and by heart, by its practitioners (priests, monks, clerics, religious) provided the language of expression and structure of thought for the clerical class—that is, for the class of people who wrote or composed almost all of the texts that we plumb, at least for the early period, for our understanding of the crusading movement. Even scripture, that root source of legitimacy and truth, was generally mediated through knowledge and recitation in the prayer of liturgy, and the interpretation of scripture was often inflected by its liturgical application and interpretation. The liturgy was thus central to the ideological apparatus that incorporated holy war into the story of salvation history. As we will see, liturgy also increasingly enveloped lay society into its crusading project. And so, we can learn something important about the culture and values of crusading by listening carefully to what was being said to God through the liturgy.

The second premise is that liturgy comprises a particular category of cultural evidence worth studying, both for what it said and for what it *did*. Because liturgical texts and liturgical actions inherently convey, express, and even constitute sacrality, the application of liturgical rituals and language to crusading was one of the mechanisms by which the crusades were sacralized as holy war. In a sense, liturgical sacralization was *the* thing that made holy war holy—that elevated crusading out of the hands of men and placed it squarely in God's hands. It was the liturgy that made crusading redemptive. And it was the liturgy that, through prayers, masses, rituals, and formal intercessions, integrated the temporal campaign measured by earthly gains into the eschatological war against the devil. If, as some have argued, the institutionalization and routinization of crusading in the thirteenth century militated against crusading as a spiritual exercise,[23] its steady integration into the ritual life of the Church and Christian society worked in the other direction, to insist on what William Chester Jordan called the "perpetual alleluia."[24]

---

23. Tyerman, *God's War*, 486–488, 889–893.

24. William Chester Jordan, "Perpetual Alleluia and Sacred Violence: An Afterword," *International History Review* 17, no. 4 (1995): 744–752.

Finally, by concentrating on the crusades to the Levant as the principal focus of the analysis, and in a sense also the principal focus of this book's structure, I do not wish to come down on the side of those who confine crusading to crusading for Jerusalem. For my part, I use the term *crusade* to refer to any military engagement sanctioned by the pope, the fighting of which garnered spiritual merit (indulgences). Generally, these were, following 1099, military programs on which and for which soldiers wore the cross. I use the term *holy war* somewhat more expansively to refer to any war or warfare fought for religious reasons and the fighting of which had religious meaning. These are obviously overlapping, but not identical, terms, and in and of themselves do not privilege Jerusalem. That said, however, the sources used here have often prioritized and thus justify the focus on the crusades to Jerusalem, making an argument for what the historiography has labeled the "traditionalist's" definition of crusade (as opposed to the "pluralist," the "popularist," and the "generalist" views).[25] For instance, a full rite, as we shall see, was established after 1099 to celebrate the capture of Jerusalem. No such comparable liturgical tradition was established in 1204, after the capture of Constantinople; after 1212, in commemoration of Las Navas de Tolosa; or in the 1240s in celebration of the conquest of Prussia.[26] The liturgical evidence for the rite of departure also slowly favored Jerusalem over other destinations.[27] And although we have a good deal of ancillary evidence for the use of the liturgy to support the Albigensian crusade, very few of the rites that were copied into books are rubricated for the Albigensian effort. We should certainly be willing to imagine the use of—the performance of—these rites in a variety of non-Jerusalem crusade undertakings. But what evidence exists for them suggests that they were imitative of those rites that were originally invented for the Jerusalem cause. That this study itself should focus primarily on the Jerusalem crusade and its successor crusades against the Ottomans (that is, crusades looking Eastward), is driven by the fact that, when the sources do concern themselves with geography, they too tend—like cathedral choirs—to look to the Levant. The liturgy, in any event, supports the traditionalist view of crusading. For many reasons, Jerusalem always lay at the heart of the eschatological economy in which the liturgy traded.

25. On these divisions, see Giles Constable, "The Historiography of the Crusades," in *The Crusades from the Perspective of Byzantium and the Muslim World*, ed. Angeliki Laiou and Roy Parviz Mottahedeh (Washington, DC: 2001), 1–22.

26. For a very local exception, see Megan Cassidy-Welch, "The Stedinger Crusade: War, Remembrance, and Absence in Thirteenth-Century Germany," *Viator* 44, no. 2 (2013): 159–174.

27. M. Cecilia Gaposchkin, "The Role of Jerusalem in Western Crusading Rites of Departure (1095–1300)," *Catholic Historical Review* 99 (2013): 1–28.

Plan of Inquiry

The structure of the book mimics the liturgy's role in the process of crusading itself, beginning in Europe (chapter 1), taking the cross (chapter 2), going to the Levant on crusade (chapter 3), establishing the Kingdom of Jerusalem (chapter 4), then returning, crusaderlike, to Europe with the news of the First Crusade (chapter 5), and finally adapting the larger vision of crusade to subsequent defeats (chapters 6 and 7). Although the book moves in broad terms chronologically, beginning in the eleventh century and ending in the fifteenth, a number of chapters, because they treat the development of a discrete liturgical form, themselves move through time, from the First Crusade to the later period. I have wanted to deemphasize the standard narrative chronology of the crusades, with their convenient numbering system. Instead, I have allowed the sources themselves to establish turning points. The result reveals seminal moments of creativity and change that occur against the larger backdrop of continuities and slow developments. Those moments are 1099, 1187–1213, 1308, and 1453. This book thus requires a basic knowledge of the standard history of crusading. For readers lacking this, I offer a brief outline of events that can be skipped by those who know the basic contours of the received narrative. (See the Preliminaries chapter that follows this introduction.) But I hope readers will note that the narrative told through the liturgy resists the traditional way of telling the story of crusading in European history and argues that the liturgy was one of the mechanisms that constructed the Latin West as a crusading society, defined not by specific and easily numbered campaigns, but rather, a general and ongoing commitment to warring with the infidel embedded in ritual and social life.

The first chapter begins before 1095, with rites and ideas contained in the liturgy prior to Urban II's epochal speech calling for the First Crusade at Clermont (1095). It establishes the basic liturgical language that influenced both crusading and the ideology of crusade, discussing the image of Jerusalem in the Western liturgy, and the rites of penitential pilgrimage, warfare, and the cross on which crusading drew. Each of these liturgical traditions would come to play a role in crusading, and their origins expose the processes by which the First Crusade was inflected by monastic ideals and grew out of, but recombined, existing devotional and ideological paradigms. It was these texts that allowed crusading to be so smoothly integrated into a larger eschatological scheme that mapped fighting Muslims onto fighting the greater battle against the devil. The second chapter traces the development of the departure rite for crusaders, in which rites of pilgrimage and rites for the cross came together to create a new liturgical ritual that gave specific definition and status to crusade. It was through this rite that crusaders were defined as armed pilgrims. The liturgy sanctioned the crusader as a temporary religious (that is, responsible for a time to heightened religious, quasi-monastic expectations of conduct) and thus set the devotional quality of the journey and the mission. That definition changed over time, reflecting both the development of the institution of crusade and evolving crusade spirituality. The third chapter leaves the Latin West and follows the First Crusade in some detail, and then more briefly the later crusades, with an eye to how and when crusaders on campaign employed the liturgy and what liturgy they employed. The liturgical rites deployed on the march and in the field were mostly penitential rites, designed to showcase humility before God and mark participants as deserving of His favor in fighting His enemy. The liturgies thus confirmed the status of the crusade as a penitential act in keeping with its status as a pilgrimage.

With the successful conclusion of the First Crusade, the crusaders established the Latin Kingdom of Jerusalem and immediately established a liturgical thanksgiving for what they saw as the miracle of the First Crusade. The fourth chapter thus looks in detail at the feast day that was established shortly after 1099 to commemorate the 15 July victory and capture of the city. The liturgy expressed the providential and perhaps even apocalyptic outlook of the early crusades, expressing an utterly triumphant interpretation of the Franks' role in providential history, confirming a new stage in the history of the Church and God's promise to these new Israelites of a new Jerusalem. The fifth chapter follows the returning crusaders back to the West, with their memories of 1099, to examine the ways in which the story of the First Crusade was commemorated liturgically. Looking mostly at France—the heartland of the crusades and the area for which the overwhelming majority of the evidence survives—we see the ways in which the fact of the great victory was inscribed into the liturgical worldview. Formal commemoration was rare, local, and idiosyncratic, but it expressed in liturgical form the same kind of gritty, bellicose triumphalism that we find in the monastic accounts of the early crusade historians.

The final two chapters follow the reaction in the West to successive losses in the Levant. Starting with the wholesale defeat of the forces of the Crusader States at the Battle of Hattin and the fall of Jerusalem in 1187, the Church, and specifically the papacy, began to call for coordinated, widespread, and institutionally organized programs of liturgical intercession and supplication to ask God to crush the enemy. As crusading was increasingly rationalized, institutionalized, and regularized, it was the liturgy at home that continued to do the work of defining it as part of God's great plan. The practice of asking God for help within the framework of liturgical supplication was explicitly seen as a kind of liturgical warfare, which fused both the penitential and belligerents strands in crusade liturgy. Chapter 6 traces the immediate response to Hattin in the formal programs of liturgical warfare inaugurated by the papacy. Although the program began with Gregory VIII and Clement III at the end of the twelfth century, the real architect of the program was Innocent III in his preparations for the Fifth Crusade. The book's title—"Invisible Weapons"—comes from an episode in this stage of the story, as Innocent's successor, Honorius III, renewed liturgical programs in support of crusaders who had departed for the East. Around this time it became axiomatic that crusade success in the East depended on the spiritual health of Latin Christendom.[28] Embedded in these programs, thus, were dual prerogatives of wroth upon the enemy and sincere reform penance and penitence. In addition to prayer, the latter was ritually communicated through the imposition of regular expiatory processions in which both laymen and churchmen were enjoined to participate. This was a mechanism by which lay society was increasingly incorporated into the sacralized ritual of the liturgy, in which liturgy reached ever more widely into Christian society, sacralizing crusading, delivering with it the Church's definition of crusade and crusading, and making crusade a normative aspect of Christian life. By the beginning of the fourteenth century, the pope could thus order that three special prayers "against the perfidy of pagans" be recited as part of every single mass performed in Christendom.[29] The final chapter traces the institution of these forms through to the end of the fifteenth century, in an examination of the intercessory rites that were written primarily for military help against the Ottomans. The center of gravity here moves eastward to the area between Vienna and Augsburg along the Danube, the region most threatened by the "new Turk." On the cusp of the Reformation and the collapse of a unified Christendom, the evidence for liturgical appeals against the Ottomans testifies to a devotional vitality at the same time that it reveals material and apocalyptical anxiety indebted to a medieval worldview.

As the formal expression of Christian devotion, the liturgy expressed the devotional character of the West's commitment to crusading. By tracing in this way the ongoing conversation of medieval Europeans with God over more than four centuries, we may uncover something of the devotional character of the spirituality and ideals of a crusading society as it related to the project of holy land recovery, crusading warfare, and personal salvation. Through what remains in sacramentaries, missals, ordinals, breviaries, and pontificals, we are given a portrait of just how the crusading

28. C&C 24–28.
29. *Regestum Clementis Papae V*, 9 vols. (Rome: 1888–1892), no. 2989, 3:161.

project and its successes and failures became central to religious life in general, and fit, over time, into the eschatological worldview of the Latin West. In the prayers of the liturgy and the collective rites of supplication and thanksgiving intended to call forth God's favor or stay his wrath, taking the cross, achieving victory over Muslims, and attaining individual and social salvation were all currencies of a single salvific economy. That economy connected individual sin with military defeat, Muslims with the devil, and the Cross with victory. And thus, reflecting crusading's twin roots in penitential pilgrimage and belligerent war, the liturgy of crusade, as with the ideology of crusade in general, always worked between the two poles of beseeching forgiveness and demanding God's vengeance. The liturgy thus evoked a dual battle: the internal battle against vice and sin on which the external battle against the earthly enemies of Christ depended. And the two battles were increasingly connected. Likewise, crusade itself was increasingly central to Christian devotion and identity. Over time, all Christians were to become, through their participation in the practices of prayer and supplication on behalf of crusading goals, fighters for the faith—that is, crusaders. In this way, through the liturgy, and with long-lasting implications, medieval Europe placed the crusading project at the very heart of Christian society and of the Christian faith.

Preliminaries

This study seeks to bring together two areas of historical inquiry—on the crusades and on the liturgy—each of which has its own received narratives, specialized debates, and technical vocabularies. The following pages offer two mini-essays designed for readers who might wish an introduction to or overview of either of these areas as it relates to this book. The first offers a short discussion of crusades to the Levant with the aim of reviewing the main events and introducing the principal sources that will recur in this book. The second offers an overview of the various types of sources (that is, types of books) used in the discussion of the liturgy and some of the liturgical terms that recur herein. Neither is argumentative, and neither is comprehensive. The hope is to assure a shared vocabulary with readers.

Crusading to the Levant, 1095–1500

The traditional starting date of the First Crusade and thus crusading in general is 27 November 1095. This is the date on which Pope Urban II preached a sermon at the Council of Clermont that sparked the movement we have come to call the crusades. Historians have long discussed the political and religious backstory for this call to arms, the most immediate reason for which seems to have been a request for military aid by the Byzantine Emperor Alexius Comnenus I (d. 1118) for help against the Seljuk Turks, who had been making vast territorial gains in Anatolia. Urban's speech has not survived, although various reports of it have. Despite lingering controversy, most historians now agree that Urban had in mind Jerusalem as the ultimate goal of the military venture and that he presented it as a kind of pilgrimage to free Eastern Christians and liberate the Holy Sepulcher from the hands of the enemy (Jerusalem and environs had been under

Muslim control since the seventh century). For those undertaking the call, Urban promised a remission of sins, which in time would come to be known as an indulgence.

The response was immediate, and much larger than anyone seems to have anticipated. It is in this sense that we can talk about the First Crusade as a religious and devotional movement rather than merely a military expedition. Urban put his papal legate, Adhémar of Monteil, the bishop of LePuy, in charge of the ecclesiastical leadership of the crusade. At the expedition's head were a group of princely leaders: from Lower Lorraine, Godfrey of Bouillon and his brothers Baldwin and Eustace; from northern Francia, Duke Robert of Normandy, Count Robert II of Flanders, Count Stephen of Blois, and Hugh of Vermandois (brother of the king of France); from Provençe, Count Raymond IV of Toulouse; and from Norman southern Italy, Bohemond of Taranto and his nephew Tancred. The volunteers left in several waves, passing through Constantinople and then crossing the Bosphorus and moving on through Anatolia and then downward toward Jerusalem. The first armies to depart, however, left from Normandy and the Rhineland and were independent of the princes. These smaller contingents perpetrated the first pogroms against Jews in the West, conflating Jews and Muslims as enemies of Christ. This early wave of crusaders (formerly called "the People's crusade," under the leadership of Peter the Hermit) was all but wiped out upon reaching Anatolia. Then, a little later, the princes' armies won a series of battles against the Turks around Nicea and at Doryleaeum. One contingent, under Baldwin's leadership, took possession of Edessa in March 1098. The bulk of the army marched to Antioch. After a long siege (October 1097–June 1098), the crusaders captured the city and ultimately won what was seen as a miraculous victory against a Turkish relief army from Mosul. With the city secure, the Franks set up the Latin Principality of Antioch under Bohemond's rule. A year later the army reached Jerusalem, and after a month-long siege brutally captured the city (15 July 1099), killed a vast number of its inhabitants, expelled all remaining non-Christians, and established the Kingdom of Jerusalem. The Franks quickly set up secular and ecclesiastical governments, electing as their first ruler Godfrey of Bouillon and installing Latin clergy in the Holy Sepulcher to celebrate the Latin rite. When Godfrey died the following year, his brother Baldwin marched from Edessa to take the crown. A fourth principality under Latin rule, centered on the coastal city of Tripoli, was established by 1109, completing the map of Frankish rule in the Latin East of the twelfth century.

Our knowledge of the events of the First Crusade is mostly drawn from an extraordinary set of sources that were written within a decade or so of 1099. The anonymous *Gesta Francorum et aliorum Heirosolimitanorum* (usually referred to simply as the **Gesta Francorum**, or just the *Gesta*) is closely related to the account written by **Peter Tudebode**, a French priest who was on the campaign. Another is the eyewitness account by **Raymond of Aguilers**, a chaplain in Raymond of Toulouse's army. **Fulcher of Chartres**, who served as chaplain to Baldwin of Edessa (later King Baldwin I of Jerusalem) and as canon of the Holy Sepulcher, wrote a history of the campaign and early years of the Latin Kingdom, probably completing an initial draft by 1106. These accounts (and especially the *Gesta Francorum*) found readers in Europe and were the basis of a series of rewritings by Benedictine authors eager to grapple with the larger historical meaning of crusade. **Baldric of Bourgueil** (later archbishop of Dol) began writing around 1105; **Guibert of Nogent**, probably, around 1107 or so, and **Robert of Reims** (who, although not on the campaign itself, seems to have been at Clermont in 1095) probably as early as 1106. Robert's *Historia Iherosolimitana* was the most widely copied and widely read, surviving in over eighty manuscripts. A generation later, around 1130 or so, an anonymous monk probably used the *Gesta* for yet another account (called by its most recent editor the *Hystoria de via et recuperatione Antiochiae atque Ierusolymarum*, although referred to in the earlier scholarship as the *Historia Belli Sacri* or the *Montecassino Chronicle*). This family of texts includes also an epic poem about the crusade by **Gilo of Paris**. Other accounts outside the *Gesta* tradition include one by **Ekkehard of Aura**, a German abbot, who went on a follow-up crusade in 1101; **Albert of Aachen**, another German who wrote a massive account of the crusade based in part, apparently, on interviews and other oral testimony of returning crusaders; and **Ralph of Caen**, who served in Bohemond's entourage after 1106. Back in Syria, **Walter the Chancellor** wrote an account of the first years of the County of Antioch. **William of Tyre**, the archbishop and chancellor of Tyre and an important official in the Kingdom of Jerusalem, writing in the 1170s and 1180s, also covered the years following the establishment of the four principalities using these and other now lost sources.

After 1099 and a series of less successful campaigns, powers in the Muslim world began to regroup. In 1144 a Turkish warlord named Zenghi took Edessa and slaughtered the city's Christian inhabitants, prompting Pope Eugenius II to call a new crusade (the Second Crusade, 1147–1149). Eugenius's teacher, Bernard of Clairvaux, played a pivotal role in preaching this campaign. The model, of course, was the First Crusade, which was evoked repeatedly. King Louis VII of France and Conrad III of Germany both took the cross. But the result was a disaster and an embarrassment. The crusaders set their sights on Damascus, a center of Muslim power, and mounted a siege in 1148. But the siege lasted only four days and the crusaders returned to Europe as failures. We know about this campaign primarily through the writings of two participants, **Odo of Deuil** and **Otto of Freising,** and the later reflections of William of Tyre (d. 1186). Where the First Crusade had succeeded because of disunity among Arab and Turkish polities, the Second Crusade revealed their underlying strengths. Zenghi's son, Nur-al-Din (a Turk, d. 1174), and Nur-al-Din's ambitious general Salah ad-Din Yusuf Ayyub (a.k.a. Saladin, a Kurd and founder of the Ayyubid dynasty, d. 1193), revived Muslim power, mounting what historians sometimes call a countercrusade. Nur-al-Din and Saladin made strong territorial gains throughout the 1170s and 1180s. On 4 July 1187, the Latin forces of Jerusalem under the leadership of King Guy of Lusignan met Saladin in battle at Hattin, a valley between a twin-peaked mountain ("the Horns of Hattin") and were utterly annihilated. Jerusalem fell shortly thereafter. Members of the Military Orders (Templars and Hospitallers) who survived at Hattin were executed, and the king himself was taken captive. When news reached the papacy of the debacle, Gregory VIII called the Third Crusade, even before learning that Saladin had retaken Jerusalem on 2 October through a negotiated surrender. The organization of the Third Crusade was accompanied by a call for internal reform and purification, on the premise that Jerusalem had fallen because of Christian sin. King Philip II ("Augustus") of France, Richard I ("Lionheart") of England, and Emperor Frederick I ("Barbarossa") all took the cross. Frederick drowned during his journey, but Philip, and then Richard, joined a siege of Acre, the coastal city northwest of Jerusalem. After the Franks had won the siege, Philip returned to France, but Richard stayed for a little over a year longer. Although Richard did not take Jerusalem, he did help buttress the strength of the exiled kingdom of Jerusalem, now centered at Acre. He left for England after negotiating a three-year truce with Saladin.

The character and definition of crusading altered significantly in the thirteenth century, largely due to the vision of Pope Innocent III (1198–1216). It was Innocent who called both the Fourth and Fifth crusades. The Fourth Crusade (1202–1204) never reached the Levant, and ended instead by capturing the Byzantine capital and establishing the Latin Empire of Constantinople, which lasted until 1261. Our principal reporters of the Fourth Crusade are two Frenchmen, **Geoffrey of Villehardouin** and **Robert of Clari.** The Fifth Crusade (1217–1221) was the first Western venture that targeted Egypt, the center of Ayyubid rule, whose destruction seemed a necessary precondition for taking and maintaining Jerusalem. After the long siege and capture of the coastal city of Damietta, the crusaders marched toward Cairo, got caught in the spring rise of the Nile River, and, stymied, ultimately had to retreat and abandon Egypt altogether. We are informed about these events primarily by two participants, **Oliver of Paderborn** and **Jacques de Vitry,** and an extraordinary set of anonymous but obviously clerical accounts that seem to have been prepared during the campaign itself (edited together as the **Quinti Belli Sacri Scriptores Minores**).

Pope Innocent III's effect on the history of crusading extends far beyond the calling of these two campaigns. First, Innocent dramatically widened out the use of crusade (papally sanctioned warfare which garnered spiritual benefits, and for which one "took the cross"), calling crusades against Cathar heretics ("Albigensians") in southern France and against political enemies. Innocent III was building on twelfth-century precedent here. Previous popes had offered spiritual rewards for fighting Muslims in Spain and pagans in the Baltic. But Innocent III was aggressive in pressing these powers. Second, he reformed crusade financing in the form of taxation and the redemption of crusading vows for cash such that he accelerated the transformation of crusade from a movement to an institution. Third, as part of these institutional innovations, he dramatically widened the scope of those who could participate in crusading. One could be a crusader—that is *crucesignatus*—without actually taking up arms, by financing another crusader or by redeeming a vow to go on crusade. One could thus achieve the spiritual benefits of crusading without actually going to war, a move that fed the theological development and the spiritual inflation of the indulgence in the thirteenth century. These changes in funding practices, still hazy, were also part of the process by which crusading moved from being an individual devotional enterprise to an organized military undertaking. Finally, expanding dramatically on the view of Gregory VIII and his successors that success in the East required reforms at home, Innocent inaugurated a wide-scale program of clerical and pastoral reform and renewal, a project that coalesced with his calling of the Fourth Lateran Council of 1215.

Innocent had died during the prosecution of the Fifth Crusade, and papal leadership was assumed by Honorius III. After the failures of 1221, the Emperor Frederick II, whose arrival in the Levant had been long anticipated, led another army to the East. In 1229, he reestablished a Frankish presence in the city of Jerusalem through a treaty with Al-Kamil, the Ayyubid sultan, giving both Christians and Muslims access to the city—a compromise that seems to have pleased neither side. The Franks returned to Jerusalem and the Latin canons reoccupied the Holy Sepulcher until 1244, when Christian Jerusalem fell to a new marauding force, the Khwarazmian Turks. In 1240, during Gregory IX's papacy, Earl Richard of Cornwall, Count Peter of Brittany, and Count Thibaut IV of Champagne mounted what we call the Barons' Crusade and made a number of territorial gains in the Holy Land. In 1244, King Louis IX of France took the cross and undertook the biggest and best-organized crusade venture to date. Although Innocent IV sanctioned the crusade, it was really Louis's venture. Consisting mostly of Frenchmen, Louis's army followed the path of the Fifth Crusade, attacking and taking Damietta, and marching south toward Cairo. But it suffered a catastrophic defeat at Mansurah on 8 February 1250, and two months later, Egyptian forces captured or killed what remained of the army. Our chief source for these events is the memoir written by Louis's friend, **Jean de Joinville.** Louis himself spent a month in captivity before being ransomed. He returned to France only in 1254, after spending a few years in Acre doing what he could to reinforce the Latin Kingdom. In 1267 he announced plans for a new crusade, which left in 1269 for the coast of North Africa (besieging Tunis), but ended when illness ravaged the army and the king himself died (25 August 1270). Although remnants of the expedition, under Edward I of England, went on to the Levant, Louis's second crusade too had ended in failure.

During the period between the Third Crusade and Louis IX's second crusade, Muslim leaders steadily consolidated their power in the Levant. After Louis's Egyptian defeat in 1250, the Mamluks (military slaves in Egypt who ousted the Ayyubids during the time of Louis IX's captivity and established a new dynasty) won a series of victories in Syria in the 1250s and 1260s, and more significantly, halted the westward advance of the Mongols at the Battle of Ain Jalut in 1260. The Mamluks then turned their attention to the Franks and took Antioch in 1268, Tripoli in 1289, and finally, in 1291, Acre. This signaled the end of Latin rule in the Levant and has often been considered the "stop date" in traditional histories of the crusades. But crusading, and in particular crusading with the aim of retaking Jerusalem, did not end in 1291. The papacy continued to call crusades, to offer indulgences, and to mount expeditions to fight for control over the Holy Land. Clement V, for example, organized a papally funded relief effort to help shore up the Christian communities in Armenia in 1308. Yet with the rise and expansion of Ottoman power in the fourteenth century, the front lines of crusading moved steadily westward. New crusades were called for after the Ottomans captured the Greek city of Constantinople in 1453. Philip of Burgundy made plans to take the cross against the Ottomans in 1454. John Hunyadi, heir to the Hungarian throne, won a victory against Mehmet II in 1456, which was hailed in Rome as a miracle on par with the First Crusade. Pope Pius II called a new crusade in 1460 (which fizzled when the pope himself died at Ancona in 1464). But for all the effort, perennial calls for crusade mustered forces and funds but did little until the Battle of Lepanto (1571) to stop Ottoman military conquest.

The received narrative of crusades numbered one through nine belies the extent to which crusading was something of a constant feature of medieval society. Certainly, in the twelfth century men spoke of the Second Crusade as the *secunda motio* and the Third as the *tertio motio,* and historians have long told the story of the crusades according to the numbering system established in the sixteenth century (which clearly breaks down after the Fifth Crusade).[1] And there were, to be sure, particular waves of recruitments, usually following a papal call to take the cross. Yet it seems increasingly clear that crusading was something of a continuous project. Crusaders regularly took the cross and departed in aid of the Holy Land, or joined other campaigns that had been awarded the crusading imprimatur. And many historians now emphasize the extent to which crusading was, although punctuated at some points with particular campaigns, an increasingly common feature of the social order in medieval Europe, particularly as it gained caché and prestige among a secular class as a source of authority and virtue.

It is hard, and probably not necessary, to identify the last crusade. Riley Smith noted that a crusade league was still fighting at the very end of the seventeenth century.[2] Men could still take the cross as late as the nineteenth century.[3] But it is worth considering how much the character of crusading had evolved between the years 1095 and ca. 1500, in everything from organization, to goals, to funding, to religious and spiritual meaning. Standing armies had been formed. Kingdoms had arguably evolved into states. The very idea of a unified Christendom was about to be challenged by Martin Luther and his followers. By 1500 crusade was part of the fabric of European society, as much affected by military, political, social, and religious changes as having played a role in effecting those changes. And although the notion of crusade continued unabated throughout the period, what it signified had changed as much as had the Christendom-turned-Europe that it helped forge.

Standard English-Language References for the History of the Crusades

Thomas F. Madden. *A Concise History of the Crusades.* Critical Issues in History. 3rd ed. Lanham, MD.: 2013.
Hans Eberhard Mayer. *The Crusades.* Translated by John Gillingham. 2nd ed. Oxford: 1988.
Jonathan Riley-Smith. *The Crusades: A History.* 3rd ed. London: 2014.
Christopher Tyerman. *God's War: A New History of the Crusades.* Cambridge, MA: 2006.

The Liturgy and Its Books

The term *liturgy*—which is not even a medieval term—comprises an enormous range of ecclesiastical and para-ecclesiastical ritual prayer, worship,

---

1. Constable, "The Historiography of the Crusades," 16; Christopher Tyerman, *The Debate on the Crusades* (Manchester: 2011), 48.
2. Jonathan Riley-Smith, *The Crusades, Christianity, and Islam* (New York: 2008), 1.
3. Riley-Smith, *The Crusades, Christianity, and Islam,* 51–52.

supplication, and celebration. A narrow definition of liturgy restricts the use of the term to eucharistic celebration and the Divine Office, labeling other forms of ritualized, corporate prayer "paraliturgical" or "extraliturgical." This is merely terminological. Increasingly, historians have been willing to expand the term to wider forms of activity, including forms of worship that might involve laity, be performed in the vernacular, or outside the confines of the Church. This more expansive use of the term allows a wider scope and an assessment of liturgical activity as a dynamic element of expression and communication within the medieval world. One way or another, services that are not liturgically canonical belong to the wide set of devotional practices that form the skein of medieval prayer and praise at the heart of the liturgy.

There are (and were) thus many forms of liturgy and many various uses of the liturgy. One way of categorizing the liturgy—or at least, the medieval liturgy—is by the books or parts of the books in which the various elements of the liturgy were recorded. This is somewhat artificial because, especially early on, books were individual to their use (that is, to local practice). And the categorization of modern terminology itself belies the fluidity often found in the books themselves. Yet introducing these roughly in terms of their development allows us to define the various types of books and the liturgy they contained, while contextualizing the use of these types of books broadly within the larger history of liturgical celebration. This is far from a complete list. It discusses only the forms and terms used with frequency in the following pages and is at best skeletal. But it will sketch the information needed to understand the rest of this book, and in so doing hopefully offer, in broad strokes, a framework for interpreting the rites and prayers and rituals *in* history.

The first set of books deals with **the Mass**—the Eucharistic celebration performed by a priest that lay at the very heart of the Christian rite.

Sacramentary: A sacramentary is a book that contains the prayers needed for a priest to celebrate the mass. The form as it survives seems to have emerged in the eighth century. Several competing, overlapping, and interrelated traditions evolved in tandem in this early period, including what are referred to as the Visigothic, Roman, Gallican, and Gregorian sacramentaries. Because the mass was divided up between common items (that is, prayers and text said in *every single* mass; otherwise known as the Ordinary) and proper items (that is, prayers and texts said only for specific feasts or occasions), the sacramentary provided the text for both the daily liturgy and for specific occasions. Thus, sacramentaries might include liturgy for the different weekly masses during the year (which change according to the season) and votive masses such as masses *pro iter agentibus* (for those going on a journey), *contra paganos* (to be said against pagans), or as we will see, *pro terra Ierusalem*. In the twelfth century, the propers found in a sacramentary tended to be the **collect**, the **secret**, and the **postcommunion**. They might also include short **versicles**, or other associated prayer texts. These were only a few of the dozens of texts that made up the mass, and when celebrated, were embedded in a much longer script for the mass involving people other than the celebrating priest. The collect, secret, and postcommunion were three prayers recited by the celebrant that were proper (specific) to a particular feast. Other parts of the mass could be found in a gradual (containing the text and often the music for the chants sung by the choir), the evangeliary (or gospel book), and the epistolary (containing the portions of scripture recited by the deacons and subdeacon respectively). The evangeliary and the epistolary could be combined in a book simply called a lectionary. Sequences (*prosae*, sing.: *prosa*)—special mass hymns recited after the Alleluia—were increasingly written for special occasions and might be collected separately in a sequentiary, or might also survive separately in a kind of liturgical or paraliturgical miscellany.

Missal. With the increasing complexity of the texts and variability of the mass, the thirteenth century saw the development of the missal. The missal was the heir to the sacramentary, in that it grew out of it and functionally replaced it. But the missal brought together the various elements of the mass so that in theory only the single book was needed to provide all the various materials for the celebration of any given mass. So instead of just containing the items needed by the celebrant, the missal would include in addition the chants, readings, and so forth. As with sacramentaries, often the special prayers, votive masses, and clamors that were to be said in the service of the crusades were copied into missals. Over the course of the twelfth, thirteenth, and fourteenth centuries, we find these often interpolated into manuscripts or added in a later hand. If they were integral to the copying of the manuscript, these texts would often be found at the end among the long series of proper services.

An entirely different set of books was required in order to sing the **Divine Office**. The Divine Office, the *Opus dei*, was the praise sung to God, at prescribed times throughout the day and throughout the year, and was the main work of monks and canons. It was noneucharistic, and involved the singing of the entire community. It included the eight services (that is, "offices" or "hours") of **matins, lauds, prime, terce, sext, none, vespers,** and **compline**, which were sung throughout the day beginning with matins (in the middle of the night) and ending with compline (in the evening). Important celebrations often began the evening *before* the feast day with first vespers (with the evening service on the feast itself being called second vespers). Each service was made up primarily of a series of different psalms that were framed by **antiphons, responsories (and their verses), versicles and responds, hymns,** and **lections** (readings). These chants and readings were interpretive and shaped the interpretation of the Psalm in light of the particular feast or day. An antiphon is a line of proper chant that precedes the singing of a canticle or a Psalm (or part of it). Antiphon texts are often drawn or adapted from scripture, but can equally be individual or specifically composed for a particular occasion. Versicles and responds are each a kind of short prayer. Hymns are longer, newly composed texts, written in stanzaic meter which can vary in length, and are usually sung at vespers, matins, lauds, and in the little hours (prime, terce, sext, and none). In addition to antiphons and hymns, the matins service, the longest of the services, included a series of lections (three, nine, or twelve, depending on the solemnity of the feast and whether it was a monastic or secular cursus), that were followed by responsories. The lections might be passages from the Bible, or sections of hagiography or sermons. The reading of each passage was followed by a sung responsory (another newly composed text) by one-half of the choir, and its accompanying verse by the other half of the choir. Although I treat these primarily as texts for what they say, most of these were set to music and sung, and it is helpful to think of them as song, or as musical poetry. (Even lections, that is, "readings," were chanted to one or more fixed tones.) Important feasts often had proper texts and chants written specifically for the celebration of that particular feast or event.

Breviary: To sing the Divine Office, one needed a Psalter, an office antiphonal, a lectionary, a responsory, a collectary, a hymnal, and a martyrology. Each contained the relevant textual and musical material for different elements of the office. The lectionary included the readings from Scripture and the Patristics. The office antiphonary included the chant and music needed by the choir, and so forth. But as with the development of the missal out of the constituent components of the mass, the various elements for the singing of the office were, around the thirteenth century, brought together in the **breviary**. A breviary thus provided all the basic texts needed to sing the Divine Office over the course of the year, including all items, both chanted and recited (intoned), the basic templates of the Ordinary (regular liturgy), and proper items for feasts in the Temporale and the Sanctorale. The breviary would thus have included all the chant and sung texts, in order, for any particular office. This would have included all the proper antiphons of the major hours (first vespers, matins, lauds, and second vespers), the lections (readings) and great responsories (made up of responses and verses) of the matins service, the hymns recited at the major hours (again, first and second vespers, matins, and lauds), and other relevant proper items, such as short versicles or other responsories.

Pontifical: The pontifical was a book made specifically for bishops that contained the material needed in their ceremonial function. Many thus included the **ordo** (the liturgical prescriptions; that is to say, the order of service) for crowning and anointing a king, queen, or emperor, even though most bishops during their careers would never have occasion to do this. Other rites that might be found in a pontifical included the rite for the dedication of a church, the ordination of a monk, or the consecration of an altar. Pontificals also included a series of **blessings** for various occasions including, for our purposes, the rite for blessing the pilgrim's scrip and staff and, later, the rite for blessing departing crusaders. A collection of texts compiled in the tenth century that we have come to know as the **Romano-Germanic Pontifical (RGP)** was highly influential and frequently (if not completely) copied.[4] But this was only one tradition among many.[5] A collection of texts used at the papal curia seems to have come together at the end of the eleventh or early twelfth century in Rome, much influenced by the RGP, and was revised and augmented over time. Michel Andrieu identified several stages in this development, and edited what he called the **Roman Pontifical of the Twelfth Century** and then the **Pontifical of the Roman Curia** in the thirteenth century, each of which itself developed in several steps.[6] The fact of the editions, which hypostasize particular forms of the text, belies the constant evolution or shifting of whatever text was in fact used at the Roman Curia. Yet although Andrieu's clear reconstruction has been called into question and complicated by more recent scholarship, his framework still allows us to trace the broad evolution of the form and the influence of the Roman (papal) tradition in Europe. At the end of the thirteenth century, William Durandus, who was bishop of the diocese of Mende in southern France, compiled a pontifical for his own use.[7] He relied on existing sources but composed a pontifical that was so clean, so elegant, and so beautiful, that it was widely copied and used elsewhere throughout Europe. The influence of these texts was wide, but by no means universal, and there always remained local traditions. Even when adopted, they were frequently adapted to local uses.

4. Cyrille Vogel and Reinhard Elze, eds., *Le Pontifical romano-germanique du dixième siècle*, 2 vols., Studi e testi 226–227 (Rome: Vatican City: 1963); Henry Parkes, *The Making of Liturgy in the Ottonian Church: Books, Music, and Ritual in Mainz, 950–1050* (Cambridge, UK: 2015), 133–223.

5. Richard Kay, *Pontificalia: A Repertory of Latin Manuscript Pontificals and Benedictionals* (Lawrence KS: 2007).

6. Michel Andrieu, "Le Pontifical d'Apamée et autres textes liturgiques communiqués à Dom Martène par Jean Deslions," *Revue Bénédictine* 48 (1936): 321–348. Michel Andrieu, ed. *Le Pontifical Romain au Moyen-Age: Tome I: Le Pontifical Romain du XIIe siècle* (Vatican City: 1938); Michel Andrieu, ed. *Le Pontifical Romain au Moyen-Age: Tome II: Le Pontifical de la Curie Romaine au XIIIe siècle* (Vatican City: 1940).

7. Michel Andrieu, ed. *Le Pontifical Romain au Moyen-Age: Tome III: Le Pontifical de Guillaume Durand* (Vatican City: 1940).

Ordinal: The ordinal was the book that brought everything together and prescribed overall ritual instruction. The ordinal as a genre appeared sometime in the twelfth century, in lockstep with the increasing complexity of the different elements of the overall rite. An ordinal often gave robust explanatory rubrics and allowed the cantor (the master of ceremonies, as it were) to organize the overall rite, but unlike the breviary or missal, it gave only the incipits of all the chant and sung texts, for which the participants would need to go to other books to get the complete texts (assuming they did not know them by heart to begin with). So, for instance, the Templar Ordinal that was copied around 1170 in Jerusalem and represents the "order of the Holy Sepulcher" (see chapter 4) prescribed the entire rite for the entire year. Thus, in addition to the regular liturgy, it gave the instructions for extramural processions and other liturgical rites that were not part of the mass and office strictly defined, such the liturgy for the Rogation days, when the entire community—lay and clerical—were to come out and engage in a penitential procession. When available, the ordinal gives the best overall view of a community's daily and yearly liturgy.

Calendar: The yearly liturgical cycle comprised two interlocking series of feasts. The first, the Temporale, is a series of celebrations following the seasons that celebrate the lives of Christ and Mary, and, keyed to Easter, are moveable (in that they depend on the lunar calendar and do not occur on the same day every year). The second, the Sanctorale, is fixed, occurring on the same day every year. (Thus the feast of Saint Augustine is always on August 28, and the feast of the Assumption is always on August 15, and so forth.) The calendar, usually placed at the beginning of liturgical books, listed the fixed feast days—the Sanctorale, usually in honor of the saints. The calendar was specific to the locality, so that, for example, in Amiens it might include Saint Firmin (d. ca. 303), the local evangelizing bishop, but in Durham it would include Saint Edmund Martyr (d. 869).

All of this bespeaks an important aspect of these sources, which is that they are at once descriptive (in that, in many cases, they are codifying an existing practice) and especially prescriptive, in that they offer instructions.[8] Historical analysis can expose the ways in which individual liturgical scripts found in the books themselves would be, or would have to be, adapted to local circumstance, geography, or events.[9] And thus, as sources, they necessarily suffer from the problem of ritual texts, which articulate an ideal—often an ideal that reveals notional power relationships and ideological worldviews—but

---

8. Carol Symes, "Liturgical Texts and Performance Practices," in *Understanding Medieval Liturgy: Essays in Interpretation*, ed. Helen Gittos and Sarah Hamilton (2015), 239–267.

9. Louis Hamilton, *A Sacred City: Consecrating Churches and Reforming Society in Eleventh-Century Italy*, Manchester Medieval Studies (Manchester: 2010), 56 and throughout.

that, when measured against other historical (often narrative) sources we can observe being ignored, challenged, or strained.[10]

It should also be said that this typology of book forms, useful as it is for us, reflects a later set of categories and an attempt to understand the early evolution of the books that were used to perform the liturgy. Those who study these books often find these terms insufficient or misleading in describing any particular manuscript, whose makers rarely set out to copy a volume that conformed to later practice or scholarly categorization. (This is not the case for the liturgical forms themselves. Medieval practitioners knew exactly what a responsory, or a lection, or an antiphon was.) But for our purposes, this vocabulary helps in providing the language needed in discussing the historical production, composition, performance, and reception of the liturgy.

Fuller English-Language Introduction to the Medieval Liturgy

John Harper. *The Forms and Orders of Western Liturgy from the Tenth to the Eighteenth Century: A Historical Introduction and Guide for Students and Musicians.* Oxford: 1991.

David Hiley. *Western Plainchant: A Handbook.* Oxford: 1993.

Andrew Hughes. *Medieval Manuscripts for Mass and Office: A Guide to Their Organization and Terminology.* Toronto: 1982.

Aimé Georges Martimort, Pierre Marie Gy, Pierre Journel, and Irénée Henri Dalmais. *The Church at Prayer: An Introduction to the Liturgy.* 4 vols. Collegeville, MN: 1985–1988.

Eric Palazzo. *A History of Liturgical Books from the Beginning to the Thirteenth Century.* Collegeville, MN: 1998.

Cyrille Vogel. *Medieval Liturgy: An Introduction to the Sources.* Revised and translated by William G. Storey, Niels Krogh Rasmussen O.P., and John K. Brooks-Leonard. Studies in Church Music and Liturgy. Washington, DC: 1986.

---

10. On the limits of liturgical texts in the study of ritual, see Philippe Buc, *The Dangers of Ritual: Between Early Medieval Texts and Social Scientific Theory* (Princeton: 2001); This is beautifully negotiated in Hamilton, *A Sacred City.*

1

The Militant Eschatology of
the Liturgy and the Origins
of Crusade Ideology

On 27 November 1095, at an ecclesiastical council held at Clermont in central France, Pope Urban II preached the First Crusade, in which it seems he enjoined the armed class of Christendom to take up arms, travel east, rescue Eastern Christians from the tyranny and torture of the Seljuk Turks, and (probably) recapture the Holy City of Jerusalem from the bondage of Muslim dominion. Urban was responding to a plea for help from the Byzantine emperor, Alexius Comnenus I, whose lands in Anatolia were being overrun by the Seljuks, a Turkic people who, in the process of their migration westward, had converted to Islam. And the pope offered to compensate the arms-men of Christendom with the spiritual benefit of sin forgiveness. Anyone who would take up the journey could, in the language of the privilege that Urban issued, "substitute the journey for all penance for sin." Urban then put Adhémar of LePuy, the papal legate, in charge of the crusade's ecclesiastical leadership. The response was overwhelming, far greater than anything that either the pope or the emperor had envisioned. Not limited to just the warrior class, men, women, and children took up the call, made a vow, and headed eastward. The rapidity with which the call to crusade was answered and mobilized is astonishing. Some of the contingents had left by the early months of 1096.

Very quickly, the crusade came to be seen as an army on pilgrimage to free Jerusalem, whose special emblem was the sign of the cross. In the account of a chronicler writing some three decades later, Pope Urban

> instituted and ordered that soldiers and footmen, that is anyone who was able to go to Jerusalem for the purposes of delivering Jerusalem and the other churches of Asia from the power of pagans, for the love of God and in order to obtain the remission of all their sins, should set forth as one bearing their arms, . . . and likewise he arranged that all going there should wear

the sign of the cross marked on their clothing somewhere on the shoulder or on their front, by which they would show themselves to be religious travelers or pilgrims to anyone who would care and by this would not be impeded.[1]

The account, of course, is retrospective, and we have no idea what Urban actually preached, but it is useful in identifying the ideological and mythic elements that came to be associated with the origins story of the First Crusade. For each of the elements credited to Urban—Jerusalem, pilgrimage, war, the cross—there was an established liturgical and devotional context that had flourished in the century before the First Crusade. These traditions are central for understanding the role that liturgy played in the crusades—both as liturgical practices that would be performed on crusade and as traditions that provided a language and an ideological context crucial in the development of the language and ideology of crusades. The chants, texts, prayers, and readings would have been known to the clerics and laymen who went on crusade from their practice of the liturgy. And from their books—books such as the recently discovered eleventh-century sacramentary from the cathedral church of LePuy en Velay, Adhémar of LePuy's own cathedral in the heart of the Auvergne, which was itself at the heart of the crusader movement, and which we will return to throughout this chapter.[2]

This chapter is about the salvific ideals and the language provided by the liturgy that would bear on the ideology and practice of crusade. It treats the period before 1095 in order to demonstrate the richness of the tradition that bequeathed a language of service, sacrifice, militancy, victory, and eschatology, and argues that the core elements of crusade ideology were furnished by the liturgy of early medieval Francia. A bellicose language pervades these texts. Devotion to Christ, remission of sin, and victory over the enemy are core themes that, looking backward from a later date through the lens of crusade, will seem recognizable as furnishing the wellspring of ideals that would constitute the building blocks of crusade ideology. The ways in which the liturgy imparted rites and ideals to the crusaders is a central part of how crusading was constituted as the first lay religious movement, a movement indebted to monastic ideals and framed through a monastic vocabulary,[3] and should be set alongside such other phenomena

1. HdV 1.16 (p. 4–5).

2. This manuscript is in private hands. I will cite it throughout as simply the LePuy Sacramentary (LePuy Scr.). On dating and provenance, see Robert Klugseder, "Bedeutende, bisher unbekannte liturgisch-musikalische Quellen aus Salzburg und Le Puy-en-Velay," *Beiträge zur Gregorianik* 59 (2015): 159–170.

3. Jean Leclercq, *The Love of Learning and the Desire for God: A Study of Monastic Culture*, 3rd ed. (New York: 1982); Purkis, *Crusading Spirituality*, 12–29; Giles Constable, *Crusaders and Crusading in the Twelfth Century* (Burlington VT: 2008).

as the Peace of God and the Gregorian Reform movement as part of the culture and context that invented crusading. The discourse articulated by the liturgy in the medieval West constructed the devotional imagination in which the crusades took root. It was the liturgy that provided the eschatological vision of time and history into which the crusaders jumped, and out of which an ideology of crusade was built.

The Image of Jerusalem in the Western Liturgy

We begin with Jerusalem. Jerusalem was always present in the liturgy and in the churches that purported to be images of the new Jerusalem. This was especially but not exclusively true of the Advent-Christmas-Epiphany cycle and during the Easter cycle. But this was the Jerusalem of the future, the Jerusalem of the heavenly kingdom. Paul Bradshaw opened an essay on "the Influence of Jerusalem on Christian liturgy" by writing:

> A search of Christian liturgical texts from all time periods and in all ecclesiastical traditions reveals the regular occurrence of reference to Jerusalem, but the word is almost invariably employed as a symbol of the eschatological age to come, picking up on the language of the book of Revelation, which speaks of "new Jerusalem, coming down out of heaven from God" (21:2; see also 3:12, 21:10); of St. Paul, who refers to "the Jerusalem above" (Gal. 4:26); and of the Letter to the Hebrews, which talks of "the heavenly Jerusalem" (12:22).[4]

Jerusalem and its cognate, Sion,[5] permeated the language and imagery of the liturgical cursus. This was in part because so much of the liturgy was built upon scripture, and in particular the Psalms, which were preoccupied with the holiness of Jerusalem as God's city and had been, since Saint Benedict, recited in full in the monastic rite each week.[6] The Psalms, in addition to being the basis for the core liturgical cycle of the office, bequeathed its poetry to a huge number of antiphons, verses, responsories, and chants in the liturgy.[7] Moreover, the use throughout the liturgy of the prophets who had written about the exile from Jerusalem and the desire to return—especially Isaiah, Jeremiah, Ezekiel, and Daniel—opened up the meaning of Jerusalem

4. Paul Bradshaw, "The Influence of Jerusalem on Christian Liturgy," in *Jerusalem: Its Sanctity and Centrality to Judaism, Christianity, and Islam*, ed. Lee I. Levine (New York: 1999), 251.

5. S. Krauss, "Zion and Jerusalem: A Linguistic and Historical Study," *Palestine Exploration Quarterly* 77 (1945): 15–33.

6. Psalms 47, 50, 78, 86, 121, 126, 131, 134, 136.

7. André Rose, "Jérusalem dans l'année liturgique," *La Vie Spirituelle* 86 (1952): 389–403; James McKinnon, "The Book of Psalms, Monasticism, and the Western Liturgy," in *The Place of the Psalms in the Intellectual Culture of the Middle Ages*, ed. Nancy van Deusen (Albany: 1999), 43–58; Joseph Dyer, "The Psalms in Monastic Prayer," in *The Place of the Psalms in the Intellectual Culture of the Middle Ages*, ed. Nancy van Deusen (Albany: 1999), 59–89.

(and Sion and Israel) to eschatological interpretation.[8] The possibilities of this interpretation were echoed at various points throughout the year. The readings for Advent, for instance, ran through Isaiah, beginning with Isaiah 1:1, "The prophet complains about the sins of Judah and Jerusalem." The prophets' Jerusalem became the Church, and ultimately the heavenly city. But it was more than this. The prophets furnished almost endless references to a desired, longed-for Jerusalem that was incorporated in its Christianized interpretation throughout the divine office.

The liturgy, building on a deep patristic theology establishing the relationship between the Old and New Testaments, was the mechanism by which material from the Old Testament was given Christian meaning. Responsories (chants that follow or "respond to" a liturgical reading) and other verses commented on and thus interpreted scriptural readings and other prayers. Antiphons were chosen in the office to shape and guide the core idea of a psalm. The liturgy thus was constantly engaged in an exegetical discourse with itself and the scripture on which it was based. And in turn, the meaning of Jerusalem in the liturgy could be informed both by the multiple ways of reading scripture (literally, historically, allegorically, tropologically) and on deep traditions of exegesis that informed these readings.[9] John Cassian (d. 435), glossing Galatians, had long before explained that Jerusalem should be understood according to history as the city of the Jews; according to allegory as the church of Christ; according to anagogy as that heavenly city of God which is the mother of us all; and according to tropology as the soul of man.[10] In this way, the Jerusalem of the Psalms became, in Christian hands, the New Jerusalem of the New Dispensation. The Advent antiphon, "Behold, the great prophet comes and he shall make the new Jerusalem,"[11] was paired with Psalm 146, which began "The Lord builds up Jerusalem; he will gather together the dispersed of Israel." The interplay between prayers and texts and the inherited exegetical tradition that they absorbed thus turned the historical Jerusalem into the Church and ultimately into the community of the blessed. By the time the liturgist John Beleth (d. 1182) was writing, around 1160 sometime between the

8. Daniel and the Minor Prophets were read during the night office and also probably in the refectory during the month of November. Isaiah was read in December as part of the Advent cycle.

9. Henri de Lubac, *Medieval exegesis*, trans. Mark Sebanc, 3 vols. (Grand Rapids, MI: 1998): 2:28; Susan Boynton, "The Bible and the Liturgy," in *The Practice of the Bible in the Middle Ages: Production, Reception, and Performance in Western Christianity*, ed. Susan Boynton and Diane J. Reilly (New York: 2011), 10–33, especially at 10–11.

10. Bernard McGinn, "Iter Sancti Sepulchri: The Piety of the First Crusaders," in *Essays on Medieval Civilization*, ed. Bede Lackner and Kenneth Philp (Austin, TX: 1978), 40–41.

11. CAO 2552.

Second and Third Crusades, he, in speaking of the fourfold interpretation, defined the historical Jerusalem as "the city to which pilgrims go," the allegorical one as the Church militant, the tropological as the faithful soul, and the anagogical as the celestial Jerusalem.[12] For Beleth, the Jerusalem celebrated daily in the liturgy was the earthly city then under Frankish control. And it in turn signified salvation.

Of the many ways that "Jerusalem" was present in the West through and throughout the liturgy, one of the most important was the liturgy for the dedication of the church, the rite celebrated to consecrate and reconsecrate the church edifice that was the very theater of this liturgy. Through the complex interplay of the elements of the liturgy, the office for the dedication of the Church made the argument that the building was allegorically a version—a vision—of Jerusalem.[13] In the rite prescribed by the highly influential Romano-Germanic Pontifical, the deacon sings, "O how awesome is this place; truly this is none other than the house of God and the doorway to heaven."[14] The Church was the gateway to heaven, and also its image here on earth. The liturgy was predicated on a comparison between the New Jerusalem, as described by John in Revelation, and the physical structure of the earthly church. The dedication hymn, "Urbs beata," drew on John's dream and described the Church in the language John had used for heaven.[15] This was only one part of a whole series of scriptural evocations of the heavenly Jerusalem that was inscribed into the dedication liturgies.[16] The entire office was constructed so as to celebrate the physical structure of the church as an image of, and a portal to, the New Jerusalem.[17] The standard reading for all dedication rites drew on Rev. 21:2: "I saw the holy city, the New Jerusalem, coming down from heaven from God."[18] The version in the LePuy Sacramentary connected the heavenly Jerusalem (from Rev. 21:2–3) with the Tabernacle (Lev. 26:11, from the Old Testament), the Temple of God (from 1

12. Johan Chydenius, *Medieval Institutions and the Old Testament* (Helsinki: 1965), 83. See John Beleth, *Summa de ecclesiasticis officiis*, CCCM 41A, ch. 113, 212–213.

13. Hamilton, *A Sacred City*; Ann R. Meyer, *Medieval Allegory and the Building of the New Jerusalem* (Woodbridge, UK: 2003), 69–97; H. Ashworth, "*Urbs beata Jerusalem*: Scriptural and Patristic Sources," *Ephemerides Liturgica* 70 (1956): 238–241; Jennifer A. Harris, "Building Heaven on Earth: Cluny as *Locus Sanctus* in the Eleventh Century," in *From Dead of Night to End of Day: The Medieval Customs of Cluny—Du Coeur de la Nuit à la fin du Jour: Les Coutumes Clunisiennes au Moyen Âge*, ed. Susan Boynton and Isabelle Cochelin (Turnhout: 2005), 137–138.

14. RGP XL.26 (vol. 1:136), *O quam metuendus est locus*. Cf. Gen. 28.17.

15. Ashworth, "*Urbs beata Jerusalem*," 238–241.

16. The many different *dedicatio* liturgies in use in the West generally all shared this essential interpretation. CAO, vol. 1, no. 127: 372–376, for secular uses; and CAO vol. 2, no. 127: 714–719, for monastic uses. Hamilton, *A Sacred City*, exploits these variations.

17. Meyer, *Medieval Allegory and the Building of the New Jerusalem*, 81, offers an elegant reading of the liturgy at St.-Denis.

18. CAO 7871.

Cor. 3–9, from the New Testament), and finally the foundation, "which is Jesus Christ" (from 1 Cor. 3:11).[19] Consecrating the Church in this world was to bring the New Jerusalem to earth, to make the Church, and the living souls who prayed in it, the embodiment of the salvific community and salvation to come.[20]

Monasteries in particular were considered images of Jerusalem.[21] This came from the Augustinian precept that the faithful (past, present, and future) made up the City of God, that "the true Sion is the church of Christians,"[22] and that the saved were traveling in life to the New Jerusalem. The monk was the ideal pilgrim, journeying spiritually toward the New Jerusalem through a corporate liturgy that continually reaffirmed it. Because of the central role of the *laus perrenis* at Cluny, Jerusalem may have been especially potent within the Cluniac worldview in which Urban II, himself a former Cluniac monk, was nurtured. It was conviction in the idea that the monastery was the better Jerusalem on earth that prompted Anselm of Bec in 1086 to urge a young man to become a monk instead of going on pilgrimage, and Peter the Venerable in the twelfth century to counsel a young knight to enter a monastery—the better Jerusalem—rather than go on crusade.[23] Anselm wrote, "Put aside the Jerusalem which is now the vision not of peace but of tribulation . . . and begin the way to the heavenly Jerusalem, which is the vision of peace, where you will find treasures which can be received only by those scorning the other ones."[24] The idea of the vision of peace (*visio pacis*) came from Ezekiel 13:16,[25] but eleventh- and twelfth-century monks would have known it equally through the dedication liturgy, which equated the *visio pacis* with the earthly Church: "The city of Jerusalem," it began, "called a blessed vision of peace (*pacis visio*), which is constructed in the living heavens out of stones and by the angels, is crowned

19. LePuy Scr., 152r–v.

20. Hamilton, *A Sacred City*, throughout, but especially chapter 2.

21. Kirsti Copeland, "The Earthly Monastery and the Transformation of the Heavenly City in Late Antique Egypt," in *Heavenly Realms and Earthly Realities in Late Antique Religions*, ed. Annett Raanan S. Boustan (Cambridge, UK: 2004), 142–158.

22. Augustine, *Ennarationes in Psalmos*, "Vera sion ecclesia est christianorum," CCSL 39, 75. See also Meyer, *Medieval Allegory and the Building of the New Jerusalem*, 60–65; Thomas Renna, "The Idea of Jerusalem: Monastic and Scholastic," in *From Cloister to Classroom: Monastic and Scholastic Approaches to the Truth: The Spirituality of Western Christendom, III*, ed. Rozanne Elder (Kalamazoo, MI: 1989), 96–109.

23. Giles Constable, "Opposition to Pilgrimage in the Middle Ages," *Studia Gratiana* 29 (1947): 132–133; Giles Constable, "The Vision of Gunthelm and Other Visions Attributed to Peter the Venerable," *Revue Benedictine* 66 (1956): 106.

24. Constable, "Opposition to Pilgrimage in the Middle Ages," 133.

25. Jerome presented an etymology for Jerusalem as meaning *visio pacis* that was repeated by Augustine and Isidore. McGinn, "Iter Sancti Sepulchri: The Piety of the First Crusaders," 40.

as bride in her entourage."[26] The conviction that a monk could obtain this vision of peace at home was at the heart of a broader opposition to monks going on pilgrimage, and later, on crusade.[27] Instead, the monk sought Jerusalem through the liturgy, and the liturgy throughout bespoke the glory of the future Jerusalem.

By the first decade of the twelfth century, the monastic chroniclers who began the work of historical interpretation of the First Crusade reimagined the crusaders' achievement precisely as the soldierly equivalent of their own monastic vocation. In this view, for the crusaders who captured Jerusalem on 15 July 1099, taking the earthly Jerusalem signified attaining the heavenly Jerusalem. Baldric of Bourgeuil, a monastic author rewriting the received accounts of the First Crusade from his monastery in northwest Europe around 1105, imagined a preacher telling the crusaders storming the wall of the actual Holy City that "truly, if you consider it rightly, this Jerusalem, which you see here, to which you have come, which is present before you, prefigures and points toward that other city, the celestial Jerusalem."[28] Giles of Paris, another monk writing in the same decade, described Godfrey of Bouillon, one of the great heroes of the First Crusade, fighting on 15 July, as "fighting for a twofold kingdom, since he was looking forward to both Jerusalems: he fought in the one so that he might have life in the other."[29] Guibert of Nogent, a third Benedictine monk who undertook an account of the First Crusade, said that the terrestrial Jerusalem was "renewed" by the crusades so that it might serve as the "vision of celestial peace" (again, the *visio pacis*).[30] Albert of Aachen, our fourth chronicler, spoke of "the city of Jerusalem, which is the gate of the heavenly homeland."[31] These monastic chroniclers imagined the crusades themselves as the worldly and knightly equivalent of the monastic life. It was a view of the earthly Jerusalem necessarily conditioned by the monastic liturgical ideal.

The Liturgy of Pilgrimage

If, at the close of the eleventh century, monks attained Jerusalem through prayer, pious laymen increasingly sought to reach the Holy City by foot on pilgrimage. And of course, the First Crusade itself was dependent on the

---

26. AH 51:110 (no. 102); CAO 8405, *Urbs Jerusalem beata dicta pacis visio*. In 1195, Celestine III lamented Jerusalem as the "quondam pacis visio." Ralph of Diceto, *Radulfi de Diceto decani Lundoniensis opera historica. The Historical Works of Master Ralph de Diceto, Dean of London*, ed. William Stubbs, RS 68 (London: 1876), 2:133.

27. Constable, "Opposition to Pilgrimage in the Middle Ages."

28. BB 108.

29. Giles of Paris, *The Historia vie Hierosolimitane of Gilo of Paris, and A Second, Anonymous Author*, trans. C. W. Grocock and J. E. Siberry (Oxford: 1997), IX:280 (pp. 244–245).

30. GN 7.21 (lat. 305, tr. 143).

31. AA vi.27 (pp. 438–439).

paradigm of penitential pilgrimage.[32] The practices of penance, which were all undergirded by liturgical regimes, and the larger penitential ideal they underwrote, thus lay at the heart of the First Crusade. And liturgical rites of penance were often occasions where the (lay, elite, or comparatively elite) men-of-arms that constituted the traveling and fighting forces of the First Crusade had interacted with monastic and clerical culture. Well into the eleventh century, the Church continued to maintain that a soldier practicing his vocation as part of a just war still had to do penance for killing the enemy in battle.[33]

These interactions informed the practices of penance and the ideal of penitential pilgrimage, which around 1000 gained its own liturgical rite. Penitential pilgrimages grew out of the tariffed penances of an even earlier period that were assigned by a confessor as expiation for sins. Initially, penitential tariffs were assigned *by* churchmen *to* churchmen, and initially the goal was Rome, where Saint Peter held the power of binding and loosing, and thus absolution. But in the tenth and eleventh centuries, laymen increasingly went on penitential pilgrimages, and increasingly it was to the Holy Land that they traveled to fulfill the penance.[34] The goal of penitential pilgrimage thus shifted from Rome, the land of the Vicar of Christ, to Jerusalem, the land of Christ himself. Robert I, Duke of Normandy is an apt example. In the 1030s, he undertook a penitential pilgrimage to Jerusalem after assassinating his brother Richard.[35]

As they departed on their sacred journey, pilgrims were likely to participate in a ritual in which the insignia of their pilgrimage status—the scrip (or "satchel," "wallet," or "purse"; the Latin is either *capsella, sporta*, or *pera*) and staff (or "walking stick" or "rod"; *fustis, baculum*) were blessed by the bishop or local priest.[36] These rites emerged over the course of the eleventh century and were often attached to the earlier practice of special ceremonies for those leaving on a journey (*pro iter agentibus*) that had emerged in the eighth or ninth century.[37] The rubrics of these travel rites

32. Hans Eberhard Mayer, *The Crusades*, trans. John Gillingham, 2nd ed. (Oxford: 1988); Jonathan Riley-Smith, *The First Crusade and the Idea of Crusading* (Philadelphia: 1986).

33. Cyrille Vogel, "Le pèlerinage pénitential," in *Pellegrinaggi e culto dei Santi in Europa fino alla 1 Crociata* (Todi: 1963), 82–83.

34. Vogel, "Le pèlerinage pénitential," 56–61. For other examples, see Bull, *Knightly Piety*, 204–249.

35. Vogel, "Le pèlerinage pénitential," 59–60.

36. RR 7 (tr. 81, where *benedictione* is translated as "permission"): "Quippe nec laicis expedit peregrinari, nisi cum sui benedictione sacerdotis"; FC I.vii.1 (lat. 164, tr. 75): "et ab eo benedictione suscepta."

37. *Iter agentibus* formulas are not found in the earliest of surviving manuscripts, the Verona Scr., the old Gelasian, or the Missale Francorum. For early examples, see, Alban Dold and Klaus Gamber, eds., *Das Sakramentar von Monza*, Texte un Arbeiten 3 (Beiheft: 1957), 79–80 (no. 248); Liber Ordinum col. 346–347. Early examples of scrip and staff prayers are often

suggest that the earliest travel benedictions were composed for monks, but over time rituals would come to encompass laymen as well who wanted to beseech divine protection.[38] The increasing laicization and secularization of these texts in the period from 800–1200 bears on the ideological dynamic by which the laity were, in the wake of the Gregorian Reform movement, increasingly brought into the liturgical fold of the Church. The benedictions in the Gallican and Gregorian texts emphasize God's direction of and involvement in a safe journey, emphasizing God as the leader and the guide.[39] In the eleventh century, various rites adapted some of these texts and new texts expanded on themes of desire for a safe journey, the request to be directed by God, and the request for the angelic companion (often Raphael, who in the Book of Tobit accompanied Tobias into Medea).[40] The sense of the whole is the physical safety of journey in an uncertain age. "May [God] lead you along a direct route, up steep mountains, through the vaults of valleys, through open plains, the fords of rivers, the hidden spaces of woods."[41] The physical journey was, over time, turned into a metaphor for spiritual journey, being not merely the physical dangers of travel but the moral temptations of the devil. One prayer asks that Christ's "invincible shield" [*inexpugnabilis clipeus*] protect the pilgrim so that he "might be relieved of the misfortunes to body and soul."[42] Another asked that Raphael, Tobias's guardian, might stay with the traveler, so that he might "avoid human and diabolical trickery" and that the pilgrim should merit having the company of Christ himself as guide.[43]

The eleventh century, within the context of flourishing local and international pilgrimages, and in particular the rise in the practice of penitential pilgrimage, witnessed the composition of specific prayers for the departing pilgrim.[44] What characterized the pilgrim over and above the mere traveler

---

attached to "pro iter agentibus" or "pro fratribus in via dirigentibus" rites. See for instance the LePuy Scr., 80v–82v; and Roda Pnt., LXVII (537–544).

38. Gregorian Scr., 1313–1319 (1:437–439).

39. Gregorian Scr., 1318 (1:438); LePuy Scr. 82r; Autun Scr., 1814, Gellone Scr., 2797, Gelasian Scr., 1319. *Deus infinite misericoride* . . .

40. Gellone Scr. 2794; Gelasian Scr. 1317; Saint Amand Scr. 392; Autun Scr. 1811; LePuy Scr., 81v; Liber Ordinum, col. 93.

41. CBP 1881; Gellone Scr. 2098; Angoulême Scr. 1855.

42. H.M.J. Banting, *Two Anglo-Saxon Pontificals (the Egbert and Signey Sussex Pontificals)* (London: 1989), 105–106; Henry A. Wilson, ed. *The Benedictional of Archbishop Robert* (London: 1903), 55.

43. Banting, *Two Anglo-Saxon Pontificals*: 105; Wilson, *The Benedictional of Archbishop Robert*, 55.

44. On these blessings, see Jürgen Bärsch, "'Accipe et hunc baculum itineris,' Liturgie- und frömmigkeitsgeschichtliche Bemerkungen zur Entwicklung der Pilgersegnung im Mittelalter," in *Wahrheit auf dem Weg*, ed. Jürgen Bärsch (2009), 76–99; Adolph Franz, *Die kirchlichen Benediktionen im Mittelalter*, 2 vols. (1909; reprint, Bonn: 2006), 2:271–289; Derek A. Rivard,

were three things: first, pilgrims probably took a pilgrimage vow, although this is not clear before the turn of the twelfth century;[45] the second was that the *loca desiderata* of the travel rites was a *locus sanctus* and thus the enterprise had a sacred and pious aura that was absent in mere travel; finally, the pilgrim himself (or herself) was "marked" (*insignatus*)—that is, distinguished in appearance by aspects of dress, the hat, the tunic, and particularly by the scrip and the staff. It was these attributes that denoted the particular status—legal and devotional—of the pilgrim, who took on imperatives of a temporary monk and who, since at least the eighth century, had been afforded certain rights and protections by the Church for the length of his journey.[46]

The early rites for pilgrims were thus all structured around the blessing of satchels and staffs, and were often attached to the votive Mass or prayers for travelers.[47] In the LePuy Sacramentary, for instance, standard blessings for scrip and staff were added at the head of an unusually long list of prayers for travelers, testifying to a robust culture of pilgrimage in the eleventh-century Auvergne.[48] The ceremony designated the pilgrim as a pilgrim, and thus as legally and canonically entitled to certain privileges and spiritually obligated to certain codes of conduct that made them quasi-monks for the period of their pilgrimage.[49] It also allowed the pilgrim to *perform* his (or her) penitence in public. That is, pilgrims enacted their penitence before the bishop, the community, and especially, before God. This was a classic "performance"—a ritualized act which engenders various transformations and where the participants are *both* the performers and the audience.[50] Theoretically this public performance was transformative (making pilgrims *into* penitents) and inaugurated a defined period of Turnarian liminality in which the pilgrim (or group of pilgrims in *communitas*) participated in a religiosity that took them outside the practices and confines of their normal devotions and community.[51]

Blessing the World: Ritual and Lay Piety in Medieval Religion (Washington, DC: 2009), 134–155.

45. James A. Brundage, *Medieval Canon Law and the Crusader* (Madison: 1969), 17–18.

46. Francis Garrisson, "A propos des pèlerins et de leur condition juridique," in *Études d'histoire du droit canonique dediées à Gabriel Le Bras* (Paris: 1965), 1178–1181; Brundage, *Medieval Canon Law and the Crusader*, 14–17.

47. Alejandro Olivar, ed. *El Sacramentario de Vich*, Monumenta Hispaniae Sacra, Serie liturgica 4 (Barcelona: 1953), 215–217, CCXCVII. Roda Pnt. LXVII (pp. 537–544); Darmstadt Hessische Landes-und Hochschulbibliothek 3183, 181–184.

48. LePuy Scr., 80v–82v.

49. Riley-Smith, *The First Crusade*, 22; Brundage, *Medieval Canon Law and the Crusader*, 30–39.

50. Richard Schechner, *Performance Theory*, rev. and expanded ed. (New York: 1988).

51. Victor and Edith Turner, *Image and Pilgrimage in Christian Culture: Anthropological Persepctives*, Lectures of the History of Religions, ns 11 (New York: 1978).

The ceremony itself varied regionally, though the Roda Pontifical (ca. 1000, in Catalonia) provides rubrics that give a sense of how the ceremony would have unfolded. The rubrics are in the plural, suggesting that the ceremony was done for a number of pilgrims setting off at once. The rite sanctioned the pilgrimage as part of a penitential regime, the aim of which was the remission of sins. A number of its prayers were in fact taken from Lenten rites and the giving of penance (*penitenciam dare*) from other parts of the sacramentary.[52] Liturgically, then, penitential pilgrimage took its place alongside the liturgical rites for private penance and public penance in the liturgical apparatus of the central Middle Ages, and its function sort of straddled the two.[53] In this rite, in Roda at the turn of the eleventh century, the pilgrim would confess "any kind of sin or crime" to God and to the bishop (or, absent the bishop, to any available priest); after the bishop assigned the pilgrim his penance, he would prostrate himself on the ground before the altar and the seven penitential psalms and the litany would be chanted over him. The bishop would then offer a series of prayers, asking for pardon and grace, and for God to grant remission of all sins.[54] One prayer expressed the hope that in the future the pilgrim might be worthy of the company of angels, archangels, and saints. The pilgrim would then get up from the ground, and the bishop would place the scrip on him and give him the staff. Two specific prayers would be said at this point. As the bishop handed the pilgrim the scrip, he asked that the pilgrim "take on this scrip, the *habitum* of pilgrimage, so that you might merit to arrive well clean, saved, and purified at the threshold of the apostles Peter and Paul (or of other saints where you might desire to go), and having finished your journey, you might merit to return to us in safety."[55] The bishop recited another prayer as he handed over the staff, in which he asked that the pilgrim arrive at the threshold of the blessed Apostles Peter and Paul and other saints safely, and that they also return "to us" in joy.[56] In the final blessing, the bishop asked God to guide the journey, to give the pilgrim the

---

52. Editor's note, in Roda Pnt. 197. Other examples associate travel/pilgrimage rites with penitential rites, as with Liber Ordinum, col. 93–94.

53. There were competing types of penance—what older scholars had categorized as "public penance" and "secret penance," categories that have more recently been understood to be fluid and overlapping. For the classic older formulation of categories, see Cyrille Vogel, *Le pécheur et la pénitence au Moyen Age* (Paris: 1969). For more recent approaches, see Sarah Hamilton, *The Practice of Penance, 900–1050* (Woodbridge, UK: 2001); and Rob Meens, *Penance in Medieval Europe, 600–1200* (Cambridge, UK: 2014).

54. Roda Pnt. LXVII.10 (p. 541).

55. Roda Pnt. LXVII.18 (p. 543). This was a version of a common prayer, known widely north of the Pyrenees as well. See for example Gellone Scr. 3058; Avignon BM 178 155v.

56. Roda Pnt. LXVII.19 (p. 544). This too was a version of a common prayer, appearing for instance in LePuy Scr. 811; and Gellone Scr. 3059.

Archangel Raphael as a companion, to kindly fulfill the pilgrim's pious vow, and to allow him ultimately to arrive at eternal bliss. Arrival at the locus sanctus was thus equated with the attainment of heaven. The whole was then followed with a mass *Pro iter agentibus.*

Because the rite was associated with penitential pilgrimage, a crucial theme common to the many different versions of this rite was the promise of *remissio peccatorum*, or even *remissio omnium peccatorum*. An English rite of the eleventh century speaks broadly of God's clemency, power, indulgence, remission, pity, and compassion, which the pilgrim leaving on the "journey of penitence," hopes will be granted for his crimes. He asks for "prosperity, the remissions of sins, and eternal life," since he hopes to be "improved through the new bath of penitence and pilgrimage."[57] In Spain, the Vich Missal of 1038 speaks of the pilgrim returning, joyful in the remission of sins.[58] The Roda Pontifical includes a prayer that asks God to give the pilgrim "remission from all sins" after he confesses.[59] In France, the Reims Pontifical of about 1100 asks God to grant an "indulgence and remission of all of your sins."[60] The eleventh-century recension of the RGP asked that the pilgrim "might merit in this world to receive the remission of all sins and, in the future, to be in the company of all the blessed."[61] The rite followed by asking that God "absolve [the pilgrim] from all sins" so that he might be crowned on the Day of Judgment when sinners are separated from the just.[62] The rubrics in a Benevantan Pontifical of about 1100 specified that confession be given after the bishop (or abbot) handed over the staff and before the final prayers.[63]

Initially, the rite assumed pilgrims going to Rome, that is, to the seat of Saint Peter, from whom the power of binding and loosing was derived. Despite the increase in pilgrimage traffic to Jerusalem in the century before the crusades, penitential pilgrimages were still primarily associated with

---

57. London BL Cotton Vitellius E.XII, 157r (York Pontifical) and Cambridge Corpus Christi College 163, 289r: "precamur ob noxiis flexis poplitibus tuam clementiam, potentiam, indulgentiam, remissionem, miserationem, compassionem; ut hunc [hos] famulum [famulos] tuum [tuos], illis tuam pietatem exorentem suaque delicta deflentem, nec non ad iter penitudinis euntem et asylum sanctissime, tue habitationis pro suis facinoribus requirentem; nunc novo lavacro penitentie peregrinationis."

58. Vich Scr. 1146 (p. 174): "letetur remissione peccatorum." Roda Pnt. LXVIII.C.9 (p. 550).

59. Roda Pnt. LXVII.10 (p. 541): "det uobis remissionem omnium peccatorum uestrorum."

60. Reims BM 341, 2r: "Indulgentiam & remissionem omnium peccatorum vestrorum [tuorum] tribuat vobis [tibi] omnipotens dominus."

61. RGP CCXII.2 (2:362): "mereamini in hoc seculo accipere remissionem omnium peccatorum et in futuro consorcium omnium beatorum."

62. RGP CCXII.2 (2:362).

63. Richard Gyug, "A Pontifical of Benevento (Macerata, Biblioteca Comunale 'Mozzi-Borgetti' 378," *Mediaeval Studies* 51 (1989): 402.

Rome, and in 1095 none of the rites yet assumed Jerusalem.[64] This is in line with the motivation for going on the greater pilgrimages, and especially to Rome, since there—the home of Saint Peter, the holder of the keys—one might hope to obtain the absolution of sins.[65] In the RGP, it was specifically the Apostle—that is, Peter—who was envisioned as offering the remission of sin. The notion that pilgrimage itself would enjoin a remission from all sins, central to the pilgrim liturgies of the eleventh and twelfth centuries, would be integrated in the crusading rites that grew out of them. This explains in part how the idea of penitential warfare as it developed around 1095 was so closely associated with pilgrimage, because it was the liturgical apparatus of pilgrimage that provided the mechanism that allowed for the remission of sin. That is, it was the pilgrimage liturgy that marked crusaders out as pilgrims, but also, critically, as penitents. When Robert of Reims (who was probably at Clermont) recounted Urban's speech, he reported the pope urging that people "take up, thus, this journey, in the remission of your sins."[66] Robert further reported Urban saying that laymen ought not leave "unless they have received the blessing of their priest [*benedictione sacerdotis*]."[67]

The Liturgy of War

If the liturgy of pilgrimage made crusading a penitential activity, it was the liturgies of war that sacralized the business of war itself. These were not unrelated, since a long exegetical tradition had equated spiritual warfare (against vice) with actual warfare (against worldly enemies) such that the two worked in cohort toward an ideal of virtue, peace, and justice.[68] The Old Testament, which would play such a strong role in the development of crusade ideology, offered many examples of prayer and penitence in the face of military losses. The very idea that military failures were God's punishment

---

64. Gaposchkin, "The Role of Jerusalem," 5–7.
65. Benedicta Ward, *Miracles and the Medieval Mind* (1982; rev ed. Philadelphia: 1987), 115–126; Debra Birch, *Pilgrimage to Rome in the Middle Ages: Continuity and Change* (Woodbridge, UK: 1998), 39–41.
66. RR 7 (tr. 81).
67. RR 7 (tr. 82).
68. Gerard Caspary, *Politics and Exegesis: Origen and the Two Swords* (Berkeley: 1979); Philippe Buc, "Some Thoughts on the Christian Theology of Violence, Medieval and Modern, from the Middle Ages to the French Revolution," *Rivista di Storia del Cristianesimo* 5 (2008): 9–28; Philippe Buc, *Holy War, Martyrdom, and Terror: Christianity, Violence, and the West* (Philadelphia: 2015), 67–111; Katherine Allen Smith, *War and the Making of Medieval Monastic Culture*, Studies in the History of Medieval Religion (Woodbridge, UK: 2011). This was not unimportant for Urban II: Alfons Becker, *Papst Urban II (1088–1099)*, 3 vols., Schriften der Monumenta Germaniae Historica 19 (Stuttgart 1964–2012), 2:333–376.

for sin—and that military victory was bestowed on the chosen people—was biblical. Repeated cycles of sin, military loss, repentance, and forgiveness leading to victory were found in the Old Testament, including, in particular, the story of Joshua before the Battle of Ai and the procession around the city of Jericho before its fall (Joshua 6); of the Israelites who were granted victory against the Benjaminites after fasting and making burned offerings (Judges 20:26); of the Ninevites who wore sack cloths and repented in order to stave off God's wrath (Jonah 3); and of Judas Macchabeus, who prepared his army through fasting and prayer (1 Mach 3:18–19). 1 Maccabees 3:19 proclaimed that "the success of war is not in the multitude of the army, but the strength coming from heaven." The theme of these stories was communal repentance before the Lord. Perhaps the most important model, cited repeatedly in later years in defense of crusade liturgies, was Moses, from Exodus 17:8–13, whose prayer permitted Joshua and his army to prevail over the Amalechites.

> Moses said to Joshua, choose your men and go forth to fight Amalec . . .
> Joshua did as Moses had told him, and he fought against Amalec; but Moses
> and Aaron and Hur went up to the top of the hill. And Moses raised up his
> hands [to God in prayer], and Israel conquered; but if he let them down a little,
> Amalec overcame. And Moses' hands became heavy; so . . . Aaron and Hur
> held up his hands on either side of him. And it happened that his hand did not
> weary until sundown. And Joshua put Amalec and his people to flight by the
> edge of the sword. (Exodus 17:9–13)

This material was all recited each year as part of the liturgy: Exodus between Septuagesima and Passion Sunday; Jonah in the period leading up to Advent; and Maccabees in what is known as the Summer Histories, such that, starting in October, the story of Judas Maccabeus was parceled out over several weeks. These histories were in line with the tone of much of the liturgy, which, since its foundation, and its early dependence on the Psalter (the basis of much of the liturgical cursus), had always had a deeply bellicose edge, steeped in a militant language of spiritual warfare.[69]

The patristics had, early on, spiritualized the warfare of the great Old Testament narratives within Christianity's irenic ideal—war was war against vices—The central text here—a New Testament text that grappled with Old Testament bellicism—was Ephesians 6:11–17. Origen (d. 254), more than anyone, explained how Christians fought a spiritual battle for virtue through prayers, "putting on the whole armour of God" (cf. Ephesians

---

69. Smith, *War and the Making*, 9–38. Many of these values were absorbed into saints' offices. Roman Hankeln, "Reflections of War and Violence in Early and High Medieval Saints' Offices," *Plainsong and Medieval Music* 23, no. 1 (2014): 5–30.

6:11–17).[70] By the fifth century, in his *Psychomachia*, the poet Prudentius staged a full-scale war between the virtues and vices. It was monks, not soldiers, who were the *milites christi* fighting what the liturgy called the "invisible enemy" (the devil), while knights and soldiers fought real, actual enemies.[71] Yet there always remained a relationship between spiritual and material warfare that made the latter dependent upon the former. These Old Testament stories of purification, supplication, and warfare linked the two in the Christian theology of war. Prayer, and particularly the formal prayer of liturgy, thus assumed a central role in the waging of wars. Early on, Gregory of Nyssa (d. 395) referring to Exodus 17, had extolled the efficacy of prayer in this regard: "Through [prayer] good prospers, evil is destroyed, and sinners will be converted. . . . Through prayer, the Israelites triumphed over the Amalechites, and 185,000 Assyrians were slain in one night by the invisible sword."[72] For Gregory and many following him, Exodus 17 was the proof text for the fact that liturgical prayer could play a critical role in military success. For Augustine, the battles were complementary: "Others [i.e., monks] fight for you [soldiers] against invisible enemies by praying; you work for them against visible barbarians by fighting."[73] And since Christian warfare was mapped onto the eschatological divide, the great battle that monks waged through prayer every day against the devil was waged in smaller ways by fighting the enemies of the Church, or the enemies of Christ. This was particularly true when monks prayed specifically for victory in battle. A letter attributed in the Middle Ages to Augustine advised that in preparing for war one should: "Take up your arms with your hands, and let the prayers strike the ears of The Creator, because, when a battle takes place, God looks down from the heavens and, observing which side is just, grants there the palm [of victory]."[74]

From the very outset of the crusades, prayers were juxtaposed to swords as a way of fighting the enemies of God. One of the earliest monastic chroniclers of the First Crusade, Baldric of Bourgeuil, evoked the Moses trope for Urban II in 1095 describing him as saying at Clermont: "You who are about to go [on the First Crusade], you will have our prayers for you; we will have you fighting for the people of God. Our [job] is to pray; let

70. Buc, *Holy War, Martyrdom, and Terror,* 72–100.

71. Smith, *War and the Making,* 28–37. We can only talk properly about knights by the thirteenth century: Jean Flori, *L'Essor de la chevalerie, XI^c–XII^c siècles* (Geneva: 1986).

72. Gregory of Nyssa, *The Lord's Prayer. The Beatitudes,* Translated and annotated by Hilda C. Grae (Westminster, MD: 1954), 24–25.

73. Caspary, *Politics and Exegesis,* 128–129; Smith, *War and the Making,* 32; Buc, *Holy War, Martyrdom, and Terror,* 79.

74. PL v. 33, col. 1098, Ep. 13.

yours be to fight the Amalechites. We will raise our unwearied hands, like Moses, praying to the heavens; you, like intrepid fighters, must go forth and brandish your swords against Amalec."[75] Baldric also compared Adhémar to Moses and Raymond of Toulouse to Aaron to argue that the crusade was supported by both *sacerdotium* and *regnum, clericalis ordo et laicalis.*[76] As early as 1098, the bishop of Grenoble, upon forwarding news from the princes writing from Antioch to churchmen in France, said that "some of you will answer their rightful requests with prayers and alms, while others will hasten to them with arms."[77]

THIS premise—that prayer could effect military outcomes—lay at the heart of liturgical supplication for God's help in war. In 1935 Carl Erdmann pointed to liturgical texts that sanctified war, the implements of war, and the men of war who carried them, in arguing that the militarization of the Church in the century before Clermont was instrumental in building the ideology of crusade.[78] Liturgical appeal of this sort in fact went back to the earliest centuries of Christian rulership in the Roman Empire, in ritual texts that prayed for the military success of the universalizing polity.[79] A year earlier, in 1934, Gerd Tellenbach had traced brilliantly how these war prayers evolved during the late Roman and early medieval period to accommodate both the evolving ideal of Christian empire as well as the military realities and political identity of the Carolingian world.[80] These prayers were a crucial element in the Christianization of the state that followed from the time of Constantine's conversion and reign. In the years between, say, Constantine and Charlemagne, the Roman duty to bring peace to the uncivilized world became the obligation to ensure the unencumbered worship of God's name. Romans became the Christians of the new Frankish Empire. Barbarians became the pagans of the Carolingian world.

75. BB 10.
76. BB 11.
77. Epistulae XII (p. 154) (tr. *Letters* 26).
78. Carl Erdmann, *The Origin of the Idea of Crusade*, trans. Marshall W. Baldwin and Walter Goffart (Princeton, NJ: 1977), 28–31.
79. Robert Folz, *The Concept of Empire in Western Europe from the Fifth to the Fourteenth Century* (London: 1969), 4–7; Tellenbach, *Römischer und christlicher Reichsgedanke in der Liturgie des frühen mittelalters*, Sitzungsberichte der Heidelberger akademie der wissenschaften. Philosophisch-historische klasse. (bd. 25) jahrg. 1934/35, 1. abh. (Heidelberg: 1934). Erdmann certainly recognized this.
80. Gerd Tellenbach, *Römischer und christlicher Reichsgedanke.* Tellenbach's work can be updated with Michael McCormick, *Eternal Victory: Triumphal Rulership in Late Antiquity, Byzantium, and the Early Medieval West* (Cambridge, UK: 1986); and Ildar Garipzanov, *The Symbolic Language of Authority in the Carolingian World (c. 751–877)* (Leiden: 2008), 43–100.

Specific liturgical attention to the martial aims of the state, and particularly the person of the king, appeared with renewed vigor in the eighth and ninth centuries as a product of the strength of royal power in Visigothic Spain and Carolingian Francia, developing in response both to expansionist efforts and to their defensive needs. In Iberia, starting in the eighth century, particularly during the reign of Alphonse III (866–910), the liturgy was enlisted to aid the military efforts of the Visigoths to conquer territory from Muslim powers.[81] A Visigothic mass against enemies asked God to recall Moses, who overcame the power of Amalec (who trusted in the power of his army), not by fighting with swords but by fighting with holy prayers.[82] North of the Pyrenees, Charlemagne sponsored special supplications for military campaigns in the 790s. The Church wrote new appeals and developed a whole series of new liturgical rites, including votive masses, special benedictions, supplicatory litanies, and processions. The original context for masses and blessings was the Carolingians' expansionist efforts into non-Christian lands that were paired with a policy of conquest and conversion by the sword.[83] The prayers associated with the military leadership of the king were in step with the Carolingian appropriation of the ideal of Christian kingship and its obligations to protect subjects and ensure peace.[84] The rites were adopted widely in the following centuries as Carolingian liturgical reform engendered the production of new manuscripts throughout Francia—that is, throughout the geographical expanse that would supply the "Franks," the term our sources often use for crusaders.[85]

These rites were part of the larger ideological program that constructed holy war as holy. They were performed both on the home front (in monasteries and secular churches) and in the field while on campaign (by priests and bishops accompanying the army in order to serve the pastoral needs of the soldiers).[86] As a group, they drew on the tradition rooted in the Old Testament, of God as avenger against sinners, and against those that acted against His interests or those of His people, assuming His people were

---

81. Alexander Pierre Bronisch, *Reconquista und Heiliger Krieg: die Deutung des Krieges im christlichen Spanien von den Westgoten bis ins frühe 12. Jahrhundert* (Munster: 1998); Patrick Henriet, "L'idéologie de guerre sainte dans le haut moyen âge hispanique," *Francia. Forschungen zur westeuropäischen Geschichte* 29 (2002): 171–220.

82. *Liber Ordinum*, 413.

83. Michael McCormick, "The Liturgy of War in the Early Middle Ages: Crisis, Litanies, and the Carolingian Monarchy," *Viator* 15 (1984); McCormick, *Eternal Victory*, 352–362; Bachrach, *Religion and the Conduct of War*, 33–43.

84. Tellenbach, *Römischer und christlicher reichsgedanke*.

85. On the notion of "Frank," see Matthew Gabriele, *An Empire of Memory: The Legend of Charlemagne, the Franks, and Jerusalem before the First Crusade* (Oxford 2011).

86. Bachrach, *Religion and the Conduct of War*, 33–43.

righteous.[87] War rites proposed that the individual warrior and his weapons were agents of God's will in His larger battle against the devil. The rites foster the equivalency of material and spiritual (or visible and invisible) enemies elaborated by ninth-century exegetes.[88] Together, they served to construct a theology of war—a theology which, pace Erdmann, was funneled directly into the theology of crusading—in which the fighter participated in the temporal manifestation of the larger eschatological battle of salvific history. The collect for the popular *in tempore belli* mass asked:

> O God, You who crush wars and who, by the power of Your defenses, conquer those who fight against [us] who hope in You, bring aid to those imploring in Your mercy, so that, the savagery of all gentiles [=nonbelievers] having been suppressed, we may offer You praise in unwearied thanksgiving.[89]

These rites thus connected faith, service, and humility to temporal victory and in turn eternal salvation. For the most part, the prayers asked God to protect the king and his army so that they would be victorious, but some of the language beseeched God's active help in crushing, conquering, subduing, vanquishing, or destroying the enemy (using forms of words such as *comprimere, superare, expugnare, prevalere, subdere*).[90] God is the "ruler over all kings and kingdoms,"[91] the "one who will anger at those who offend him,"[92] the one who will "subdue the enemies of the Christian name, with the power of Your majesty"[93] and who will "crush wars and conquer those who assault those who hope in You with the force of Your defense."[94]

Both the Visigothic tradition (in northern Iberia) and the Gallican tradition (rites that flourished in the same areas that formed the core catchment area for participants of the First Crusade) evoked the Israelites.[95] In the LePuy Sacramentary, for instance, the king whose army is the object of

---

87. Susannah Throop, *Crusading as an Act of Vengeance, 1095–1216* (Farnham, UK: 2011), 88–96.

88. Buc, "Some Thoughts on the Christian Theology of Violence," 90–103.

89. CO 1501, *Deus, qui conteris bella . . .*

90. *Comprimere*: CO 3726, 3846; *Superare*: CO 3848, 5746, 5747; *Expugnare*: CO 2475, Autun Scr. 1792 (same as Gellone Scr. 2768); *Prevalere*: CO 4071, Gelasian Scr. no. 1498 (p. 217); *Subdere*: Autun Scr. 508, Angoulême Scr. 661, Gelasian Scr. 406 (p. 65); *Depellere*: CO 1803a.

91. Gelasian Scr., 1479: *Deus regnorum omnium regumque dominator.*

92. Gregorian Scr., 2564 (2:164), *Domine deus qui ad hoc irasceris . . .*

93. Gregorian Scr., 1336 (1:442), *Omnipotens deus christiani nominis inimicos . . .*, from the Aniane supplementary.

94. Gregorian Scr., 1332 (1:441), *Deus qui conteris bella . . .*, from the Aniane Supplementary.

95. Tellenbach, *Römischer und christlicher reichsgedanke*, 21–22. Bronisch, *Reconquista und Heiliger Krieg*, 62–75, 102–111; Henriet, "L'idéologie de guerre sainte dans le haut moyen âge hispanique," 175–176.

these votive prayers was compared to Moses, Aaron, and Abraham.[96] A mass for those leaving for battle compared the entreating Christian army to the Israelites leaving Egypt in need of God's defense.[97] Another prayer asked, "Just as You freed the sons of Israel from the church of the Egyptians, would You now liberate Your Christian peoples from the oppression of the heathens."[98] Elsewhere, God is beseeched to protect princes with His shield as He had David,[99] and to spare His people as He had the Ninevites.[100]

The rites proposed the free, unencumbered worship of the Christian religion (or "the Christian name") as the desired state of the Christian polity, allowing for the "perpetual Alleluia" praising God and his power.[101] "Conquer the obstacles that oppose Your servants so that, the terrors of war having been lifted, untroubled liberty and worship might be at peace."[102] And "avert the terrors of all hostilities from us so that the untroubled liberty of the Christian name might always exult in Your devotion."[103] This ideal was rooted, we saw, in the late antique ideal of bringing the (Christianized) Roman peace to the uncivilized world but was easily adapted to the purpose of the crusades. As Riley-Smith has insisted, the notion of the liberty of Christian worship in the Holy Land was one of the guiding impulses of the First Crusade.[104]

A particular strand of votive mass emerged in the ninth century to call for help against pagans. Additions to the Gregorian sacramentary included *contra paganos* prayers and masses, asking God to crush the enemy or repulse the hostilities the pagan people (*gentem paganam*).[105] The LePuy Sacramentary included, in addition to the traditional *in tempore belli* mass

---

96. CO 3873. LePuy Scr., 202v and Angoulême Scr. 2308: "ut sicut Moysi et Aaron fuisti propitius in Aegypto, ita dignare famulo tuo illo cum omni exercitu suo liberare de tirannorum terrore." For other examples, see Angoulême Scr. 2309 and 2316; Autun Scr. 1643; also Corbie Sacramentary as transcribed in Flori, *L'Essor de la chevalerie*, 378.

97. LePuy Scr., at 80v. Also found in Angoulême Scr. 2309: "et sicut israheli properanti ex aegypto securitatis prebuisti munimen." A variant is found in Gellone Scr. 2750, and a version was adopted in RGP CCXLV (2:380).

98. LePuy Scr., 202v: "sicut liberasti filios israhel de manibus egyptiorum"; See also Angoulême Scr. 2307 = CP 5467.

99. Angoulême Scr. 2317.

100. Gregorian Scr. 2570 (2:165).

101. Jordan, "Perpetual Alleluia," 744–752.

102. CO 1803a. Gelasian Scr., 1477; Gellone Scr., 2768; Gregorian Scr., 2579 (2:166), *Deus qui misericordiae . . .*

103. CO 4285. See also CO 5746–5748, and O.S.B. Heiming, Odilo, ed. *Das Sacramentarium triplex. Die Handschrift C 43 der Zentralbibliothek Zürich*, Corpus Ambrosiano-liturgicum 1 (Münster: 1968), no. 3054 (p. 287).

104. Riley-Smith, *The First Crusade*, 17–22.

105. Gregorian Scr. 2564–2569 (2:164–165).

(discussed above), two *contra paganos* masses, one of which compared the army leaving for war to the Israelites.[106] In the eleventh century an old prayer used in the Easter liturgy, *Omnipotens sempiterne deus in cuius manu*, was updated as *contra paganos* mass.[107] *Omnipotens sempiterne deus* asked God to look favorably upon the beseechers "so that the heathen [*gentes*] who put trust in their own ferocity might be vanquished by the power of Your right hand."[108] This prayer had originally spoken of the Roman Empire, but later versions replaced Rome with the Franks, or spoke of the "Christian empire," before, in the crusading context, adapting it for the interest of the Christian armies.[109] The conceit of the various war rites was that military setbacks against enemies and pagans were caused by sin, and that the enemy was thus the scourge of God, the instrument of punishment for sin and pride.[110] Another *contra paganos* prayer, found in the Gregorian Sacramentary as well as the LePuy Sacramentary and then adopted by later crusading rites, asked that those entreating God might be free "of the pagan people who are prevailing over us, we know, because of our sins."[111] The word *paganus* or phrase *gentes pagani* did not appear in the Vulgate bible, but it was a common enough phrase in Frankish Christendom. Under the Carolingians, the term probably referred to the Saxons. Gregorian texts for masses against pagans incorporated into the Spanish sacramentaries of the eleventh century were presumably repurposed for the reconquest.[112] The phrase would be crucial after 1095, since during the crusades, Muslims were, of course, routinely described as pagans.

The continued applicability of these war rites and the addition of similar compositions fed into the militarization of the Church and ecclesiastical ideology that made the First Crusade possible.[113] A great number of these texts continued to be copied, with some adaptations and some new compositions, into liturgical books of the tenth and eleventh centuries.[114] At times

---

106. LePuy Scr., 202v, *Sempiterne trinitas deus* . . . See also Angoulême Scr., 2307 (p. 358).

107. CO 3846. For earlier examples of this prayer in *contra paganos* liturgy, see Nevers Scr. 351 and Heiming, *Das Sacramentarium triplex*, no. 3013. Both manuscripts date to the eleventh century.

108. CO 3846, *Omnipotens sempiterne deus* . . .

109. See variants of CO 3846.

110. An idea central to the theological-historical conceptualization of Urban II himself. Becker, *Papst Urban II*, 2:361.

111. Gregorian Scr. 2564 (2:164); LePuy Scr., 203r; CO 2304b, with citations, *Domine deus qui ad hoc irasceris* . . . . For examples in other prayers, see also Missale Franc., 70 (p. 20); and Gelasian Scr., 1482 (p. 215).

112. Vich Scr. 1172–1174 (p. 178) *Missa contra paganos*; Ripoll Scr. 1660–1663 (p. 224)

113. Erdmann, *The Origin of the Idea of Crusade*; Jean Flori, *La guerre sainte—la formation de l'idée de croisade dans l'Occident chrétien* (Paris: 2001); Tomaž Mastnak, *Crusading Peace: Christendom, the Muslim World, and Western Political Order* (Berkeley: 2002).

114. LePuy Scr., 202v–203r (*missa contra paganos*); Vich Scr., 1139–1141 *pro pacis* (p. 173), 1171–1174 *contra paganos* (p. 178), 1175–1178 *contra inimicis et persequentibus* (p. 179),

the rubrics were updated.[115] In France, one *contra paganos* rite talked about invasion against Normans.[116] In England, another was used against the Danes.[117] Romans were replaced with the Franks.[118] Liturgical texts often evolved to meet the needs of new contexts. At the same time, new rites were composed that maintained the essential features of the genre.[119] The frequency with which these masses were copied into service books of the tenth and eleventh century suggests both their continued need and applicability (these being the centuries of weak secular leadership and the Peace of God). It also points to ecclesiastical appropriation of one of the core functions of secular society—military defense. In this way churchmen, whose weapon, Moses-like, was prayer, participated in the broader social and military goals of their political community.[120]

NEWER to the scene in the eleventh century were blessings of the weapons of warfare (the sword, the shield, the war standard) and ultimately blessings laid on the soldier himself (see Fig. 1.1). These rites were performed as crusaders prepared for and departed for crusade.[121] The tradition of blessing the swords of knights grew out of the coronation ceremonies for kings and emperors, in which the king was vested with the sword as an emblem of his secular power, designed to ensure peace and do justice. These rites asked God to bless the sword, which was conferred on the king for "avenging evil doers," so that, through the power of the Holy Spirit the king might be able to withstand or eject all his enemies and all the adversaries of the holy Church, entrusted to him, through the authority of Jesus Christ the "invincible victor."[122] In this way, the ideology behind the sword as a symbol of

---

1184–1193 *tempore belli* (pp. 180–181); Ripoll Scr., 1586 *pro pace* (p. 216), 1660–1663 *contra paganos* (p. 224), 1664–1667 *in tempore belli* (p. 224), 1668–1674 *Pro exercitu ad bellum contra paganos* (p. 225); Henry Austin Wilson, *The Missal of Robert of Jumièges* (London: 1896), *Missa pro pace* (pp. 264–265), *missa in tempore belli* (p. 267), *missa contra paganos* (p. 268); Leofric Scr. 185–186, *missa contra paganos*; Nevers Scr., *Missa pro pace* (p. 344), *pro invasione gentium* (p. 351); Heiming, *Das Sacramentarium triplex*, 2985–2991 *pro pace* (pp. 281–282), 2992–3005 *pro regibus* (pp. 282–283), 3006–3029 *in tempore belli* (pp. 283–285).

115. CO 3007, *Hostium nostrorum.* . . . Autun Scr. no. 3014 and Ripoll Scr. no. 1674 (p. 225, "missa pro exercitu ad bellum contra paganos"); Gellone Scr. 2756 (p. 432, "Missa in profectionem hostium eontibus in prohelium"); Heiming, *Das Sacramentarium triplex*, no. 3014 (p. 284, "alia missa contra paganos").

116. Paris BNF Lat. 2293, 211v: "gentem normannorum."

117. CBP 1228: "Benedictio in tempore belli, sive contra Danos."

118. CO 3846b, with variants listed.

119. Eg., CO 1160, 1249.

120. Barbara Rosenwein, "Feudal War and Monastic Peace: Cluniac Liturgy as Ritual Aggression," *Viator* 2 (1971): 129–157; Smith, *War and the Making.*

121. EA *Chron* 142. EA *Hier* 19.

122. Flori, *L'Essor de la chevalerie*, 370. See here the Erdman Ordo (Ordo XIII); Antonio Staerk, *Les manuscrits latins du Ve au XIIIe siècle conservés à la Bibliothèque impériale de*

Figure 1.1. The blessing of swords, from a copy of the pontifical of William Durandus, ca. 1357. Sainte Genevieve 0143, 181v. © Bibliothèque Sainte-Geneviève, Paris, cliché IRHT.

God's power delegated was over the course of the tenth and eleventh century slowly adapted to (or adopted by) the emerging "knightly" class, as that class developed a coherent corporate ideology that imbibed ideals of Christian warfare.[123] In the RGP, the formula for the sword blessing was grouped with other services for the departing army, and for the battle standard.[124] The RGP's battle standard blessing was also copied into the LePuy Sacramentary, alongside the prayer for the army. It asked God to sanctify the standard

> that has been prepared for use in war, so that it might prevail against adversaries and rebellious nations, and, surrounded by Your protection, may it be terrifying to the enemies of the Christian people. . . . You are indeed the God who crushes wars and gives the aid of celestial protection to those who have hope in You.[125]

In tenth-century England the blessing of weapons asked God to bless swords or lances or shield or helmets or battle standards so that "through the power of Your power they might remain unconquered by the enemies fighting

---

Saint-Pétersbourg; description, textes inédits, reproductions autotypiques, 2 vols. (Saint Petersburg: 1910), a transcription of Saint Petersburg Codex Q.v.I, no. 35, at 97r. Nevers Scr. 109.

123. Flori, *L'Essor de la chevalerie,* 43–115.

124. RGP CCXLIV (2:379).

125. LePuy Scr., 80v; RGP CCXLIII (2:378) "*quod bellico usui preparatum est.* . . . Erdmann, *The Origin of the Idea of Crusade,* 45.

against us."[126] In an eleventh-century ordo "for the arming of a defender of the church or another warrior," the warrior's battle standard, lance, sword, and shield were each blessed separately, before the soldier himself.[127] The bishop girded the warrior and asked him to stand strong against all enemies and all adversaries of the holy Church of God. The sacralized function of the warrior was thus an appropriation of the obligations of sacral kingship, with the protection of and the interests of the Church as legitimate objects of warfare.[128] Herein we find one of the paths by which penance would be replaced by chivalry in crusading ideology.[129] But more important is the way in which this praxis insisted that the soldier was participating in God's eschatological fight, that the warrior was an arm of God's justice, wielding His sword. A chronicler of the Albigensian crusade would later make this case. He described Aimery of Montfort, following a solemn mass, proclaiming: "Today I take my arms from Your altar, so that as I prepare to fight Your battles, I receive from You the instruments of battle."[130]

Throughout these various war-rites, the liturgy expressed a binary between God and his people on the one hand, and between the devil and the enemy on the other. The enemy was both an enemy of the army and also an enemy of God, or of the Church; and the fighters were described as "the faithful," "those trusting in You," or those "believing in You."[131] The prayers asked God to "protect the kingdom of Christians subject to You" so that it might be victorious over all other kingdoms.[132] In the early war masses, the adversary was identified as *hostes, inimicos,* or *adversarios*—that is, generic terms for "enemy." "Crush the enemies of Your people."[133] Strike the "enemies of the Christian name."[134] "Let us be freed from hostile enemies."[135]

---

126. Banting, *Two Anglo-Saxon Pontificals,* 138–139: "per virtutem potentie tuae ab hostibus contra nos dimicantibus invicta permaneant." Discussed in Flori, *L'Essor de la chevalerie,* 50, 84–85.

127. Cologne 141, 171v–174v; and Bamberg Staatliche lit. 56. Text found in Franz, *Die kirchlichen Benediktionen,* 2:295. Flori, *L'Essor de la chevalerie,* 379–382, example 26.

128. Jean Flori, "Chevalerie et liturgie," *Le Moyen Age* 84 (1978), 409–442; Jean Flori, "Les origines de l'abouement chevaleresque: étude des remise d'armes et du vocabulaire qui les exprime," *Traditio* 35 (1979), 209–272; Jean Flori, *L'idéologie du glaive: préhistoire de la chevalerie* (Geneva: 1983); Flori, *L'Essor de la chevalerie.*

129. Jonathan Riley-Smith, *The First Crusaders: 1095–1131* (New York: 1997), 64.

130. PVC §450 (lat. 3:143, tr. 205).

131. "Fidelium," "in te confidans," and "in tua virtute fidentes." E.g.: Angoulême Scr. 2310; Linder RA 107–108; CO 1189 and 1190.

132. Gregorian Scr., 1331 (1:441).

133. CO 826; Gelasian Scr., 1483; Autun Scr., 1780; Angoulême Scr., 2331; Nevers Scr., 29: "Contere quaesumus domine, hostes populi tui."

134. "Christiani nominis inimicos." See: CO 6760; Gregorian Scr. 1336 (1:442); Leofric Scr. 185; Dold and Gamber, *Das Sakramentar von Monza,* 990. Gregor Richter and Albert Schönfelder, eds., *Sacramentarium Fuldense Saeculi X: Cod. Theol. 231 der K. Universitätsbibliothek zu Göttingen,* Quellen und Abhandlungen zur Geschichte der Abtei und der Diözese Fulda 9 (1912; reprint, Henry Bradshaw Society 101, 1977), 1945.

135. CO 2675, 2676: "ab infestis liberetur inimicis."

The terms were always plural. In these instances, the 'enemy' usually indicated a military enemy, and was often used in military contexts, but the terms could shade into metaphysical categories that equated military opposition with the great eschatological battle against the ancient enemy. Enemies might be "visible" or "invisible," and of course, the invisible enemies were associated with the greatest, the most ancient, enemy—Satan.

Indeed, these very terms were also used to refer to Satan, the devil, demons, or malignant forces—that is, any metaphysical enemy that labored in the eschatological battle of which human life was only a small part. In the liturgy, Satan was routinely the "ancient enemy" (*antiqui hostis, antiquum adversarium, inimicus*).[136] The cross was the weapon against the enemy (*hostem*), the devil.[137] The visible and invisible enemies of liturgical prayer thus referred to the entire spectrum of hostile forces. Several prayers asked God to render the king invincible against visible and invisible enemies (*hostes* and *inimicos*).[138] One prayer that begged God to protect the beseechers from the enemy was originally written as a mass against the temptations of the devil but was later adapted for times of war and against pagans.[139] It would later be used in crusading.[140] The adaptions of prayers that assumed the devil as the enemy to ones that assumed a military enemy undergirded a broader ideological matrix in which war was understood as following a larger divine scheme, with Christian armies identified with God's plan and the enemy with the devil.[141]

It is in this way that the liturgy brought war into the divine scheme and made it possible for violence to be made sacred. In its earliest form, the violent imagery of combat and victory was the language of spiritual struggle within the context of an ostensibly pacifist Christianity, and the liturgy naturally absorbed images of warfare as monks took on the mantle of being the soldiers of Christ. Increasingly spiritual and material warfare were interdependent. The appropriation of sacrality by kings and emperors— the war leaders—blurred the categories of good and evil, of allies and enemies. Under the Visigoths and the Carolingians, the militancy of the liturgy was thus partly deallegorized, and prayer explicitly instrumentalized toward the earthly aims of war.[142] In turn, because physical warfare against

---

136. Many examples, including CO 351, 1204; CBP 228, 744, 985, 1825, etc.
137. RGP XL 99 (1:158).
138. CO 2801. See also CO 1384b.
139. CO 4746, *Protector noster.*
140. Rome Biblioteca Angelica 477, Paris BNF Lat. 12056, 276v. *Regestum Clementis Papae V*: no. 4769 (p. 313).
141. A theme developed in Smith, *War and the Making.*
142. There are earlier examples of this. Constantine was clearly the model, and this even has Roman roots. But it was the Carolingians who instrumentalized prayer warfare. The

pagans had explicitly religious aims, warfare itself took on spiritualized meaning, thus reversing the initial allegoricization of Old Testament bellicism undertaken by Origen and Jerome.[143] And thus it was in these Old Testament texts that the framework was established for the belligerent texts of the liturgy, a framework that equated the enemy, or pagans, with the devil; that drew on Old Testament models of holy war; that understood military setbacks as caused by pride and sin; that linked military struggle to God's cause; and ultimately that associated military victory in the temporal world with eschatological triumph and individual salvation. In this sense, the central images of devotional ideology that defined the First Crusade had been established in the liturgical discourse of the tenth and eleventh centuries.

The Liturgy of the Cross

This brings us to the most militant of the liturgical texts—the liturgy of the cross. If the liturgy of pilgrimage sacralized the penitential aspects of crusade, and the liturgy of warfare the bellicose, then in the liturgy of the cross, which was at once both militant and penitential, we have the reason that the cross itself became the central symbol of crusade. The cross was militant, in that it was the power that crushed the enemy (the devil), but it was also a sign of service and passion, ultimately the mechanism of individual salvation. The symbol encompassed a dialectical synthesis of the opposites—victory and defeat, conquest and humiliation—that was at the heart of Christianity. Between the ninth and the twelfth centuries, devotion to the cross moved in emphasis from the mystical and eschatological to the personal and passion centered.[144] The shift related to a move in devotion from divine Christ to human Christ; from (pace Rachel Fulton) Christ as Judge to Christ as Sufferer. The earlier phase, which characterized the Cross as a symbol of victory over the devil, gave way in the years around 1100 to a celebration of the Incarnation and a valorization

---

relationship between internal battle (in the Church, for reform) and external battle against pagans (mostly in Spain) in the thinking of Urban II is explored in Becker, *Papst Urban II*, 2:333–376.

143. Buc, "Some Thoughts on the Christian Theology of Violence"; Buc, *Holy War, Martyrdom, and Terror*, 45–61.

144. Jean Leclercq, "La dévotion médiévale envers le crucifié," *La Maison Dieu* 75 (1963): 119–132; Rachel Fulton, *From Judgment to Passion: Devotion to Christ and the Virgin Mary, 800–1200* (New York: 2002); Giles Constable, "The Ideal of the Imitation of Christ," in *Three Studies in Medieval Religious and Social Thought* (Cambridge, UK: 1995), 143–248; Dominique Iogna-Prat, "La croix, le moine et l'empereur: dévotion à la croix et théologie politique à Cluny autour de l'an mil," in *Haut Moyen Age: Culture, éducation et société. Etudes offertes à Pierre Riché*, ed. Michel Sot (Nanterre: 1990), 449–475; Colin Morris, *The Sepulchre of Christ and the Medieval West: From the Beginning to 1600* (Oxford: 2005).

Figure 1.2. Altar cross, (a) front and (b) back, from the treasury of the cathedral church at Münster, ca. 1090. (a) The front *crux gemata* represents victory and splendor. (b) On the back is engraved an image of Christ, between the sun and the moon, victorious over death. Photo © Stephan Kube, Greven.

Figure 1.3. Reliquary crucifix. 1125–1175, showing Christ suffering. Made in Spain, ca. 1125–1175. Metropolitan Museum of Art 17.190.221. © The Metropolitan Museum of Art.

Image source: Art Resource, NY.

of the salvific value of Christ's suffering. The former never disappeared, but the emphasis shifted. And this shift, well known in art and literature, was also manifest in the liturgy.[145]

The crusades, begun in the crucible of the transition from victory to passion, drew on both strands of cross devotion in carving out a spirituality and devotion specific to crusading. By all accounts the dominant motif of crusading spirituality from its inception, the cross pervades the early sources of the crusade. Urban had reportedly emphasized the cross even at Clermont, and the line from Matthew 16:24, "If any man will come after me, let him deny himself and take up his cross and follow me," became the rallying cry for crusading thereafter. The rhetoric of the cross emerging from the liturgical texts of the precrusade period was in some parts a language of service to God, and in others a militant language of combat and victory. It is perhaps not too much to say that, in this interplay, we see the seeds of crusade spirituality as it unfolded over the next two centuries.

THE cross permeated the liturgy as a symbol of the singular event of human salvation. It was central to the sacred ceremonial of Holy Week, especially the Adoration of the Cross on Good Friday. In the West, the practice, which coalesced around 700, was centered, when available, on a relic of the True Cross, and involved ritual prostration before the relic.[146] In addition were the feasts of the Invention of the Cross (May 3) and the feast of the Exaltation (September 14). The Invention feast was introduced into the Gallican rite in the West in the seventh century, apparently to commemorate the Byzantines' recovery of the True Cross from the Persians by the Emperor Heraclius.[147] The feast of the Exaltation, which commemorated Helena's discovery of the True Cross in Jerusalem, dates back to the fourth century in the Holy Land and was imported West, to Rome, also in the seventh century (probably around 630), also fueled by the enthusiasm that followed Heraclius's recovery of the Cross.[148] As part of the developing cult, the poet Venantius Fortunatus (d. ca. 600) composed three hymns to

---

145. Joseph Szövérffy, "'Crux fidelis . . .' Prologomena to a History of the Holy Cross Hymns," *Traditio* 22 (1966): 1–41; André Wilmart, "Les prières de Saint Pierre Damien pour l'adoration de la croix," *Revue des sciences religieuses* 9 (1929): 513–523; André Wilmart, "Prières médiévales pour l'adoration de la croix," *Ephemerides liturgicae* 46 (1932): 22–65.

146. Wilmart, "Prières médiévales pour l'adoration de la croix," 22–65; Louis van Tongeren, "Imagining the Cross on Good Friday: Rubric, Ritual and Relic in Early Medieval Roman, Gallican and Hispanic Liturgical Traditions," in *Envisioning Christ on the Cross, Ireland and the Early Medieval West*, ed. Juliet Mullins, Jenifer Ní Ghrádaigh, and Richard Hawtree (Dublin: 2013), 34–51.

147. G. Manz, "Ist die Messe *De inventione S. Crucis* im Sacramentarium Gelasianum gallischen Ursprungs?" *Ephemerides Liturgicae* 52 (1958): 192–196.

148. Louis van Tongeren, *Exaltation of the Cross: Toward the Origins of the Feast of the Cross and the Meaning of the Cross in Early Medieval Liturgy*, Liturgia Condenda 11 (Leuven: 2000).

the cross.[149] Meanwhile, in Rome, a liturgy developed around the adoration of a Roman relic of the True Cross (the "Exaltation" referring to the relic's elevation as part of the ceremony). From there the feast spread north, not without alteration and adaptation, as part of the move to Romanize the liturgy under the Carolingians. In the cross-fertilization of liturgical traditions in the eighth and ninth centuries, both feasts survived in the Western calendar.[150] At the end of the eleventh-century, for instance, Adhémar's church in LePuy celebrated both.[151] By the thirteenth century, these two feasts would be used as principal days on which to preach the cross.

The liturgical texts for the mass celebrated the salvific power of the cross and the redemption of Christ's sacrifice, along with the eternal victory of the cross against the powers of the devil in the ongoing eschatological battle. Cross liturgies were replete with triumphalist imagery in which the cross was both protector and savior. The LePuy Sacramentary offered the following prayers for the Invention Mass:

> God, who in the extraordinary invention of Your salvific cross enkindled the miracle of Your passion, grant for the price of the tree of life that we might attain the suffrage of eternal life.

> O God, look kindly upon this sacrifice we offer so that it might free us from all the evils of war and that, towards the destruction of the threat of the power of our enemies, through the standard [*vexillum*] of His son's holy cross, it might place us in the safety of Your protection.

> Filled with nourishments from heaven and refreshed by the spiritual cup, we beseech, Almighty God, that You defend us from the malignant enemy, who, through the wood of the holy cross of Your son, You ordered to vanquish with the arms of justice from the salvation of the world.[152]

The prayers envisioned an eschatological battle whose principle weapon was the cross. The central prayer asked specifically that the cross destroy enemies and protect from wars. These were the dominant themes in other traditions as well. Elsewhere, refrains included "Protect, O Lord, Your people by the sign of the holy cross from all the snares of all Your enemies."[153] "Through

---

149. On hymns to the Holy Cross, Szövérffy, "'Crux fidelis . . . ,'" 1–41; van Tongeren, *Exaltation of the Cross*, 209–212; The connection to crusade spirituality is discussed in Friedrich Wilhelm Wentzlaff-Eggbert, *Kreuzzugsdichung des Mittelalters: Studien zu ihrer geschichtlichen und dichterischen Wirklichkeit* (Berlin: 1960), 31–59.

150. Gerald Ellard, "Devotion to the Holy Cross and a Dislocated Mass-Text," *Theological Studies* 11 (1950): 333–355; van Tongeren, *Exaltation of the Cross*.

151. LePuy Scr., 170v–171v.

152. LePuy Scr., 170v–171v. The three prayers CO 1741 (*Deus qui in preclara*), 5217c (*Sacrificium Domine*), and 5040 (*Repleti alimonia celesti*). They are also attested in the other Gallican Sacramentaries, such as Angoulême Scr., Gellone Scr., and Autun Scr.

153. Cantus Index g00376. *Missale Romanum* 454; SMRL 2:298, 319; van Tongeren, *Exaltation of the Cross*, 168–169: "Protege domine plebem tuam per signum sancte crucis ab omnibus insidiis inimicorum omnium."

the sign of the cross [*Per signum crucis*], O Lord, free us from our enemies."[154] Here again the enemies (always in the plural) were spiritual enemies—the demons and the devil; the *inimicorum invisibilium* of some of the earlier texts which slowly shifted to *inimicorum visibilium et invisibilium*, enemies both actual and spiritual. As we saw with respect to the war rites, both terms—*inimicus* and *hostis*—were used for the devil. The cross texts also spoke of the adversaries (*adversarios*), always in the plural, denoting the host of temptations, dangers, and obstacles working in the devil's stead. Cross liturgy spoke of the "snares of adversaries" and the "wickedness of adversaries," which God is asked to crush by the power of the cross.[155] Venantius Fortunatus's hymn *Vexilla regis* used the image of the cross as Christ's royal battle standard in the eternal fight against the devil and other *inimicos Christi*.[156] In the mass, the cross is the *sanctificatum vexillum* (the sanctified war banner) which secures salvation through its triumph.[157] Behind this imagery lay the legend of Constantine's adoption of the Cross on his standard (here: the labarum) at the Battle of Milvian Bridge, a legend recited on the feast of the Exaltation.[158] In the tenth and eleventh centuries, new sequences for the cross could be found in manuscripts at St.-Martial, Cluny, and Fleury—that is, in what would become the heartland of the crusades.[159]

This eschatological triumphalism was also found in the Divine Office. An antiphon used in both the Invention and Exaltation feasts, for example, echoed the famous liturgical acclamation, *Christus vincit*: "The sweet cross shines, through which salvation was rendered to the world; the Cross conquers, the cross rules, the cross drives out all sins." But because the Divine Office was often structured as a narrative and included historical readings, it was here that the cross's triumphalism was given historical explication.[160] Several references to the Persian King Chosroes's capture of the cross in 614 and its retrieval by the Byzantine Emperor Heraclius (d. 641) reflect the

154. CAO 4264; *Missale Romanum* 330, 381: SMRL 2:281, 298, and see also 319 for a votive mass for the cross: "Per signum crucis de inimicis nostris libera nos deus noster."

155. For *insidias adversariorum*, CO 5217c; *nefas adversariorum per auxilium sanctae crucis digneris contere*, CO 156a and b; Leofric Scr. 225. These prayers appear widely in the sacramentaries of the ninth, tenth, and eleventh centuries.

156. AH 50:74, no. 67. See also, Fulbert of Chartres's (d. 1029) poem "Vexillum regis venerabilie cunta regentis." Frederick Behrends, *The Letters and Poems of Fulbert of Chartres* (Oxford: 1976), 244–247.

157. Leofric Scr. 159; van Tongeren, *Exaltation of the Cross*, 93.

158. Further hymns and sequences and votive masses were composed in France, Spain, and Germany in the ninth, tenth, and eleventh centuries. Ellard, "Devotion to the Holy Cross," 333–355; Gerald Ellard, "Alcuin and Some Favored Votive Masses," *Theological Studies* 40 (1940): 37–61. The dominant tradition was effectively codified in the tenth century in RGP XL.96–104 (1:157–160).

159. Szövérffy, "'Crux fidelis . . . ,'" 19.

160. For the early sources, see CAO nos. 92 (for the monastic cursus, in vol. 1) and 110 (for the secular cursus, in vol. 2). On the narrative nature of the Divine Office, see Ritva Jonsson, *Historia. Études sur la genèse des offices versifiés* (Stockholm: 1968).

Exaltation feast's origin in the celebration of the relic's return to Jerusalem in 631. One chant ran: "Chosroes, former infidel (*profanus*) king of the Persians, had carried off the holy Cross of Jerusalem through fighting, which then the clement Heraclius took back from the impious."[161] The liturgical readings further rehearsed stories of the cross's military power against pagans.[162] These were recited during the matins service, in conjunction with the great responsories (chant), and were often taken from the martyrology, that is the book containing the lives of the early martyrs and other Christian narratives. The lessons for the feast of the Invention told the story of Helena's discovery of the True Cross, but began with Constantine's fighting the "great race of barbarians" on the Danube (and not at the Milvian bridge) and the story of his miraculous vision of the great cross in the sky, and his great victory.[163] Constantine is told, "In hoc signo vinces"—"In this sign you will conquer"—echoing the *crux vincit* acclaim in the office. And the episode concludes with Constantine's great victory "over the barbarians."[164] "And on that day [God] gave victory to king Constantine through the power of the holy cross."[165] The cross's militancy and victory is thus associated as much with the story of Constantine's temporal victory as with its eschatological powers. In turn, the readings for the Exaltation feast told the story of Heraclius's recapture of the cross from the Persian king and its victorious return to Jerusalem.[166] The latter was yet another historical narrative of military triumphalism, valorizing the power of the cross, set in a military conflict between a Christian ruler and his pagan enemy, celebrating the role that God, and the ruler's devotion to God, played in the military outcome of events. In one passage, because "a mound of sins required God to let the Christian people be chastised by the viciousness of pagans," Chosroes entered Jerusalem, ravaged the city, and took away the "salvific wood that the pious Empress had left there as a testimony of power."[167] In the end, the Emperor Heraclius is victorious.

161. CAO 6275; CAO 6398.

162. Stephan Borgehammar, "Heraclius Learns Humility: Two Early Latin Accounts Composed for the Celebration of Exaltatio Crucis," in *Millennium: Jahrbuch zu Kultur und Geschichte des ersten Jahrtausends n. Chr.—Yearbook on the Culture and History of the First Millennium C.E.* (Berlin: 2009), 151–157; Barbara Baert, *A Heritage of Holy Wood: The Legend of the True Cross in Text and Image*, Cultures, Beliefs and Traditions, Medieval and Early Modern Peoples 22 (Leiden: 2004), 140.

163. BHL 4169. For the text, see Boninus Mombritius, *Sanctuarium, seu Vitae sanctorum*, 2 vols. (Paris: 1910), 1:376–379.

164. *gens multa barbarorum congregate est super Danubium fluuium ad debellandum contra Romanos.*

165. BNF Lat. 3779, 171r: *Deditque victoriam regi constantino in illa die per virtutem sancte crucis.*

166. BHL 4178; BNF Lat. 8895, 62–63v; Anselm Davril, "Le Lectionnaire de l'office à Fleury," *Revue Bénédictine* 89, no. 110–164 (1979): 110–164.

167. Borgehammar, "Heraclius Learns Humility," 181–183.

"Finally, battered by the tears of the Christians, the Lord Christ gave His faithful servant Heraclius victory over his enemy through the power of the Holy Cross, to which the said prince had intently commended himself on that day."[168] The power of the cross was the source of military victories, which God granted because of Christian penitence ("tears").

Themes of victory and triumph dominant in the Roman tradition were naturally absorbed in the Gallican rites, although the Frankish liturgy emphasized more than did the early Roman mass texts the cross as a symbol of Christ's redemptive sacrifice.[169] They emphasized passion over triumph; service over victory. The new prayers composed in Frankish territories introduced into the overall scheme Christ's sacrifice and death: "Christ our Lord, who has mounted the Cross, poured out His blood and delivered the whole world from sin. He is himself the lamb of God. He who has Himself taken away the sins of the world. He, being sacrificed, never more dies, and dead, lives forever. Praise him."[170] With this came commemoration of the cross as a symbol of passion and suffering, and of Christ's service to the Father, less in evidence in the Roman texts. It was through Christ's "suffering of the Cross" (*passionem crucis*) that he redeemed the world.[171] One text recalled the wood to which Christ permitted himself to be nailed which blotted out original sin, and then sins of man.[172] In another, Christ is the lamb of God.[173] The cross is called the "gibbet that was the punishment for criminals."[174] The votive mass for the Holy Cross composed by Alcuin embraced the Frankish themes of humanity and sacrifice. For Alcuin, the cross was the standard (*vexillum*) of the living cross, but also the altar of the cross (*ara crucis*) on which all offenses were purged.[175] Although the Roman theme of eschatological victory dominated overall in both feasts, those of passion and humanity were embedded and thus available later on as the crusading valorized service and suffering in the thirteenth century.

Finally, this combative theology was also inscribed into cross blessings.[176] These were originally written for consecration of liturgical crosses found in churches and used in processions, although they would ultimately be adopted to bless the cross worn by the crusader during the departure

168. Borgehammar, "Heraclius Learns Humility," 185.

169. van Tongeren, *Exaltation of the Cross*, 123–170.

170. van Tongeren, *Exaltation of the Cross*: 140–141.

171. Gregorian Scr. nos. 1609, 1667 (I: 530, 549); See van Tongeren, *Exaltation of the Cross*, 134.

172. van Tongeren, *Exaltation of the Cross*, 137. See also Angoulême Scr. 942.

173. Leofric Scr. 159.

174. van Tongeren, *Exaltation of the Cross*, 141: "beatae crucis patibulum quod erat scelestis ad paenam."

175. Gregorian Scr. 1835 (2:44): "vivificae crucis vexillum."

176. For the range, see CPB, indexed in 1:xxv.

ceremony. The Gellone Sacramentary, dating to the end of the eighth century, includes a long series of benedictions for a liturgical cross, including:

> O Lord, bless this cross of Yours, through which you rescued the world from the power of the demon and You conquered the suggestion of sin through Your passion, [the demon who] rejoiced in the prevarication of the first man, through the boldness of the ancient wood. Sanctify, O Lord Jesus Christ, this sign of Your passion, so that it might be an obstacle of Your enemies, and for those believing in you might prove to be an unending standard of victory.[177]

The prayer was taken up by the RGP as part of a series of benedictions for liturgical vestments and instruments, including the blessings for liturgical stoles, censers, and altars,[178] and from there widely disseminated on the continent.[179] This set of texts associated the cross with combative imagery that exalted the powers of the cross within the great adversarial conflict of eschatological battle. Another blessing in the Gellone Sacramentary called the cross the "protection and guard against the cruel darts of the enemies" (*contra seva iacula inimicorum*, a phrase we will return to),[180] the triumph over death, and the most sacred standard (*sacratissimumque vexillum*). The cross fortifies both spiritually and in actual conflicts; it is the strength of those who have faith through a "protection fortified by your standard," and is also "the defense in adversity, help in prosperity, victory in foreign lands, and protection of the city, protection in the field, and support at home."[181] The language permitted a whole host of talismanic and protective functions to be attributed to the cross. Drawing directly on the liturgy's claim that the cross defeats the ancient enemy, the sign of the cross was used to ward of the devil.[182] The cross was routinely used in rites of healing; relics of the cross even more so.[183] And this is why, of course, the crusader was, from the very beginning, "protected by the sign of the cross."[184]

177. Gellone Scr. 2447 (p. 370); cf. Autun Scr., 1485; the Angoulême Scr., 2050, Leofric Scr 225; and the RGP XL.97–98 (1:157).

178. RGP XL.96–104 (1:157–160).

179. For example through RP12 XXVI: *Benedicito crucis novae* (pp. 204–205).

180. Gellone Scr., 2448. See also CAO 4744 for similar language regarding the *saeva iacula inimicorum*.

181. RGP XL.102 (1:159).

182. See bibliography at Constable, "The Cross of the Crusaders," 51.

183. Constable, "The Cross of the Crusaders," 51; Karen Louise Jolly, "Cross-Referencing Anglo-Saxon Liturgy and Remedies: The Sign of the Cross as Ritual and Protection," in *The Liturgy of the Late Anglo-Saxon Church*, ed. Helen Gittos and M. Bradford Bedingfield, *Henry Bradsaw Society, Subsidia 5* (Woodbridge, UK: 2005), 218.

184. The phrases use formulations such as "undique signo crucis armatus," "munitus," praemunitus," and "protectus." E.g.: GF 15, 37, 40, 68; PT 26 (tr. 49), 111 (tr. 86), 112 (tr. 88), 129 (p. 107); FC III.xi.6, p. 650 (tr. 236); AA vi.43 (pp. 458–459); HdeV 8.18 (p. 27), 9.152 (p. 51), 13.26 (p. 87), 15.84 (p. 100). Or the "power [*virtutem*] of the cross," EA *Chron.* 176.

It is also why the crusade enemies were always deemed "enemies of the cross."[185] As always, physical and metaphysical enemies were not unrelated. Exegetes explicated the deep alliance between invisible enemies and their visible counterparts—evil rulers, pagans, heretics, and the like, who were in the service of the invisible.[186] Thus, in time, as liturgical texts were deployed in new contexts, the definition of the enemy shifted, or layered, to include actual enemies. So, for example, a collect for the feast of the Exaltation of the Cross that spoke of God destroying the wickedness of adversaries through the aid of the holy cross was in the tenth century put to liturgical use against actual, temporal enemies (*inimicos*).[187] In the late twelfth or thirteenth century, the popular *Per signum crucis* antiphon, long used in both the Mass and office of both the Invention and the Exaltation feasts, would be adapted to the rites during which the crusader's cross was blessed on his departure.[188] A blessing specifically written for blessing the crusader's cross said that it was the "obstacle against the cruel darts of enemies, both visible and invisible." (*seva iacula inimicorum visibilium et invisbilium*), drawing directly on earlier language of the cross's power against the cruel darts of the *ancient* enemy.[189] A version of the prayer for the Invention of the Cross from the LePuy Sacramentary quoted above was used in a votive mass in times of war and also in one for the army departing for battle.[190] This dual applicability underlies a real and tangible belief in the power of the cross, made more tangible by the fact that armies carried relics of the cross into battle, and that the military standard sometimes bore an image of the cross.[191] But above all it

185. Cf. Philippians 3:18. Beverly Mayne Kienzle, "Preaching the Cross: Liturgy and Crusade Propaganda," *International Medieval Sermon Studies Society* 53 (2009): 13. RR 105 (tr. 208). EA *Chron.* 138, EA *Hier.* 16. For precedent, Becker, *Papst Urban II*, 2:346. My impression is that this became much more common starting with the Second Crusade. Giles Constable, "Second Crusade as Seen by Contemporaries," *Traditio* (1953): 213–279, and especially at 234, 247 (for Bernard of Clairvaux's use). WT 11.11 (lat. 511. tr. 479). OP pp. 136, 256. Jacques de Vitry, "Epistolae," in *Serta Mediaevalia: Textus varii saeculorum X-XIII, in Unum Collecti*, ed. R.B.C. Huygens, CCCM *171* (Turnhout: 2000), 582, 607, 628. Peter of Blois, *Tractatus duo*, ed. R.B.C. Huygens, CCCM 194 (Turnhout: 2002), ll 65, 180, 248, 363, 0123. Christoph T. Maier, *Crusade Propaganda and Ideology: Model Sermons for the Preaching of the Cross* (Cambridge, UK: 2000), 186. Salimbene de Adam, *Chronica*, ed. G. Scalia, CCCM 125-125A (1998–1999) (Turnhout: 1965), 181, 320. Innocent III's crusading clamor (see chapter 6) includes "inimicorum crucis." Joseph F O'Callaghan, *Reconquest and Crusade in Medieval Spain* (Philadelphia: 2003), 16. This became very common in later years. E.g., Ludwig Mohler, "Bessarions Instruktion für die Kreuzzugspredikt in Venedig (1463)," *Römische Quartalschrift* 35 (1927): 339.

186. Becker, *Papst Urban II*, 2:377–413; Buc, *Holy War, Martyrdom, and Terror*, 78–79.

187. CO 156; Dold and Gamber, *Das Sakramentar von Monza*, 1987 (missa pro inimicis).

188. Graz UB 186, fol, 81r (Pennington, "The rite for taking the cross," 433); Avignon 143, 173r (Antiphon for, *Ordo cum datur crux in signum peregrinationis vel visitationis sancti sepulcri domini*).

189. Text found in Franz, *Die kirchlichen Benediktionen*, v. 2:283

190. CO 5217a-b, with list of early sources.

191. Giles Constable, "The Cross of the Crusaders," in *Crusaders and Crusading the Twelfth Century* (Farnham, UK: 2008), 45–91; George Dennis, "Religious Services in the Byzantine

underscores the ways in which the Christianization of warfare itself mapped the salvific binary onto military engagement, and in particular the crusades. The prayer was ultimately adapted in *contra paganos* rites, and, by the end of the Middle Ages, was adapted again for the secret in a mass *Pro recuperatione Terrae Sanctae.*[192] As the discourses shaded into one another, temporal echoes of eternal victory could be achieved more immediately.

The power of the cross, Christ's own war banner against the devil, in this way directly applied against the pagan enemy of the crusades. Yet, the liturgy had defined the meaning of the cross as a powerful defense against the enemy, and also a sign of service to God, and an instrument of His protection. The dual nature of the cross—victory on one hand; service, renunciation, and suffering on the other—thus also provided the room needed for the complex devotional ideology of crusade to create the peculiar blend of militancy, service, and later, suffering in imitation of Christ that so quickly characterized crusading spirituality.

IT IS NOT difficult to underscore the importance of these liturgical and ritual contexts for the experience of crusading. Jerusalem was the gateway to heaven. The cross was the *signum* of protection against the enemy. Enemies were both material (Danes, Saracens) and spiritual (the devil, or vices), and meaning could slip easily between the two, or even encompass both at once. When the time came, these were the texts that were called upon in undertaking crusade. By the end of the twelfth century, as liturgists began compiling rites that they labeled "pro terra sancta" and "Missa devote ad recuperandam terram sanctam," it was to the early war masses that they turned. In Catalonia at the end of the twelfth century, liturgists took the traditional *contra paganos* mass collect derived from the Gregorian tradition, which asked God to extend a hand to the lapsed

> so that we might feel ourselves freed by Your mercy from the pagan people which we know are prevailing over us because of our sins[193]

and adapted it specifically for the fight in the East, changing it to read

---

Army," in *Eulogēma: Studies in honor of Robert Taft, S.J.*, *Studia Anselmiana* 110 (Rome: 1993), 31–39.

192. Rome Angelica 477 165v–166r; Paris BNF Lat. 12056, 268r–v. The related prayer is used for the Invention at 12056 at 191r–v; for Franciscan, and thus ultimately Roman, use, see SMRL 324, and confirmed by BNF Lat. 827, 241v, and BNF Lat 8887, 209v. See also *Missale Romanum* 474; *Regestum Clementis Papae V:* no. 4769 (p. 313); W.G. Henderson, *Missale ad usum percelebris Ecclesiae Herfordensis* (Leeds: 1874), 417–418. The missal dates to 1502.

193. CO 2304b. Gregorian Scr. 2564 (2:164), *Domine deus qui ad hoc irasceris.*

so that we might feel ourselves freed by Your mercy from the pagan people which we know are prevailing over us *and over the land and city of holy Jerusalem* because of our sins.[194]

The hymns *Vexilla regis* and *Salve crux sancta* where sung as part of preaching the cross in the thirteenth century.[195] Blessings for crosses were said, in time, over crusaders as they departed on pilgrimage. And the militant power of the cross in the liturgy came to be directly associated with the military victory of the cross in the field. A chronicler could thus associate the liturgy of the Exaltation of the Cross with a field victory: "The prayers of bishops and good men, devoutly celebrating the Exaltation of the Holy Cross, were with [the army] on that day, when God's champions overcame the enemies of the Cross. Returning triumphant to their camps from the enemy camp they gave thanks to the Lord Jesus Christ, who had deigned to grant them, few as they were, victory over so numerous an enemy."[196]

More broadly, the language of liturgy sanctified the values and worldviews that were central to crusading, all assuming a state of opposition, an imminent danger, or an enemy. The earliest travel rites worried primarily about the physical dangers of traveling through valleys, rivers, and mountains, though later adaptions assumed that the dangers of physical progress might be matched with invisible dangers threatening spiritual progress. The war rites assumed actual, physical, military enemies, who were the temporal shadows of immanence. In the liturgy of the cross, the enemy was "The Enemy"—the ancient adversary. Satan. The devil. But it was also any number of adversaries (in the plural) that made up the temptations, or spiritual dangers, that sought to do the devil's bidding. These were together the visible and invisible enemies. Indeed, at the end of the twelfth century, a crusader was described as leaving for Jerusalem to go fight "visible and invisible Saracens."[197] The language of the liturgy was fluid, and interpretable, in that the cross's enemy could be secularized, and the cross thus evoked to help ward off an invading army.

And the opposite could also happen, since the worldly adversary, seen as a scourge of God existing as a punishment for sin, was part of the eschatological battle between His forces and its opposition. The liturgy thus expressed a world divided in two. On the one side was God, the cross, the clerical beseecher, and his community. On the other was *the* Enemy (the devil), other enemies both visible and invisible, pagans, and infidels. The

194. Linder RA 108, 150–151.

195. Humbert of Romans, "Liber de predicatione sct. Crucis, transcribed and edited by Kurt Villads Jensen," http://www.jggj.dk/saracenos.htm.

196. WP ch. 21 (lat. 86, tr. 49). The context is the Albigensian crusade. William was also evoking 1 Macc. 3:19, discussed above.

197. Buc, *Holy War, Martyrdom, and Terror*, 319n125.

crusades would take place in the world defined by this imaginary. That is why the collect for the Friday following Easter could be appropriated for a votive mass against pagans in the eleventh century, or why the secret for the Mass of the Invention of the Cross written in the ninth century could then be deployed, during the crusader period, as a mass "for the recovery of the Holy Land." And also why Baldric, writing as early as 1107, imagined a preacher telling crusaders storming the walls of Jerusalem that "our visible enemies deny us this [city of Jerusalem], the path to which our invisible enemies, against which we fight with spiritual warfare, persist in threatening us now."[198] Two decades later, according to Walter the Chancellor, the king going into battle "forearmed with the sign of the Holy Cross" (the relic of the cross), said to his troops "Come, soldiers of Christ! If we fight lawfully to protect God's law we shall easily overcome not only the countless attendants of demons, we shall indeed overcome even the demons themselves."[199] The battles were one and the same.

198. BB 108.
199. WC II.16 (lat. 113, tr. 169).

2

From Pilgrimage to Crusade

"In the year of our Lord 1101," reads a fragmentary chronicle from the Benedictine abbey of Saint Florent-de-Samur, "in the second week of Lent, Viscount Herbert of Thouars and his brother Geoffrey, with William Count of Poitou, and an incredible number of his men—almost of all them undertook the Jerusalem pilgrimage [*Jerosolimitanam peregrinationem*]."[1] Count Herbert was a crusader. He had been in Palestine already in 1098, and he would die at Jaffa in 1104. And as he prepared to join the host of his lord, William IX of Aquitaine, on the Crusade of 1101, he made a series of arrangements. He traveled to Saint Florent, with which his family had ties, confirmed some gifts to the monastery, and asked the monks to pray for him. He made it known that he wished his body to be buried at the church of la Chaise-le-Vicomte. Then, at Poitiers, he asked the bishop, Peter II, to bestow on him the habit of pilgrimage (*habitum peregrinationis*).[2] And from there, he set off on crusade.

There is no doubt that in the years following Urban II's call to arms, the men who set off for Jerusalem saw themselves as pilgrims. The chronicles all refer to them as pilgrims (*peregrini*) and the journey as a pilgrimage (*peregrinatio*), and the crusaders themselves routinely called themselves pilgrims.[3] No matter the ultimately martial goal of conquest, the paradigm of the journey was that of pilgrimage. And thus from the outset many crusaders submitted to some sort of ritualized blessing of the insignia of pilgrimage (*signum peregrinationis*)

1. Paul-Alexandre Marchegay, *Cartulaires du Bas Poitou (Département de la Vendée)* (1877), 6.
2. Marchegay, *Cartulaires du Bas Poitou*, 6.
3. Purkis, *Crusading Spirituality*, 15–18; Riley-Smith, *The First Crusaders*, 67–69; Léan Ni Chléirigh, "*Nova Peregrinatio:* The First Crusade as a Pilgrimage in Contemporary Latin Narratives," in *Writing the First Crusade: Texts, Transmission, and Memory* (Woodbridge: 2014), 63–74.

that, we saw last chapter, had become standard over the course of the eleventh century. Because Urban II had himself instituted the wearing of the cross for the Jerusalem pilgrimage,[4] because of the richness of the cross's meaning, and because of the rapidity with which the symbol of the cross would become central to crusading devotion and identity, the blessing of the cross would ultimately be added to the blessing of the scrip and staff to bring the departure ceremony in line with the identity of the new form of pilgrimage. That this would take the better part of the following century testifies to the processes and timeline of the institutionalization of crusading.

The ceremony for departing crusaders should not be mistaken for the ritual (or inspirational) moment of a crusader "taking up the cross"—that is, making the *votum crucis*, vowing to crusade and affixing the cloth cross that marked him as a crusader to his garb. The language here can be confusing, since "taking the cross" came to mean making the vow, which made one *crucesignatus*, that is, signed by the cross, and ultimately came to define the crusaders over and above the mere pilgrim. In the early days, these two moments seem to have been quite proximate, but in time, the vow generally occurred well before departing on crusade and was often described as taking up (*assumens, baiulens*) the cross in language inspired by Matthew 16:24. It was the vow that made the crusader, and thus it was from this point that he incurred spiritual and temporal benefits ensured by the Church.[5] And it was also at this point that the crusader began to "wear" the cross—usually a cloth cross, on his garb. In time, special prayers and blessings developed to be said at this moment. Blessings *ad suscipiendum signum crucis* appear in a few later manuscripts independent of the scrip and staff blessings and may have been intended or used at the time of the taking of the vow.[6] In the fifteenth century, papal legates provided a special prayer to be invoked as a red cloth cross was placed on a crusader's breast (*pectore*) on the occasion of taking the cross, beseeching the Lord to extend to the cross wearer His heavenly protection.[7] But these prayers are later and represent a different ritual moment than the

---

4. *Epistulae* XVI (p. 164). BB 10.

5. Brundage, *Medieval Canon Law and the Crusader*, 17–18.

6. Bamberg Staatliche lit. 56, 171v–173r, printed in Franz, *Die kirchlichen Benediktionen*, 2:283–284; Trier Bistumarchiv 570, 282r–v. These two are both are titled *Ordo ad suscipiendum signum crucis*, and are close to identical. See also London BL Add. 39762, 162r-v, *Benedictio ad imponendam crucem*. Both Paris Bibliothèque d l'Arsenal 332, 24v–25v, and Cambrai BM 223, 146r–147r, include a *Benedictio signaculi crucis*, which has been edited by Pick, "*Signaculum Caritatis*," 413–414.

7. František Palacký, *Urkundliche Beiträge zur Geschichte des Hussitenkrieges vom Jahre 1419 an*, 2 vols. (Prague: 1873), 1:115; Robert Swanson, "Preaching Crusade in Fifteenth-Century England: Instructions for the Administration of the Anti-Hussite Crusade of 1429 in the Diocese of Canterbury," *Crusades* 12 (2013): 192; Mohler, "Bessarions Instruktion," 342.

ceremonies prescribed in the missals and pontificals. The ritual of bestowing the cross, scrip, and staff, which historians have sometimes called "the rite for taking the cross,"[8] came at a later point—at times well after the vow—after preparations had been made, affairs for one's absence put in order, and reconciliation effected, at the moment that the crusader left his home and took up the journey. A case in point is Louis VII, who took the sign of cross—his crusading vow—from Bernard of Clairvaux in a field in Vezelay on Easter, but received the pilgrim's insignia directly from Pope Eugenius III at St.-Denis in June 1145.[9]

Pilgrims on Crusade

Scattered evidence for the months and years following Urban's speech show that any number of crusaders, as they were preparing to leave, participated in some sort of sacralized ritual of blessing and ecclesiastical sanction upon departure.[10] Herbert of Thouars is one example. Another is Fulk Doon, who received from the abbot of Lerins, a monastery on an island south of Cannes, a ceremonial cloth and the pilgrim's walking staff before the abbot "enjoined him to undertake the Jerusalem pilgrimage for his penance."[11] The model was of course the departure ceremony for the pilgrim that included the scrip and staff blessing, but that the insignia vary in these different accounts points to the fact that the ceremony was still unstable. Ekkehard of Aura, a monk at Corvey who participated in the Crusade of 1101 (and later became abbot of Aura), spoke not only of the crosses sewn onto the knights' garb but of the rite—a "new rite" (*novum ritum*)—in which this was done. Speaking of the rush—divine and human—of activity that followed Urban's call, he wrote:

> No few men displayed the sign of the cross, stamped upon them from heaven on their front or on their clothing or on some part of their body; and having been signed in this way, they understood themselves to be ordered into the army of the Lord. And then others, pricked by a sudden change of mind or instructed by a night-vision, determined to sell their lands and family

8. Brundage, "Cruce signari"; Pennington, "The Rite for Taking the Cross."

9. Odo of Deuil details the two events definitively as two separate occasions. Louis VII took the sign of cross from Bernard of Clairvaux (that is, he took his crusading vow) in a field in Vezelay on Easter, but underwent the rite of departure for crusade later, directly from Pope Eugenius III at St.-Denis in June 1145. Odo of Deuil, *De Profectione Ludovici VII in Orientem; The Journey of Louis VII to the East*, trans. Virginia Gingerick Berry (New York: 1948), 8–9, 16–17.

10. Riley-Smith, *The First Crusaders*, 69–70, 81–83.

11. He. de Flamare, ed. *Cartulaire de l'abbaye de Lérins*, Société niçoise des sciences naturelles et historiques (Nice: 1885), 311–312.

possessions and sew the sign of the cross [*signum mortificationis*] on their clothing; and in all these things—it was truly unbelievable—people [ran] to churches in a frenzy, and, in a new rite, the sacerdotal benediction spread to the swords [*gladios*] along with staves [*fustibus*] and scrips [*capsellis*].[12]

Ekkehard described as part of his new rite two elements: distribution of swords and the blessing of pilgrim's scrips and staves. For the latter, he used the vocabulary for scrips and staves found in the rubrics of the German liturgical manuscripts of the period. We do not know, of course, what happened in these churches—or even the one church that Ekkehard might have been thinking of. But we do know that German pontificals of the late eleventh century routinely included both pilgrimage rites and blessings for swords and other arms of war ("Benedictio ensis noviter succincti").[13]

Mostly likely, Ekkehard's new rite was some kind of spontaneous amalgam of the two liturgical traditions hastily brought together for this new type of knightly activity, the armed pilgrimage.[14] It would have been easy enough for bishops or local priests to have added a simple sword blessing to the rite for pilgrims, in which case the rite would have consisted of a series of blessings for the scrip, staff, and sword. Several twelfth-century manuscripts pair the pilgrimage texts with the rites of war in precisely this way. For example, in Bamberg Staatliche Bibliothek ms. Lit. 58, a Salzburg pontifical, the RGP's blessings for the sword ("Benedictio ensis") appeared alongside the RGP's blessings for scrip and staff ("Benedictio super capsellas que fustes"), and the blessing of the military standard ("Benedictio vexilli").[15] The sword blessing spoke of how the newly girded servant of Christ was to protect the Church (and widows, orphans, etc.) against the "cruelty of pagans."[16] He is inspired to take up the sword by God in order that, so blessed, the sword shall keep him safe.[17] The benedictions ask that the fighter, girded by piety in the Lord, be able to "oppress visible enemies beneath his feet, and through victory over all things, remain always unharmed."[18] And finally that he, girded by this mighty sword, be "armed by celestial protection against all adversity and disturbed by nothing in this time of the tempests of war."[19] The language echoed Psalm 44:3–4, which

---

12. EA *Chron.* 142; EA *Hierosolymita* 19.

13. RGP CCXLIV (2:379). On the liturgy of the sword, see Flori, *L'idéologie du glaive*; Flori, *L'Essor de la chevalerie*, 81–115.

14. Garrisson, "A propos des pèlerins," 1174; Vogel, "Le pèlerinage pénitential," 89–90.

15. Bamberg Staatliche Bibliothek Lit. 58, 63v–64v, combining RGP CCXLII (2:378), RGP CCXLIV (2:379), and RGP CCXII (2:362) in sequence.

16. *Sevitiam paganorum*: RGP CCXLIV.1 (2:379). Note that the word *miles* is not used yet.

17. RGP CCXLIV.2 (2:379): *Alia: Famulum tuum N, quesumus . . .*

18. RGP CCXLIV.3 (2:379): *Benedic, domine, sancte pater omnipotens . . .*

19. RGP CCXLIV.5 (2:379): *Omnipotens sempiterne Deus . . .*

was sung as an antiphon: "Gird your sword upon your thigh, O you, most mighty," thereby linking the entreaty to the scriptural legitimization that sacralized the request.[20] If we assume Ekkehard's Germanic context, then, the rituals for scrips and staves, which emphasized sacred journey, an apostolic model, and the remission of sins, was combined with war blessings that emphasized the defense of the Church against the cruelty of pagans under the protection of God. Herein is the crux of the ideals, rhetoric, and spirituality that surrounded the First Crusade.

During this initial period, Church authorities probably cobbled together appropriate ceremonies for crusading from the fund of blessings and rites available in their books. But beginning in the second half of the twelfth century, scribes copying new liturgical volumes began to group together pilgrimage blessings with blessings for weapons. Two other German manuscripts copied sometimes around 1180 grouped together the "Benedictio super baculos et capsellas peregrinantium" with the "Benedictio ensis noviter succincti," both derived from the RGP but not normally copied in sequence.[21] Another manuscript, this one from Normandy, grouped the travel benedictions from the RGP (*pro iter agentibus*) together with blessings for war (*in tempore belli*).[22] A ritual from Soissons, almost certainly produced on the instructions of Nivelon of Soissons (who participated in the Fourth Crusade) included a votive mass for war followed immediately with the scrip and staff blessings.[23] In England, by the mid-twelfth century, a pontifical, likely from Canterbury, paired pilgrimage blessings with the *Benedictio super hominem pugnaturum* that included blessings for shields.[24] The "benedictio crucis peregrinationis" is added in a later hand, presumably after (as we will see) the cross blessing had been firmly established as a necessity for the rite.[25] There are other examples.[26] This seems to have been an ad hoc or experimental solution to the need for new rites. But the

20. Cf: BB 11. In Baldric's account of the Council of Clermont, Urban II quotes this very Psalm-verse in his call to arms to the military class.

21. Darmstadt Hessische Landes-und Hochschulbibliothek 3183, pp. 180–181 (a sacramentary from Mainz); Walter Von Arx, *Das Klosterrituale Von Biburg* (Budapest, Cod. lat. m. ae. Nr. 330, 12 Jh.), Spicilegium Friburgense 14 (Freiburg: 1970), 260–263.

22. Bamberg Staatliche Bibliothek Lit. 60, 108v–109v.

23. Paris BNF Lat. 8898, 208r–209r, edited in A. E. Poquet, *Rituale seu Mandatum insignis ecclesiae Suessionensis* (Soissons: 1856), 260.

24. Edited in Henry A. Wilson, *The Pontifical of Magdalen College: With an Appendix of Extracts from Other English mss. of the Twelfth Century* (London: 1910), 207. The manuscripts cited are: London BL Cotton Tiberius B. VIII, 152r–157r; and Oxford Magdalene College, ms. 226, 242r–243v. See Wilson, 207n3.

25. For related discussion, see Flori, *L'Essor de la chevalerie*, 321.

26. For instance, Munich CLM 29345(8, a twelfth-century *Rituale*, a fragment in which are grouped the sword blessings with pilgrimage blessings. See Leroquais, Pontificaux, 1:188, for Lyon BM 570. Deslions's copy of the *Pontificale vetus Ambianense* appears at 178–218; the blessings are found at 214r–215r.

practice may not have been limited to these few examples, as any bishop or priest would have been able to combine aspects of both rituals in practice even if they were found in different parts of his service book.

In France, a tradition emerged that paired the scrip and staff rites with the blessing of the military standard (*vexillum*). Military standards, we saw, were one of the instruments of war for which blessings had been composed over the course of the eleventh century. As Erdmann, and later Flori, have shown, the sacralization of the military banner (*vexillum*) was part of the process of sacralizing warfare in the tenth and eleventh centuries,[27] and it is possible that crusaders marched under a banner marked with a cross. In the late twelfth and thirteenth centuries pontificals copied in the Ile-de-France wedded one of the standard series of prayers for the blessings of scrips and staves with the *benedictio vexilli* derived, ultimately, from the tradition of the French Coronation *ordines*.[28] The rite may not have been unrelated to royal practice. In Odo of Deuil's description of Louis VII's departure on the Second Crusade, he writes that "when the banner [*vexillo*] had been taken from above the altar, after he had received the pilgrim's wallet [*pera*] and a blessing from the pope, [Louis] withdrew."[29] Louis seems to have conflated the traditional ritual of taking the *Oriflamme* (*vexillum*, which Odo accurately says was "always the custom of victorious kings")[30] with the rite of scrip and staff. Philip Augustus, leaving for the Third Crusade, and Louis IX, leaving for his first crusade in 1248, both repeated the ceremony.[31] As with the blessing of the bestowal of the sword, the reception of the Oriflamme by French kings before battle was, as Odo acknowledged, long customary and associated with the departure for war. The wedding of this ritual with the existing liturgical tradition of the blessing of the scrip (and, presumably, staff) brought together themes

27. Erdmann, *The Origin of the Idea of Crusade*, 35–56; Flori, *La guerre sainte*, 145–152.

28. For the rite and its sources, see M. Cecilia Gaposchkin, "From Pilgrimage to Crusade: The Liturgy of Departure," *Speculum* 88, no. 1 (2013): 88–90, appendix 2. For derivation from the Coronation Liturgy, see Maurice Keen, *Chivalry* (New Haven, CT: 1984), 71–77; Flori, "Chevalerie et liturgie," 266–278, 409–442; Flori, "Les origines de l'adoubement chevaleresque," 209–272.

29. Odo of Deuil, *De Profectione*, 17.

30. Odo of Deuil, *De Profectione*, 16.

31. For Philip Augustus, see Rigord, *Histoire de Philippe Auguste*, Sources d'histoire médiévale 33, edited by Élisabeth Carpentier, Georges Pon, and Yves Chauvin (Paris: 2006), 244–245 (where it says Philip *signum sancte crucis assumpserunt*) and 272–275 (where it says that Philip he received the *sportam et baculum peregrinationis* from the abbot and too the *Oriflamme* and "weapons against the enemy" from the altar at Saint Denis. For Louis IX, see Sébastien Le Nain de Tillemont, *Vie de Saint Louis, Roi de France*, 6 vols. (Paris: 1847–1851), 3:176–177; But see alternatively William Chester Jordan, *Louis IX and the Challenge of the Crusade: A Study in Rulership* (Princeton: 1979), 109, who has Louis receiving scrip and staff at Notre Dame de Paris before going to Saint Denis.

of pilgrimage and themes of war and war leadership. The *vexillum* of Saint Denis (the Oriflamme) and its particular role in the history of French kings leaving for war may indicate a unique liturgical pairing specific to the Capetians, though this "working downwards" from rites of kingship to rites of knighthood and warfare was evident in other aspects of the liturgy as well in this time period.[32]

Here too the themes were entirely appropriate to the developing ideology of holy war: the *benedictio vexilli* called for the intervention of the Archangel Michael, and the aid of God's right hand, and evoked Abraham's victory against the five kings and King David's triumph. Then: "May You sanctify this standard [*vexillum*], so that for the defense of the holy church against hostile madness, in Your name, the faithful and the defenders of the people of God, through the power of the holy cross [*virtutem sancte crucis*], might rejoice to acquire triumph and victory against their enemies."[33] The military standard (the *vexillum*) was thus equated here with the *vexillum Christi*, Christ's standard—the cross. And so here we see how old language appropriates its new context. With the *benedictio vexilli*, the traditional prayer was appropriate to its new context, calling on the individual to defend the Church against God's enemies, and calling on the power of the cross.

The use of arms blessings (either sword or standard) in conjunction with the pilgrimage blessing thus emphasized sacred violence as part of the developing ideal of crusade. This was an active and militant piety, not the penitential piety of the pilgrimage rites alone. The sword blessings and the blessing of the standard both derived ultimately from royal consecration rites, in which the king was understood to effect God's sovereignty on earth. The liturgy, as we saw, understood the sword and military standard to be instruments of God's power and, thus delegated to the knight, understood the army and armsmen to be doing God's work. This was part of the sacralization of the arms bearer (later, knight) that played such an important role in the chivalric elements of crusading that would gain momentum over the course of the later twelfth and thirteenth centuries.[34] What was emphasized here was not penance, but the justness of sacred violence and its alliance with Providence. The knight (as the king) represented and wielded the might of God, delegated on earth, to do the will and effect the power of God. The penitential aspects of crusade inherent in its identity as

32. Flori, *L'Essor de la chevalerie*, 81–115; Flori, "Chevalerie et liturgie"; Flori, "Les origines de l'adoubement chevaleresque"; Keen, *Chivalry*, 71–77.
33. Gaposchkin, "From Pilgrimage to Crusade," 88, *ita benedicere et sanctifare. . . .*
34. Flori, *L'Essor de la chevalerie*; Richard Kaeuper, *Holy Warriors: The Religious Ideology of Chivalry* (Philadelphia: 2009); Flori, *La guerre sainte*.

pilgrimage are overtaken here by sacred violence. In this form, the departure rite promoted an active and aggressive piety that understood sacred violence, executed by God's agents, as part of God's plan.

The Centrality of the Cross

And yet, ultimately, it was not the sword that defined the crusader, but rather the shield—Christ's shield—which was the cross, and with it the cross's power to destroy the enemy. Starting in the second half of the twelfth century scribes copying out new liturgical books began grouping the pilgrimage rites with the blessing of a cross—the *benedictio crucis*. There is no evidence that the cross was used as a symbol of pilgrimage— Jerusalem or otherwise—before 1095.[35] But from the earliest moment, it was above all the sign of the cross that distinguished the status of the crusader.[36] At Clermont, Urban almost certainly evoked Matthew 16:24 and had cloth crosses at the ready for crusaders to take up.[37] The choice of the cross emphasized on the one hand both self-denial (i.e., penitence) and service to Christ, but its great potency—and Urban's sheer brilliance in choosing it as the symbol for the First Crusade—was rooted in the cross's protective virtue and combative power against the forces of evil and the enemies of Christ. Even during the crusade itself, the sign of the cross (*signum crucis*) was identified as the symbol of the vow that crusaders had made to reach Jerusalem, just as the scrip and staff represented the *signum peregrinationis*, the sign of their pilgrimage vow.[38] The earliest chronicle evidence also emphasized that the sign—*signum*—that distinguished crusaders from mere travelers or even pilgrims and sacralized them as crusaders was the cross that was sewn onto their clothes. Fulcher indicated that these crosses were sewn on "by command of the pope after they made the vow to go" because "it was proper that the soldiers of God who were preparing to fight for His honor should be

35. A reference in an account of the great pilgrimage of 1064–1065 describes the pilgrims as "taking up the cross and following Christ" (*viam crucem baiolantes Christum secuti sunt*), though the account was written in the twelfth century (that is, after the advent of the First Crusade), and seems to have been more an allusion to Matthew 16.24 than any insignia of pilgrimage per se. See MGH SS 12:230 (*Vita Altmanni Episcopi Patavensis*).

36. Giles Constable, "Jerusalem and the Sign of the Cross (with particular reference to the cross of pilgrimage and crusading in the twelfth century)," in *Jerusalem: Its Sanctity and Centrality to Judaism, Christianity, and Islam*, ed. Lee I. Levine (1999); Constable, "The Cross of the Crusaders," 371–381.

37. BB 10. See also the crusade princes' statement of this: *Epistulae* XVI (p. 164, and again on 165).

38. *Epistulae* XV (p. 160), XIX (p. 175), and XX (p. 176). The terms are *signum salutiferae crucis, qui huius militae voto crucis signa sumpserunt*, and *signum crucis*.

identified and protected by this emblem of victory."[39] In the *Gesta Franco-rum*, when Bohemond, learning of the First Crusade, asked about the participants, he was told, "They are well-armed, they wear Christ's cross [*crucem Christi*] on their right arm or between their shoulders, and as a war-cry they shout all together 'God's will, God's will, God's will!' "[40] Even Ekkehard of Aura (in the passage quoted above) stressed that it was above all the cross that distinguished the crusader. The cross—its symbol, devotion to it, the meaning of sacrifice and salvation it emblemized, the ideal of the *imitatio christi* that it implied—was at the very center of the motivations and meaning of crusade.[41]

It was thus the blessing of the cross that came to redefine the rite of departure. Just as in the pilgrimage liturgies in which the pilgrim was handed the blessed scrip and staff as the *signum peregrinationis*, the new procedures incorporated the bestowal of the *signum crucis* as *the* thing that constituted a crusader.[42] The use of the cross in the departure ceremony was probably a local response to this new form of pilgrimage and may have begun in some fashion on an ad hoc basis early on. A charter of 5 June 1100 to Cluny has one knight (a certain Stephen of Neublens) receiving the "signum salutis, id est, sancte crucis" and a ring from the abbot as he departed.[43] By 1120, another crusader spoke of how "he received the cross as a sign of pilgrimage, as requires the custom for this kind of pilgrim."[44] By the time of the Third Crusade, chroniclers could talk of the "cross of pilgrimage" with which one was signed as a member of a Jerusalem crusade.[45] And it was about this time that new rites which brought together the pilgrimage ordo and a blessing of the cross began to be copied into new manuscripts.

As with the liturgical formulas themselves, the practices of bestowing the scrip and staff varied in time and place in details. Blessings in themselves were not eucharistic, and the rite of blessing the instruments of pilgrimage and crusade did not necessarily need to be performed in conjunction with a mass, or even within a church. But clearly they were

39. FC I.iv.4 (lat. 140–142, tr. 68).

40. GF 6–7. I have altered Hill's translation slightly.

41. Norman Housley, *Fighting for the Cross: Crusading to the Holy Land* (New Haven: 2008), 49–53; Constable, "The Cross of the Crusaders," 45–91; Tyerman, *God's War: A New History of the Crusades*, 70–71; Purkis, *Crusading Spirituality*, 30–47.

42. For the *signum crucis* or *signum sancte crucis*, see Graz UB 186; Troyes BM 2140; Rome Biblioteca Casanatense 614, Avignon BM 143, PWD 2.XXX.1–2, Cambridge, University Library Ff.6.9, Vat Lat. 9340, and others (for the twelfth and thirteenth century)

43. Constable, *Crusaders and Crusading*, 99.

44. Constable, *Crusaders and Crusading*, 99.

45. "Ottonis de Sancto Blasio Chronica" in MGH SS Rerum Germanicarum 47: 2, 4, 44, 48, 59.

often associated with the mass, and were often performed in the church with the insignia placed on the altar and the crusader/pilgrim prostrate before it. In earlier sacramentaries, the scrip and staff rites were often added on to the old votive mass for travelers,[46] and a number of the more explicit crusader rites specify that the cross blessing was to be performed with the traditional *missa pro iter agentibus*.[47] The rite in a Spanish ritual for scrip, staff, and cross "for those who wish to go to Jerusalem" indicates that the pilgrim "veniat in ecclesiam ante altare."[48] In England, the ceremony was built on a votive Mass for Travelers. The scrip, staff, and cross are placed on the altar, while the pilgrim prostrates himself before it. After the singing of dedicated psalms, the crusader rises; the blessings of the scrip, staff, and cross are pronounced; and the cross is placed on his vestments. After the mass, further prayers are said over the pilgrim, who again prostrates himself before the altar.[49]

This suggests that crusaders, regardless of their Latinity, were active participants in the ceremony, performing their humility and service to Christ before the altar. Some might do more. The twelfth-century Italian ordo for taking the cross is a remarkable example.[50] The rite specified that the blessings were to follow the Mass for the Holy Cross. The rubric read:

> The order for the taking up of the *signaculum* of the holy cross for those going to Jerusalem. First the Mass of the Holy Cross is sung, as found in the sacramentary, and after the mass has been sung, those who are preparing to leave prostrate themselves in the form of a cross, and they place the garments [*vestimenta*] and the *signaculum* [of the cross] upon the altar and they sing the following psalms.[51]

Although the rite was built on the old scrip and staff rite, the new crusade ritual was utterly rooted in the imagery of the cross. It was intended to follow the votive mass for the cross, and it had the crusaders themselves perform the Christomimesis (of prostrating themselves in the form of a

46. For instance, Roda Pnt., LXVII:18 and 19 (pp. 543–544); Darmstadt 3183, pp. 181–183;
47. Graz UB 186; Cambridge University Library Mm.3.21; Paris BNF Lat. 969; Rome Bibliotheca Casanatense 614; Norman-Sicilian rite, see Gaposchkin, "From Pilgrimage to Crusade," 90–91 (app. 3).
48. San Cugat del Valles 73, 23r: "Ordo ad sportas dandas. His qui peregrinandi sunt. Primum veniant in ecclesiam ante altare, et sacerdos accipiat sportas & baculos."
49. Paris Bibliothèque d l'Arsenal 135, 225r–v. Exeter Cathedral Library 3513; see Ralph Barnes, ed. *Liber pontificalis of Edmund Lacy, Bishop of Exeter* (Exeter, UK: 1847), 242–246; Cambridge University Library Mm.3.21; Brundage, "Cruce signari," 307–310.
50. Graz UB 186, 81r–84r, ed. Pennington, "The Rite for Taking the Cross," 433–434. Translated in C&C 42–47.
51. Graz UB 186, 81r.

cross) before the altar (at which Christ's sacrifice on the cross was reen-acted). And it included no less than six separate blessings of the cross. The bishop or priest would then offer several prayers, with dedicated blessings for the moment of handing over the insignia of crusading to the crusaders. And the crusaders themselves, if possible (*si fieri potest*), were to recite the following antiphon: "Sanctify us, O Lord, through the sign of the holy cross, that it might serve as a shield for us against the cruel darts of our enemies. Defend us, O Lord, through the holy wood and through the just price of Your blood with why You redeemed us."[52] The crusaders asked for God's protection, using this old prayer from the Exaltation Office that lay at the heart of the meaning of the crusader's cross.

The cloth insignia of the cross that was blessed was usually the cloth cross that crusaders had, upon making the vow, sewn onto their clothing. The earliest sources are clear on this point.[53] Plenty of narrative and docu-mentary evidence exists from the twelfth and thirteenth centuries of crusad-ers (and pilgrims) sewing crosses to their outer clothing as a symbol of their status, and contemporary iconography shows pilgrims and crusaders with crosses either pinned to their satchels (*peram*) or on their clothing.[54] The Italian rite quoted in the previous paragraph includes precise instructions that the garments (*vestimenta*) ought be placed on the altar at the start of the ceremony. And the rubrics make clear that the cross is usually the cross placed on the crusader's garb. One English rite includes a blessing specifi-cally for a *vestimentum crucis*, and another to be said as the *vestem cruce signatum* is handed over to those leaving for the Holy Sepulcher.[55] In later years, these might be illustrated. An illumination in a Durandus pontifical from around 1400 illustrating the cross prayer appears to show a bishop handing over the cross badge to an armored knight (See fig. 2.1). Other illu-minations of bishops handing over book-sized crosses give the sense of somewhat larger crosses (See figs. 2.2–2.3).

52. Graz UB 186, 82r: "Levate. Postea ipsi, si fieri potest, cantent hanc antiphonam: 'Sanctifica nos domine signaculo sancte crucis ut fiat nobis obstanculum contra seva iacula inimicorum, defende nos domine per lignum sanctum et per pretium iusti sanguinis tui cum quo nos rede-misti.'" = CAO 4744 (from *Exaltatio* and *Inventio* feasts)

53. FC I.iv.4 (lat. 140–141, tr. 68); BB 10.

54. See Constable, "The Cross of the Crusaders," 45–91; Constable, "Jerusalem and the Sign of the Cross," 371–381; Robert Plötz, "'Benedictio perarum et baculorum' und 'corona-tio peregrinorum; Beiträge zu der Ikonographie des Hl.Jacobus im deutschen Sparachgebiet," in *Volkskultur und Heimat. Festschrift für Josef Dünninger zum 80 Geburtstag* (Würzburg: 1986), 339–376.

55. Paris, Bibliothèque de l'Arsenal 135, 225v.

Figure 2.1. Blessing and bestowal of the cross, from a late fourteenth-century copy of the pontifical of William Durandus. Cambridge, Harvard University, Houghton Library, MS Typ 0001, fol. 34v.

Figure 2.2. Philip Augustus and Henry II take the cross. From a copy of the *Grandes Chroniques of France*, 1332–1350. ©British Library Board. London British Library MS Royal 16G VI, 344v.

Figure 2.3. The blessing of the cross. From a pontifical of Beauvais, dating to the second quarter of the thirteenth century. Besançon BM ms. 138, 157v. © Bibliothèque muncipale de Besançon. Cliché IRHT.

The Rite Coalesces

Integrated departure rites for crusaders began being copied into new liturgical books sometime between the Second and Third crusades. In 1144, the crusader states suffered their first truly major reversal when the Turkish warlord Zenghi captured Edessa. Pope Eugenius III immediately called a new crusade. It is at this stage that the idea of crusade became something more than the single miraculous campaign of 1096–1101. The Second Crusade (1147–1149) solidified the idea of crusade and its particular association with the sign of the cross.[56] Bernard of Clairvaux famously preached the cross, handing out cloth crosses to men who would take the vow. He asked men to "take the sign of the cross" and identified the enemy with the "enemies of the cross."[57] The term *crucesignatus* appears in the sources (although not yet in official correspondence) near the end of the twelfth century.[58] As with the term, the incorporation of a blessing of the cross only came into real use at the end of the century, probably surrounding the events of the Third Crusade, called by Pope Gregory VIII after the loss of Jerusalem and the True Cross to the Ayyubids under Saladin's leadership in 1187. All three monarchs who undertook the Third Crusade—Philip Augustus, Richard the

56. Constable, "Second Crusade as Seen by Contemporaries."
57. Purkis, *Crusading Spirituality*, 89.
58. Michael Markowski, "*Crucesignatus:* its Origins and Early Usage," *Journal of Medieval History* 10 (1984): 158.

Lionheart, and Frederick Barbarossa—participated in a departure ceremony which was described in terms of the traditional insignia, the scrip and staff.[59] In many manuscripts, a *benedictio crucis* (or a grouping of several) was simply copied in succession with the traditional rite for scrip and staff. The cross texts were often derived from one of the RGP's blessings for a new liturgical cross that had been found in manuscripts grouped with blessings for other liturgical instruments, such as a chalice, a paten, or a portable altar.[60] A number of robust formularies for departing crusaders were confected in Italy by the end of the twelfth century, perhaps because so many people left for crusade from the Italian coast. A rite incorporated into the liturgy of Norman Sicily was in place in Palermo by at least 1167,[61] and Pennington published two remarkable rites for ports from the Benevento that seem to date to the last third of the twelfth century.[62] In England, in the diocese of Canterbury, someone added a *Benedictio crucis peregrinationis* to the scrip and staff prayers after the manuscript's original composition, sometime in the last quarter of the twelfth century[63] and a new cross blessing was composed to be used at Ely in the same period.[64] In Spain, the rite took longer to coalesce (probably because there were initially fewer Spanish participants),[65] and, if we take as representative the documentation of Adolf Franz, we do not find strong evidence of similar rites in Germany until the fourteenth

---

59. For Philip Augustus (16 September 1190), see WT Cont., ch. 101 (lat. 102, tr. 92); and Rigord, *Histoire de Philippe Auguste*, 272–275. For Richard the Lionheart (June 1190) see RH *Chron.* 2:141, who says Richard was in Tours. RH *Gesta*, 2:11, says Richard was in York. For Frederick Barbarossa (15 April 1189, Hagenau), see: MGH SS 21:566 (*Gisleberti Chronicon Hanoniense*) 21:566. See, for the Second Crusade, Odo of Deuil, *De Profectione*, 16–17.

60. The RGP blessings are found grouped together at RGP XL.96–105 (1:157–161).

61. The rite in Milan Ambrosiana A92, which is dated to sometime before 1170, indicates that a rite was in place before the Third Crusade. See Kay, *Pontificalia*, no. 473, p. 93. Edited in Gaposchkin, "From Pilgrimage to Crusade," 90–92 (app. 3).

62. Pennington, "The Rite for Taking the Cross," 429–435; these are Graz 186 and 239.

63. Oxford Magdalene College, ms. 226, edited in Wilson, *The Pontifical of Magdalen College*, 207, and see 201n1.

64. The Ely rite appears *near* but not *next to* the scrip and staff rites in both Cambridge Trinity College Library B.XI.10, and Cambridge University Library Li.2.10. The texts are edited by Brundage in Brundage, "Cruce signari," 303–306. Brundage was mistaken when he wrote (at page 293n13) that only Li.2.10 includes the new *Benedictio crucis* (it appears on 103r–104v). Cambridge Trinity College Library B.XI.10 also includes the prayer at 77v–78r. It comes in the same order as Cambridge University Library Li.2.10.

65. This is the conclusion I draw from Janini's highly detailed catalogues. Rites for scrip, staff, and cross appear only with the influence of RP13 or Durandus in the fourteenth and fifteenth centuries. José Janini, *Manuscritos liturgicos de las bibliotecas de España*, 2 vols. (Burgos: 1977–1980); José Janini, Ramón Gonzálvez, and A. M. Mundó, *Catálogo de los manuscritos litúrgicos de la catedral de Toledo* (Toledo: 1977); José Janini, José Serrano, and Anscario Mund, *Manuscritos litúrgicos de la Biblioteca nacional* (Madrid: 1969).

century,[66] although it is difficult to imagine, especially in light of Ekke-hard's comments, that German crusaders did not submit to departure cere-monies. (We know at least that Frederick Barbarossa did.) In any event, most of the earliest examples of these expanded rites are found in pontifi-cals, although by the second half of the thirteenth century new cross-scrip-staff rites were increasingly copied into missals, which meant that its bestowal was also by priests (rather than bishops only) and was probably becoming more and more common.[67]

Old Texts, New Meanings

Initially the adaption of the pilgrimage rite for crusaders constituted the addi-tion of an existing blessing for the cross that celebrated the cross's eschatolog-ical power against the eternal enemy (that is, Satan), the meaning for which would have taken on new resonances within the crusade context. In many manuscripts, the cross blessing was taken directly from the Romano-Germanic Pontifical (RGP) or its derivatives, texts which themselves can often be traced back to the seventh or eighth century. Take for instance the sequence of prayers from a Senlis pontifical dating to the first half of the thirteenth cen-tury. The standard blessing set for scrip and staff known since the eleventh century was preceded by two short prayers for the cross derived from the RGP.

> *The Blessing of the cross*: Bless, O Lord, this Your cross, through which You rescued the world from the power of demons and conquered by Your Passion the one who promotes sin, who had been rejoicing in the prevarication of the first man through the presumption of the forbidden tree.

> *Another*: Sanctify, O Lord, this, the insignia of Your passion, so that it might be an obstacle to Your enemies [*inimicis*] and, for those who believe in You, make it a standard [*vexillum*] in perpetuity.[68]

The prayers emphasize the Fall and Christ's redemption through the cross, played out in the timeless tension between God and the devil. These

---

66. Franz, *Die kirchlichen Benediktionen*, 2:271–289.

67. For missals, see for instance Paris Mazarine 406, 385r–v; Paris BNF Lat. 824, 262v–263r;; Paris BNF Lat. 831, 353v–354r; Paris BNF Lat. 861, 340r–340v. There are *many* more.

68. Paris, Bibliothèque de la Compagnie des prêtres de Saint-Sulpice, MS. R 4, 140v–141r: "Benedictio crucis: Benedic domine hanc crucem tuam per quam eripuisti mundum a potestate demonum et superasti passione tua suggestorem peccati qui gaudebat in prevaricatione primi hominis per ligni vetiti presumptionem. Qui tecum: Item: alia: Sanctifica domine signaculum istud passionis tue ut sit inimicis tuis obstaculum, et credentibus in te perpetuum perfice [*for* efficiatur victoriae] vexillum." I extend my gratitude to Patricia Stirnemann for her help on dating the manuscript to 1230–1245. Compare to RGP XL.97, 103 (1:157, 159–160). The brackets include the text as it appears in the RGP.

were only two of the nine orations of RGP's prayer sequence for the cross. There were infinite possible variations on this additive principle, pointing to the fluidity and malleability of constructing a rite for departing crusaders. As a whole the early cross prayers (as we saw in chapter 1) focused on the eschatological powers of the cross to overcome the devil and redeem mankind. The crusading rites thus imported the protective and salvific power of the cross over the eternal enemies. For instance, the prayer for the cross in a southern Italian pontifical of the twelfth century drew chant from the office of the Exaltation of the Cross, and asked: "Oh God, free us from our enemies [*inimicis*] by the sign of the cross . . . the sign of the cross will be in the sky when the Lord will come to judge us,"[69] and then drew from a prayer from the Roman Mass set for the Exaltation of the Cross in asking God "with the standard of the holy cross, to destroy the crimes of our enemies [*nefas adversariorum*] with the standard [*vexillum*, updated from *auxilium*] of the holy cross, so that we can attain the port of salvation."[70] The result inherited from an earlier devotional theology the cross's eschatological and salvific power; its talismanic, protective function; and a confidence in its power against the enemy. Transferred to its new context—the departing crusader—these values were contextualized, secularized to the earthly struggle against the enemies of God, the occupiers of the Holy Land, the enemies of the Church. The tradition of military prayers that entreated success against the enemies of the Church used much the same vocabulary to refer to pagans and "heathens" (*gentes*) and other temporal enemies.[71] It is hard to imagine that after 1095, in this new configuration, the *inimicos* and *adversarios* were not understood to indicate the Muslim occupiers that successive popes, in their calls for crusade, labeled as the enemies of the cross, or the enemies of Christ.

Small adaptations were made that sharpened their association with crusading (replacing, for instance, "auxilium sancte crucis" with "vexillum sancte crucis,"[72] or "hoc lignum crucis," with "hoc signum crucis"),[73] but

69. Graz UB. 186, 81r: *Per signum crucis de inimicis* . . . (Pennington, p. 433); cf. CAO 4264, 1287, 6845, 4686.

70. Graz UB 186, 82r, *Adesto domine, quesumus familie,* quoted above. Cf. Autun Scr. 843. For Roman mass set, see van Tongeren, *Exaltation of the Cross,* 89.

71. A very few examples from *contra paganos* rites: For forms of "inimici," see Heiming, *Das Sacramentarium triplex* 3015 ("inimicorum"); Staerk, *Les manuscrits latins,* 169–170 ("inimicos christiani nominis," = CBP 568). Also, in a blessing for the military banner, RGP CCXLIII (2: 378). For forms of "hostis," see Angoulême Scr. 2310; Heiming, *Das Sacramentarium triplex* 3014; Leofric Scr., 186. Vich 1674. For forms of "adversarios," see BNF Lat 12052 ("sancte dei ecclesie adversarios"; granting of the sword); Gellone Scr., 2095. The more common term for temporal enemies in the ninth and tenth century materials is *adversarii*. Later, *inimici* becomes common for both temporal and spiritual enemies. There are many more examples.

72. Graz UB 186, in item quoted above.

73. RGP XL.97 (1:157), uses *lignum crucis.*

mostly it was the new context of the crusades that altered their meaning and offered new interpretations. Old texts might take on evocative new resonances in their new crusading context. The apotropaic and talismanic protective function of the cross was certainly reflected in early sources.[74] The narratives are replete with descriptions of battle and warfare in which the cross is hailed as a victorious badge of military valor and of protection. Repeatedly, crusaders enter battle "protected (*muniti*) by the sign of the cross,"[75] "armed (*armati*) on all sides by the sign of the cross,"[76] "protected by the victory of the standard of the holy cross,"[77] "protected and signed with the sign of the holy cross."[78] In the *Gesta Francorum*, the Franks are urged to place their trust "in Christ and in the victory of the holy cross";[79] the Count of Flanders was "armed with the sign of the cross," and Bohemond was "protected on all sides by the sign of the cross."[80] Albert of Aachen, putting words into the mouth of Godfrey of Bouillon, even quoted from the standard blessings of the cross, saying that the "sign of the holy cross [*signum sancte crucis*] by which we are protected and sanctified is beyond doubt a spiritual shield against all the darts of the enemies [*contra omnia iacula inimicorum*]."[81] Elsewhere Albert explained that "it is certainly clear that the power of the holy cross prevails not only against the darts of invisible enemies [*invisibilium iacula inimicorum*], but also against the weapon of the visible ones."[82] The image of the darts of the enemy was liturgical.[83] The enemy was originally envisioned as the devil, who appears throughout the early Western liturgical texts as the ancient enemy. But Albert's text suggests how easily the text could be repurposed.

Local Innovations

Although many exemplars of the expanded rite adopted existing cross texts (mostly from the RGP), the production of new cross texts in other manuscripts demonstrates local devotional and interpretive responses to crusading. They ranged in emphasis—some evoking a rhetoric of militarism, others emphasizing the penitential ideals associated with *imitatio christi*. Some

74. Housley, *Fighting for the Cross*, 184. See further chapter 1.
75. GF 37, 68; PT 112, 129; FC II.xxi.14 (lat. 453); HdeV 13.45 (p. 88).
76. GF 15, 40; PT 66, 72; FC III.xlii.9; HdV 6.18 (p. 27), 9.152 (p. 51)
77. PT 26, 53.
78. AA vi.43 (pp. 458–459).
79. GF 19–20. Cf. HdV 7.15 (p. 31).
80. GF 31, 37. Cf: FC III.xi.6 (lat. 650, tr. 236).
81. AA vi.43 (pp. 460–461). Cf: Gellone Scr. 2448; Autun Scr. 1486; Anjoulême Scr. 2051. RGP XL.98 (1:157). RP12 XXVI.3 (p. 204). Banting, *Two Anglo-Saxon Pontificals*, 121.
82. AA vii.68 (pp. 580–581). For an example from the Albigensian crusade, where the power of the cross in the liturgy is actualized in a military battle, see WP ch. 21 (lat. 86, tr. 49).
83. CAO 4744, *Sanctifica nos domine* . . . ; and above.

transferred the expectation of the salvific powers of the cross onto the crusader himself. As a group, then, the new blessings for vesting the departing crusader with the cross composed starting in the second half of the twelfth century demonstrate the variety of devotional and ritual responses to the crusades and the local nature of new productions.

The cross blessings increasingly took the pilgrim-crusader himself as the focus, as the hoped-for beneficiary of the powers of the cross. For instance, a new cross blessing, the *benedictio crucis peregrinationis*, added to an English Pontifical in the late twelfth century read:

> Bless this cross, and grant, through the invocation of Your most holy name, that whomever should wear this sign upon himself, defended by the protection of Your piety, might be worthy to overcome the attacks of the enemy, visible and invisible.[84]

The prayer explicitly grouped visible and invisible enemies together. Likewise, a southern French pontifical asks that God bless the cross so that his servants, "in memory and recollection of Your most blessed Passion, will carry the sign of Your salvific cross upon them, that they might be spared from visible and invisible enemies."[85] (Again, with the visible and invisible enemies.) A twelfth-century Italian text reworked an older Gelasian prayer to read, "Bless the sign of this holy cross . . . so that he who picks it up or bears it on him might gain health of body and protection of soul."[86] Another pontifical from the south (from Saint Pons de Thomiérs, near Montpellier) included instructions that, as the bishop placed the cross on the crusader's right shoulder, he was to say: "Accept this sign of the saintly cross in remission of your sins, in the name of the father, and the son, and the holy spirit. Amen. Accept this cross through which you shall be able to conquer the devil and merit to obtain sempiternal life."[87] The eschatological claims were familiar, except that the offer of "remission of sins" formerly embedded in the pilgrimage rites had now been transferred to crusading.

---

84. Oxford Magdalene College, ms. 226. *Voluisti benedicere dignare hanc . . .* , edited in Wilson, *The Pontifical of Magdalen College,* 207.

85. Avignon BM 143, 173v: "ut hi famuli qui in memoriam et [*illeg*] recordationem tua beatissime passionis salutifere crucis tue signum super se portaverint, sint ab omni visibili et invisibili hoste liberati."

86. Graz UB 186, 81r. *Benedic domine hec signacula sancte crucis . . .* (Pennington p. 433).

87. Vat Lat. 9340, 47v: "Accipe signum sancte crucis in remissionem peccatorum tuorum. In nomine patris et filii et spiritus sancti, amen. Accipe crucem per quam dyabolum vincere possis et vitam consequi merearis sempiternam."

Some texts flirted explicitly with a language of sacralized militarism. A blessing specifically for the *signaculum crucis* found in pontificals from Paris and Cambrai addresses those who assume (*assumere*) the cross:

> Kindly inspire, in courage, Your knights [*milites*] present here, who are to be born again for Your military service, and give them the security and pledge of eternal blessedness that You will be their protection when they are in danger, their counsel in what they must do, their refreshment in the face of temptations, their meal in hunger, their [source of] regulation in the use of Your consolation. As their commander in the journey, their rewarder when they are in their own country, in order that they may carry upon themselves these here symbols of the most venerable cross of Jesus Christ and, aided by You, advantageously fulfill their unconquerable vow, make them firm in their strong spirit lest they revert to secular ways through apostasy.[88]

The benediction is now focused squarely on the person of the crusader, on whomever might bear on himself the sign of the cross, asking God specifically to aid, console, and fortify him to "fulfill" the unconquerable vow. It directly addresses the knight (miles). The Holy Spirit has an army. God is the *dux* of the journey.[89]

In the matrix of an evolving liturgical language of crusading, one of the most powerful images of Christian militarism was the *vexillum crucis*, which melded at once the christic and the militant, the eschatological and the devotional, and the sign (the signum; the cross) and its signifier (the sacrifice; salvation). In its simplest form, the *vexillum* just indicated the military standard (or banner), and as such, the RGP (for instance) included its blessing of the war standard (*vexillum bellicum*) as part of a series of blessings for the instruments of war.[90] But it was also used as a synonym for the cross in the RGP's rite for blessing a new liturgical cross, where the *crux fidei* was identified with the *vexillum* as part of the protection and benefits offered by the cross, which included "victory against enemies" (*sit ei in hoste victoria*).[91] The image of the *vexillum crucis* was also used for the relic of the holy cross—both in battle and not[92]—and after 1095 it came

---

88. Cambrai BM 223, 146r–147r; Paris Bibliothèque d l'Arsenal 332, 24v–25v: *Sanctificator et gubernator . . .* (ed. in Pick, "*Signaculum Caritatis*," 414.)

89. Riley-Smith, *The First Crusade*, 99, 126; Housley, *Fighting for the Cross*, 197.

90. RGP CCXLIIII (2:378).

91. RGP XL.102 (1:159).

92. Giuseppe Ligato, "The Political Meanings of the Relic of the Holy Cross among the Crusaders and in the Latin Kingdom of Jerusalem: An Example of 1185," in *Autour de la Première Croisade. Actes du Colloque de la Society for the Study of the Crusades and the Latin East (Clermont-Ferrand, 22–25 juin 1995)*, ed. Michel Balard (Paris: 1996), 315–330. Alan V.

also to refer to the image of the cross borne on the crusader's clothes, the standard of the cross (that is, a banner with a cross on it) carried into battle, *and* the cross *as* a battle standard carried into battle.[93] Thus Baldric of Bourgeuil could write of the *sancte crucis vexillum* that Urban II instructed crusaders to sew onto their outer clothing.[94] These associations were all embraced as the RGP's blessings for a new liturgical cross were routinely redeployed as part of the new rites of departure. A number of pontificals, we saw, simply adopted cross blessing from the RGP that spoke of the *vexillum crucis*.[95] Others incorporated the image of the *vexillum* into other older formulas; for instance, a twelfth-century Italian manuscript adopted a Gelasian prayer for the exaltation of the cross that spoke of the *auxilium Christi*, replacing *auxilium* with *vexillum*.[96] One Italian pontifical drew on the image twice, emphasizing both the penitential aspects of crusading, and the militant and salvific:

> Take up, my brother N. [indicating that the celebrant should here say the crusader's name], the most victorious standard [*vexillum*] of the holy cross, through which you will be able to safely conquer the evil of all your enemies, and, victorious, to form an army with others following Jesus Christ, so that, in the end, at the time of retribution, the enemies having been laid low, [you] returning with the palm of victory from war, by our Lord Jesus Christ, the greatest emperor, may receive the unfading crowns of glory, and in his eternal palace be worthy to reign with him without end.[97]

The text is specific to the crusade endeavor, referring to the army of Christ, victory over the enemy, and the final reward of the crown of glory. It melds perfectly the eschatological battle against the devil inherited from the ancient cross theology with the earthly battle against temporal enemies, placing the crusader's battle into an eschatological frame ("at the time of retribution"). Its use of the *vexillum crucis* demonstrates how the inherited images of

---

Murray, "'Mighty Against the Enemies of Christ': The Relic of the True Cross in the Armies of the Kingdom of Jerusalem," in *The Crusades and their Sources: Essays Presented to Bernard Hamilton*, ed. John France and William G. Zajac (Aldershot: 1998), 217–238.

93. Constable, "The Cross of the Crusaders," 69; Erdmann, *The Origin of the Idea of Crusade*, 36–37.

94. BB 10. For other examples, see FC III.xi.6 (lat. 650, tr. 236); Charles Wendell David, *De expugnatione Lyxbonensi = The conquest of Lisbon*, trans. Charles Wendell David (1936; reprint New York: 2010), 146–147, 156–157, 174–175; Maier, *Crusade Propaganda*, 102–103.

95. RGP XL.102 (1:159); Montpellier Bibl. Univ. Section Medicine, 399; Troyes BM 2140, Sens BM12, Besancon BM 138. The adoption of this prayer was identified by Pick in Montepellier Bibl. Inter. Med. 339,142r–143r; Sens BN 12 (104v–105v; and Besançon BM 138 (157v–161v). On the importance of the RGP, see Pick, "Signaculum Caritatis," 388.

96. Graz UB 186, 81r–84r, at 82r. *Adesto domine, quesumus familie tue . . .* (Pennington, 433–434.) Cf. *Gellone Scr. 1450; Anjoulême Scr. 1321.* These are for "*Exaltatio Sancti Crucis.*"

97. Graz UB 239, 145v. *Suscipe frater mi N victoriosissimum . . .* ed. Pennington, 432.

eschatological power were taken up in the crusading rhetoric—how the developing language of crusading drew from a deep well of devotional and liturgical ideas and symbols but redeployed them with new meanings or enriched associations within its new context.

Other new blessings for the crusader's cross evoked ideals of penitence, the love of Christ, and the Holy Land. As the rites increasingly became associated with Holy Land pilgrimage/crusade, references to the Holy Land rose in number, and with them attention to aspects of crusading devotion that grew out of, or along with, devotion to Jerusalem. Jerusalem, we saw, had long been evoked in liturgy of all kinds, usually as the heavenly Jerusalem, the salvific goal.[98] But now the terrestrial Jerusalem or (more broadly) the Holy Land as a geographical goal came more squarely into focus.[99] References to Abraham, the paradigmatic *peregrinus*, the patriarch to whom God promised the Holy Land (*terra repromissionis*), who had been evoked the pre-1095 rites for pilgrims,[100] became more pronounced after 1095. The Norman-Sicilian rite began with a reading from Genesis 12:1–4, in which God commands Abraham to "go forth out of the country and from your kindred and come into the land which I shall show you,"[101] a clear type for crusaders as the new chosen people. In France, a blessing for the *signaculum crucis*, found in pontificals for Paris and Cambrai, compared the sanctification of the crusader's cross with God's sanctification of "Abraham our patriarch, with the sign of just faith."[102] In England, a rite from Ely dating to the last quarter of the twelfth century incorporated traditional scrip and staff prayers and several known cross texts along with a new text for the moment of blessing the cross that associated the pilgrim with Abraham:

> Take up the yoke of Christ [*iugum Christi*], the burden of which is light [*leve onus*] to the faithful, with the sign [*signo*] of the holy cross having been ensigned [*insignus*], so that, going forth with the right side signed, you, like Abraham, may, with the aid of our Lord Christ, merit to possess [*possidere*] the land of the living [*terram viventium*], where is the most beloved haven of faithful souls.[103]

---

98. See chapter 1.

99. Gaposchkin, "The Role of Jerusalem," 5–13.

100. Vich Scr., 1430 (p. 215). Roda Pnt., LXVII:13 (p. 541). RGP CCXII.3 (2:362). On the shift from *terra repromissionis* to *terra sancta*, see Erdmann, *The Origin of the Idea of Crusade*, 300.

101. Gaposchkin, "From Pilgrimage to Crusade," 91. See also Rome Biblioteca Casanatense 614, 18v, edited in Derek A. Rivard, "*Pro Iter Agentibus*: The Ritual Blessings of Pilgrims and Their Insignia in a Pontifical of Southern Italy," *Journal of Medieval History* 27 (2001): 378. Rivard discusses the meaning of the Abraham trope.

102. Paris Bibliothèque d l'Arsenal 332, 24v–25v; Cambrai BM 223, 146v–147r.

103. Cambridge Trinity College Library B.XI.10, 103r–v, Cambridge University Library Ll.2.10, 77v. *Suscipe iugum Christi . . .* (Brundage, "Cruce signari," 305).

The crusader is signed with the cross on his right side (where we know he wore it) just as Abraham, signed by faith, was led by the right hand of God from Ur into the promised land.[104] The injunction to possess (*possidere*) the land of the living evoked crusading goals. The *terra viventium* (land of the living) was a biblical phrase employed in the Old Testament to refer specifically to life on earth and thus the temporal world, though medieval liturgical use of the phrase tended to allegorize it to heaven.[105] Here it is defined eschatologically as the *portus animarum*, the haven of souls, which was of course one of the devotional goals of serving Christ through crusade. It thus mixed and melded the temporal Jerusalem and the heavenly Jerusalem: to possess the (temporal) land of the living, following Abraham, so as to possess the heavenly reward. Baldric of Bourgeuil's imagined sermon (quoted in chapter 1) had said precisely this.

As emphasis shifted from an eschatological focus to a territorial one, the departure rite increasingly emphasized Christ's humanity and the Passion over the salvific powers of the cross and the penitential ideals associated with the *imitatio christi*. The twelfth-century Italian rite cited above brought together traditional blessings for scrip and staff with newly composed texts centered on the cross,[106] and from there, Christ, the life of Christ, and his geographical location in Jerusalem. With the blessing of the cross, the celebrant read:

> He, because of the love of Your name, rejects all impiety and secular desires, and *hurries to go to the place where our Lord Jesus Christ wished to be born of the Virgin, to die, and to rise in the flesh*. In his revelation, the prophet said this about him: "*We will worship in the place where his feet stood*" [Ps. 131:7]. Hear, kindly, his prayers and clemently breathe life into his vows, and because human frailty is to do no worthy fruit of penitence without You, bestow upon him aid and protect him with the protecting power, and watch over him with care.[107]

Psalm 131:7 was a standard of the devotional Holy Land pilgrimage literature for its specific focus on Jerusalem and had often been deployed in crusading texts.[108] Its use here emphasized Jerusalem the place, and with it

---

104. Cf. Hebrs. 11.8; Jac. 2.23.

105. Job 28:13; Ps 26:13, 51:7, 141:6, Is. 38:11, 53:8, Jer 11:19, Ezk 26:20, 32:23–27, 32:32. On allegorization, Albert Blaise, *Le Vocabulaire latin des principaux thèmes liturgiques* (Turnhout: 1966), 297, §167.

106. Graz UB 239,143v–146v (Pennington, 431–432.) For earlier texts: Gellone Scr. 2797; Autun Scr. 1815.

107. Graz UB 239, 143v, *Domine deus pater omnipotens . . .* (Pennington, 431.) Only the second half of the prayer is quoted here.

108. FC I.xxxiii.15 (lat. 331–332, tr. 131); Sylvia Schein, *Gateway to the Heavenly City: Crusader Jerusalem and the Catholic West (1099–1187)* (Aldershot, UK: 2005), 78. See also Constable, *Crusaders and Crusading*, 318; Purkis, *Crusading Spirituality*, 96, 113.

Christ's humanity, His lived life and death in the Holy Land, and the physical geography that was the very goal of the crusade. No longer exalting the salvific power of the cross, the benediction enjoined the devotional contrition of the person being signed with it. The sign and symbol of the cross thus embraced the penitential aspects of crusade ideology, linked to penitential pilgrimage to Jerusalem. In this same way, a monastic rite from southern France instructed the pilgrim or crusader to "accept the sign of the passion of our Lord Jesus Christ, and proceed forth to the church of Jerusalem, where the glorious tomb of our redeemer is known to all humanity, where with the rivulet of your tears streaming forth before Him, you may be able to wash away the filth of your crimes, with the Lord our Jesus Christ smiling upon you."[109] Another prayer underscored the importance of confession and the truly contrite disposition of the crusader in gaining salvific merit, proclaimed that as a pentitent, he might demonstrate "the outward humility of the confession in his penance," and expressed the hope that he might be granted "the true innocence of the soul and purgation of his sins."[110] This shift away from militancy and victory was tied up in the increasing emphasis on the crusader's interior disposition and penitential motivations that emerged in lock step with the increasingly spiritualized theology of crusading. The themes were now penitential rather than triumphant, centered on the cross, and the living Christ as human, temporal, sufferer, and then redeemer, as well as the penitential disposition of the crusader himself.

Crusade and Pilgrimage in the Papal Rite

These were all singular innovations, known in single examples. This fact itself underscores the importance of local contexts in the crusading cultures of Europe, the fluidity of individual responses, and the ad hoc nature of the rituals during the first century and a half of crusade. Yet the very variety of individual examples may in part be explained by the fact that the papacy itself was so slow to adopt any rite at all for pilgrims *or* crusaders. This is surprising, especially given the importance of the papal rite for the development of liturgy on the continent, which thus lagged behind the development of canon law on the issue. But the early form of pilgrimage

---

109. Avignon BM 178, 155r: "Iesu Christi domini nostri passionis signum accipe frater, et perge ad ecclesiam iherosolimitanum, in qua gloriosum sepulcrum nostri redemptoris secundum humanitatem constat adesse, quatinus profusis coram eo riuulis tuarum lacrimarum, abluere valeas sordes tuorum facinorum annuente ipso domino nostro Iesu Christo. Qui cum patre et filio."

110. Graz UB 239, 144v–145r, *Benedic domine hanc crucem . . .* (Pennington, 432).

rituals known in certain manuscripts of the RGP was never adopted in Rome,[111] and it was only around 1250 or so, probably under the pontificate of Innocent IV, that the Roman liturgy finally incorporated a rite for scrip, staff, *and* cross into the curial pontifical.

Popes conferred the blessing on departing crusaders, probably from the earliest years,[112] but it was not until midcentury that the papacy's own ritual included a departure ritual. The overall rite was for the scrip and staff (*Benedictio pere et baculi peregrinantium*; that is, for pilgrimage in general), but it included an optional blessing for the cross that could be used for those going to Jerusalem (*Super crucem eius qui iturus est in Iersosolimam*), which made it appropriate to crusaders.[113] This cross prayer deployed the language of militant victory and conquest:

> God of unconquered power, immense majesty, and the aid of consolation to all those who are on pilgrimage, who assigns to Your servants conquering arms, we beseech that You deign to bless these crosses so that the standard of the venerable cross [*crucis vexillum*] might be to them an invincible source of strength against worthless temptations of the ancient enemy. Let them be a defense in this journey; let them be a protection and home and a protector everywhere.[114]

The text itself was not a curial innovation. It predated the ~1250 compilation of the second recension of the Roman Pontifical of the thirteenth century and seems to have been derived from the Norman-Sicilian rite that developed in the last third of the twelfth century.[115] It also found its way into exemplars in England, France, Spain, and Italy, and thus was far more broadly disseminated than other new texts.[116] It reveals the strong continuities of old ideas (entreating God to protect travel; the cross to be a defense everywhere) that took on particular meaning in a crusader context. But the cross blessing, composed originally for liturgical instruments, was now explicitly intended for a pilgrimage. It used a militant language of might and victory: the "unconquered power," the "conquering arms," the "invincible stronghold," and of course the image of the *crucis vexillum* that was so

111. M. Cecilia Gaposchkin, "Origins and Development of the Pilgrimage and Cross Blessings win the Roman Pontificals of the Twelfth and Thirteenth Centuries (RP12 and RP13)," *Mediaeval Studies* 73 (2011): 261–286.

112. For Urban II: FC I.vii.1 (lat. 164, tr. 74–75). For Eugene III: Odo of Deuil, *De Profectione*, 17. For Innocent IV: MP 5:23 (tr. 2:269).

113. RP13 XX (pp. 418–420).

114. RP13 XX.6 (p. 420). *Deus invicte potentie* . . .

115. Gaposchkin, "From Pilgrimage to Crusade," 90–92 (app. 3, on 91, *Deus invicte virtutis* . . .).

116. Paris Bibliothèque d l'Arsenal 35, 125v; Troyes BM 2140, 22v; Cambridge University Library Ff.6.9, 85v; Rome Biblioteca Casanatense 614, 20v.

deeply implicated in eschatological and victorious images of Christianity, and here evoked the larger discourse of conquest and power. The "ancient enemy" was, we keep noting, the devil, but the devil was easily and often equated with the enemies of Christianity, the enemy of crusading.[117]

Innocent IV's pontifical, though, and the militant tone of its departure blessing, was soon supplanted by the penitential rite of William Durandus, bishop of Mende (d. 1296), the greatest liturgist and liturgical commentator of his age.[118] Durandus, in the years between 1293 and 1295, immediately after the fall of Acre, wrote and revised a pontifical for the Episcopacy of Mende that, thoroughly rooted in Roman models, for all intents and purposes standardized the rite for the Roman Church. It gained wide circulation throughout the Christian West in the fourteenth and fifteenth centuries, ultimately becoming the standard pontifical of the Roman rite.[119] It was an extraordinary achievement. Durandus cleaned up the mess that had become the inherited tradition, rationalizing the structure of the pontifical and the liturgy it contained. He never simply recopied an available text; instead, he took over the ideas and language and reworked these into a cohesive and elegant whole.

Durandus's pontifical included a rite for pilgrims, one for crusaders, and liturgical rites for "the liberation of the Holy Land from the enemies of the faith."[120] The cross blessing for those "departing to aid the Holy Land" was clearly a *crusading rite*, for crusaders going to fight for Jerusalem. The rubric for *subsidium terrem sancte* used the language popes used in calling for crusades. It drew from the pilgrimage and cross texts known from eleventh century recensions of the RGP, incorporated other known texts, and composed a few new ones. The rite for the blessing of the scrip and staff could be performed with the cross rite for Jerusalem crusaders, or independently of the crusading rite for "mere" pilgrims, since it envisioned the intercession of both Peter and Paul (inherited from a text from RGP, suggesting Rome as a destination) and James (added in this version, indicating Santiago of Compostela). Durandus incorporated into the "cross" blessings a number of motifs drawn from the pure pilgrimage tradition, thus injecting the crusaders cross with longstanding pilgrimage ideals. The final pilgrimage oration, for instance, was based on the Gelasian formula for the

---

117. John Victor Tolan, *Saracens: Islam in the Medieval European Imagination* (New York: 2002); Debra Higgs Strickland, *Saracens, Demons, and Jews: Making Monsters in Medieval Art* (Princeton: 2003).

118. PWD 2.XXX–XXXII (pp. 541–546).

119. Cyrille Vogel, *Medieval Liturgy: An Introduction to the Sources*, trans. William G. Storey, Niels Krogh Rasmussen O.P., and John K. Brooks-Leonard, NPM studies in church music and liturgy (Washington, DC: 1986), 253–255.

120. PWD 3.XVI (pp. 630–631): "Ordo pro liberatione terre sancte a fidei inimicis."

ad iter agentium ordo and other texts known from eleventh-century versions of the RGP, embellished with language taken from RP13.[121] The priest asked God to bless the pilgrim so that "in this world he might receive remission of all sins and in the future be in the company of all the blessed."[122] Here we are reminded of long continuities that imbued themes of sacred travel from the pilgrimage traditions that were incorporated into the rites for crusaders.

What was new was the pointed emphasis on the humanity of Christ, the Passion, and above all the incorporation of the line of scripture—Matthew 16:24—that more than any other had embodied the aims of crusading since its inception. The opening prayer exalted, again traditionally, the salvific function of the cross: God consecrated the "sign of the cross through the precious blood of [his] son," and the "power [*virtus*] of the cross freed the human race from the indenture of the ancient enemy."[123] But then, the "sign of passion and of the cross" is born specifically on the crusader. The prayer beseeches God, just as he blessed Aaron's staff (*virgam Aaron*, drawing from the RGP), to bless the cross with his right hand so that the cross might grant prosperity of body and soul to the one bearing it. After blessing the cross itself, the bishop would bless the crusader who received it. Here, Durandus incorporated—for the first time—the biblical line central to crusade ideology: "If any man will come after me, let him deny himself, and take up his cross, and follow me" (Matt. 16:24). The blessing beseeched Jesus Christ, the living son of God, "who asserted to [His] disciples, that whomever wished to come after You, may deny himself and, carrying his cross, follow You" (*ut quicumque vult post te venire, seipsum abneget et suam crucem tollens te sequatur*). Then: "We beseech Your immense clemency, that this faithful servant of Yours, who according to Your words, desires to deny himself and take up his cross and follow You [*seipsum abnegare suamque crucem tollere et te sequi desidera*], and may he hasten towards Your tomb, may You always and everywhere protect him and pluck him up from every danger and absolve him from the chains of sin."[124]

Fully embedded into the rhetoric of crusade, routinely used by crusade preachers, the clearest scriptural referent for the ideal of crusading Christo-mimesis, Matthew 16:24 was the natural choice for the ceremony in which

---

121. PWD 2.XXXI.5 (p. 545), *Deus infinite misericordie . . .* ; Cf. Gellone Scr. 2797, and common.

122. PWD 2.XXXI.3 (p. 544): "ut per eam mereamini accipere remissionem omnium peccatorum." Cf RGP CCXII.2 (2:362).

123. PWD 2.XXX.1 (p. 542).

124. PWD 2.XXX.2 (p. 542).

the crusader, in fact, placed the cross on his body in order to "follow Christ" to the land where he had walked.[125] It is something of a surprise that it was not adopted earlier. Finally, in the third prayer, as the bishop places the cross on the crusader, he says, "Take up the sign of the cross, in the name of the Father, the Son, and the Holy Ghost, in the image of the cross, of the Passion, and of the death of Christ, and for the defense of your body and soul, so that, by the grace of divine goodness, after having completed the journey, saved [*salvus*] and corrected [*emendatus*] you might be able to return to us."[126] The prayer was loosely based on one of the pilgrimage prayers that dated back to the eleventh century and made its way into the Roman Pontifical of the thirteenth century.[127] But Durandus added the "image of the cross, of the Passion, and of the death of Christ," thus encapsulating what the crusaders' cross had come to mean within the context of sacrifice and suffering on crusade. It still retained its apotropaic function as a sign of protection, but its meaning had given way from militant and eschatological victory, to Passion, suffering and death.

The symbol of the Crusader's cross had shifted from militant victory over the enemy to salvific suffering. This new emphasis on the *imitatio christi* as passion and suffering was in line with the larger devotional developments in crusading ideology. Over the course of the thirteenth century, within the broader devotional discourse of crusading, the interpretation of Matthew 16:24 had become increasingly penitential; the cross was interpreted not as the sign of eschatological victory, but rather of Christ's penitential passion, against the backdrop of which the scriptural line came to represent the penitential aspects of the crusading enterprise.[128] Taking up the cross was, in Durandus, not only the commission to crusade, but the call to suffering and penitence enjoined by following Christ in his footsteps in crusade. The focus of the rite is the living Jesus, specifically; the evocation of his tomb at once recalled his humanity and his death, and of course, the Holy Sepulcher that was the very goal of crusade (Jerusalem). The emphasis on Christ's Passion was not new. The Passion had been evoked in the ninth- and tenth-century prayers for the Exaltation of the Cross and other cross benedictions, and these had on occasion been adopted in cross rites. But the emphasis had always been on the eschatological promise of redemption effected by Christ's suffering on the cross. Indeed, over the course of

---

125. Constable, *Crusaders and Crusading*, 111. Maier, *Crusade Propaganda*, 56–68. On Christomimesis, see Purkis, *Crusading Spirituality*, 30–47.

126. PWD 2.XXX.3 (p. 543): *Accipe signum crucis . . .*

127. See Vich Scr. 1434 (p. 216); RP13 XX.2 (p. 419), *In nomine domini nostri Iesu . . .*

128. Maier, *Crusade Propaganda*, 51–68; Jean Leclercq, "La dévotion médiévale envers le crucifié," *La Maison Dieu* 75 (1963): 119–132.

the late twelfth and thirteenth centuries the emphasis on the humanity of Christ and the consequent valorization of the salvific role of bodily suffering (in general, and on crusade specifically) had animated much of the theology and spirituality of the crusade. Durandus's rite—wherein the crusader actually took up the physical symbol of the cross—ritually instantiated that ideal.

3

On the March

On Friday, 8 July 1099, three and half years after leaving home, the Franks, wearing their crosses, were camped outside the Holy City.[1] They had arrived a month earlier, on 7 June, and two camps had been set up on either side of the city to conduct the siege. But the mood was uneasy. One attempt to take the city had already failed. The Franks suffered from a lack of water. Infighting was brewing among the commanders. And aside from the constant threat of ambush or a well-aimed arrow from within the city, the arrival of a relief force from Cairo was imminent. Peter Tudebode, a priest from the south of France, who was an eyewitness to the events, wrote the following:

> When our lords saw these atrocities, they were greatly angered and held a council in which the bishops and priests recommended that the crusaders hold a procession around the city. So the bishops and priests, barefooted, clad in sacred vestments, and bearing crosses in their hands, came from the church of the Blessed Mary, which is on Mount Zion, to the church of Saint Stephen, the Protomartyr, singing and praying that the Lord Jesus Christ deliver His holy city and the Holy Sepulcher from the pagan people and place it in Christian hands for His holy service. The clerks, so clad, along with the armed knights and their retainers, marched side by side.[2]

The image of the Frankish clergy and soldiery engaging in a barefoot procession, bearing crosses, chanting prayers, and begging their Lord to help

---

1. For what follows, the primary accounts are GF 90; PT 137 (tr. 115). RA 143–145 (tr. 121–123). AA vi.7–8 (pp. 412–415). For general accounts, see Jay Rubenstein, *Armies of Heaven: The First Crusade and the Quest for Apocalypse* (New York: 2011), 273–280; John France, *Victory in the East: A Military History of the First Crusade* (Cambridge Eng; 1994), 325–350.
   2. PT 137 (tr. 115).

them take the city, while the Muslims from Jerusalem stood atop the city walls mocking crosses and jeering at their besiegers, is one of the most famous from the First Crusade.[3] And, of course, because the city fell to the Franks a week later, on 15 July, the liturgical supplication to God and the ritual show of communal penitence and devotion was naturally understood as having been instrumental in the ultimate military success.

The episode underscores the liturgical and devotional nature of much crusader warfare, revealing at once both its militant and its penitential nature. Jonathan Riley-Smith argued that the liturgiosity of the march bespeaks the character of the First Crusade as a whole, observing that it was the liturgical apparatus that most keenly manifested the crusade's character as a pilgrimage—that is, as an essentially religious and devotional activity—and that the crusade's processions and other liturgical rituals demonstrated its penitential nature.[4] He described the army, "constantly at public prayer," marching toward Jerusalem as a "military monastery on the move," the religiosity of which became increasingly heightened as the forces faced the rigors of deprivation and as they marched closer to Jerusalem.[5] The whole enterprise was first and foremost a religious act, and the explicitly devotional and penitential nature of the campaign necessarily conditioned the meaning and import of the liturgy in its context. So, surely, did the Holy Land itself, since much of the liturgy was intentionally mimetic of the Holy Land and the salvific events that occurred there. A penitential procession in Jerusalem could only have emanated eschatological resonance for being performed on the same ground on which Christ himself processed on Palm Sunday.[6]

This chapter looks at the liturgy of crusade in an attempt to appreciate the devotional and religious texture that the rites of prayer and intercession brought to the crusading experience. Unlike most of the rest of this book,

---

3. On the liturgical activity of the First Crusade, see Riley-Smith, *The First Crusade*, 82–86; McGinn, "Iter Sancti Sepulchri: The Piety of the First Crusaders," 33–71; Michael McCormick, "Liturgie et guerre des Carolingiens à la première croisade," in *Militia Christi' e crociata nei secoli XI–XII: atti della undecima settimana internazionale di studio Mendola* (Milan: 1992), 209–240; Michael McCormick, "The Liturgy of War from Antiquity to the Crusades," in *The Sword of the Lord: Military Chaplains from the First to the Twenty-First Century*, ed. Doris L. Bergen (Notre Dame: 2004), 45–67; Bachrach, *Religion and the Conduct of War*, 108–150; Guy Lobrichon, *1099: Jéruslem conquise* (Paris: 1998), 103–107.

4. Riley-Smith, *The First Crusade*, 84–85.

5. Riley-Smith, *The First Crusade*, 2, 83–84.

6. RA 144 (tr. 122); On the theme of Christomimesis, see: Katherine Allen Smith, "Glossing the Holy War: Constructions of the First Crusade, c. 1095–1146," *Studies in Medieval and Renaissance History* 10 (2013): 11–13; Iris Shagrir, "The *Visitatio Sepulchri* in the Latin Church of the Holy Sepulchre in Jerusalem," *Al-Masaq: Islam and the Medieval Mediterranean* 22, no. 1 (2010): 57–77; Wolf Zoeller, "The Regular Canons and the Liturgy of the Latin East," *Journal of Medieval History* 43 (2017), forthcoming.

which is organized around the evidence found in the liturgical volumes themselves, this chapter draws primarily on narrative accounts of crusading, paying particular attention to the role of liturgy, prayer, and ecclesiastical ritual in underwriting the goals and sacrality of the First Crusade and crusading in general. It is clear from the sources themselves that liturgical rituals were more frequently performed in the First Crusade (or at least, as more frequently represented in the written accounts) than in other campaigns in a way that suggests that the rites played a heightened role—that is, a more frequent or at least more meaningful role—on the campaign. But we should note that their performance were also strategic, and the way in which the devotional and strategic aspects of liturgical intervention intertwined is central to the quality of crusade as holy war. Just as visible and invisible enemies were linked within the larger eschatological economy, so temporal victories were intimately associated with virtue and worthiness, and thus with grace. Enactment of liturgy was crucial precisely because the entire crusade was in a sense a sacramental act—that is, a religious act or ceremony that is regarded as an outward and visible sign of inward and spiritual grace, or could even impart that grace.[7] It was because of this that the liturgy, with its eschatological frame and its transformative capacity, took on such resonance during the First Crusade, and probably why the sources for the First Crusade, much more so than those of the later crusades, both recalled and emphasized liturgical acts as central to the crusade experience. The liturgy, the vehicle for communicating and communing with God, routinely connected the First Crusade, with its eschatological and perhaps apocalyptic tenor, to the providence that was God's plan.

Liturgical prayer and liturgical performance would impart meaning to the crusade and for crusaders in different ways. The clergy's role on crusade was largely if not primarily liturgical, and we assume their Latinity to have enabled them to understand the words and the meanings of the liturgy. But what of the other crusaders, whose motivation was (at least in part) religious while their vocation was soldierly?[8] What would the liturgy have meant to these crusaders? This must have been highly variable. A segment of the laymen on crusade—especially those who had contacts with monasteries in the West or had been educated in their schools—would certainly have had a degree of liturgical literacy, as evidenced by penitentials and *libri precum* written for a nonclerical audience in this period.[9] These libri

7. Definition adapted from Oxford Dictionaries.

8. Enrico Cattaneo, "La partecipazione dei laici alla liturgia," in *I Laici nella "Societas Christiana" dei secoli XI e XII. (Atti della terza Settimana internazionale di studio, Mendola, 21–27 Agosto 1965* (Milan: 1968), 386–427.

9. Michael Driscoll, "Penance in Transition: Popular Piety and Practice," in *Medieval Liturgy: A Book of Essays*, ed. L. Larson-Miller (New York: 1997), 121–163.

precum included the Psalms, the litanies, and many of the votive prayers that were part of the ritual that laymen might access in the West and that were, in turn, invoked on the crusade.[10] Peter Bartholomew, a pilgrim and probably a layman soldier or perhaps a low-level parish priest, was described as knowing a little something (*aliquantulum*) about the liturgy. When pressed and, in a flurry of nerves, forgetful of what he knew, Bartholomew still could remember the *Pater Noster*, the *Credo in Deum*, the *Magnificat*, the *Glori in excelsis Deo*, and the *Benedictus Dominus Deus Israel*.[11] These were all core prayers from the Mass and the office—two canticles and the greater doxology, in addition to the Credo and the Pater Noster—and suggests (at least for this one man) some level of knowledge about or involvement with the liturgy. Certainly, it was the case that Peter was trying to claim that his visions were remarkable and authentic, and thus wanted to emphasize his status as an *illiteratus* (that is, one who did not know Latin), but the passage indicates what basic liturgical literacy might look like. At one point, soldiers were instructed to recite the *Pater Noster* as they marched into battle.[12] At other point, they recited the *Kyrie eleison* in thanksgiving upon return and upon victory.[13] The *Kyrie* was the opening invocation of the litany of the saints, that is, the series of prayers that were said in the litany/processions in which laymen in Latin Christendom would have participated during the Greater and Lesser Rogations. This all suggests rudimentary familiarity with Western liturgical practice. The Latinity and liturgical literacy of the nonclerical crusaders must also have shifted dramatically over the course of the crusading centuries. With the rise of literacy and the revolution of lay devotion in the West in the twelfth and thirteenth centuries, it is not surprising to find increasingly sophisticated knowledge of and involvement in liturgy by laymen on crusade. Joinville is perhaps our best example, and even if we assume he is an outlier, he still represents the direction of the trend. His memoirs of Louis IX's first crusade (1249–1250) are replete with references to the liturgy, often in close juxtaposition to fighting, in ways that reveal the different registers in which the crusades could be experienced; he even composed his own Credo upon return, a sure mark of his liturgical and devotional sophistication.[14]

It may have been as much or more the ritual, performative, and participatory aspects of the liturgy that, for men of arms, endowed meaning to

---

10. Driscoll, "Penance in Transition," 128–134.

11. RA 76 (tr. 58). See comments in France, "Two Types of Visions," 7.

12. RA 78 (tr. 60).

13. PT 108 (tr. 83); RC 94 (tr. 128), 104 (tr. 141); HdV 9.321 (p. 66), 17.110 (p. 121); Caffaro 105 (tr. 112)

14. Lionel J. Friedman, "Text and Iconography for Joinville's *Credo*," (Cambridge, MA: 1958).

the crusade, or at least iteratively reinforced the superstructural proposition of the crusade. The rituals themselves undergirded the essential truths of the community—in this case, that their project was religious in nature, and that it required the sanction and help of God. For the *illiteratus*, the ritual, gestural qualities of the liturgy rather than its literal (that is, strictly textual) qualities may well have conveyed more about the function and meaning of the liturgy and in turn the crusade. The rituals of communion, of procession, and of prayer that litter the sources enveloped the crusaders in the liturgical community and thus the theological project of the campaign. Participation in any individual liturgical act, and perhaps especially those done in groups, allowed crusaders to perform their humility, devotion, penitence, or thanksgiving before one another and, above all, before God. The rituals could also be transformative, literally turning one *into* a penitent, or shifting one's status from sin to grace.[15] Here again, regardless of the literal comprehension of the prayers and hymns, the regular and repeated use of liturgy certainly undergirded the sacramental nature of the crusade project as a whole. And no matter their level of Latinity or liturgical literacy, all participants would have (or should have) recognized the central rituals of the Catholic faith as a devotional act. Communal rites in particular (such as processions), or rites done communally (such as prebattle communion) would have cemented the host specifically as a Christian community, certainly reinforcing their allegiance to and defense of the Christian God as the defining feature of the campaign.

The First Crusade

Throughout the course of the campaign, from the First Crusade onward, there was an attempt to maintain a regular routine of liturgical ceremonies while on the march and in camp. When possible, the Franks venerated in local churches.[16] The eyewitness chroniclers refer to events that occurred while the crusaders were on the march or camped in tents by the liturgical calendar such as to indicate that crusaders were at least keeping track of the passage of time, and thereby their place in the devotional year.[17] Mass continued to be performed regularly, even in transit and during sieges, presumably on portable altars.[18] Priests whose function was to perform the

---

15. Schechner, *Performance Theory*; Turner, *Image and Pilgrimage*.
16. FC I.viii.9 (lat. 175–176, tr. 78). PT 132–133 (tr. 111).
17. GF 11, 14–15, 82, 85, 86; PT 42 (tr. 26), 65–66 (tr. 45), 73 (tr. 52), 132–134 (tr. 109–111); AA iv.47 (p. 321), v.41 (p. 397); RR 20 (tr. 104), 94 (tr. 192); HdV 9.47 (p. 42), 15.75 (pp. 99–100), 15.100 (p. 102), 15.111 (p. 103), 15.114 (p. 104).
18. GF 4; PT 36 (tr. 20).

mass must have carried the minimum liturgical instruments. Robert of Reims, writing later from the West, spoke of crosses, relics, and altars.[19] Chroniclers invariably mention celebration of the mass for, and the observance of, the principal feast days.[20] Sermons were regularly delivered.[21] Accommodations of the regular feast day were done on a makeshift basis, especially when the crusaders were still on the march. Fulcher of Chartres recounts how, after the establishment of the Kingdom of Jerusalem, he and others "gathered in the tent of the king and heard the Mass of the Nativity of the Blessed Virgin Mary, to which event the day was sacred."[22] Robert of Reims, drawing on the *Gesta*'s version of the campaign, imagined how difficult it was for the Franks to celebrate the Christmas rite in tents during the long siege of Antioch.[23] Easter of 1099 was celebrated outside of Acre,[24] Pentecost in a camp pitched outside Caesarea.[25] Clergy maintained their liturgical dress and are regularly described wearing their white stoles or priestly vestments, even—or especially—in battle or at moments of chaos.[26] (One can only imagine that the white stoles were dirty.) During the division of spoils, the clergy "who administered their masses" were granted a fortieth.[27] Three-quarters of a century later, William of Tyre imagined Godfrey of Bouillon along the entirety of the march followed by a train of monks, diligently celebrating the Divine Office according to canonical hours, following the use of his home church.[28]

Regular liturgical functions had to be maintained, particularly, not surprisingly, around confession (so that one would be prepared for the dangers of battle), last rites, and burial. It was part of the individual preparation for battle that soldiers confessed and took communion before combat. It seems soldiers did so en masse prior to battle.[29] In a letter to France during the

---

19. RR 98 (tr. 199). See also AA vi.9 (414–415) for relics.

20. GN IV.4 (lat. 173, tr. 77); GN VI.23 (lat. 265, tr. 123).

21. PT 35 (tr. 19), 117 (tr. 93); AA ix.47 (p. 702–703); Caffaro 106 (tr. 113); Rubenstein, *Armies of Heaven*, 70.

22. FC II.xiii.1 (lat. 417–418, tr. 160).

23. RR 37 (tr. 123). See also Hagenmeyer, *Chronologie*, 115.

24. April 10, 1099; GF 85; Hagenmeyer, *Chronologie*, 222–223, gives other sources.

25. May 28–29, 1099; AA v.41 (396–397); RR 94 (tr. 194).

26. GF 68, 78, 94; FC I.xi.9 (lat. 196–197, tr.85–86), I.22.3 (lat. 252, tr. 104); RC 104 (tr. 141); RA 81 (tr. 62–63); PT 110 (tr. 86), 123 (tr. 100), 145 (tr. 122); AA vi.9 (pp. 414–415), xii.56 (pp. 564–565); HdV 13.24 (pp. 86–87).

27. RA 111 (tr. 91); PT 122 (tr. 99).

28. WT ix.9 (lat. 1:431, tr. 1:392).

29. GF 67. AA iv (pp. 320–321), vi.43 (pp. 458–459), xii.55 (pp. 564–565); HdV 13.19 (p. 86); RA 79 (tr. 61). On communion, see Bachrach, *Religion and the Conduct of War*, 117. For a Spanish context, Joseph F. O'Callaghan, *Reconquest and Crusade in Medieval Spain* (Philadelphia: 2003), 185–190.

campaign itself, Count Anselm of Ribemont told the archbishop of Reims that the entire army had confessed and taken communion before the Battle of Nicea, and again before Antioch.[30] Anselm himself confessed on his deathbed during the march to Jerusalem.[31] Confession and communion were still a comparatively rare event for laymen, being prescribed more than a century later to be performed *at least* once a year.[32] Soldiers thus seem to have taken communion more often when on campaign than when at home. In spite of the aura or mystique of the possibility of martyrdom that surrounded the First Crusade, canonically speaking dying on crusade was a guarantee of heaven only if one had properly confessed.[33] Since dying on crusade alone thus did not guarantee salvation, men sought the consolation of confession and communion when they were on the brink of death.[34] Crusaders who perished en route of illness and exhaustion were buried in situ and given proper burial rites.[35] Frankish soldiers who died during the month-long siege of Jerusalem were buried in a local Christian cemetery outside the city, and "Christian priests carried out the funeral rites for them."[36] The issue of giving proper rites to those who died in battle was equally urgent. Robert of Reims imagined crusaders venturing onto the battlefield the day after the Battle of Doryaleaum, identifying crusaders by the crosses they wore and burying them "with as much honor as could be managed. The priests and clerics" he wrote, "sang the funeral service."[37]

The Liturgy of Battle

The prosecution of battle was also undergirded by liturgical practices. Confession and communion were of a piece with battle-time prayers, the point of which, of course, was both to aid the army in toto and also to prepare the individual for salvation in the case of death.[38] Prayers were said

---

30. *Epistulae* VIII (p. 144), XV (p. 160). For Baldwin, see also AA vii.67 (pp. 578–579).

31. RA 108–109 (tr. 88–89).

32. Norman P. Tanner, *Decrees of the Ecumenical Councils* (London: 1990), 1:245 (statute 21).

33. H.E.J. Cowdrey, "Martyrdom and the First Crusade," in *Crusade and Settlement: Papers Read at the First Conference of the Society for the Study of the Latin East and Presented to R.C. Smail,* ed. Peter W. Edbury (Cardiff: 1985), 46–56; Jean Flori, "Mort et martyr des guerriers vers 1100. L'exemple de la première croisade," *Cahiers de civilisation médievale* 34 (1991): 121–139.

34. RA 46 (tr. 28–29); WT iii.18 (lat. 1:220, tr. 1:177).

35. AA iii.27 (182–183). See also WT iii.18 (lat. 1:221, tr. 1:178), vi.2 (lat. 1:308, tr. 1:263), IV.7 (lat. 1:242, tr.1:197).

36. AA vi.5 (410–411).

37. RR 28 (tr. 112).

38. RA 79 (tr. 61).

or a mass performed upon departing for battle.[39] The eyewitness accounts recall bishops and priests offering exhortations or making sermons prior to battle. Adhémar of LePuy was renowned as a preacher to both the clergy and the men of arms, and he gave a memorable sermon to the army before the Battle at Nicea.[40] But other priests and clergy are also described as giving battlefield exhortations. Albert of Aachen composed a series of such exhortations that suggests the imagined flavor of such battlefield sermons.[41] Baldric, we saw, imagined a priest exhorting crusaders to take the earthly Jerusalem so that they might attain the heavenly Jerusalem.[42]

A bishop, or the legate, would bless the army as it set out for battle.[43] This was, according to canon law, one of the legitimate functions of a bishop or cleric on campaign, who were theoretically otherwise barred from bearing arms.[44] At Dorylaeum, Adhémar and four other bishops "humbly besought God that He would destroy the power of our enemies [*ut virtutem hostium nostrorum prosterneret*] and shed upon us the gifts of His mercy" as the leaders set out for battle.[45] The language here echoes one of the standard masses against pagans (*Hostium nostrorum quesumus domine elide superbiam et dexterae tuae virtute prosterne*).[46] Raymond Aguilers, describing the Battle of Antioch, explained that priests stood on the walls "invoking God to protect His people, and by a Frankish victory bear witness to the covenant which He made holy with His blood."[47] Raymond, too, was echoing the language of a *contra paganos* mass.[48] The author of the *Hystoria de via* (formerly known as the Montecassino Chronicle) described "our bishops and priests and clerics and monks, all dressed in sacred vestments, leaving with us, carrying crosses, praying and imploring God that He might make us safe and guard us and liberate us from all danger and all evils"; then "they stood upon the walls of the city holding saintly crosses in their hands, signing and blessing us. And we, thus ordered, and protected by the sign of the cross, began to exit from the city through the doorway, which is called the Mohametrie."[49] Speaking of preparations for

---

39. RA 79 (tr. 61); WT vii.22 (lat. 1:374, tr. 333); Caffaro 107 (tr. 114); WC I.5 (lat. 72, tr. 97, 98).

40. AA ii.27 (pp. 106–107); GF 74. Rubenstein, *Armies of Heaven*, 107, 232.

41. AA iv.38 (pp. 306–309), vi.7 (p. 413), vi.9 (pp. 414–415); ix.47 (pp. 702–703).

42. BB 107–109.

43. Riley-Smith, *The First Crusade*, 83.

44. Ivo of Chartres, Decretum, cap. 333 (PL 161, col. 424).

45. FC I.xi.9 (lat. 196–197, tr. 85).

46. CO 3007.

47. RA 81 (tr. 63).

48. Cf. CO 2422 (*Missa contra paganos*).

49. HdV 13.24–26 (pp. 86–87). Evocative is also William of Tyre's later description of the battle. Taken up by WT vi:16 (lat. 1:329, tr. 1:285–286). See also FC I.xxii.3 (lat. 252, tr. 104).

a battle in 1115, Walter the Chancellor, described the blessing: "The renowned bishop, bearing in a spirit of humility the cross of holy wood in his reverent hands, circled the whole army; and while he showed it to all of them he affirmed that they would claim victory in the coming battle through its virtue [or power, *virtutem*], if they charged the enemy with resolute heart."[50]

After the establishment of the Kingdom of Jerusalem (and taking possession of its relics), as Walter here makes clear, the blessing might be accompanied by a saint's relic or even a relic of the True Cross. Leading up to the Battle of Ascalon (12 August 1099), the bishop gave a blessing before the leaders made plans for the prosecution of the battle and the protection of the city.[51] Albert of Aachen reported that Arnulf of Chocques, the recently elected patriarch, sanctified the entire army with the holy cross in a blessing from his own hand.[52] This probably meant that he held the relic of the True Cross in the hand with which he made the blessing. The papal legate (Maurice of Porto) blessed the army following a battlefield exhortation by Patriarch Arnulf during the Crusade of 1101.[53] That year, the bishop of Milan gathered the army, urged them to confess their sins, granted them indulgence, and "sanctified and blessed them all with the arm of the blessed Ambrose bishop of Milan."[54] Presumably, he had brought this relic with him from home. The practice of engaging a saint—particularly an arm reliquary—in the ritual blessing was common in the West.[55]

One might imagine the bishop here using one of the many *in tempore belli* or *contra paganos* blessings known from the Gallican sacramentaries, the language of which infuses the narrative sources. It is also possible, given the fact that crusaders wore crosses and clergy blessed crusaders while holding the cross in their hands, that the cleric employed one of the prayers used to bless liturgical crosses in churches. These were, as chapter 1 discussed, so militant in tone that historians have sometimes assumed that intended as a battlefield blessing (they were not).[56] The RGP blessing referred to the cross as the *victoriae vexillum* and asked God to grant that

50. WC I.5 (lat. 72–73, tr. 99).

51. RA 154–155 (tr. 131–133); WT ix.11 (lat. 1:433–434, tr. 395).

52. AA vi.44 (460–461).

53. EA *Chr.* 174.

54. AA viii.15 (p. 605).

55. Cynthia Hahn, *Strange Beauty: Issues in the Making and Meaning of Reliquaries, 400–circa 1204* (University Park, PA: 2012), 135–141.

56. Eric Goldberg, "'More Devoted to the Equipment of Battle than the Splendor of Banquets': Frontier Kingship, Martial Ritual, and Early Knighthood at the Court of Louis the German," *Viator* 30 (1999): 66; Bachrach, *Religion and the Conduct of War*, 40. I extend my thanks to Dr. Goldberg for his correspondence with me on this matter.

his servant be armed by the standard which is the cross.[57] The cross borne on crusaders' clothing was also called the *vexillum*. Baldric of Bourgeuil imagined bishops and priests before the Battle of Antioch "signing all with the most reverend sign of the cross."[58] After the capture of Jerusalem the True Cross itself came to be called the *vexillum crucis*, mapping back onto the relic the liturgical imagery developed in praise of its power.[59]

The cross blessings may have also been appropriate if crusaders marched into battle beneath a military standard bearing an image of the cross. The textual evidence can be unclear, though, since the term *vexillum* was also used to mean the insignia of the cross itself. When the *Gesta* describes Raymond of Toulouse as being *undique signo crucis armatus* (armed on all sides with the sign of the cross),[60] and the ranks being *signo cruci protecti*,[61] or when Peter Tudebode relays a battlefield exhortation where the Franks are encouraged to be "protected by the victory of the standard of the holy cross" (*sanctae crucis vexilli victoria muniti*),[62] do they mean that the soldier(s) were going into battle under a battle standard that bore an image of the cross, that the soldier(s) were going into battle wearing the sign of the cross on their own garb (which of course we know they did), or that they were armed by the cross in that they were spiritually fortified by their faith in Christ? Probably some combination of the three. The Latin *signum*, too, could also mean banner, or battle standard, rendering layered meanings to the many instances, particularly in Peter Tudebode, of crusaders being described "signo crucis muniti" or "signo crucis armantur."[63]

Even if the language of the early chronicles is unclear, it does appear as if at least some of the crusaders' standards bore an image or the shape of a cross.[64] (See examples in figs. 3.1–3.3) Ralph of Caen speaks explicitly of a cloth banner in the shape of a cross."[65] By the mid-twelfth century, the cross itself (*vexillum*) and the war banner (also *vexillum*) were being intentionally

---

57. RGP XL 102–103 (p. 159). See also CBP 792.
58. BB 79.
59. See Fulcher's description of the expedition against the Turks in 1122, for which Baldwin II brought the True Cross. FC III.xi.6 (lat. 650, tr. 236–237). For other examples, see WC I.2 (lat. 66, tr. 86), I.5 (lat. 72–73, tr. 97, 98), II.3 (lat. 83–84, tr. 121), II.10 (lat. 100; tr. 147).
60. GF 15; HdV 6.18 (p. 27), 9.152 (p. 51).
61. GF 68.
62. PT 53 (tr. 35).
63. PT 49, 66, 72, 76, 111, 112. See also FC II.xxi.14 (lat. 453, tr. 173), III.xlii.9 (lat. 765, tr. 279). HdV 15.84 (p. 100).
64. Erdmann, *The Origin of the Idea of Crusade*, 35–56, with examples on pp. 39, 54 and 55. Constable, *Crusaders and Crusading*, 55–56, 63–89. McCormick, "The Liturgy of War," 55–56.
65. RC 74 (tr. 106). See also HdV 7.23.

Figure 3.1. The blessing of the war standard. From a copy of the pontifical of William Durandus, ca. 1357. Sainte Genevieve 0143, 181v. © Bibliothèque Sainte-Geneviève, Paris, cliché IRHT.

Figure 3.2. Blessing and the giving of the cross for those going in aid of the Holy Land, from a fifteenth-century copy of the pontifical of William Durandus. Boulogne Sur Mer 85, fol. 192. © Bibliothèque municipale de Boulogne-sur-Mer, cliché IRHT.

Figure 3.3. Moralization of 1 Kings 5:3–6. In the top roundel, the Philistines, described as Saracens, find the image of Dagon lying on the ground before the Ark with his head and hands cut off. In the bottom roundel the personification of the Church, holding a battle standard bearing a cross, tramples the devil beneath her feet. Oxford Bodelian 270v, 131v. Ca. 1235. Moralized Bible, after Alexandre de Laborde, *La Bible moralisée illustrée conservée à Oxford, Paris et Londres.* Paris: 1911–1927.

conflated. Of the Lisbon expedition during the Second Crusade, right before battle, the priest, holding up a bit of the True Cross, urged crusaders: "Under this standard [*hoc vexillo*], if only you falter not, you shall conquer. Because if it should happen than anyone signed [with the cross; *hoc insignitum*] should die, we do not believe that life has been taken from him, for we have no doubt that he is changed into something better. Here, therefore, to live is glory and to die is to gain."[66] That same decade, Hugh of Poitiers could talk of Louis VII "going to Jerusalem with a great army under a banner inscribed with the life-giving cross [*vexillo vivificae crucis*], to fight the race inimical to the faith."[67] The standard (or banner) of the holy cross appropriated the power and prestige in the liturgy of fighting for Christ. A half century later Barbarossa's army was described achieving a military victory "through the leadership and guidance of God and under the standard of the holy cross."[68] During the Fifth Crusade, in June when the crusaders captured the Tower, they placed the *vexillum crucis* on top of the tower, in part so the Egyptians could see their claim to victory.[69] The meaning was visualized in a moralized bible allegorization of 1 Kings 5:3–5 at about this same time (ca. 1230, fig. 3.3). The Philistines, called Saracens in the biblical synopsis of the upper roundel, find an image of Dagon, their idol, lying on the ground before the Ark with its feet and hands cut off. The allegorization beneath reads: "Dagon, who prostrate has lost his feet and hands signifies the devil who is conquered, destroyed, and thrown into confusion by the church, lies abject on the ground."[70] The lower roundel shows Ecclesia, holding a standard bearing the cross, who tramples and thus conquers the devil (associated with Saracens) beneath her feet.

Back to the First Crusade. Clergy accompanied the Frankish soldiers into battle, reciting prayers and beseeching the aid of God and the saints. Some clergy may have participated in the fighting—Anna Comnena would tell a story of a priest who entered the fray, shooting off several arrows and fighting violently;[71] and later, Joinville's own priest entered a melee with a

---

66. David, *De expugnatione Lyxbonensi*, 156–157. I have altered the translation slightly.

67. Hugh of Poitiers, *Chronicon abbatiae Uizeliacensis*, ed. R. B. C. Huygens, CCCM 42 (Turnhout: 1976), part 4, line 2996; Hugh of Poitiers, *The Vézelay Chronicle and Other Documents from MS. Auxerre 227 and Elsewhere*, Medieval & Renaissance Texts and Studies (Binghamton, NY: 1992), 308.

68. HdE 174 (tr. 170). See also 176: *et cum vix sexcenti equites essemus, sub signo vivifice crucis*.

69. QBS 120, 163.

70. Oxford Bodeleian 270b, 131v: "Dagon qui prostratus pedes and manus amisit significat diabolus qui ab ecclesia victus destructus iacet et confusus."

71. Anna Comnena, *The Alexiad of the Princess Anna Comnena, Being the History of the Reign of Her Father, Alexius I, Emperor of the Romans, 1081–1118 A.D.*, ed. And trans. Elizabeth A. S. Dawes (London: 1928), 256 (book 10).

spear and was later celebrated for routing eight Saracens.[72] Priests and bishops certainly accompanied soldiers into the field. They were present at all the principal battles of the First Crusade: Dorylaeum,[73] Antioch,[74] Ma'arrah,[75] Jerusalem,[76] and Ascalon.[77] Adhémar of LePuy had his own retinue which he led into battle, even if he himself did not bear arms. Adhémar had led the rear guard at Nicea, and also a contingent in the Battle of Dorylaeum.[78]

But for the most part, bishops and priests were meant to pray. Their prayers were understood as the spiritual equivalent of swords, as militarily efficacious in battle. A vivid portrait of liturgical warfare emerges from the multiple descriptions of the Battle of Antioch of 28 June 1098, when, after the taking of the city, the Franks faced Kerbogha and his army outside of the city walls.[79] Adhémar actively led his division into the mountains, having Raymond of Aguilers carry the recently discovered Holy Lance as his battle standard.[80] With the participation of vested and chanting clergy, the march into battle took on the character of a liturgical procession. Raymond of Aguilers describes the advance in precisely such terms: "In typical clerical procession we advanced and, may I add, it was a procession. Priests and many monks wearing white stoles walked before the ranks of our knights, chanting and praying for God's help and the protection of the saints."[81] He repeated the image later, in describing the retreat from Arqua.[82] Fulcher of Chartres also described how the army set forth against Kerbogha: "The footmen and horsemen were organized into companies and squadrons preceded by their banners. Amongst them were the priests vested in white. These latter, weeping for the whole people, sang to the Lord and poured out many prayers from the depths of their devout souls."[83] The clergy were probably reciting the litany of the saints, invoking the prayers of the saints

---

72. Joinville §§258–260.

73. FC I.xi.9 (lat. 196–197, tr. 85–86); RR 27–28 (tr. 111–112). For an earlier episode, see GF 4; PT 35 (tr. 19).

74. FC I.xxii.3 (lat. 252, tr. 104); PT 110–111 (tr. 86); HdV 13.24 (pp. 86–87).

75. GF 78–79; PT 123 (tr. 100); RR 86 (tr. 184); HdV 15.31 (p. 96).

76. GF 90; PT 137 (tr. 115).

77. GF 94; PT 146 (tr. 123).

78. PT 54 (tr. 36.) J. H. Hill and L. L. Hill, "Contemporary Accounts and the Later Reputation of Adhemar, Bishop of Puy," *Medievalia et Humanistica* 9 (1955): 30–38; James A. Brundage, "Adhémar of Puy; the Bishop and his Critics," *Speculum* 34 (1959): 201–212; Riley-Smith, *The First Crusade*, 82.

79. GF 67–68; FC I.xxii.3 (lat. 252–253, tr. 104); RA 81 (62–63); PT 110 (tr. 86). See also AA ix.47 (320–323), ix.53 (332–333); RR 72 (tr. 167–168); RA 81 (tr. 63).

80. AA iv.47, 54 (320–321, 332–333).

81. RA 81 (tr. 62).

82. RA 125 (tr. 104–105).

83. FC I.xxii.3 (lat. 252–253, tr. 104).

for aid. The litany called individually on the saints to "pray for us" and ended with a series of more specific invocations.[84] But the petitions to the saints may have been understood quite literally. It was later reported that some of the soldiers saw saints George, Demetrius, and Theodore (or Maurice) ride to their aid.[85] The *Gesta*'s account was complementary: "Our bishops and priests and clerks and monks put on their holy vestments and came out with us, carrying crosses, praying, and beseeching God to save us and keep us and rescue us from all evil, while others stood above the gate with holy crosses in their hands, making the sign of the cross and blessing us."[86] If the author of the *Gesta* was being precise here, the clergy standing on the walls and blessing the Frankish soldiers while holding the cross were probably making some kind of war blessing, or possibly a blessing of the cross which would have enjoined conquering the enemy.

The richness of our description of the Battle of Antioch in the narrative accounts is exceptional, but references littering the sources suggest that clergy were often on the front lines. A few months later, during the Battle of Ma'arrat-an-Nu'mān in November 1098, according to Peter Tudebode, "knights and retainers battled, while priests and clerks dressed in sacred garments stood behind the tower praying and imploring our Lord Jesus Christ to protect his people, give victory to the knights of Christ, glorify sacred Christianity, and destroy heathenism. Thus they fought until sundown."[87] The author of the *Gesta* said that vested priests stood behind the siege tower beseeching "God to defend his people, and to exalt Christendom and cast down paganism."[88] These, we have seen, were precisely the requests in the *contra paganos* and *in tempore belli* prayers. Robert of Reims, writing within a decade, said (or imagined) that during the attack priests stood at the siege tower reciting scriptural verses, including Isaiah 33:2 ("O Lord have mercy on us; be our arm in the morning, and our salvation in the time of trouble"); Psalm 78:6 ("Pour out Your wrath upon the nations that have not known You; and upon the kingdoms that have not called upon Your name"); and Psalm 58:12 ("Scatter them by Your power, and bring them low, O Lord, my protector").[89] In 1099, during the siege of Jerusalem, Raymond took "up position with two bishops from Italy before the

84. Michael Lapidge, *Anglo-Saxon Litanies of the Saints*, Henry Bradshaw Society 106 (Woodbridge, UK: 1991).

85. GF 69 (Mercurius); PT 112 (tr. 87, Theodore); HdV 7.27 (p. 32; Maurice). On this episode, see Elizabeth Lapina, *Warfare and the Miraculous in the Chronicles of the First Crusade* (University Park, PA: 2015). See for later HdE 176.

86. GF 68. See also GN VI.7 (lat. 237–238, tr. 109).

87. PT 123 (tr. 100).

88. GF 78–79.

89. RR 86 (tr. 184).

doorway" of the Tower of David.[90] The evidence of liturgical interventions near or in battle accelerates as the crusade advanced toward Jerusalem, and continued after its capture. Fulcher himself remembers that, at the start of the Battle of Nahr al-Kalb (24 October 1100), "we, with contrite and pure hearts, devoutly prayed that as we encountered the foe, aid would come from Heaven."[91] After the taking of Jerusalem, clergy would carry the (re)discovered relic of the True Cross into battle. Albert of Aachen identifies two bishops, "Gerard and Baldwin," who "carried the Lord's cross before them to confound and blind the Saracens" during the Battle of Ascalon.[92] Two years later, in the siege of Caesarea in April 1101, Daimbert of Pisa, the patriarch, was described "wearing a holy and white robe instead of a breastplate" and carrying "the cross of our Lord before them for protection and defense of the Catholic people, and the whole army of warriors did not hesitate to follow him right up to the walls."[93]

If bishops and priests sung liturgical prayers as they marched, processionlike (if we follow Raymond Aguilers) into battle, soldiers made battle cries. The standard cry was *Deus lo volt!* In Latin: *Deus vult.*[94] The *Gesta* says that Bohemond learned the war cry when learning about the crusade. Others suggest that Urban himself instituted the cry.[95] But there were other options, some of which suggest liturgical inspiration and influence. Peter Bartholomew reported that God instructed soldiers to give alms and repeat the *Pater Noster* five times before entering into battle.[96] Ralph of Caen described soldiers returning to the walls from battle singing the *Kyrie eleison*, the traditional invocation that served as the popular response or choral refrain during the recitation of the litany. Like the Pater Noster, the Kyrie, we saw, was an invocation that laity would have been accustomed to saying as part of their role in popular liturgy.[97] In Antioch, in the face of the imminent battle with Kerbogha, Peter Bartholomew explained that God had instructed the army to desist using the triumphant *Deus vult:* "Your battle cry should be 'Deus adiuva.' And God will thus aid

90. AA v.46 (402–403). See also BB 107–109.

91. FCII.ii.3 (lat. 359, tr. 139).

92. AA vii.66 (p. 579); PT 146 (tr. 124).

93. AA vii.56 (pp. 564–565). For further examples, see also AA vii.67–68 (pp. 578–579, 580–581), AA ix.49 (pp. 708–709); WT x.17 (lat. 1:473, tr. 439); WT xi.3 (lat. 1:498, tr. 464–465).

94. GF 7 (*Deus vult*); HdV 3.21 (p. 14: *Deus lo volt*); PT 40 (tr. 24: *Deus hoc vult*), 86 (tr. 64, *Deus lo vult*); RR 7 (tr. 81), 14 (tr. 92), 26 (tr. 109, *Deus vult*; GN 3.1, 5.5 (lat. 136, 205, tr. 57, 92, *Deus id vult*).

95. RR 7 (tr. 81).

96. RA 78 (tr. 60).

97. RC 94 (tr. 128), 104 (tr. 141). See also HdV 9.321 (p. 66). On the *Kyrie eleison*, David Hiley, *Western Plainchant: A Handbook* (Oxford: 1993), 150–156. McCormick, "The Liturgy of War," 48–49.

you."[98] The shift to *Deus adiuva* signaled the shift from the confident militarism of the war liturgies to the penitential supplication of the pilgrimage rites. The new prayer, echoing a penitential battle cry from Second Maccabees (8.23, "signum adiutorium Dei"), was in line with the long list of petitions to individual saints and to God repeated in the Litany of the Saints and during Rogations: "Exsurge Domine, adjuva nos" and (from Psalm 69:6) "Deus adjuva me," which would have been recited during the penitential processions. In this same passage, Raymond reported that heavenly assistance came to the army. Heavenly assistance, protection, and intercession are at the heart of the litany. Raymond himself associated this battle cry with divine success in the field.[99] This then became the standard cry. In the battle for Jerusalem on July 15, 1099, the Franks, as they entered the city, shouted *Adiuva Deus* (God, help us!).[100] Fulcher describes it in use in later years as well.[101]

The litanic and liturgical source of the battle cries further enveloped the practice of war in a sacral aura. Another cry used at moments of greater optimism was the *Christus vincit, Christus regnat, Christus imperat* invocation. This too was litanic, also associated with the recitation of the Litany of the Saints.[102] Ralph of Caen described how, after a victory, the crusaders sang out *Christus vincit, regnat, imperat*.[103] Fulcher of Chartres explained that in 1105, in the aftermath of a penitential procession, the army used it as a battle cry."[104] As we know from Ernst Kantorowicz's classic study, the *Christus vincit* triad, rooted in late antique emperor acclamations, was a Gallican practice that coalesced and was incorporated into the litany in the century or so before 1095, injecting into otherwise penitential and supplicatory pleas calls to the "militant nature of the victorious Christ," the "conquering God—Christ the victor, ruler, and commander— and acclaim in Him; with Him, or through Him, His imperial or royal vicars on earth along with all the other powers conquering, ruling, commanding, and safeguarding the order of this present world."[105] Transferred from the West to the very land of Christ, and to the effort to take back His

---

98. RA 78 (tr. 60). Raymond had evoked the liturgical line itself at 60 (tr. 42). See also 105 (tr. 86), and 115 (tr. 95).

99. RA 105 (tr. 86). I am extremely grateful to Philippe Buc for the reference to the biblical precedent for *Deus adiuva* in II Macc 8.23. He tells me that *Deus adiuva* was also used in the Byzantine army.

100. FC I.xxvii.10 (lat. 299, tr. 121).

101. FC III.xlii.9 (lat. 765, tr. 279), III.l.8 (lat, 789, tr. 290). See also John France, "The Text of the Account of the Capture of Jerusalem in the Ripoll Manuscript, Bibliothèque Nationale (Latin) 5132," *English Historical Review* 103, no. 408 (1988): 646.

102. Lapidge, *Anglo-Saxon Litanies of the Saints*, 49–50.

103. RC 41 (tr. 65).

104. FC II.xxxii.5 (lat. 497, tr. 186).

105. Ernst H. Kantorowicz, *Laudes Regiae: A Study in Liturgical Acclamations and Mediaeval Ruler Worship*, University of California Publications in History (Berkeley: 1946), 14.

patrimony and serve His kingship, the invocation ceded its allegorical affect and became in a sense a literal evocation of Christ's authority, alongside the crusaders, to rule in the Holy Land. As throughout the campaign, the allegorical and spiritualized meaning of liturgical prayers were being actualized.

From the start, the crusaders repaid victory with the liturgical expressions of thanksgiving.[106] Robert of Reims reported that following the Battle of Dorylaeum the soldiers returned to their tents with priests and clerics chanting the following hymn to God: 'You are glorious in Your saints, O Lord, and wonderful in majesty; *fearful in praises, doing wonders*" (Ex 15:11). The makeshift hymn drew from Exodus (Ex 15:6, 7, 19, and 13) in thanking God for dashing the enemy to pieces, overthrowing them, and drawing His sword on them.[107] The hymn was made up of verses that celebrated the militant God of the Old Testament who, through his chosen people, destroyed and scattered the enemy. After defeating Kerbogha in late June 1098, Fulcher exclaimed, "Then all in exultant voice blessed and glorified God." The language that follows echoes liturgical orations and suggests the nature of the prayers that were offered up: "In righteous compassion He had freed them from the cruelest of enemies, those who, placed in great need and tribulation, had still trusted in Him. In His might He had scattered in conquered state the Turks who up to then had almost conquered the Christians."[108] The language in these descriptions again resonates with the wartime liturgies.[109] The victory in Jerusalem resulted in joyful celebrations at the Holy Sepulchre.[110] Thanksgiving was performed with the jubilant recitation of the "Te Deum Laudamus."[111] Fulcher twice says the "Te Deum" was sung in Jerusalem as part of a thanksgiving procession, once on the return of the True Cross to the city, and again upon receiving the news that Tyre had been captured.[112]

Processions

God's military support was premised on the Frankish forces being worthy, free of sin, and appropriately penitent. Strategic setbacks or defeats in battle

---

106. PT 66 (tr. 46); RA 61 (tr. 43).

107. RR 27–28 (tr. 111–112).

108. FC I.xxiii.6 (lat. 257, tr. 106–107). For other examples in Fulcher, see I.xii.5 (lat. 198, tr. 87); I.xxxiii.1 (lat. 322–323, tr. 128–129), II.viii.4 (lat. 398, tr. 152); III.li.3 (lat. 795, tr.292). Also WT vi.22 (lat. 1:339, tr. 295).

109. Cf. CO 1501: *Missa tempore belli.*

110. See next chapter, and for 1105, AA ix.47 9.48 (pp. 704–705).

111. McCormick, *Eternal Victory*, 357; O'Callaghan, *Reconquest and Crusade*, 203.

112. FC III.xix.1 (lat. 668, tr. 243), and III.xxxiv.4–6 (lat. 736, tr. 266–267). See also PT 108 (tr. 83).

were understood as God's punishment for sin and the withdrawal of His favor. Penitence and internal reform were always linked to spiritual, and ultimately, to actual, or material, warfare.[113] The Old Testament, we have seen, furnished repeated examples, in the stories of Joshua, of the Ninevites, of Judas Maccabeus, of military victories being contingent on religiosity, and of the role of prayer, penitence, and liturgical intercession in convincing God to tip his hand and ensure victory, all of which were rehearsed in the liturgy. This was certainly on the minds of the crusaders. For one, the chroniclers themselves made reference to these very stories.[114] For the Franks, then, a principal tactic at heightened junctures was to effect penance and demonstrate to God worthiness, which was done liturgically through communal repentance, most visibly with a penitential and expiatory procession. Bernard McGinn has discussed the course of these rituals as a "dialectic of sin-repentance-special providential intervention."[115] These cycles of fasting, prayers, alms, and processions were called in moments of need or crisis, in what the language of the liturgical rubrics called the "necessitatis causa," or the "laetania proquacumque tribulatione."[116] At Dorylaeum, for instance, hemmed in by the enemy and expecting to be wiped out, as Fulcher said, "It was clear to us that this was happening because of our sins."[117] The Franks confessed and prayed, and the clergy beseeched God "to overthrow the strength of our enemy" (*ut virtutem hostium nostrorum prosterneret*, again, echoing standard wartime liturgy).[118] The sins included luxury, avarice, pride, and plunder, as well as ones sexual in nature, all of which would have been a violation of the temporary religious status that crusaders took on as part of their vow.[119] Military victory was in turn attributed to the force of these prayers. "God, appeased no doubt by their prayers," wrote Fulcher about a later episode, "was pleased to end the labor of His people who had daily poured fourth beseeching supplications to Him."[120]

At four points during the First Crusade (30 December 1097, 25–27 June 1098, 8 July 1099, and 10 August 1099), and then again in the years that followed, the ecclesiastical authorities called for crusaders to participate in processions in order to beseech God for help in a coming battle and

---

113. Buc, "Some Thoughts on the Christian Theology of Violence," 23–26. Buc, *Holy War, Martyrdom, and Terror*, 89–105.
114. RA 15 (editors' discussion), 53 (tr. 35)). Lapina, *Warfare and the Miraculous*, 107–108.
115. McGinn, "Iter Sancti Sepulchri: The Piety of the First Crusaders," 55. At 50 he speaks of "the cycle of sin-repentance-providential confirmation."
116. BNF Lat. 2290, 8v–9r; BNF Lat. 2293 226r.
117. FC I.xi.8 (lat. 195–196, tr. 85).
118. FC I.xi.9 (lat. 196, tr. 85–86). Cf. CO 3007.
119. FC I.xv.13–14 (lat. 222–223, tr. 95).
120. FC I.xvii.1 (lat. 230–231, tr. 98).

convince Him of their worthiness.[121] At the very end of 1097, during the long siege of Antioch, the Franks were camped in pitched tents outside the walls of the city, harassed by Turkish attacks, short of food, and suffering illness. Omens in the form of a comet and earthquake suggested God's anger. Raymond of Aguilers recalls that at this point, Adhémar of LePuy organized three days of prayers, fasting, and processions:

> Although God had so scourged His army in order that we might turn to the light which arose in the darkness, yet the minds of certain ones were so dense and headstrong that they were recalled from neither riotous living nor plundering. Then Adhémar urged the people to fast three days, to pray, to give alms, and to form a procession; he further ordered priests to celebrate masses, and clerks to repeat psalms. Thus the blessed Lord, mindful of His loving kindness, delayed His children's punishment lest it increase the pride of their adversaries.[122]

The call for fasting, praying, and almsgiving was the staple biblical triad of penitential life (see Tobit 12:8), enshrined in the penitential system established in the Carolingian period and thus familiar from the penitential culture that the crusaders would have brought with them East.[123] What Adhémar of LePuy was ordering here was a traditional three-day litanic procession based on the rogations of the Minor Litany (we'll come back to this). Six months later, after the taking of the city on 3 June 1098, the emir of Mosul, Kerbogha marched his forces down to relieve the city. (This is the scene with which this book's introduction opened.) Imprisoned by Kerbogha's siege within the walls of the city they had just captured, the priest Stephen of Valence had a vision in which Christ Himself instructed that He would ensure military victory if "they would return to Him." In Peter Tudebode's account, Stephen of Valence said that Christ Himself had instructed him to tell the army to take up penance (*accipiant poenitentias*), by performing barefoot processions throughout the city and giving alms to the poor. Priests, in turn, should say the Mass and offer up communion. Christ also instructed the Franks to sing the responsory *Congregati sunt*, along with the versicle (*cum versu*). Only then, said Christ, should they take up battle, and He "would send to them a mighty help."[124] *Congregati sunt*, the prayer that Christ requested of the crusaders, ran: 'Our enemies have gathered together, and they are boasting of their power. Destroy their strength, O Lord, and scatter them. That they may know that there is no

---

121. Godfrey of Bouillon's smaller procession around the walls of Jerusalem after the capture of the Holy City could be counted as a fifth. See AA vi.25 (pp. 436–437).

122. RA 54 (tr. 36).

123. Driscoll, "Penance in Transition," 125.

124. GF 58. PT 100 (t. 75).

one who fights for us but You, our God. [v] Scatter them by Your power and destroy them, O Lord, our protector.' "[125] The verse was on point for the moment. It originated with the daily office for the Thursday of the first week of October (part of the summer histories), in which the lessons were taken from the Book of Maccabees and the whole of which dealt with God's power and holy war. The liturgical cycle was dominated by the Israelite victories against the Canaanites and Philistines. And, of course, the crusaders themselves were routinely compared to the Maccabees as holy warriors with divine backing.[126] In the regular liturgy *Congregati sunt* was the responsory paired to a lesson from Maccabees (1 Macc 2:64–69), which introduced Judas Maccabeus as "the leader of Your army" who "shall wage the war of the people." It had also been used for the Cluniac monastic clamor by about 1075[127] and appears to have been used routinely for rites in times of war.[128] It would later be incorporated into special liturgical rites for the crusades.[129] It called to God, the divine protector, to use His power to destroy the enemy that was threatening, to crush their strength, and to scatter them. It made a clear division between those favored by God and those whom He would destroy. And it made clear that it was God's power that would be responsible, should He so choose, for military victory.

It is hard to know exactly what happened in Antioch in the first week of June 1098. The *Gesta* said only that God issued the order. Peter Tudebode said that He instructed the entire army to chant the litanies along with the *Congregati sunt* responsory for five (rather than three) days.[130] Raymond of Aguilers said that the army was to recite the responsory *as* they marched into battle.[131] When Guibert of Nogent retold the story, he presumed that it would be accompanied by the standard litany, that is, the long appeal to the saints and a series of short hortatory appeals.[132] It was probably one of a handful of such texts that was used in an ad hoc fashion. As Stephen of Valence reported his vision, God was calling on the Franks to repent. The

---

125. CAO 6326: "*De Machabaeis*. Response to the third lesson for the Thursday of the first week of October. Translation taken from Catholic Church, *The Hours of the Divine Office in English and Latin* (Collegeville, MN: 1963), 3:1206.

126. See most recently Lapina, *Warfare and the Miraculous*, 97–121.

127. Lester Little, *Benedictine Maledictions: Liturgical Cursing in Romanesque France* (Ithaca, NY: 1993), 20.

128. Terence Bailey, *The Processions of Sarum and the Western Church* (Toronto: 1971), 120n3.

129. Linder RA 167, 183, 196. Later ordinals prescribe *Congregati sunt* as the responsory for special processions called *in tempore belli*. J.B.L. Tolhurst, *The Customary of the Cathedral Priory Church of Norwich: Ms. 465 in the Library of Corpus Christi College, Cambridge*, Henry Bradshaw Society 82 (London: 1948), 212.

130. PT 99–110 (tr. 75).

131. RA 73 (tr. 56).

132. GN V.17 (lat. 220, tr. 100).

sin was one of sexual continence. "Behold," relates the *Gesta*, "I gave you timely help and put you safe and sound into the city of Antioch, but you are satisfying your filthy lusts both with Christians and with loose pagan women, so that a great stench goes up to heaven."[133] The crusaders needed to demonstrate their deep repentance. And with it, they called on God to help them crush Kerbogha's forces.

So, what were these processions? In the West, litanic Rogation processions were a regular part of the Latin liturgy, and in which—this is crucial—laymen and women were meant to participate along with the clergy in asking God for aid ("rogation" comes from "rogo, rogare"—to ask). They occurred twice a year in the Roman and Gallic liturgy, in April (the "Major Litany") and before Ascension (the "Minor Litany").[134] The Major Litany was the ritualized commemoration of a penitential procession Gregory the Great had organized in Rome in the sixth century after the city of Roman had been devastated by plague. The Minor Litany, in turn, was rooted in a supplicatory procession called in Vienne in 470 by the bishop (Marmetus) to supplicate God following a number of earthquakes. Both origin stories evoked the Ninevites, a detail repeated in the liturgy as well as by the commentators, and thus served to link the entire rite to the Old Testament models for communal repentance.[135] The Major Litany lasted only one day, but the Minor Litany was generally performed over the three days preceding Ascension. In both, the entire community—laymen as well as clergy—gathered at the main church and then went in procession from church to church ("stations") throughout the city, saying prayers of supplication and evoking the help of the patron saints of individual churches. The liturgical books instructed everyone to wear simple clothes and walk barefoot. Later commentators explained that because everyone sinned, everyone had to pray for forgiveness, and thus everyone had to participate in the procession's show of ritual humility.[136] The cycle of prayers sung during the procession—the *Letania*—came to denote the supplicatory procession itself.

Ecclesiastical authorities could call upon *Letania* at moments of crisis or special need. Prayers in liturgical books include special antiphons and prayers

---

133. GF 58.

134. Gregory Nathan, "Rogation Ceremonies in Late Antique Gaul," *Classica et Medievalia* 21 (1998): 276–303; Joyce Hill, "The *Litaniae maiores* and *minores* in Rome, Francia and Anglo-Saxon England: Terminology, Texts and Traditions," *Early Medieval Europe* 9, no. 2 (2000): 211–246.

135. Gregory of Tours HF X.1 (for the Major Litany), and HF II.34 (for the Minor Litany); RGP XCIX.77 (2:22); John Beleth, *Summa de ecclesiasticis officiis*, ed. H. Douteil, CCCM 41–41a (Turnhout: 1976), 2:234 (ch. 122.e).

136. Sicard of Cremona, *Mitralis de officiis*, ed. Gábor Sarbak and Lorenz Weinrich, CCCM 228 (Turnhout: 2008), 574; William Durandus, *Rationale divinorum officiorum*, ed. D. A. Davril and T. M. Thibodeau, 3 vols., CCCM 140–140b (Turnhout: 1995–2000), 2:503–504.

for rain, drought, plague, and in times of war. That is, the function of these processions was to beseech God for *worldly aid*. The *Ordo Romanus*, which recorded papal liturgical practice, indicated that the Major Litany should be used to protect the harvest from the ravages of war and from inclement weather,[137] and the RGP spoke of its use "for the relentlessness of wars."[138] The specifics of the litany itself varied according to regional use,[139] but in general it began with the *Kyrie eleison*, invoked the Trinity, the Virgin, archangels, apostles, martyrs, confessors, and virgins, asking each individual or group to pray for the beseeching community ("Ora pro nobis"), and ended with a series of short prayers asking for various forms of favor. The petitions were about the community, beseeching God on behalf of "us" or "the Christian people" (*populum Christianum*). Relevant to the corporate identity that the crusaders were fostering may have been other common refrains: "Save Your servants, trusting in You, O my God." And "let not the enemy prevail against us at all." Other petitions asked to be protected from all evil, that God see fit to "crush the enemies of the holy church of God," and to "defend us, O Christ, from all of our enemies."[140] The Romano-Germanic Pontifical included a petition to "defend us both here and in eternity from pagan peoples."[141] The petitions were specifically penitential, but they were also explicitly communal, beseeching God on behalf of "us" or "the Christian people" (populum Christianum).

And so, in June 1098, in order to demonstrate contrition and penitence, ecclesiastical authorities organized a classic Letania.[142] The *Gesta's* version said that the crusaders then spent three days fasting and going "in processions from one church to another," then confessed their sins, received absolution, and took communion.[143] In this instance, the procession probably began at the Church of Saint Peter, and then onward to various shrines or churches in the city. The procession would have begun with the standard antiphonal call to God, *Exsurge domine*: "Rise up, O Lord, and help us; and free us on account of Your name."[144] Other standard rogational

137. Joseph Dyer, "Roman Processions of the Major Litany (*litaniae maiores*) from the Sixth to the Twelfth Century," in *Roma Felix—Formation and Reflections of Medieval Rome* (Aldershot: 2007), 113–137.

138. RGP XCIX.419 (2:119).

139. For this paragraph, see Lapidge, *Anglo-Saxon Litanies of the Saints*.

140. Lapidge, *Anglo-Saxon Litanies of the Saints*, 101, 119, 147, 151.

141. RGP XCIX.434 (2:131).

142. This is made absolutely explicit from Spanish materials from 1212. The rite discussed and translated in Martín Alvira Cabrere, *Las Navas de Tolosa 1212: Idea, liturgia y memoria de la batalla* (Madrid: 2012), 139–140, includes incipit for standard items from typical rogations.

143. GF 67–68. Cf. 13.19 (p. 86).

144. CAO 2822, 8072.

Figure 3.4. The Franks perform penitential processions prior to the Battle of Antioch. From an illustrated history of William of Tyre. Mid fourteenth century. BNF Fr. 352 fol. 47v.

Figure 3.5. The Frankish army leaves the city to fight the Battle of Antioch. From an illustrated history of William of Tyre. Mid fourteenth century. BNF Fr. 352 fol. 47v.

antiphons may have held particular resonance in the context of their goals in 1098, namely, the *De Ierusalem exeunt*: "The remnant comes out from Jerusalem and deliverance from Mount Sion, therefore there will be protection for this city and it will be saved on account of David, the servant of the Lord. Alleluia."[145] It was standard fare in the West, but nothing could have been more appropriate in Antioch, as the crusaders looked on Jerusalem as their ultimate goal. Clergy and those laymen who were able would have chanted the long series of petitions of Christ, Mary, and the saints, asking to be freed from harm, and freed from enemies. The crusaders and their clergy would have born a cross, relics, almost certainly the recently discovered Holy Lance, and gone barefoot, intoning the litany of the saints, Psalms, and special invocations, including *Congregati sunt*. As a series of wonderful illuminations in a thirteenth-century copy of William of Tyre makes clear, the demonstration of humility was a layer of military strategy. The images juxtapose the procession, marching out from the city holding crosses, croziers, censes, and relics, with the army, also marching out from the city, holding banners, spears, shields, and axes (figs. 3.4 and 3.5). They represent parallel forms of warfare. In both, God blesses them from above.[146]

And it was not the last time. The most famous episode, of course, was the penitential procession performed around the walls of the Holy City on 8 July 1099, a week before the fall of Jerusalem to the Franks, with which this chapter opened. All the early "eyewitness" narrators include the event. Peter Tudebode said that he participated in the procession himself and saw it with his own eyes.[147] The author of the *Gesta* said that the bishop and priests preached to the crusaders, telling them to go around Jerusalem in procession, to pray, to give alms, and to fast.[148] Raymond of Aguilers said that Adhémar had returned from the beyond, advising crusaders to "turn back on your sin; Then, take off your shoes and in your naked feet walk around Jerusalem, and don't forget to fast."[149] Albert of Aachen later explained that it was the advice of a hermit on the Mount of Olives that all Christians should perform a three-day fast, and a procession around the city

145. CAO 2109.
146. Note that there are in fact nine illuminations on this one folio, one of them showing the procession and the others showing departure for battle. Only two are reproduced here. With my thanks to Susannah Throop. On the image cycle in general, see Susannah Throop, "Mirrored Images: The Passion and the First Crusade in a Fourteenth-century Parisian Illuminated Manuscript (Paris, Bibliothèque nationale de France, MS fr. 352)," *Journal of Medieval History* 41 (2015): 184–207.
147. PT 138 (tr. 116).
148. GF 90.
149. RA 144 (tr. 122).

in constant prayers, "and after this they would more surely with God's aid carry out an attack on the walls and the Saracens."[150] Camped outside the city, the crusaders were unable to perform the Letania stationally from church to church, although there was certainly Western precedent for litanic processions around the outside of the walls of a city—the *circuitus murorum*—in the early medieval period."[151] The procession began at the Church of Saint Mary at Sion, south of the city in the environs of the Provençals' camp, and proceeded around the west side of the city up to the Church of Saint Stephen Protomartyr, which stood at the north point, and where Godfrey and Robert of Normandy were camped. The Franks walked barefoot, chanting the litany of the saints.[152] Peter Tudebode, we saw, wrote that the Franks sang and prayed that the Lord Jesus Christ would deliver Jerusalem and the Holy Sepulcher from the pagan people.[153] The request echoes the cadence and timber of the litanic petitions. "Please deign to destroy the pagan people" and "deign to humiliate the enemies of the church," "deign to protect the Christian people whom You redeemed with Your precious blood," and "deign to give our kings and princes peace, true concord and victory."[154] From the Church of Stephen Protomartyr, the Franks then processed clockwise down the east side of the city and up the Mount of Olives. Here the geography was such that the Egyptians standing on the city walls could observe them closely. Atop the Mount of Olives, Arnulf of Chocques preached a sermon on forgiveness and God's mercy. The crusaders then retraced their steps down to the Blessed Mary of Jehoshaphat, recited a stational prayer at the church, and returned to the Mount of Olives. Peter does not say, but presumably, they continued back to their starting point, at the Church of Mary at Mount Sion, thus completing an entire circuit of the city (or some may have marched back north to the church of the Protomartyr). A decade later, Guibert of Nogent explicitly compared the procession around Jerusalem to Joshua circling the walls of Jericho: "The bishops" he said, "remembered what had once happened at Jericho, that the walls of the perfidious city had fallen when the Israelites'

150. AA vi.7 (pp. 412–413).

151. McCormick, *Eternal Victory*, 343.

152. RA 144 (tr. 122). AA vi.9 (pp. 414–415) speaks of a procession, litany, and prayers.

153. PT 137 (tr. 115). The whole passage is quoted at the start of the chapter. AA vi.9 (pp. 414–415).

154. Rome Angelica 477, 62r–62v: "Ut regibus et principibus nostris pacem et veram concordiam atque victoriam donare digneris," "Ut cunctum populum christinum precioso sanguine tuo redemptum conservare digneris," "Ut inimicos sancte ecclesie humiliare digneris," and "ut gentem paganam comprimere digneris." Continental versions of these prayers existed in the West by the end of the eleventh century. See Lapidge, *Anglo-Saxon Litanies of the Saints*.

trumpets sounded, and they marched seven times around the city, carrying the sacred ark, and the walls of the faithless city fell down."[155]

As with the comparison to Jericho, military successes ratified confidence in the effectiveness of the liturgical tactics. Robert of Reims imagined that the great processions "with crosses, relics, and holy altars" occurred on 15 July while the great battle was taking place on top of the city walls.[156] Albert of Aachen spoke of clerics, wearing albs, bearing the relics of the saints.[157] Gilo of Paris imagined Christians carrying "Christ's standards around Jerusalem, banners, crosses, and holy altars."[158] Banners (*vexillum*) and crosses (*cruces*) were the symbols (*insignia christi*) of Christ's victory over the enemy (devil and others). The sources are more reticent on examples of their failures. The use of the crisis procession continued, naturally, into the existence of the crusade states. In the lead up to the Battle of Ascalon on 12 August 1099, Peter the Hermit organized a series of barefoot processions in Jerusalem in which both Greeks and Latins participated, and in which they carried out both the True Cross and the Holy Lance.[159] This time, a procession was done (presumably from the Holy Sepulcher) to the Temple, "where they sang masses and prayers that God would defend his people."[160] And votive processions of this sort were employed repeatedly during the life of the Latin East. Fulcher himself participated in a procession on 27 August 1105, as battle was looming between Baldwin I and al Afdal.[161] Back in Jerusalem, Latins joined with Greeks and Syriacs to pray for the battle and to perform a barefooted procession to all the churches in Jerusalem. This time, relics, and in particular, relics of the True Cross, were involved.[162] Likewise, in 1119, the holy cross was incorporated into the Letania at Antioch, when the king and "the entire city, people and clergy" set out for battle.

Walter the Chancellor describes a textbook Rogation procession performed in Antioch in that year that demonstrates the close connection between communal practice and battle, between spiritual and material warfare. He explains that the clergy, people, and whole town gathered at the main church (Saint Peter's), where the patriarch addressed those going to battle. He "advised them and prepared them for battle and signed them with his heavenly patriarchal benediction," and then performed the mass. After prostrating themselves, they,

155. GN VII.6 (lat. 276, tr. 129).
156. RR 98 (tr. 199).
157. AA vi.9 (pp. 414–415).
158. Gilo of Paris and a second anonymous author, *The Historia vie Hierosolimitane*, trans. C. W. Grocock and J. E. Siberry (Oxford: 1997), IX:267 (pp. 244–245).
159. GF 94. PT 146 (tr. 123). See also RR 103 (tr. 205–206), GN VII.17 (lat. 295–296, tr. 138).
160. GF 94.
161. FC II.xxxi.12 (lat. 665, tr. 184).
162. Murray, "'Mighty Against the Enemies of Christ,'" 229–231.

"with the Lord's cross" at the head of the procession, the entire group, "beseeching the litany and other prayers to God," all in humble clothing and barefoot, then walked in procession through town. At the point where the procession divided into two, the patriarch took up the cross and blessed them. And then Walter explained that "with the sign of the holy cross in front, the king returned to war, the clergy to the church, the people to their homes, entreating and praying earnestly that the Author of supreme justice who destroyed wars from their foundation would destroy their adversaries by a charge of His people, who were heaping praise on His name."[163] Then the patriarch blessed the army with the relic of the True Cross, explaining that, redeemed by His blood and freed from sin, they should be confident in the triumph of victory.[164] The liturgical volumes from the Latin east that survive for the period before 1187 all include the appropriate prayers that the rite would require.[165]

These litanic processions were central to the meaning of the crusade. The whole rite, as the whole crusade, married the demonstration of individual penance with the call for wroth on the enemy. Unlike the penitential rite of departure, which was about individual contrition and salvation, the expiatory processions understood penance as a social construct, inheriting an older idea of a chosen people, the Israelites, the people of God. They thus fostered a culture of penitence, not tied, as with the first, to a specific individual or specifically identifiable and claimable sins for which individual atonement (that is, penance) was necessary for personal salvation. They were rather broadly social exercises targeting the entire community as responsible before God as a community devoted to him and leading a righteous existence. And, unlike rites of individual penance, where the goal was the forgiveness of sin itself, here the goal was the request for earthly favor. This drew on an Old Testament model of communal responsibility for individual and common sin, a model that was evoked repeatedly in later crusades. This is why Guibert of Nogent's likening the procession of 8 July to Joshua before Jericho is so illuminating. This was a different way—a corporate way—of performing penance, and in so identifying with a biblical narrative, appropriating biblical sacrality. The army as a whole was expected to participate in both the regular and extraordinary liturgies precisely because favor before God was a communal responsibility. The two were linked, since victory in war was linked with communal favor and thus salvation of *Christianitas* as a whole.

163. WC II.10 (lat. 100, tr. 148).
164. WC II.10 (lat. 100, tr. 147–148).
165. Rome, Biblioteca Angelica 477, 62r; Paris BNF Lat. 12056, 302r; London BL Egerton 1139, 192v–197v.

Crusading after the First Crusade

The liturgiosity of the First Crusade has long been understood as a key component of its progress and in turn the spirituality of its experience and the interpretation of the events. Yet the principal elements of that liturgiosity—making confession and taking communion before battle, offering battlefield exhortations, using special votive masses, performing expiatory processions—were all common in the prosecution of wars before and after the First Crusade.[166] Bachrach has argued that these were simply a standard part of medieval warfare.[167] My own sense is that the liturgical supplications performed throughout the First Crusade were more than that; that these practices and rituals ratified the crusade as a sacramental act. And so the question is one not only of scale, but above all, of meaning. Was the First Crusade marked in some real way as more highly religious, more explicitly liturgical? Or was the liturgical quality of the First Crusade a product of the nature of our sources and the larger intellectual project of the clerical writers in emphasizing the divine and thus religious aspects of holy war? That is, was the First Crusade in this sense extraordinary, actually differing in this sense from other types of warfare?[168] And, if so, did the crusading campaigns that followed—those campaigns that saw themselves explicitly as modeled on and hoping to imitate the First Crusade—exhibit this quality of religious engagement and religious strategy, particularly as crusading itself became more institutionalized and, in a sense, professionalized?

The regular performance of the liturgy is easy to establish for the history of subsequent crusading. In successive papal calls for crusade, popes routinely outlined the purpose of having clerics in the Christian army: they were to devote themselves to prayer and exhortation, teach crusaders by word and example, and be available to offer penance and absolution. Clergy on the crusades were described as "armed with spiritual and material weapons" with which "to fight the enemies of the faith, relying not on their own power but rather trusting in the strength of God."[169] The chronicles also report priests and bishops offering prayers for knights and soldiers during the course of battle.[170] Whether these rites were employed more frequently, or with a greater sense of religious urgency, in these later campaigns is a matter of interpretation. Yet, a rapid review shows ample evidence in subsequent campaigns of all the same basic ritual elements that the early sources allowed us to trace for the First Crusade: the effort to

---

166. McCormick, "Liturgie et guerre," 220.
167. Bachrach, *Religion and the Conduct of War*.
168. Discussed in Rubenstein, *Armies of Heaven*, 199–203.
169. Tanner, *Decrees of the Ecumenical Councils*, 1:267, 297.
170. PVC §462 (tr. 210), §526 (tr. 236). Peter Tudela and Continuator, *Song of the Cathar Wars*, laisse 188 (tr. 132).

maintain regular liturgical functions;[171] confession and communion before battle invocations,[172] sermons and blessings to God before and during military engagements;[173] the use of relics in battle (the use of the True Cross during the Battle of Hattin being perhaps the most famous);[174] the singing of "Te Deum" and other standard hymns in battle or in thanksgiving;[175] and the performance of expiatory processions at times of crisis or before imminent battle.[176] Some examples: during the Second Crusade, Louis VII and his familiars celebrated the Feast of Purification in a small tent (the larger ones having been abandoned).[177] The king always took communion before attacking enemy forces and requested the singing of the office when he returned from battle.[178] Thirty years later, after the Battle of Hattin in which the Ayyubids wiped out the crusading forces and as Saladin's forces marched on Jerusalem, monks, nuns, and priests performed a crisis procession inside the wall of the Holy City.[179] ("Our Lord did not deign to hear the prayers or the clamors that were made in the city. For the stench of adultery, of disgusting extravagance, and of sin against nature would not let their prayers rise to God. God was so very angered at that people that He cleansed the city of them.")[180] On the Third Crusade it was reported that knights marched into battle chanting the *Christus regnat* litany[181] and that mass was chanted alongside as they marched into battle.[182] Three days later the entire army attended mass and took communion before engaging

171. David, *De expugnatione Lyxbonensi*: 57, 61, 71, 84–85, 96–97. HdE 26, 70, 84, 119, 184, 180, 185. OP 198–199 (tr. C&C 177). JV Ep. 2 (p. 570). QBS 151–152. MP 6: Additamenta 153. Janet Shirley, ed. *Crusader Syria in the Thirteenth Century: The Rothelin Continuation of the History of William of Tyre with Part of the Eracles or Acre Text* (Aldershot: 1999), 85. Joinville §297–299.

172. HdE 84; *Letters* 72; RClari 108–109, 156–157 (tr. 68, 93–94); QBS 83, 154.

173. David, *De expugnatione Lyxbonensi*: 126–127, 146–147, 158–159; HdV 63; OP 161, 182–184, 202–207, 257 (tr. C&C 160, 170–171, 179, 206); QBS 105–106, 135, 162; Ludwig Pastor, *The History of the Popes: From the Close of the Middle Ages. Drawn from the Secret Archives of the Vatican and Other Original Sources*, trans. Frederick Ignatius Antrobus (London: 1894–1899), 2:395.

174. Flori, *La guerre sainte*, 149. David, *De expugnatione Lyxbonensi*, 146–147. "Historia peregrinorum," MGH SS Rerum Germ. 5:119 (tr. HdE 138); *Letters* 73; Andrea *Sources*, 288–289; OP 214 (tr. C&C 182); QBS 78; Jean Sarrasin, *Lettre à Nicolas Arrode* (1249), ed. Alfred Foulet, Lettres Françaises du XIIIᵉ siècle (Paris: 1924), 3–4, §§7–8, tr. C&C 357. MP 6: Additamenta 153; Pastor, *The History of the Popes*, 2:395.

175. PVC § 276 (lat. 1.272, tr. 138–139); QBS 76, 86, 113–114, 120, 136, 163; OP 185, 294 (tr. C&C 171); Joinville § 163; Joseph F O'Callaghan, *The Last Crusade in the West: Castile and the Conquest of Granada* (Philadelphia: 2014), 51, 59, 65, 76, 131, 164, 190.

176. WT Cont., ch. 54 (lat. 67, tr. 59); QBS 81, 122–123, 147; OP 257 (tr. C&C 204); JV Ep 4 (p. 589) and Ep. 5 (p. 601); Joinville §§ 128–129, 180–181.

177. Odo of Deuil, *De Profectione*, 129.

178. Odo of Deuil, *De Profectione*: 143.

179. WT Cont., ch. 54 (lat. 67, tr. 59).

180. WT Cont. (lat. 67, tr. 59). I have slightly altered Edbury's translation.

181. HdE 86 (tr. 111).

182. HdE 80, 84 (tr. 105,110–111).

in battle with the Turks.[183] After their victory, they sang the *Kyrie*.[184] Routinely throughout the twelfth century crusaders were described entering battle "armed with the sign of the holy cross."[185] During the Fourth Crusade, outside Constantinople, soldiers confessed and took communion before "attacking the Greeks, for they were the enemies of God,"[186] and they carried the relic of the True Cross into battle.[187] Prebattle attendance of Mass, communion, and confession were also a regular practice during the Albigensian Crusade.[188]

We do find some innovations. In the thirteenth century the popular and versatile hymn to the Holy Spirit, "Veni Creator Spiritus," became associated with the crusades. Attributed to the ninth-century theologian Rabanus Maurus, the hymn was composed for Pentecost, but thereafter used on a variety of occasions during the liturgical year. It included the refrain "May You drive our enemies far off, and give directly to us peace; with You as our leader, let us avoid all evil."[189] It seems to have been the standard invocation for ships setting off,[190] and it became the standard war cry of the northerners during the Albigensian Crusade as they entered battle,[191] such that one of the contemporary chronicles even claimed that, during the siege of Lavaur, the clergy sung the "Veni Creator Spiritus" and that "our enemies . . . feared those who sang more than those who fought, those who recited the psalms more than those who attacked them, those who prayed more than those who sought to wound."[192] The hymn might be adapted in the moment to emphasize God's militant help. In 1212 crusaders sang the "Veni Creator Spiritus," "imploring the Lord to help them . . . when they came to the verse 'May you drive our enemies far off' [*hostem repellas longius*], which they repeated three times, the enemy were filled with divinely inspired fear and driven back."[193] Later, Humbert of Romans, in his manual on preaching,

---

183. HdE 84 (tr. 111). On March 17, 1190.

184. HdE 63 (tr. 89).

185. For example, Ralph of Diceto, *opera historica*, 2:71.

186. RClari 108–109, 156 (tr. 68, 93–94).

187. Andrea *Sources*, 104.

188. PVC, with particular attention paid to the habits of Simon de Montfort; §191 (lat. 1:193, tr. 100), §253 (tr. 1.252, tr. 129–130), §270 (lat. 1:267, tr. 136), §297 (lat. 1:291, tr. 146), §450 (lat. 2:143, tr. 205), §453 (lat. 2:144–145, tr. 206), §457 (lat. 2: 149, tr. 207–208), §462 (lat. 2:151–153, tr. 210), §476 (lat. 2:170, tr. 216), §§577–578 (lat. 2:270–271 tr. 259); WP ch. 20 (lat. 82, tr. 47), ch. 36 (lat. 130, tr. 78).

189. Heinrich Lausberg, "Der Hymnus 'Veni creator spiritus,'" *Jahrbuch der Akademie der Wissenschaften in Göttingen* (1969): 26–58.

190. RClari 62 (tr. 42); Joinville § 126.

191. PVC §§226 (lat. 1:226, tr. 116), § 526 (lat. 2:221, tr. 236). See also §431 (lat. 2.123–124, tr. 197). Peter Tudela and Continuator, *Song of the Cathar Wars*, laisse 114 (tr. 57).

192. PVC §226 (lat. 1:225–227; tr. 116).

193. PVC §351 (lat. 3:118, tr. 164).

instructed crusade preachers to end a recruitment sermon by singing "Veni Creator" or another one of the hymns to the cross.[194]

But for the most part, the forms of liturgical supplication and thanksgiving we find in the sources are mostly the standard ones. Outside of the First Crusade, the tropes of liturgical warfare are most systematically attested for the Fifth Crusade. This may be because the clerical leaders of the expedition had been studying the accounts of the First Crusade. The Damietta campaign included regular liturgical supplication and adopted the sin-prayer/penance-victory framework.[195] In 1219, the army carried a surviving fragment of the True Cross, which they called the "standard" (vexillo), ahead of them as "they advanced in orderly array."[196] Clergy regularly offered up prayers at moments of need, crisis, or during battle.[197] A wide range of prayers and rituals, liturgical and quasi-liturgical, were evoked during the long siege and occupation of Damietta.[198] Psalms were sung liturgically in votive supplication,[199] and in preparation for or while on the battlefield.[200] Other prayers were apparently invented on the fly or were adapted for the moment.[201] The crusaders performed penitential processions on at least three occasions in 1218,[202] 1219,[203] and 1221.[204] The chroniclers who reported this compared the army to the Israelites.[205]

The same is true for the crusades of Louis IX. The king's chamberlain recounts that on the eve of the disembarkation at Damietta the army was counseled to make confession and draw up their wills. The king heard the Divine Office the next morning and attended a mass for travelers at sea celebrated aboard the ship immediately before launching the attack. The legate, Odo of Chateauroux, "held the True Cross and blessed the armed men

---

194. Humbert of Romans, "Liber de predicatione," ch. 1; Riley-Smith, *The Crusades, Christianity, and Islam*, 38.

195. QBS 98–99.

196. OP 164 (tr. C&C 161). Oliver later calls the relic the "signo crucis" (p. 167 of Latin). See also QBS 78.

197. OP 183–185 (tr. C&C 170–171); QBS 78, 163.

198. QBS 81, 83–84, 93,124, 148–149, 154.

199. QBS 84.

200. QBS 78, 125, 128.

201. QBS 98–100, 105–106, 156. Cf. QBS 154 with CBP 1429.

202. OP 182 (tr. C&C 170); JV Ep. 4 (p 589); QBS 81, 122–123, 147. For the liturgy of the fifth crusade, see also Jessalynn Bird, "Rogations, Litanies and Crusade Preaching: The Liturgical Front in the Late Twelfth and Early Thirteenth Centuries," *The Papacy, Peace, the Crusade and Christian-Muslim Relations: Essays in Memory of James M. Powell*, ed. Jessalynn Bird (Routledge, 2017).

203. QBS 53, 92. JV Ep. 5 (p. 601).

204. OP 257 (tr. C&C 204). Note that the army also performed a procession of Thanksgiving in spring 1220. See JV Ep. 6 (p. 614).

205. OP 245 (tr. C&C 196).

who had entered the boats for the landing."[206] Joinville typically, gives us our most compelling, vivid evidence. His experience was punctuated with allusions to liturgical ritual and intercession in such a way as to demonstrate the fluid integration of liturgy into the experience of war and crusading. He refers routinely to his prayers, to the performance of mass, to confession. The regular performance of the mass was in fact so important that at one point, while Joinville was sick in bed, he insisted that "his" priest, who was celebrating the mass at the foot of his bed, despite having passed out in the middle of the rite, be awoken to finish it.[207] The proper rites were particularly necessary at the moment of crisis. At another point, as the Egyptians boarded their ship and, on the verge of what they thought was certain death, laymen confessed to one another.[208] This was canonically allowed in the absence of a priest at moments of need, though it is not clear whether Joinville knew this.[209] Later, when the French got ashore, they performed votive masses. Charles of Anjou, years later, explained that when Louis found himself in captivity, he had his chaplain recite the votive Mass of the Cross, and other prayers "that he knew to be useful in such a situation."[210] Elements of the crusade also employed the litanic procession.[211] For a procession they were planning on performing aboard ship, a priest explained the efficacy: "There has never been an instance of suffering in his parish, whether as a result of drought or excessive rains or any other affliction, that God and his Mother had not delivered them from as soon as they had made three processions on three successive Saturdays."[212] A few months later the papal legate (Odo of Chateauroux), because the processions at sea had been successful, organized three new processions in Damietta."[213] Joinville explains how these processions too successfully induced God's aid.

None of this ended in 1291. With the routinization and professionalization of actual crusading, much of the liturgical activity was accomplished by Christians on the home front (see chapter 6). Yet historians are increasingly aware of the sustained vigor of the crusades in the fourteenth and fifteenth centuries.[214] Men who left on crusade made arrangements for the continual

---

206. Jean Sarrasin, *Lettre a Nicolas Arrode*, 3–4, §§7–8, tr. C&C 357.
207. Joinville §§ 299–300.
208. Joinville §§ 354–355.
209. Vogel, *Le pécheur et la pénitence au Moyen Age*, 31.
210. Paul Edouard Didier Riant, "Déposition de Charles d'Anjou pour la canonisation de saint Louis," in *Notices et documents publiés pour la Société de l'histoire de France à l'occasion du cinquantième anniversaire de sa foundation* (Paris: 1884), 172.
211. Joinville §§ 128–129.
212. Joinville § 129.
213. Joinville §§ 180–181
214. See, in general, the work of Norman Housley. Now also Timothy Guard, *Chivalry, Kingship, and Crusade: The English Experience in the Fourteenth Century* (Woodbridge, UK: 2013).

prayer and liturgical intercession on campaigns. Knights filed requests with the papacy for the right to carry portable altars, as with the knight from Evreux who in 1364 was going "with the power of arms against the enemies of our Lord Jesus Christ and the Roman Church."[215] At Nicopolis in 1396, the clergy organized intercessory processions around the walls, just as in Jerusalem in 1099. "But merciful God did not hearken to these prayers," said the chronicler who reported this, "very likely because those for whom they were said, had shown themselves unworthy of grace."[216] In 1448 the pope granted a license to celebrate Mass on the battlefield.[217] Liturgical supplication was not limited to the Jerusalem crusades, or even crusades in general.[218] Although the narrative sources are less forthcoming about the types of extraordinary liturgy related to the twelfth- and thirteenth-century campaigns, we do know, for instance, that processions and solemn masses were instituted to celebrate Peter I's ("King of Jerusalem and Cyprus") victory in Adalia;[219] that the great preacher John of Capistrano preached from the shorelines carrying a crucifix in 1456 as John Hunyadi fought the Turks outside Belgrade;[220] and in fifteenth-century Spain, during "the last crusade of the West" (for Grenada), solemn masses and liturgical processions were routinely instigated in thanksgiving for victory in battles against the enemies of the faith.[221]

And yet we should not make the mistake of thinking that the meaning that the liturgy imparted on, and to, crusade was static or rote. The forms may have been the same, but the context they were performed in shifted, utterly, its weight. So, the crisis procession performed in Jerusalem in 1099 was essentially the same in form as the type established in the Latin West in the fifth and sixth centuries. And the form of the litany the crusaders sang had largely coalesced in the ninth. Still, the sources for the First Crusade suggest that the quality of the liturgy, what it meant, and how it functioned to endow meaning, was somehow something really very different than at other times. It is only by placing the rituals and their texts in particular context (serial contextualization) that we can understand that texts and

215. M-H Laurent et al., *Urbain V (1362–1370): lettres communes analysées d'après les registres dits d'Avignon et du Vatican*, Bibliothèque des Écoles françaises d'Athènes et de Rome, sér 3, 5 (Paris: 1954–1989), no. 8885. See also no 17089; and J-M Vidal, *Benoît XII (1334–1342), lettres communes*, vol. 1, Bibliothèque des Écoles françaises d'Athènes et de Rome, sér. 3, 2. (Paris: 1903–1911), 332, no. 3707.
216. Setton, *The Papacy and the Levant, 1204–1571*, 1:350.
217. O'Callaghan, *The Last Crusade in the West*, 89–90, 127–128. The example here is the Spanish theater.
218. Bachrach, *Religion and the Conduct of War*.
219. Housley, *Documents on the Later Crusades, 1274–1580*, 85.
220. Pastor, *The History of the Popes*, 2:395.
221. O'Callaghan, *The Last Crusade in the West*.

ritual forms that appear static in the manuscript copies could be dynamic in performance and context. For one, a penitential procession around the walls of Jerusalem, where Christ himself had walked, or the Easter Liturgy celebrated in the Holy Sepulcher itself on the day of the capture of Jerusalem would surely have had a different—a more intense—sacral tenor for the participants because the ritual was being done quite literally where His feet had stood (Psalm 131:7). Raymond of Aguilers says as much.[222] The liturgy may have endowed meaning to the crusade; but the crusade in turn imbued the liturgy with meaning as well.

The question may not be so much whether there was liturgy on crusade (yes, as in all warfare) but rather, what did the deployment of liturgy during crusading campaigns mean to the experience of crusading and subsequently the interpretation of the meaning of a particular crusade, or even crusading in general? Although we can trace a continuity of forms in later crusading and other warfare—that is, we can trace all the basic rituals of supplication and thanksgiving in the First Crusade's imitators—they mostly hold a different place in the narratives and thus, arguably, played a different role (or held a different meaning) during the experiences themselves. Again, meaning and force here come from context. The First Crusade—if not before the victory in Jerusalem, certainly afterward—was immediately understood as an epochal event in salvation history. Within the decade, Robert of Reims said that it was rivaled by only the Incarnation in the history of salvation. The immediate interpretation of the First Crusade was thus understood in the same terms and on the same register as the liturgy as a whole.

The key may lie in the nature and goals of the principal sources for the First Crusade. In a series of eye-opening articles, Jay Rubenstein has unpacked the complex interrelationships between the overlapping sources for the First Crusade.[223] He rejects the authorial model for most of the first-generation narratives and, in order to make sense of the high coincidence among the individual texts, suggests that many of the set pieces that have come to define the First Crusade coalesced first as self-contained narratives, as "campfire tales," that were then taken up and stitched together by subsequent narrators.[224] This is an appealing model and would explain, for instance, the surprising consistency across the sources regarding the procession of the Battle of Antioch in June 1098, and the

222. RA 144 (tr. 122).
223. Jay Rubenstein, "What Is the Gesta Francorum, and Who Was Peter Tudebode?" *Revue Mabillion* 16 (2005): 179–204; Jay Rubenstein, "Guibert of Nogent, Albert of Aachen and Fulcher of Chartres: Three Crusade Chronicles Intersect," in *Writing the Early Crusades: Text, Transmission, and Memory*, ed. Marcus Bull and Damien Kempf (Woodbridge, UK: 2014), 24–37; Marcus Bull, "The Relationship between the *Gesta Francorum* and Peter Tudebode's *Historia de Hierosolymitano Itinere*: The Evidence of a Hitherto Unexamined Manuscript (St. Catharine's College, Cambridge, 3)," *Crusades* 11 (2012): 1–17, argues that the *Gesta* is the earliest surviving source.
224. Rubenstein, "What is the Gesta?" 200, 202–203, for conclusions.

Jerusalem procession in July 1099. It is these narrative "set pieces" which offer the richest and most evocative descriptions of liturgical warfare that became emblematic of the whole campaign. Rubenstein's notion that these narratives developed as independent stories that coalesced according to oral tradition and repetition during the campaign itself explains how these liturgical stories became cemented into the developing narrative of their own experience, since these stories in particular ratified the divine favor and thus the providential implications of the events for which they sought to narrate meaning. That is, the stories of liturgical intervention took hold and were repeated and perhaps embellished precisely because they had seemed to work. They were repeated not because they themselves as practices were out of the ordinary (although they may have been used more frequently), but because the First Crusade had ended up being extraordinary. Their repetition in the sources thus amplified this particular aspect of the developing narrative as it got repeated and refined. The prominence of these stories may appear to make liturgy more common during the First Crusade than in later campaigns. On the other hand, this is itself evidence of the meaning of liturgy *to* the crusaders themselves. These were the stories that grew up and gained traction precisely because they gave shape and meaning to the narrative of the First Crusade—a narrative that began to take shape during the crusade itself and was sharpened after the victory at Jerusalem. In other words, it is quite probable that liturgical intercession and ritual were not any more common on the First Crusade than in other instances of warfare, but rather that they came to be more meaningful in context and in retrospect. Because crusaders understood themselves as participating in a religious enterprise, and because the extraordinary outcome suggested as much, the narrative of liturgical supplication and divine response helped structure the experience in a way that was meaningful, and then that memory (initially oral, then in the written narratives) of liturgical intervention and its successes gave the narrative itself its shape and meaning. The use of the liturgy during the campaign may have intensified alongside the lived experiences, precisely because these liturgical moments—sacrifice in hope of grace—ratified the idea that the entire crusade was not only a historical event but a sacramental act.

4

Celebrating the Capture of Jerusalem in the Holy City

A week after performing the litanic crisis procession, barefoot, carrying crosses and relics, and singing the litany, the Franks launched their final attack on Jerusalem. On 15 July 1099, in what they considered the final, triumphant, and indeed, miraculous act of the long expedition, the Frankish warriors who had left Western Europe more than three years earlier succeeded, after a month-long siege, in taking the Holy City. Upon securing the city, the crusaders proceeded to the Holy Sepulcher—the liberation of which was the very object of the crusade[1]—to offer thanksgiving to God. There, according to Raymond of Aguilers, at the Church of the Holy Sepulcher, where Christ had been buried and whence he had risen, the Franks performed—mid-July—the Easter Office, the Office of Resurrection.[2] And then Raymond added, "This day, which I affirm will be celebrated in the centuries to come, changed our grief and struggles into gladness and rejoicing. I further state that this day ended all paganism, confirmed Christianity, and restored our faith. *'This is the day which the Lord has made, we shall rejoice and be glad in it'* [Ps. 117.24], and deservedly because on this day God shone upon us and blessed us."[3] This was a triumphalist vision of the victory, expressed in terms of historical absolutes, confirming the truth of the Christian faith within the providential contest between Christianity and paganism. The celebration of the Easter liturgy—the liturgy that commemorated at once Christ's victory over death and the salvation of mankind—did

---

1. Schein, *Gateway to the Heavenly City*, 11–13.
2. RA (lat. 151, tr. 128). Praepositinus of Cremona discusses the Easter Liturgy as the "Officium Resurrectionis" Praepositinus of Cremona, *Praepositini Cremonensis Tractatus de Officiis*, ed. James Corbett (Notre Dame, IN: 1969), 172–173.
3. RA (lat. 151, tr. 128). Linder, "The Liturgy of the Liberation," 110–111.

not put too fine a point on it. Just as the Resurrection had signaled a new phase in salvation history, so thus did the taking of Holy City. This was a new phase in the history of the Church, associated with the providential triumph of Christ's resurrection, commemorated at the Holy Sepulcher, which had been the very goal of the Crusade. The fifteenth of July was to be a "new day" and was to be commemorated for centuries to come.[4]

The Easter liturgy was a temporary solution. After the final assault, the victorious crusaders made the rounds of holy places in the city, pouring out their tears and prayers, bearing crosses and relics, singing hymns and sacred songs.[5] The bishops and priests celebrated mass to give thanks to the Lord.[6] The city and the temple precincts were purified. Later, William of Tyre would write that the faithful "cleansed the place of the holy Resurrection from the superstitions of the gentiles."[7] The entire city of Jerusalem was being reconsecrated to Christian worship, and an early set of prayers that commemorated the capture was actually based on the mass for the dedication of a church (or its anniversary), with references to the consecration of the temple replaced with references to the acquisition of the holy city of Jerusalem (*sancte civitatis tue Ierusalem acceptionis*).[8] A week later, 22 July, the same day that the Franks asked Godfrey of Boullion to be "prince of Jerusalem," they celebrated the Octave of the capture of the city.[9] Amidst the celebrations, the authorities directed that a new feast be established to solemnly celebrate the capture of Jerusalem every year.[10]

This chapter is about that feast—the "Jerusalem feast" as it was initially called, then later "the Feast of the Liberation of Jerusalem"—and thus about the way in which the capture of Jerusalem was interpreted and memorialized liturgically at the Holy Sepulcher and in the Holy City. It is,

---

4. RA (lat. 151, tr. 128): *Nova dies.*

5. BB p. 111.

6. WT viii.21–24 (lat. 1:413–418, tr. 1:373–378). See especially viii.21 for the celebration of mass.

7. WT, viii.22 (lat. 1:415, tr. 1:375).

8. M. Cecilia Gaposchkin, "The Feast of the Liberation of Jerusalem in British Library Additional MS 8927 Reconsidered," 141–145. These are the prayers for the mass found in London BL 8927, on which, see Linder, "The Liturgy of the Liberation." Linder, 128–130, made this point about reconsecrating the entire city. The text is also found in Appendix 1, below.

9. PT 142 (tr. 120). Quoted below.

10. Kohler believed the feast was only established in the second quarter of the century, since William of Tyre's reference to it was written only at the end of the century; see Charles Kohler, "Un sermon commémoratif de la prise de Jérusalem par les Croisés attribué a Foucher de Chartres," *Revue de l'Orient Latin* 8 (1900–1901): 158. There is earlier evidence however. BB 111; HdV 18.6 (p. 126); WT viii.24 (lat. 1:418, tr. 1:378) (quoted below). For an assessment of the early evidence, see Simon John, "The 'Feast of the Liberation of Jerusalem': Remembering and Reconstructing the First Crusade in the Holy City, 1099–1187," *Journal of Medieval History* 41 (2015): 4015–422. PT 142 (tr. 120) seems to suggest that the decision was made on 17 July, 1099, on the same day that the Franks elected Godfrey.

thus, about memory—liturgical memory: how liturgy helped structure the interpretation of the First Crusade and shape the local cult to the city of Jerusalem and its liberation by the crusaders that was instituted in the Holy City itself.[11] The new liturgy written for this feast commemorated the capture of Jerusalem as a singular event in Christian history, as inaugurating a new phase of the Church, foretold by the prophets, as part of providence. It did so, by, among other things, drawing largely on the liturgy of Advent, which itself commemorated not just the coming of Christ in the Incarnation but also the Incarnation as a prelude to the Second Coming of Christ at the end of time; and within the Advent liturgy, the prophets, who foretold the return of the earthly Jerusalem to the Israelites, which in turn pointed to the return of the earthly Jerusalem to the new Israelites—the crusaders—and finally, the return of Christ again, to the New Jerusalem at the end of time. Using antiphons drawn from the books of the prophets, and particularly the Book of Isaiah, the rite situated the liberation of 1099 in relationship on the one hand to the end of the Babylonian exile in the past and, on the other, to the prophesized Second Coming in the future.[12] Just as the end of the Babylonian captivity was a precondition for the coming of Christ, so the end of the new Babylonian captivity—the Muslim occupation of Jerusalem—was a precondition for the Second Coming. The crusaders' capture of the earthly Jerusalem was therefore the fulfillment of Old Testament prophecy, the marker of a stage in providential history and, of course, the crusaders' participation in the larger scheme of God's will. It reached backward into biblical history and forward toward salvation. And it argued that the victory itself was one of those extraordinary moments in salvation history, a moment of convergence between divine and human history, a moment (not entirely unlike the Incarnation) in which the story of human events intersected with God's plan, that is, providence.[13] It was thus one of those moments foretold by the prophets that signaled a decisive rupture in salvation history.

The Latin Rite in the Latin Kingdom of Jerusalem

In the city of Jerusalem the celebration of the liturgy, especially of Holy Week, was at once reenactment and representation, playing itself out in the

---

11. On the issue of liturgy and memory specifically, M. Cecilia Gaposchkin, "The Liturgical Memory of 15 July 1099: Between History, Memory, and Eschatology," in *Remembering Crusades and Crusaders*, ed. Megan Cassidy-Welch (London: Routledge, 2017), 34–48.

12. Linder, "The Liturgy of the Liberation," 110–131; Schein, *Gateway to the Heavenly City*, 29–30.

13. Cf. RR 4 (tr. 77).

very spaces of the historical events that they were commemorating.[14] One of the earliest tasks for the Frankish churchmen who arrived as part of the conquering host was the reorganization of the clergy and the liturgy of the Holy Sepulcher according to the Latin rite.[15] Arnulf of Chocques, a Norman cleric who had traveled with the army of Count Robert of Normandy, was elected (briefly) as patriarch on 1 August 1099. One tradition reported that Arnulf forbade all local clergy to continue celebrating their own (local) rite, imposing on them instead the new Frankish forms.[16] Canons had been established at the Holy Sepulcher during Godfrey's reign.[17] Evidence from the first decade of the twelfth century suggests at least that rudimentary services were performed at the Holy Sepulcher and presumably, as they were staffed, the other preeminent churches in the city.[18] A new chapter made up of Latin clergy drawn from the ranks of Frankish conquerors was installed in 1099, and in 1114 the body was reformed in adopting the Augustinian rule.

Through the second decade of the twelfth century, and perhaps through the 1120s, the clergy probably relied on books and rites brought from the West, and it was likely only in 1114 that a comprehensive evaluation of the liturgy was done and a cohesive rite for the Church of the Holy Sepulcher confected.[19] A scriptorium does not even seem to have been established before 1130 or so,[20] and the earliest surviving liturgical manuscripts from this period, dated largely on art-historical and paleographic evidence, reflect a rite still in flux, with new feasts introduced into the calendar but not

14. Kasper Elm, "La liturgie de l'Eglise latine de Jérusalem au temps des croisades," in *Les Croisades: L'Orient et l'occident d'Urbain II à Saint Louis*, ed. Monique Rey-Delqué (Milan: 1997), 244–245.

15. On the reorganization of the liturgy, see Elm, "La liturgie de l'Eglise latine de Jérusalem au temps des croisades," 243–246; Dondi 37–60. More broadly, see Kasper Elm, "Fratres et Sorores Sanctissimi Sepulcri. Beiträge zu fraternitas, familia und weiblichem Religiosentum im Umkreis des Kapitels vom Hlg. Grab," *Frühmittelalterliche Studien* 9 (1975): 275–333; Kasper Elm, "Kanoniker und Ritter vom Heiligen Grab. Ein Beitrag zur Entstehung und Frühgeschichte der palästinensischen Ritterorden," in *Die geistlichen Ritterorden Europa*, ed. Josef Fleckenstein and Manfred Hellmann (Sigmaringen:1980), 141–169.

16. Bernard Hamilton, *The Latin Church in the Crusader States: The Secular Church* (London: 1980), 14. Arrangements were later made with the Orthodox and, somewhat later, Armenian clergy for use in the Holy Sepulcher itself. Christopher MacEvitt, *The Crusades and the Christian World of the East: Rough Tolerance* (Philadelphia: 2008), 120.

17. Denys Pringle, *The Churches of the Crusader Kingdom of Jerusalem: A Corpus*, 4 vols. (Cambridge, UK: 2007), 3:12, citing the early sources.

18. Dondi 45–46; Hamilton, *The Latin Church in the Crusader States*.

19. In general, see Dondi; Geneviève Bresc-Bautier, *Le Cartulaire du chapitre du Saint-Sépulchre de Jérusalem* (Paris: P. Geuthner), 74–77. Wolf Zöller, "The Regular Canons and the Liturgy of the Latin East," *Journal of Medieval History* 43 (2017), forthcoming.

20. Hugo Buchthal, *Miniature Painting in the Latin Kingdom of Jerusalem: With Liturgical and Palaeographical Chapters by Francis Wormald* (Oxford: 1957), 21–22.

yet incorporated into the Sanctorale.[21] The feast and almost certainly a liturgy for the 15 July commemoration were already well established by this point. Cristina Dondi has envisioned a kind of ad hoc celebration of rites, done by Latin clergy using whatever books they had at hand. But slowly, a Latin rite "of the Holy Sepulchre" solidified, and thus its use in the Latin Kingdom in general was established. The sources for this rite seem to have been mostly northern French—from Chartres, Bayeux, Evreux, and Sées.[22] As the Latin Church was established in the Kingdom of Jerusalem, the liturgy originating at the Holy Sepulcher—the mother Church—was consequently, as Dondi has outlined, "adopted by all secular religious institutions within the patriarchate."[23] Then, on the fiftieth anniversary of the capture, 15 July, 1149, the newly rebuilt (although yet unfinished) Holy Sepulcher was rededicated, and the rite was at this stage largely revised.[24]

The development of the early rite (writ large) at the Holy Sepulcher and throughout the patriarchate was surely a fluid process, with different interrelated traditions adopted at different churches throughout the city. To make sense of the history of the Latin liturgy in the Latin Kingdom, we are aided by only four surviving liturgical manuscripts produced before 1187.[25] Two of these date to before the reforms of 1149.[26] These are two sacramentaries from the Holy Sepulcher, probably dating to around 1128–1130: Rome Angelica ms. 477-Cambridge Fitzwilliam ms. McClean 49 (these are two parts of the same manuscript), and Paris BNF Lat. 12056. Both include proper items for the Jerusalem feast of 15 July. The Rome/Cambridge manuscript was compiled first, with additions and changes evident that were then incorporated into the Paris volume.[27] The third, London British Library Egerton 1139, is a psalter dating to the middle of the 1130s.[28] For the

21. Dondi 45–46; Buchthal, *Miniature Painting in the Latin Kingdom*, xxx–xxxi.
22. Dondi 47–48.
23. Dondi 44, and see also comments on 39.
24. Sebastián Salvadó, "Rewriting the Latin Liturgy of the Holy Sepulchre: Text, Ritual, and Devotion for 1149," *Journal of Medieval History* 43 (2017), forthcoming. Sebastián Salvadó, "The Liturgy of the Holy Sepulchre and the Templar Rite: Edition and Analysis of the Jerusalem Ordinal (Rome, Bib. Vat., Barb. Lat. 659) with a Comparative Study of the Acre Breviary (Paris, Bib. Nat., Ms. Latin 10478)" (Stanford University, 2011), 26–37, and throughout.
25. Rome, Biblioteca Angelica, 477; Cambridge, Fitzwilliam Museum, McClean 49; Paris BNF Lat. 12056; London BL Egerton 1139. Vatican Barb. Lat. 659. See Dondi HS[1-4] for descriptions.
26. Dondi H[1-3].
27. This is the work of Sebastián Salvadó. I am grateful to him for sharing these findings with me, and for consulting Angelica 477 for certain specific questions on my behalf.
28. Dondi HS[4]. For the Latin East more generally, we should add Lucca Biblioteca Archivescovile 5 and Paris BNF Lat 1794. Cara Aspesi has recently argued that the early portion of Lucca Biblioteca Archivescovile 5 is a breviary compiled between 1125 and 1150 that may

period following the rededication of the Holy Sepulcher and the liturgical reforms of 1149, we have an ordinal, Vatican Barberini Lat. 659, belonging to the Temple dating to about 1170, which followed the rite of the Holy Sepulcher.[29] The liturgy described in this ordinal is consonant with a fifth manuscript, an ordinal from the Holy Sepulcher, Barletta, Archivio della Chiesa del Santo Sepolcro ms. s.n. (known simply as the Barletta Ordinal) that was copied in the first decade of the thirteenth century and housed "from an early date" (meaning around 1300) at the Church of Santo Sepolcro in Barletta, in southern Italy, but appears to represent the Holy Sepulcher's liturgy from before 1187.[30] Then for the period after the loss of Jerusalem in 1187 we are helped by a variety of volumes—missals, sacramentaries, breviaries, pontificals, and psalters—that were copied in Acre, and then in Caesarea or on Cyprus, and that sought to follow and thus maintained the liturgy of the Holy Sepulcher.[31] To all of this we should add the evidence from a thirteenth-century Western manuscript that included a mass and office "In festivitate sancte Hierusalem,"[32] that Linder argued represented a pre-1149 use at the Holy Sepulcher.[33] This is not a manuscript of liturgical use, nor was it of Eastern origin, but rather it is a transcription of a single mass an office included at the back of a compilation of materials relating to the First Crusade, copied in the West (probably southern France) in the early thirteenth century for commemorative purposes.[34] It is listed here because its evidence is important for us.

The liturgy that the new (Frankish) canons established may have been based on northern French sources,[35] but it was adapted to the priorities of the new, most holy, locale, with the particular circumstances of the new Latin Kingdom accommodated in its priorities. So, for instance, the litany of the

---

represent the use of Tyre. Cara Aspesi, "Lucca, Biblioteca Arcivescovile MS 5: A Window onto Liturgy and Life in the Latin Kingdom of Jerusalem in the Twelfth Century" (University of Notre Dame, forthcoming); Cara Aspesi, "The Contribution of the Cantors of the Holy Sepulchre to Crusade History and Frankish Identity," in *Music, Liturgy, and the Shaping of History (800–1500)*, ed. Margot Fassler and Katie Bugyis (Woodbridge: forthcoming). Also, BNF Lat. 1794 is an Ordinary, which includes a note of ownership from the church at Sidon.

29. Dondi HS[5].
30. Dondi HS[9].
31. Dondi HS[5-8, 10-18].
32. Linder, "The Liturgy of the Liberation." Linder identifies this as the liturgy for the "Liberation" of Jerusalem. In the BL manuscript it is simply called the "Feast of Holy Jerusalem" *(festivitas sancte hierusalem)*. It is referred to as the liberation in the Rubrics for the Evangeliary for the feast in BNF Lat. 12056, but only there.
33. Linder, "The Liturgy of the Liberation," 110–131.
34. London BL Add. 8927 was probably of French provenance, and the liturgy was copied at the end following the narratives of Fulcher of Chartres, Walter the Chancellor, and Raymond of Aguilers.
35. In general, Dondi. For this office in particular, Linder, "The Liturgy of the Liberation," 126.

saints invoked French saints as well as saints important in pre-1099 Holy Land devotion.[36] And among the short petitions that followed were typical requests for peace and mercy, but also a few that suggest the particular conditions for Christians in the city of Jerusalem at the beginning of the twelfth century: "That You might deign to humiliate the enemies of the Christian Church."[37] That You might deign to crush the pagan peoples."[38] Other petitions included: "That You might deign to give to our king and our princes peace, true concord, and victory."[39] Several related to pilgrimage. "That You might deign to watch over and sanctify these places and all the places of the saints."[40] "That You might bestow a prosperous journey and the port of salvation to the faithful pilgrims and sailors."[41] Some were clearly specific to the new kingdom: "That You might deign to keep safe the patriarch of Jerusalem and the clergy and people committed to him in holy religion."[42] The rite also included votive masses, including a series that one imagines were put to use in the early years of the twelfth century, including ones against pagans, against enemies, in times of war, and—significantly—one for captives.[43] The votive mass for captives appears to be new or to have been taken from a contemporary Aquitainian source.[44] A number were rewritten to target specifically the "pagan" enemy. So, instead of asking God to look kindly on the "Roman empire [or, in other versions, the Christian empire, or the Frankish kingdom] that the *gentes* might be destroyed," the votive mass against pagans asked God to look kindly in aiding Christians so that the *gentes paganorum* might be destroyed.[45] This appears to be the earliest use of

36. Buchthal, *Miniature Painting in the Latin Kingdom*, 107–109.

37. Rome, Biblioteca Angelica 477, 62v: "Ut inimicos sancte ecclesie humiliare digneris."

38. Rome, Biblioteca Angelica 477, 62v: "Ut gentem paganam comprimere digneris."

39. Rome, Biblioteca Angelica 477, 62r–v: "Ut regibus et principibus nostris pacem et veram concordiam atque victoriam donare digneris." Found also in Lucca Biblioteca Arcivescovile 5, p. 55; London BL Egerton 1139, 194v.

40. Lucca Biblioteca Arcivescovile 5, p. 56: "ut locum istum et omnia loca sanctorum custodire atque sanctificare digneris."

41. Lucca Biblioteca Arcivescovile 5, p. 56: "ut iter agentibus et navigantibus fidelibus iter prosperum atque salutis portum tribuere."

42. Lucca Biblioteca Arcivescovile 5, p. 56: "Ut patriarcham ierosolimitanum clerum et populum sibi comissum in sancta relgione conservaret digneris." In Angelica 477, 62r, it reads simply "ut patriarcham nostram et omnem gregem sibi comissum in sancta religione conservare digneris."

43. Rome, Biblioteca Angelica 477, 163r, 165v–166v, 169r; BNF Lat. 12056, 269v–270r, 276v, 294r.

44. Rome, Biblioteca Angelica 477, 163r. Cf. CO1467b, 5669–5670, 4617. A version of this *Missa pro captivo* appears in a later copy of an Aquitainian missal that has been dated to 1130–1150, which is roughly contemporary with the Angelica manuscript. See J. O. Bragança, *Missal de Mateus* (Lisbon: Fundação Calouste Gulbenkian, 1975), 2887.

45. CO 3846: "respice ad romanum benignus imperium, ut gentes, quae in sua feritate confidunt, potentiae tuae dextera comprimantur." Cf. BNF Lat. 12056 268r: "respice propitius in

prayers that would in later years be widely disseminated in crusading rites.[46] The secret was also altered to specifically account for the "wickedness of pagans" (instead of the wickedness of wars),[47] and the postcommunion changed "dangers of the enemy" to the "dangers of pagans."[48] Orations common in the West were adapted to make specific reference to the pilgrims who came to "this most holy city of Jerusalem,"[49] and so on . . .

The "Festivitas Ierusalem" Commemorating the Capture of the City (July 15)

The strongest example of the specific adaptation to the Latin Kingdom was the addition to the calendar of a special feast commemorating the great victory of 15 July 1099. It was immediately determined that 15 July should be commemorated annually.[50] Raymond of Aguilers, in the passage with which this chapter opened, wrote of how the day would be celebrated (*celebrabitur*, a liturgical term) for centuries to come. Peter Tudebode reports that a week after the capture the Franks celebrated the octave as a feast "for the entire city."[51] Baldric of Bourgueil, writing in 1105 or 1106, makes reference to the institution of a "solemn day" commemorating the fifteenth of July,[52] and the Montecassino author, writing later but working with early sources, also explained that a feast was established to commemorate the liberation of Jerusalem.[53] Baldric explains that the day was considered so holy that it would henceforth be observed specially, like the Sabbath (*velut sabbatizabant*).[54] The focus was on the entire city of Jerusalem, rather than the Holy Sepulcher specifically. The early mass texts that survive in BL 8927 rework the prayers for the consecration of a church for the entire city, because as Tudebode said, they celebrated the feast "for the entire city." Both Baldric and the author of the Montecassino Chronicle (drawing from Tudebode) place this institution of the feast day, as William

---

auxilium chritianorum, ut gentes paganorum que in sua feritate confidunt, potentiae tue dextera comprimantur."

46. Linder RA 116. The *contra paganos* mass in the eleventh-century Nevers Scr., which is BNF Lat 17333, p. 351 (ed. Crosnier,also p. 351), which conforms to this sequence is in fact mistranscribed in Crosnier. The first prayer is in fact *Domine deus quia ad hoc irasceris* (CO 2304b).

47. CO 5217a: *bellorum nequitia.* Cf. BNF Lat. 12056 268r: *paganorum nequitia.*

48. CO 4746: "Protector noster adspice, deus, et ab **hostium** nos defende formidine." Cf. BNF Lat. 12056 268r: "Protector noster aspice deus et a **paganorum** nos defende periculis."

49. Gaposchkin, "The Feast of the Liberation," 139–145.

50. John, "The 'Feast of the Liberation,'" 415–422.

51. PT 142 (tr. 120).

52. BB 111.

53. HdV 18.6 (p. 126).

54. BB 111.

of Tyre would also do, as part of the early victory celebrations and thanks-givings that followed immediately on the 15 July victory. Writing later in the century, William of Tyre explained that, following the expressions of thanksgiving and joy,[55]

> In order that the memory of this great event might be better preserved, a general decree was issued which met with universal approval and sanction. It was ordained that this day be held sacred and set apart from all others as the time when, for the glory and praise of the Christian name, there should be recounted all that had been foretold by the prophets concerning this event. On this day intercession should always be made to the Lord for the souls of those by whose laudable and successful labors the city beloved of God had been restored to the pristine freedom of the Christian faith.[56]

William wrote more than three-quarters of a century after the capture of Jerusalem and was informed by the early chronicles and sources.[57] Al-though the original ordinance he refers to has not survived, he too explains that this decree was issued in the day or days immediately following the capture. William says explicitly that the feast day should celebrate the event of the capture in order to formally memorialize it, to beseech intercession for the crusaders who partook in the city's restoration to Christianity, and to recount how these events had been foretold by the prophets. It is this last point—that the feast should recount "all that had been foretold by the prophets concerning" the victory of 15 July—that should be emphasized. This is *precisely* what the office did in fact do, and (as we will note below), William quoted the office a number of times to make precisely this point.

The earliest liturgical sources refer to the 15 July feast simply as the "Feast of Holy Jerusalem" (*Festivitas sancte hierusalem*). For the liturgy of the Eucharist (the Mass) we have two early sacramentaries—one from the Holy Sepulcher and one for use at the Temple, both of which Cristina Dondi has dated to 1128–1130. Both include a special feast, which is listed in the calendar for 15 July as the "Festivitas hierusalem quando capta fuit a Christianis (or, in one, *a Francis*),"[58] and give prayers for the mass for 15

55. Kohler believed that because none of the earliest authors mention the establishment of this feast, that William had the dating wrong, and that it occurred only in the second quarter or middle part of the twelfth century. Kohler, "Un sermon commémoratif," 158.

56. WT, viii.24 (lat. 1:417, tr. 1:378).

57. On William's sources, Peter W. Edbury, *William of Tyre, Historian of the Latin East* (Cambridge, UK: 1988), 44–58. Simon John, "The feast of the Liberation" 416, doubt William's claim of proximity. As above, my own reading of PT 142 (tr. 120) suggests the commem-oration was instituted within the week of the conquest.

58. Rome, Bibl. Angelica 477 (HS¹), "Festivitas Hierusalem quando capta fuit a Christianis" (4r, in the calendar),"In festivitate civitatis s. Hiersusalem" (159r, the mass, edited in Dondi 150); BNF Lat. 12056 (HS³), "Festivitas Iherusalem quando fuit capta a Francis" (5r, the calendar),

July, copied right after a mass for the consecration (or anniversary) of the church. This made sense if 15 July was understood as the reconsecration of the entire city to Christ. We also have the mass copied into BL Add. 8927, based on the Mass for the Dedication of a Church, which appears to best represent the earliest tradition.

Three manuscripts provide information for the divine office. Until recently, we had been limited in our information to only the two ordinals that represent the state of the Holy Sepulcher rite after the reforms of 1149: Vatican Barberini Lat. 659, which includes the relevant instructions for the Mass and the Office for the feast "in liberatione sancti civitatis iherusalem de manibus turchorum,"[59] and the Barletta Ordinal, which includes an office for 15 July "in liberatione sancte civitatis Ierusalem."[60] The two versions are largely identical (at least for the rites discussed here), and thus confirm basic use for the second half of the twelfth century. Cara Aspesi has recently identified an earlier version of the office in additions made to Lucca Biblioteca Arcivescovile 5.[61] An untitled copy of this office was added in a later hand to a portion of the manuscript written after 1187 that appears, however, to represents the state of the Jerusalem office *before* 1149, and thus an earlier version of the office represented in the two ordinals before it got all tangled up in changes made to the liturgy upon the Holy Sepulcher's rededication. Finally, we also have the liturgy found in the final folios of London BL Add. 8927. Although deracinated from its liturgical context, the office is clearly related to the office found in the two ordinals and the Lucca breviary, sharing a series of major chant items, the incipit, hymns, and—consequentially—the extraordinary mass sequence *Manu Plaudant* found only by incipit in the ordinals. But the liturgy in 8927 also differs in a variety of important ways. A comparison of shared texts in the extant offices suggests that, as Linder thought originally, although the liturgy appears in a thirteenth-century Western source, it probably represents an early version of an office composed *very* early on in the history of the Kingdom of Jerusalem, which was adapted by the time the scribe was compiling the mass texts for the Holy Sepulcher in Angelica 477, or perhaps a light variation or adaption of that early liturgy that survived

---

"In liberatione ierusalem" (31v, the gospel), and "Missa de Jerusalem" (250r-v, the mass, edited in Dondi 158).

59. Vat. Barbarini Lat. 659, 101r–102r (for office) and 132r (for mass). Edited in Salvadó, "The Liturgy of the Holy Sepulchre," 630. Salvadó is currently preparing an edition for publication.

60. Barletta, Fol. 119b. Dondi HS⁹. Edited in C. Kohler, "Un rituel et un bréviaire du Saint Sépulcre de Jérusalem (XIIe–XIIIe siècle)," *Revue de l'Orient Latin* 8 (1900–1901): 427–430.

61. Cara Aspesi, "The *libelli* of Lucca, Biblioteca Arcivescvile MS 5: The Liturgy of the Siege of Acre?" *Journal of Medieval History* (forthcoming in 2017).

for use elsewhere in the city or was copied for commemoration in the West.[62] Its tone matches the triumphant, exultant, and almost haughty religious optimism characteristic of the first wave of written interpretation of the successes of the First Crusade.

It appears then that an office and mass were written early on after 1099, probably represented most closely by the materials that survive in BL Add. 8927. This liturgy was written for the entire city of Jerusalem and does not prioritize the Holy Sepulcher in any particular way, but rather understands the capture of the entire city as its rededication to Christ. It was part of the move traced by Sylvia Schein, following 1099, to celebrate the success of the crusade in terms of the sanctity of Jerusalem and her many sacred spaces rather than strictly the Holy Sepulcher.[63] The emphasis on Jerusalem over the Holy Sepulcher proper, which is evident in the early texts,[64] is also sensible if a liturgist imagined a rite that would be celebrated throughout the new territories, as churches throughout the Levant were reconsecrated to the Latin rite. When exactly the 15 July rite was composed or confected is not clear, but it was, or elements of it were, probably put together quite early on, and would have circulated independently in pamphlets. But a liturgist in the second or third decade of the twelfth century, perhaps spurred on by the reform of the canons of the Holy Sepulcher as Augustinian canons in 1114, began to revisit and revise the earlier liturgy. A new office, based on but altered from the early version, was confected, and new mass texts were composed (and copied into the Angelica sacramentary). Aspesi, who has done more than anyone to clarify the stages of the feast's development over the course of the twelfth century, suggests this new office was written sometime before the mass texts in 1130 or so.[65] I suspect, given its focus on place, that it was written specifically for the Holy Sepulcher sometime after 1114. In the Holy Sepulcher manuscripts, the mass "In festivitate civitatis s. Hierusalem" is composed of special prayers, including a collect that celebrated "the Almighty God, who tore Your city of Jerusalem away from the hands of the pagans by Your strength and returned it to Christians," hoping that the Christians might thus attain the everlasting heavenly kingdom.[66] This theme, which paired the capture

---

62. I examine these various possibilities in Gaposchkin, "The Feast of the Liberation."

63. Schein, *Gateway to the Heavenly City*, 13–15.

64. Gaposchkin, "The Feast of the Liberation," 141–148.

65. Aspesi, "The Contribution of the Cantors."

66. The collect is found in BNF Lat. 12056 (250r), Rome Angelica 477 (158), and London BL Egerton 2902, 93r. "Omnipotens deus, qui virtute tua mirabili Ierusalem civitatem tuam de manu paganorum eruisti et christianis reddidisti, adesto, quesumus, nobis propitius, et concede ut qui hanc sollennitatem annua recolimus devotione, ad superne Ierusalem gaudia pervenire mereamur. Per dominum." Dondi 150, 158; Gaposchkin, "The Feast of the Liberation," 165.

of the earthly Jerusalem through God's strength with the attainment of the heavenly Jerusalem through God's grace, was repeated again in the other two proper prayers (the secret and the postcommunion).[67] The secret asked that "we who celebrate this day, concerning the city of Jerusalem, snatched from the hands of the pagans, might merit in the end to be a citizen in the bright Jerusalem of Heaven."[68] The postcommunion simply asked that "we who celebrate the freedom of Your city Jerusalem might merit inheritance in the celestial Jerusalem."[69] The Gospel reading came from Matthew 21:10–17, on Jesus driving out the moneychangers, that is, the purification of the Temple; the reclaiming of sacred space.[70] The image of the Old Testament's Temple was appropriated by the Holy Sepulcher (we will return to this). "Hosanna to the son of David!" Finally, in 1149, as we will see below, that revised version was integrated with and to a large extent subordinated to a liturgy for the rededication of the Holy Sepulcher.

Themes of Liberation and Salvation in the Mass and the Office

The early liturgy advanced a bold interpretation of the First Crusade. Most notable in this regard is the remarkable sequence, *Manu plaudant*, prescribed in 8927 and the two later ordinals, that exulted in the Christian victory of 1099, the importance of the Holy Sepulcher, devotion to Christ, and the association of pagan defeat and Christian salvation.[71] Sequences are special liturgical hymns, which Margot Fassler describes as "distillations of scriptural, exegetical, and liturgical materials, placed in an intense and thick liturgical moment, right before the Gospel."[72] Although we have no secure date, its tone is vehement, triumphant, and, I would argue, "near," reflecting the generally heady tenor of the years immediately following the initial victory.[73]

---

67. Gaposchkin, "The Feast of the Liberation," 165.

68. Paris BNF Lat. 12056, 250r: "Secr: Hanc, domine, quesumus, hostiam quam tibi supplices offerimus dignanter suscipe, et eius misterio nos dignos effice, ut qui de Ierusalem civitate de manu paganorum eruta hunc diem agimus celebrem, celestis Ierusalem concives fieri tandem mereamur. Per." Gaposchkin, "The Feast of the Liberation," 168.

69. Paris BNF Lat. 12056 250r. "Post: Quod sumpsimus, domine, sacrificium ad corporis et anime nobis proficiat salutem, ut qui de civitatis tue Ierusalem libertate gaudemus, in celesti Ierusalem hereditari mereamur. Per." Gaposchkin, "The Feast of the Liberation," 169.

70. Paris BNF Lat. 12056, 31v.

71. Linder, "The Liturgy of the Liberation," 119–120. AH 40:71–72, no. 60, "In festivitate sanctae hierusalem." No such text is given in the list of prosae presented in Rome Angelica 477, which complicates dating and transmission if we assume, as I have, that it is an early text.

72. Margot Fassler, *The Virgin of Chartres: Making History through Liturgy and the Arts* (New Haven: 2010), 25.

73. The following translation is adapted from Fassler, *The Virgin of Chartres*, 155.

Manu plaudant omnes gentes ad
   nova miracula
Vicit lupos truculentos agnus sine
   macula
Paganorum nunc est facta humilis
   superbia
Quam reflexit virtus dei ad nostra
   servicia
O nova milicia

Paucis multa milia sunt devicta.

Venit hec victoria a christi potencia
   benedicta.
Ecce signum est levatum ab antiqua
   presignatum profecia [cf. Is. 11:12]

Quisque portat signum crucis dum
   requirit summi ducis loca pia

Redde sancta civitas laudes deo
   debitas

Ecce tui filii et filie de longuinquo
   veniunt cotidie [cf. Is. 60:4]
Ad te porta gloriae pro culparum
   veniam
Ecce honor debitus est sepulcro
   redditus.
Quod profecia presciens sic loquitur
   et sepulcrum eius honorabitur. [cf.
   Is. 11:10]

Nunc munus persolvitur
Atque laudum [h]ostia
Crucifixum adoremus
Per quem demonum videmus

Destructa imperia

Adoremus resurgentem iter nobis
   facientem ad regna celestia
O imperator unice quod incoasti
   perfice

Ut sub tua custodia pax crescat et
   victoria
Fac Christianos crescere et impios
   tabescere.
Ut regna subdat omnia tu
   omnipotentia amen.

All nations clap their hands in
   applause for the new miracles
The lamb without stain conquered
   the ferocious wolves
The pride of the pagans is now
   humbled
Which the power of God turned back
   to our service
O new knighthood!

Many thousands have been defeated
   by the few
This victory came blessed by the
   power of Christ.
Behold, the sign is raised high,
   foretold by the Old Testament
   prophecy. [cf. Is. 11:12]
Everyone bears the sign of the
   cross while he seeks the holy
   places of the highest leader.
Oh sacred city, render the praises
   owed to God.

Behold your sons and daughters this
   day come from far off [cf. Is. 60:4]
To you, the gateway of glory, for
   remission of sins.
Behold honor owed is rendered to
   the Tomb.
Because the prophet, in foreknowledge, says, "his tomb shall be
   honored." [cf. Is. 11:10]

Now the duty will be discharged
Along with the host of praises
Let us adore the Crucified one
Through whom we see the empires
   of demons destroyed.

Let us adore the Risen One, who makes for
   us the path to the heavenly kingdom;
Oh singular Emperor, finish what You
   began.

So that under Your protection, peace
   and victory may grow;
Have Christians flourish and make
   the infidel wither,
So that Your almighty power might
   subdue all kingdoms.
Amen

The stanzas move from the historical events of the military victory and the devotion at the Sepulcher to the salvific victory that the crusades thus earned and finally to the dominion and eschatological victory of which God alone is capable. The last stanza offers a glorious vision of the future, entreating God to "subdue all kingdoms, and to "make Christians grow stronger, and the infidels wither away." The entire sequence is vivid and specific, resonating closely with the energy and themes that animated the early chronicle tradition. It echoes the ideological priorities of the early narratives: Saracens as pagans, the few defeating the many, the empire of demons, a focus on the city rather than the sepulcher, the eschatological significance of Jerusalem. The singular emperor is Christ, the master of time and providence. In its narrative and thematic specificity, the hymn differs from the theological and biblical strategy taken in the rest of the Jerusalem rite. But it also fits with the rite's overall interpretive scheme. It certainly echoed Raymond of Aguilers, who said that the day "ended all paganism and confirmed Christianity." Importantly, the sequence *twice* says that the crusade was the fulfillment of Old Testament prophecy, and evoked both Isaiah 11:10 and 11:12. Isaiah 11:10–12 ran:

> In that day the root of Jesse, who stands as a standard [*signum*] for the people; him that the Gentiles shall beseech, and his sepulcher will be glorious.
>
> And it shall come to pass in that day that the Lord shall set his hand the second time to recover the remnant of his people, that come out of Assyria, Egypt, Pathros, Ethiopia, Elam, Shinar, Hamath, and from the coastlands of the sea.
>
> And he shall set up a standard [*signum*] unto the nations, and shall assemble the fugitives of Israel and shall gather together the dispersed of Juda from the four quarters of the earth. (Is. 11:10–12)

Traditionally these verses spoke of the messianic age. Here, it is the crusade itself that was prophesized. But history is not yet done. Christ is asked to continue what He has begun. Peace and victory shall grow under God's beneficent victory. The vision is one of thanks, and above all, of Christian triumph, expressing the expectation of further (temporal) victory and future glory.

The divine office echoed this triumphant tone. Constructed from monastic sources, the office situated the historical victory that constituted the taking of Jerusalem within the providential framework of Jerusalem's biblical and eschatological meaning. Making the case that the capture of Jerusalem was its reconsecration as a city dedicated to Christ, it adopted the well-known hymn and several items of chant from the liturgy for the Dedication of the Church. But most of all, it used chant from existing offices that tied 1099 to biblical prophecy. The chant items shared by both offices (and also those unique to 8927) are overwhelmingly focused on the city of Jerusalem. The Psalms with which the antiphons were paired are also about Jerusalem. (As we will see below, those chant items unique to the second-generation office eschew this emphasis on Jerusalem, underscoring instead God's power.) Finally, the chant chosen for the office was derived largely from the Advent liturgy, secondarily the Epiphany liturgy, and was overwhelming rooted in Isaiah scripture.

Indeed, the prophecies of Isaiah, and the liturgy of Advent (and to a certain extent, Epiphany) are at the core of the early "Jerusalem office" and thus the liturgical interpretation of 15 July 1099. The major chant items that are common to both extant versions of the office (twenty-nine out of thirty-six total) indicate the tone and content of the earliest office. Of the chant items that we can be sure come from the earliest office, sixteen are rooted in Isaiah, while the others come from Revelation, the Psalms, and the other prophets. Fourteen are derived from the Advent liturgy, and another eight from the Epiphany liturgy, with others taken from Easter and the Office of the Dedication of the Church.[74] (If we assume the office in BL Add. 8927 *does* represent the very earliest office, then twenty-four chant lines echo Isaiah, twenty-three items come from Advent seasons, and six from Epiphany.) Both Isaiah 11:10 and 11:12, evoked in the sequence, were echoed in the July 15 liturgy in chant lines derived from Advent.[75]

The chant items that made up the original office were thus focused relentlessly on the biblical Jerusalem and her heavenly counterpart, on the idea of the sacred city, on God's favor and protection of the chosen community in Jerusalem, and on the theme of defeating national enemies. Vespers celebrated and offered thanksgiving for God's victory, the recovery of Jerusalem from its bonds of servitude, and the return of God's (new) chosen people. Both versions, for example, used *Leva Jerusalem:* "Lift up your eyes, Jerusalem, and see how mighty is your King; Behold your Savior has come to loose you from your chains,"[76] which was taken from the first Sunday in Advent, and drew its language from Isaiah 60:4: "Lift up your eyes round about, and see . . ." The antiphon introduced and commented on Psalm 124—"Those who trust in the Lord are like Mount Zion, which cannot be moved, but abides for ever"— which was a prayer for deliverance from the enemies of the people of God. The next antiphon, "Levabit dominus signum," was also from Advent and also rooted in the language of Isaiah (here, Isaiah 11:12, which is evoked in the sequence): "The Lord will raise high the standard of victory among nations, and He will gather together the outcasts of Israel." The conquering Franks were of course the returned fugitives, the new chosen people, the inheritors of the promised land, being granted back the Holy City. The antiphon introduced the incantation of Psalm 125, another prayer of deliverance:

74. For O[1]: of the 36 major chant items (antiphons and responsories) that make up the office, 25 come from the Advent Cycle, and 24 come from Isaiah.
75. CAO 3607. O[1] VA3. O[2] VA5.
76. CAO 3606. O[1] VA2, LA5. O[2] VA3.

When the Lord brought back the captivity of Sion, we became like men
comforted.
Then was our mouth filled with gladness and our tongues with joy.
Then they shall say among the gentiles, the Lord hath done great things
for them.
The Lord has done great things for us, we are become joyful
Restored again from our captivity, O Lord, as a stream in the south. (Psalm
125:1–4)

This had obvious resonance in ca. 1100. An antiphon surviving in 8927
offered "arise, arise, stand tall, O Jerusalem, release the chains from your
neck, oh captive daughter of Sion," (cf. Isaiah 51:17), while its Psalm (136)
lamented the captivity in Babylon. In this way, the vespers service compared Muslim control of the city of Jerusalem to the Babylonian exile, the
crusaders to the chosen people; the capture of the city in 1099 to the Jews'
return to Israel and rebuilding of the Temple.

Matins, the long midnight service that includes both antiphons, the great
responsories, and lections, were focused on the glory of Jerusalem. "Alight,
alight, Jerusalem for Your light is come, and the glory of the Lord has risen
upon you" (cf. Is. 60:1).[77] This antiphon may have introduced the reading
of Isaiah 60:1–5 as the first lection for matins. A verse taken from Psalm 80
pointed to the expulsion of Muslims: "O Israel, if you will hearken unto
me, there shall no strange god be in you, neither shall you worship any
strange god for I am the Lord."[78] Lauds in turn celebrated the eschatological Jerusalem. "Sion, the city of our strength and our savior, a wall and a
bulwark shall be set there; Open your gates because God is with us" (cf. Is.
26:1).[79] Salvation suffused the service. So did quotations from Isaiah deal-
ing with the salvation of Jerusalem.[80]

THE reliance on the liturgy of Advent and Epiphany, and behind these, on
the book of Isaiah, structured the theology of the office. Advent, the four
weeks leading up to Christmas, was about the anticipation of the Messiah.
Epiphany, the feast of the Magi, celebrated His manifestation and majesty.
The Advent liturgy, in preparation and anticipation of the "coming" of

77. O[1] MR1, O[2] MR6.
78. O[1]MV2, O[2] MV1.
79. O[1] LA2, O[2] VA4. Also echoes Ezek. 13:5. The strong wall was, from the Gospels (see
Matt 16:18) onward, routinely understood as heaven, as Christ, as salvation, protected "by the
host of the holy angels and by the most high God, who is its outer wall." See also O[1] LA3, O[2]
LA3; O[1] LA4, O[2] LA4; O[1] VE, O[2] VA3.
80. MA5, from Isaiah 60:2. O[1] MA6, MA7 (from Is. 62:2); O[2] MV4. MA7.

Christ, celebrated that coming both historically in the Incarnation and, above all, eschatologically at the Second Coming. A tenth-century mass blessing for the second Sunday of Advent read:

> May God, whose only-begotten Son's past advent you believe in while waiting for the future one
> Defend you in this present life from all evil, and show Himself mild in his judgments
> So that, freed from the contagion of sin, you may fearlessly await His tremendous day of Judgment. Amen.[81]

This theology was operative in the Latin Holy Land. In the earliest surviving sacramentary from the Holy Sepulcher scriptorium, a special mass sequence for the first Sunday in Advent, *Salus eterna*, includes stanzas proclaiming to Christ: "Justify us by Your First Coming; Free us by Your Second, So that we, when You judge all things, when the great light has come, . . . May then follow your footsteps wherever they are."[82] Advent, Fassler explains, took "the participant on a journey from the dawn of time to an evolving apocalyptic present."[83] The Advent chant was heavily laden with antiphons drawn from prophets, and in particular the book of Isaiah, whose Old Testament book, written in exile, prophesized the return of Jerusalem, the "arrival" of the Messiah, and of course His return at the Second Coming. Readings for the Mass were drawn from the prophets Jeremiah, Daniel, and especially Isaiah. The Gospel readings came from Matthew 21:1–9, on Christ's entrance into Jerusalem, and Luke 21:25–33, on Christ's Second Coming and the End Time.[84] The Epistles (Rom 13:11, 15:4–13, Phil. 4:4–7, and 1Cor 4:1–5) treated Christ's fulfillment of prophecy (as did Matthew 21:1–9). New sequences composed in the tenth and eleventh centuries echoed and amplified these eschatological themes.[85] The season was (is) one of preparation, and thus of both celebration and anticipation. It also emphasized a new

---

81. Gunilla Björkvall, "'Expectantes dominum.' Advent, the Time of Expectation, as Reflected in Liturgical Poetry from Tenth and Eleventh Centuries," in *In Quest of the Kingdom: Ten Papers on Medieval Monastic Spirituality* (Stockholm: 1991), 112.

82. Rome Angelica 477 101r. This is AH 53, no. 1, and is discussed and translated in Björkvall, "'Expectantes dominum,'" 124–125.

83. Fassler, *The Virgin of Chartres*, 56. On the medieval Advent cycle in the Western Middle Ages, Fassler, *The Virgin of Chartres*, 55–78; Margot Fassler, "Sermons, Sacramentaries, and Early Sources for the Office in the Latin West: The Example of Advent," in *The Divine Office in the Latin Middle Ages: Methodology and Source Studies, Regional Developments, Hagiography: Written in Honor of Professor Ruth Steiner*, ed. Margot Fassler and Rebecca Baltzer (Oxford: 2000), 15–47. Björkvall, "'Expectantes dominum,'" 109–133; Robert C. Lagueux, "Sermons, Exegesis, and Performance: The Laon Ordo Prophetarum and the Meaning of Advent," *Comparative Drama* 43, no. 2 (2009): 197–220. Rose, "Jérusalem dans l'année liturgique," 389–394. On the meaning of the Advent cycle: For the range, see Hesbert, CAO vol. 1, no. 1 (for the roman cursus); and CAO v. 2, no. 1 (for the monastic cursus).

84. Björkvall, "'Expectantes dominum,'" 113–114.

85. Björkvall, "'Expectantes dominum'," 109–133.

phase in Christian time.[86] This would not be unimportant in crusader context, for whom the capture of Jerusalem inaugurated a new phase in the history of the Church.

This emphasis on the apocalyptic promise was almost certainly underscored by the office readings—the "lections" to which the great responsories of matins "responded" and thus guided interpretation. Three different sets of readings ("lections") are prescribed in the two different versions of our office. The office in 8927 directs the reader to the twenty-sixth chapter of the first book of the Chronicle of Fulcher of Chartres, where he describes the city of Jerusalem.[87] Fulcher was a canon of the Holy Sepulcher, and it is possible that he had a role in the confection of the early office. The description, which precedes Fulcher's account of the siege itself, is, according to one editor, "a valuable eyewitness description of Jerusalem as it appeared early in the twelfth century."[88] Fulcher describes both natural elements (Mount Zion, the Valley of Jehoshaphat, Mount of Olives) along with important historical monuments including the Tower of David, the Temple of the Lord ("round in shape"), and the Church of the Holy Sepulcher (likewise circular). And Fulcher cites scriptural passages that connect the monuments in their medieval context with their biblical identity and landscape, collapsing the space in time between the biblical, the current, and ultimately the future Jerusalem. It was, in turn, the function of the chant to connect the monuments and landscape of the earthly city to the out rolling of providential history and ultimately the Second Coming.

It is however also possible that versions of the office from an early date used lections drawn from the book of Isaiah. The office in the Lucca manuscript specifies that readings from the feast of the Epiphany were to be used.[89] Although the incipits are not specifically given, the separate (and separately written, possibly representing a different use entirely) part of the manuscript that includes the Epiphany office indicates for the first three lections Isaiah 55:1–60:10,[90] a homily on Epiphany from Pope Leo, and a homily on Matthew 2:1–12 from Gregory the Great. The version of the

86. A theme explored by Gail R. O'Day, "Back to the Future: The Eschatological Vision of Advent," *Interpretation* 62, no. 4 (2008): 357–370.

87. The lections themselves are indicated just by the incipit, "est enim civitas ierusalem in montano loco sita"; cf. FC I.xxvi (lat. 281–283, tr. 116–117). It is not clear how far into the description the readings were supposed to extend, but in the single manuscript witness, London BL Add. 8927, the prose section appears on folios 21v–22r, with an additional marginal note in a different (later) hand reading "Incipit descriptio seu denominatio civitatis sancte Jerusalem" and a line running down the side of the text ending at "ego sum qui peccavi isti qui oves sunt quid fecerunt." The text is not a perfect match for Hagenmeyer's edition.

88. See editor/translator's note at FC I.xxvi.1, at tr. 116n.1.

89. Lucca Biblioteca Archivescovile 5, A57r (for the Jerusalem feast), says simply: *Lectiones require in epiphania.*

90. Lucca Biblioteca Archivescovile 5, B51r–54v for the Epiphany lections. Lection 1–3 are Isaiah 55:1–5, Isaiah 55:6–13, and Isaiah 60:1–10. Lection 4–6 are taken from Leo's sermon on

office found in the two post-1149 ordinals indicate readings from Isaiah 60:1–62:12, a unified subsection of the book of Isaiah that constituted a paean to the glory of Jerusalem, her future, and God's people. One way or another, Isaiah 60–62 and its message of eschatological hope were at the heart of the original conception of the liturgy. The passage promises a new stage of history to the faithful, the glory of the future of Jerusalem, her restoration to God's chosen people, and the eschatological vision of her salvation. Its potential for understanding the First Crusade as the fulfillment of prophecy was palpable, and it was thus cited by the early narrative authors.[91] It contains many of the themes found in both versions of the office, because, of course, so many of the lines of scripture adopted for the offices are rooted in this passage in Isaiah.

Prophecy and Fulfillment

It is in its dialogue with Advent and with Isaiah that the Jerusalem office invoked the multiple meanings of Jerusalem's liberation.[92] All chants evoked successive layers of meaning, both temporally and allegorically, pointing on the one hand toward scripture, or sermons interpreting scripture, or other related chant, and on the other to history, both past and future. The capture of Jerusalem in 1099 was at once the fulfillment of biblical prophecy that foresaw the return of Jerusalem to the Israelites after exile, and in turn the return of Jerusalem to the crusaders, the new Israelites, after a period of submission. It also linked the capture to the Second Coming as a salvific act and as part of God's providential plan. That is, the liturgy expressed the idea that the crusaders' taking of Jerusalem in 1099 was the historical fulfillment of biblical prophecies about Jerusalem found in Isaiah, Daniel, and the Psalms. In this, the liturgy echoed (or presaged) the monastic authors of the West who, in the first decade of the twelfth century, sought to situate the First Crusade within the structure of biblical and salvific history.[93] In reordering the prophetic endpoint (that is, making Old Testament prophecy point to the crusade rather than the Apocalypse,

---

the Epiphany, found in PL 54, col. 235. Lection 7 is Matt 2:1. Lections 8 and 9 are taken from Gregory the Great's homily X on Matthew 2:1–12, found in PL 76, col. 1110.

91. RR 29 (tr. 113), 100 (tr. 201), 106 (tr. 209), 109 (tr. 212), 110 (tr. 213). See also Kohler, "Un sermon commémoratif," 161–162.

92. For the exegetical background, see Elisabeth Mégier, "Christian Historical Fulfilments of Old Testament Prophecies in Latin Commentaries on the Book of Isaiah (ca. 400 to ca. 1150)," *Journal of Medieval Latin* 17 (2007): 88.

93. Riley-Smith, *The First Crusade*, 141–143; Norman Housley, "Jerusalem and the Development of the Crusade Idea, 1099–1128," in *The Horns of Hattin: Proceedings of the Second SSCLE Conference*, ed. Benjamin Z Kedar (Jerusalem:1992), 28–29; Schein, *Gateway to the Heavenly City*, 24–25; Smith, "Glossing the Holy War," 13.

or even the crusade itself as a step toward the Apocalypse itself) they engineered a dramatic break in exegetical tradition, in which the prophets had been read spiritually rather than historically.[94] The crusaders were saying as much within weeks of the victory. In a letter to the West as early as September 1099 Daimbert of Pisa explained that God had "magnified his mercy by fulfilling through us what he had promised in ancient times."[95] Among the early chroniclers, Robert of Reims made the argument most forcefully, repeatedly evoking Isaiah prophecy.[96] Of Isaiah 55:12 he wrote that "then was fulfilled in reality what was expressed spiritually," and "we now see in that event the promise which God made through the mouth of the prophet Isaiah."[97] Robert explained that anyone who "thinks about this sequence of events so worthy of high praise will be able to discern clearly the wonders of God at work" and then he quoted Luke 1:52 and 53, and Isaiah 60:15–16. Robert also quoted Isaiah 26:1–2 (evoked in O[1] LA2), "Through these and similar symbolism comes the form and mystic sacrament of that heavenly Jerusalem, of which it is said *we have a strong city; salvation will God appoint for walls and bulwarks. Open ye the gates, that the righteous nation which keeps the truth may enter in* [Is. 26:1–2]."[98] And he explained, drawing on Isaiah 11:10 (*et erit sepulchrum eius gloriosum*), that on 15 July 1099, "as was foretold by the prophet, the Lord's sepulcher was made glorious."[99] Other authors followed suit. Baldric evoked the Psalms and the Song of Songs to foretell the crusaders on the march.[100] Guibert of Nogent offered an extended paean to the siege as a fulfillment of the prophet Zacharias, and throughout evoked prophetical passages from Job, the Psalms, Proverbs, Isaiah, and Luke as having been fulfilled by the events of the First Crusade.[101] Albert of Aachen spoke of Godfrey of Bouillon as the "fulfillment of Moses."[102] And so forth.

Ekkehard of Aura, the German monk who participated in the crusade of 1101, also understood current events to be the fulfillment of Old Testament promises, and he made this argument in part by evoking the same scripture as did the liturgy for 15 July. Speaking of the consecration of new bishops in the Levant in 1100, he wrote that events "'turned into visible history those

---

94. Mégier, "Christian Historical Fulfilments"; Lapina, *Warfare and the Miraculous*, 135–137.

95. *Epistulae* XVIII (p. 168); tr. *Letters* 34.

96. Matthew Gabriele, "From Prophecy to Apocalypse: The verb tense of Jerusalem in Robert the Monk's *Historia* of the First Crusade," *Journal of Medieval History* 42 (2016) 304–316.

97. RR 109 (tr. 212), 13 (tr. 90). Riley-Smith, *The First Crusade*, 142, and 201nn27–28.

98. RR 110 (tr. 213). Cf. O$_1$ LA2, O$_2$ VA4.

99. RR 100 (tr. 201). Gabriele, "From Prophecy to Apocalypse" emphasizes Robert's use of the past (*fuit*) in place of the Vulgate's future (*erit*) to indicate the shift in Robert's mind of the prophetic endpoint from the Second Coming to the climax of the First Crusade.

100. Riley-Smith, *The First Crusade*, 201n22.

101. GN vi.21 (lat. 301–307, tr. 141–145).

102. AA vi.35 (pp. 448–449).

things that were so far only mystical prophecy."[103] He cited *Surge illuminare Jerusalem* (cf. Is. 60:1) and *Letare Jerusalem . . . Diem festum agite qui diligitis eam* (cf. Is. 66:10), liturgical phrases drawn from Isaiah.[104] This was no accident. *Surge illuminare* was used in both the office and mass.[105] *Letare Jerusalem*, the Introit for "Laetare Sunday" (the fourth Sunday in Lent), drew on Isaiah and celebrated the heavenly Jerusalem, and was adopted for the Mass Introit.[106] *Letare Jerusalem* was one of the more recognizable refrains, and pointed to the Resurrection and the anticipated joy of the heavenly Jerusalem.[107] *Diem festum agite* was part of the *Letare* prayer in the Mass and was also invoked in the office chant.[108] Ekkehard further explained that long forgotten prophecies were now understood in the context of 1099, by invoking Isaiah 66:10–11 itself: "Rejoice with Jerusalem [*Laetamini cum Jerusalem*], and be glad for her, all you who love her."[109] And then he glossed Isaiah 66:10–11:

> These, with a thousand other prophecies of this kind, can refer through anagogy [*anagogen*] to our mother Jerusalem, which is above; but they also can serve as a substitute for the contemplation and experiences of heavenly joys by inciting members of lower orders, nurtured through the draughts of reassurances (which have been written and are still yet to be composed), to risk the dangers of the literal journeys now occurring [*historialiter*].[110]

And then, if it were not yet clear, Ekkehard told the story of a man who, in a vision heard the hymn "Letatus sum" with the alleluia (Ps. 121:1, also from the Introit).[111]

A sermon attributed to Fulcher of Chartres written for the 15 July commemoration and preserved in a twelfth-century manuscript also quoted Isaiah 66:10.[112] The sermon (the ending of which does not survive) seems to have been composed shortly after the feast had been established to be preached as part of the day's liturgy. In its praise of the heroic deeds of the first crusaders, in its use of narrative, and in its move from past oppression to current liberation, it echoes strongly the narrative in the *Manu Plaudant*

---

103. EA *Chr.* 160. See also Buc, *Holy War, Martyrdom, and Terror*, 283.
104. EA *Chr.* 160, EA *Hier.* 26.
105. O¹ Cap, M¹ Epistle; O² Cap, M² Epistle, and cf: O² Lection 1.
106. M¹ Introit, M² Introit. See Gaposchkin, "The Feast of the Liberation."
107. Rose, "Jérusalem dans l'année liturgique," 394–397.
108. O¹ VA5, O² LA2.
109. EA *Hier.* 38.
110. EA *Hier.* 38.
111. EA *Hier.* 39.
112. Kohler, "Un sermon commémoratif," 162–163. The manuscript is Paris Mazarine 1711. Kohler queried whether the sermon was written by Fulcher himself, though, as Kohler noted, there are enough passages in the sermon that appear to derive from Fulcher's chronicle that a close association seems merited.

sequence. But above all, it supports this historical and prophetical interpretation of the taking of Jerusalem. It begins by enjoining liturgical celebration and commemoration of the capture of Jerusalem, of how the holy city of Jerusalem was, by divine arrangement, unexpectedly taken from the impious hands of the pagans by the Christians and mercifully restored.[113] Quoting Lamentations, the preacher explains, the city had for a long time been oppressed, because of her sins, and suffered tribulations. The author was quoting Lamentation on the Babylonian exile, but meaning Jerusalem in the four and half centuries before the First Crusade. He continued: Yet, the Lord wept for her, and quoting Isaiah 49:14–18 and 60:14, the preacher explained that the Lord returned to her.[114] Now the temple is purified, because the Occident, signed by the sign of Christ's cross, rose up against the Orient. Inspired by faith, but having suffered much labor, famine, cold and heat, "we" persevered, guided by God, and on blessed feet, and with blessed arms, the worthy work was accomplished. And then the author quoted Isaiah 66:10: *Rejoice, Jerusalem* ("Letare Jerusalem"); and then Isaiah 66:6–9, pointing to Jerusalem's redemption as a divine miracle, and Isaiah 66:18–20, the foretelling of the Apocalypse. The liturgy invoked these verses (Isaiah 66:10; 66:19): "They shall proclaim My might unto nations, and declare My glory unto the gentiles."[115] The preacher then narrated the events of the First Crusade: may God bless all those who, enjoined by Pope Urban, wearing crosses (that special and triumphant sign) on their clothes, went as pilgrims to Jerusalem, striving for God. They marched all the way to Nicea, to Bithynia, and enormously outnumbered, faced a huge army that had gathered from all around (again, an idea echoed in the sequence). But men (and clerics, monks, women, and children) had come from all around, from Rome, from Apulia, from Hungary, from Dalmatia. Many turned back. Many died along the way. Those that stuck it out were fearfully wearied by the time they besieged Antioch. "But in the end, truly notwithstanding their labors, and God having mercy on them, they seized Jerusalem, on the ides of July, during the harvest."[116] Then the preacher shifted to the present tense. And now, the faithful hasten to the Lord's Temple and the Sepulcher of Christ, and there they pour out their pious prayers, rendering thanks owed in that very place. "Thus, we say with Isaiah, 'Rejoice Jerusalem, and be glad for her, all you who love her' . . ." (Isaiah 66:10). As the preacher said it, so did the clerics in the liturgy. Vespers drew again from Advent: "Rejoice with Jerusalem, and be glad with her, all you that love her; rejoice for joy with

---

113. Kohler, "Un sermon commémoratif," 160. The sermon is edited from pp. 160–164. The final section is lost.

114. Cf. EA *Hier.* 38.

115. O¹ MV7.

116. Kohler, "Un sermon commémoratif," 163.

her in eternity."[117] The introit for the Mass ran: "Rejoice, O Jerusalem, and come together all you that love her . . ."[118]

Two generations later, William of Tyre used the Jerusalem liturgy to make the point about prophetical fulfillment. He said explicitly that the establishment of the feast for 15 July was decreed so that "there should be recounted all that had been foretold by the prophets concerning this event."[119] Describing the first liturgical celebrations, he then quoted Isaiah 66:10 as having been literally fulfilled: "There went up from the Holy City a shout of spiritual rejoicing to the Lord, and, as if by direct command from Him, solemn rites were celebrated again and again; so that these words of the prophet seemed to be literally fulfilled: "Rejoice ye with Jerusalem (*Laetamini cum Hierusalem*), and be glad with her, all ye that love her."[120] *Laetamini cum Jerusalem*, from Isaiah 66:10, was deployed in the office.[121] In the liturgy, the line was one of joy and thanksgiving for the deliverance to the Christians of the city, itself foretelling the Second Coming. William of Tyre quoted the Jerusalem liturgy's vespers service a number of times. In a passage where he described the Franks' march toward Jerusalem, he described their first sight of the sacred city. Then he wrote: "Here indeed, the prophetic utterance of Isaiah seemed to be fulfilled and the word of the Lord to be made actual fact: 'Lift up thine eyes unto Jerusalem (*Leva Ierusalem*) and see the power of the Lord. Behold your Redeemer comes to release you from your bounds'" (Is. 51:15). And likewise, "Awake, awake [*Elevare elevare*], stand up, O Jerusalem: loose yourself from the bonds of your neck, O captive daughter of Sion."[122] In a footnote, the translators explain that these passages "resemble" the verse from Isaiah 51:15 "but is William's own version," and that "this [the second verse] is a contraction of Is. 51:17 and 52:2," but in fact, William was quoting lines of chant from the Jerusalem office. *Leva Ierusalem* was used in both versions of vespers, *Elevare elevare* survives in 8927's vespers service. Both drew on Isaiah, and both came from Advent. And both explained, as the liturgy as a whole did, and as William would later write, how it was that the prophets had foretold the capture of

---

117. O[1] VA5, O[2] LA2.

118. M[1] Introit: "Letare ierusalem et conventum facite omnes qui diligits eam; gaudete cum letitia, qui in tristia fuistis; ut exsultetis, et satiemini ab ubribus consolationis vestrae."

119. WT viii.24 (lat. 1:417, tr. 1:378).

120. WT viii.22 (lat. 1:415, tr. 1:375).

121. William may have been thinking of the office celebrated in his own day, as the line was also used in the office found O[2] LA2. On William's use of such allusions, see Alan V. Murray, "Biblical Quotations and Formulaic Language in the Chronicle of William of Tyre," in *Deeds Done Beyond the Sea: Essays on William of Tyre, Cyprus and the Military Orders Presented to Peter Edbury*, ed. Susan B. Edgington and Helen J. Nicholson (Farnham: Ashgate, 2014), 25–34.

122. WT vii.25 (lat. 1:378, tr. 1:338).

Jerusalem. Finally, William quoted Isaiah through the Jerusalem liturgy in describing the preparations in Europe in 1095 and 1096. He wrote, "To this movement the following passage from Isaiah seems to refer: The Lord 'shall set up a sign [*Levabit dominus signum*, cf. Isaiah 11:12] for the nations, and shall assemble the outcasts of Israel.'"[123] Here again, he quoted the version of the text used in the Jerusalem feast during vespers.[124]

The image of raising up the *signum* from Isaiah 11:12 was also evoked in the triumphant *Manu plaudant* sequence. As translated earlier, the sequence echoed Isaiah 11:12 in explaining that the "prophesized *signum* was raised up by the ancient prophecy." The sign of prophecy (*signum . . . presignatum profecia*) was traditionally equated with the sign of the cross, which brought salvation and released those in [spiritual] captivity, and which had conquered the devil.[125] But now of course the *signum presignatum* was the sign of the cross under the protection of which the crusades fought to secure the sacred city, which itself conquered the devil. (Fulcher's sermon also referred to the signum.) The sequence also spoke of the prophecy that foretold that His tomb would be honored, evoking here Isaiah 11:10 (*et erit sepulchrum eius gloriosum*; "and his tomb will be glorious"), and also made reference to Isaiah 60:4. This was a favorite of the monastic chroniclers.[126] Robert of Reims, writing a few years later in the West, also used both Isaiah 60:4 and 11:12 this way. He quoted 60:4—"she made her sons come from afar"—in describing the immediate aftermath of the capture.[127] Three sentences later, in his chapter describing how, after the capture, the Franks prayed at the Holy Sepulcher, he said, "On that day, as the prophet had foretold, the Sepulcher of the Lord was glorious."[128] These pointed references linked the historic references of the sequence to the biblical and eschatological frame of the office, since Isaiah 11:12 and 60:4 were also evoked in the antiphons.

IT IS possible we want to push this one step further. The liturgy was probably composed in the early period after the victory, when, according to recent historians, apocalyptic expectations were still high. The use of Isaiah, and in particular chapters 60–62, in which the prophet foretells the rise and glory of

---

123. WT i.16 (lat. 1:138, tr. 1:95). See also WT viii.2 (lat. 1:384, tr. 1:341–342) for quotation of Joel 3.1–2.

124. O¹ VA3, O² VA5.

125. Cyril of Alexandria, *Commentary on Isaiah, Translated with an Introduction by Robert Charles Hill*, 3 vols. (Brookline MA: 2008–), 1:269. See also Glossa Ordinaria, commenting on "signum": "Signum., crucis, in qua est victoria, ut sciant omnes in quo diabolus sit victus."

126. GN ii.4 (lat. 112, tr. 43).

127. RR 100 (tr. 201).

128. RR 100 (tr. 201): "Ipso die, sicut per prophetam fuerat praedictum, sepulchrum domini fuit gloriosum."

Jerusalem throughout the office, underscored the heightened expectations for the Franks' new Jerusalem. In this respect, those instances where the Jerusalem feast did not draw from the Advent or Epiphany liturgy or Isaiah-inspired antiphons make the point that the office sought to tie, perhaps equate, the taking of Jerusalem to the coming of the New Jerusalem. The liturgy adopted chant taken from Revelation, John's apocalyptic vision of the New Jerusalem. "This is Jerusalem, the great city of the heavens. . . . And the gates thereof shall not be shut."[129] The language came directly from Revelation 21:2–3 and 21:25. This was the New Jerusalem, the heavenly Jerusalem, of future times, the gateway to which was the earthly Jerusalem that the crusaders had just captured. And chant taken from the office of the Dedication of the Church spoke of John "looking at the whole mystery of the sky, he called it the holy city" and "her wall, decorated in precious stones." This was language from Revelation 21:2 and 21:11–12. A matins antiphon, drawing from Revelation 21 and 22:2 spoke of "the holy city of Jerusalem, decorated with the ornaments of the martyrs, whose streets sing out praises from day to day."[130] The liturgy linked the earthly Jerusalem to the heavenly Jerusalem, the prophesized return of Jerusalem to the Franks with the Apocalyptic return of Christ and the New Jerusalem.[131]

Revelation 21–22 was also at the heart of the office hymn.[132] Both versions of the Jerusalem feast adopted the *Dedicatio ecclesie's* hymn "Urbs beata Hierusalem."[133] It was an old hymn—attested in Western manuscripts of the eighth or ninth century—but had particular resonance in the Holy City after 1099 for the way in which it equated the earthly houses of God with the future glory. (The Franks had inscribed lines from "Urbs beata" inside the *Templum Domini* as part of their appropriation of the sacred space for Christian devotion.[134]) The hymn celebrated the vision of peace of the blessed city of Jerusalem. It was influenced by language of the Old Testament prophets—Isaiah, Daniel, and Tobias—but in the main, it drew on Revelation 21, embracing John's description of a heavenly Jerusalem, with its twelve gates of pearls, with its streets of pure gold, its walls adorned with precious stones, but without a temple. Its praise of the physical church as a vision of heaven—the *beata pacis visio* (from Jerome and Ezekiel)[135]—was, in the Jerusalem liturgy, turned back onto the actual city of the earthly

---

129. O¹ MRV3, O² MRV7.

130. O¹ MA9.

131. For further examples, see also O¹ MRV9, O¹ MR2, O¹ MRV9. Cf. O² MRV8.

132. Jordi G. Gibert Tarruell, "La 'dedicatio ecclesiae.' Il rito liturgico e i suoi principi teologici," in *L'amiata nel medioevo* (Viella: 1989), 19–32.

133. AH 51:110–111, no. 102. List of sources on p. 111–112 attest to eighth- or ninth-century origins. On its scriptural sources, see Ashworth, "*Urbs beata Jerusalem*," 238–241.

134. At least by ca. 1170: JW 95.

135. See chapter 1.

Jerusalem. The point was that the earthly Church—or, in this context, the earthly Jerusalem—was both the image of, and the gateway to, the heavenly Jerusalem. After 1099, the hymn was appropriate not because the Holy Sepulcher was being rededicated but because, in fact, the entire city was being rededicated to Christ. Its use for the Liberation feast underscored the relationship between capturing the earthly Jerusalem and ultimately attaining the heavenly Jerusalem. This was echoed in the early narratives. Gilo of Paris described Godfrey's charging of the earthly Jerusalem on 15 July, saying the duke was "fighting for a twofold kingdom, since he was looking forward to both Jerusalems: he fought in the one so that he might have life in the other."[136] The collect following the hymn was also based on a traditional dedication prayer, but instead of asking God to renew "this holy temple by your consecration" and granting grace to whomever should enter "this temple," it asked that God renew "your holy city of Jerusalem by its capture" and grant grace to whomever should enter "the city."[137]

Within the context of the earthly Jerusalem newly acquired and possessed by the Franks, in which the office was celebrated, the evocation of the physical, tangible traits of the heavenly city concretized the link between the present attainment of the earthly Jerusalem and the future attainment of the heavenly Jerusalem. Baldric, we saw in chapter one, imagined a preacher telling the crusaders that the earthly city prefigured and pointed to the heavenly one—the celestian Jerusalem.[138] And it may have done more. It may have been expressing the belief that the taking of Jerusalem was the precursor to and part of the march toward the Apocalypse. In this view—rooted in ninth-century exegetical tradition and imbibed in the liturgy as a whole—the prophets foretold the destruction and return of Jerusalem to the new Israelites, the Franks, in the image of, or as a type of, or in anticipatory promise of, the end-times.[139] Guy Lobrichon, Jay Rubenstein, and Philippe Buc have recently emphasized the apocalyptic in the thinking of participants and contemporaries in the crusade, arguing that participants understood themselves to be playing a key role in what Buc calls "moving history forward"; that is, as agents pushing forward the events that would lead to the end-times.[140] In

---

136. Gilo of Paris and a second anonymous author, *The Historia vie Hierosolimitane*: IX:280 (pp. 244–245).

137. Cf. CO 1825; Gaposchkin, "The Feast of the Liberation," 141.

138. BB 108.

139. Chydenius, *Medieval Institutions and the Old Testament*; Becker, *Papst Urban II*, especially vol. 2; Matthew Gabriele, "The Last Carolingian Exegete: Pope Urban II, the Weight of Tradition, and Christian Reconquest," *Church History* 81, no. 4 (2012): 781–814.

140. Lobrichon, *1099: Jéruslem conquise*; Rubenstein, *Armies of Heaven*; Buc, *Holy War, Martyrdom, and Terror*; Jay Rubenstein, "Crusade and Apocalypse: History and the Last Days," *Questiones Medii Aevi Novae* 21 (2016), forthcoming. Rubenstein and Buc are refining an older historiography, best known in Paul Aphandéry and Alphonse Dupront, *La Chrétienté et l'idée de croisade*, Bibliothèque de l'évolution de l'humanité 10 (1954; reprint Paris: 1995). For larger context, see

this view, the events of 1099 were either part of the Apocalypse itself, or, when the Apocalypse failed to materialize, a punctuation in the typed scheme of apocalyptic history. Multiple "liberations" or "freedoms" or "returns" could be imprints, foretold, of the greatest prophecy. In Buc's words, the progress of sacred history was "also, in part, a History including demoted apocalyptic moments. It may be that the events that had been seen in their own times as apocalyptic could transmute themselves into special nodes within Sacred History's course *precisely* because of their apocalyptic charge."[141] The capture was a fulfillment of prophecy at the same time that it pointed toward, promised, and participated in the end-times. And the liturgy, because of the way in which it spoke to Scripture, history, and eschatology, because of the multivalent readings and multiple levels on which liturgy was intended to convey, was the ideal vehicle to bridge the gap between the historical and the eschatological; to articulate the ties between the events themselves and the providence they belonged to.

The Rededication of the Holy Sepulcher in 1149

At dawn on 15 July 1149, fifty years to the day after the capture of Jerusalem, the Church of the Holy Sepulcher was rededicated.[142] The existing structure, which now served as a patriarchal see as well as a pilgrimage church, failed to meet the increased demands placed on it and, as the most important church in Christendom, surely demanded embellishment. The Franks had undertaken a massive rebuilding of the edifice in the contemporary Romanesque style favored in the West, starting probably around 1143, although we have few secure dates to work with.[143] Jaroslav Folda has argued for royal patronage and involvement. The building project unified under one roof the many churches and chapels—including most notably the Anastasis (Tomb) and Calvary—that had made up the Byzantine complex that the Franks found in 1099.[144] A number of chapels were incorporated into the unified architectural complex, including the Chapel of Saint Helena and the Chapel of the Franks, which opened on the Calvary gallery. Four altars were also

---

also Jean Flori, *L'Islam et la fin des temps: L'interprétation prophétiques des invasions musulmanes dans la chrétienté médiévale* (Paris: 2007), 250–281.

141. Buc, *Holy War, Martyrdom, and Terror*, 284.

142. Linder, "'Like Purest Gold Resplendent,'" 31–50. The reference to dawn comes from an inscription recorded by John of Wurzburg. JW 123.

143. Jaroslav Folda, *The Art of the Crusaders in the Holy Land, 1098–1187* (Cambridge, UK: 1995), 177–179. Robert Ousterhout, "Architecture as Relic and the Construction of Sanctity: The Stones of the Holy Sepulchre," *Journal of the Society of Architectural Historians* 62, no. 1 (2003): 4–23. Pringle, *The Churches of the Crusader Kingdom*, 3: 19–31.

144. On which, see Robert Ousterhout, "Rebuilding the Temple: Constantine Monomachus and the Holy Sepulchre," *Journal of the Society of Architectural Historians* (1989): 66–78.

consecrated that day, including the main altar, one in the Calvary chapel, one to Saint Peter, and one to the Protomartyr Stephen.[145] Yet the contemporary sources are surprisingly quiet about the fiftieth anniversary ceremonies.[146] The mood in 1149 may have been different than that in 1099, following just months after the catastrophic failure of the Second Crusade. An inscription placed in the Calvary chapel at the time explained that the reconsecration of the church "added no holiness" since it was consecrated by Christ's own blood.[147] Our best evidence for the ritual that occurred on that day comes, in fact, from its echoes in the liturgical ceremonies that commemorated it.

The rededication was presided over by the patriarch of Jerusalem, Fulcher of Angoulême, who occupied that office from 1146–1157. It was Fulcher, apparently, who arranged for a wide-scale revision of the liturgy of the Holy Sepulcher at this stage, focused on Christic and Marian devotion.[148] The two surviving ordinals allow us to reconstruct the general *cursus* of the liturgy as it was practiced after 1149 at the Holy Sepulcher (until 1187). These two sources are in broad agreement, and both include a prologue that explain the liturgical reforms.[149] Existing liturgical sources, the prologue explained, were used to create an integrated rite; the old rites were respected, but on occasion altered; and the new rite should henceforth be "read and sung" at the Holy Sepulcher.

Among the changes made to the rite was a large-scale revision to the liturgy for 15 July. Because 15 July was now not only the anniversary of the capture of Jerusalem, but also the anniversary of the dedication of the Holy Sepulcher, the liturgy for that day involved—atypically—a full mass and office for both the *Liberatio sancti civitatis Iherusalem de manibus Turchorum*, and *the Dedicatio ecclesie domnici sepulcri*.[150] The rubrics in both ordinals explain explicitly that "we" are to celebrate the Dedication feast according to the desire and command of the Lord Patriarch, Fulcher."[151] But at the Holy Sepulcher in particular, the day really became devoted to a

145. JW 124.

146. Folda, *The Art of the crusaders*, 177–178. Our best narrative material comes several years later, from John of Wurzburg, JW 123–125.

147. JW 123.

148. On Fulcher's responsibility for and vision of the liturgical cursus, see Salvadó, "Rewriting the Latin Liturgy of the Holy Sepulchre."

149. Dondi HS⁵ and HS⁹: Rome, Bib. Vat. Barb. Lat. 659, 26v, Barletta 34r, edited Dondi 48, 197.

150. Six copies survive of the Liberation feast (that I know of): Lucca Biblioteca Archivescovile 5 A57r; Vat. Barb. Lat. 659 101r–102r; the Barletta Ordinal, 109v–110v; a fourteenth-century copy found in an ordinal for the Teutonic Order (Wroclaw, I.Q.175, 15r); a fourteenth-century tract of music theory copied in the West that transcribed the office (UB Erfurt, Dep. Erf. CA. 8° 44, 19r); and finally a fifteenth-century Hospitaller breviary (Vienna ÖNB, Cod. Palat, 1928, 79r).

151. Vat Barberini Lat. 659, 102r. Dondi HS⁵, p. 170. Cf. Barletta 120r, Kohler 429–430.

commemoration of the Dedication of the Church. The Liberation rite was in a sense subordinated to the new Dedication rite, with its mass being shifted to the early morning "morrow" mass to give the Dedication mass pride of place.[152] And it appears that at the Holy Sepulcher, at least, the office may not even have been sung.

The liturgy for the Jerusalem Liberation that was incorporated into the day's rite had probably been composed at the Holy Sepulcher several decades earlier, in what appears to be a revision of the Advent-driven rite composed in the wake of the conquest. This version of the 15 July liturgy introduced a series of chant items from the liturgy of Epiphany and certain elements from the liturgy of the Trinity. The repeated emphasis of the chant on Jerusalem and Sion was replaced with chant items that celebrated the building, the Church, and the Temple. Praise of the city of Jerusalem was muted, and praise of the Holy Sepulcher as the house of God was put front and center. The effect was to tone down the eschatological and apocalyptic themes from the earlier Jerusalem liturgy, replacing them with an emphasis on the magnitude of God's power and the holiness of place. It adopted, for example, a known prayer for the protection of a monastery that asked God, "the architect and guardian of the city of the heavenly Jerusalem," to guard "this place" and its inhabitants, so that it might always be an abode of safety and peace.[153] The revision eschewed chant that praised the city of Jerusalem in favor of items that praised God and in particular His House. "Adore the Lord in His holy house."[154] "We have taken in Your mercy, Or Lord, in the middle of Your temple, following Your name."[155] "Worship the Lord, alleluia, in His sacred court."[156] Where they remained, the providential and prophetic themes from earlier in the century were now more allegorical than providential. In a reference to the Church as an image of heaven, the liturgy evoked Revelation 21.2–3: "I saw the holy city of Jerusalem, descending from the heavens from God, and I heard the voice from the throne, saying 'behold, here is the tabernacle of God.'"[157] The line came from the liturgy of the Dedication of a Church, and the focus now was that the tabernacle of God—the Church—was the *image* of heaven, the gateway to heaven, the place for personal salvation. It was no longer a direct evocation of the imminence of end-times.

---

152. Linder, "'Like Purest Gold Resplendent,'" 47; Salvadó, "The Liturgy of the Holy Sepulchre," 30, 171–181.
153. CO 3787, *Pro custodia monsterii et habitatorum eius.*
154. CAO 1303. O² MA1.
155. CAO 5085. O² MA4.
156. CAO 1290. O² MA7.
157. CAO 7871. O² MR8.

The tabernacle was, in the Old Testament, the tabernacle housed in the Jewish Temple, and thus, strictly speaking, a reference to the Templum Domini. The Temple was the other great holy site of the Holy City, which was served, as in the Holy Sepulcher, by a chapter of canons regular.[158] The site it was identified with was, in the Books of Kings and Chronicles, called the house of the Lord, the *domus dei*, and, of course, the temple (*templum*). There are several apparently new references in the revised Jerusalem liturgy to the Holy Sepulcher as the "tabernacle."[159] These, may have indicated a kind of liturgical assertion of superiority of the Holy Sepulcher, the mother church, the head of the patriarchate, over the Temple. Certainly, the two institutions were in competition, especially after the formal consecration of the Temple in 1141 and in view of the Temple canons' interest in appealing to pilgrims.[160] Appropriation of the term suggests perhaps the Holy Sepulcher's attempt to claim the mantle of the designation as Templum, to insist on the transition from the old to the new dispensation, and to assume the central devotional function of the city, to being, for all intents and purposes, the new temple.

This would give added meaning to the most visible and public element of the Jerusalem rite, the liturgical procession that marched from the Holy Sepulcher to the Temple and back.[161] The ordinals indicate that the procession should be performed *festive* (rather than solemnly). This was not the penitential, expiatory procession of the Rogations days, but a joyful expression of thanksgiving for the gifts and wonders of God. Linder, on the basis of a careful reading of the ordinal rubrics, has proposed that the procession was a continuation of earlier practice, done even before 1149.[162] After prime and after the Morrow Mass commemorating the liberation, at about seven in the morning, the clergy would set out in procession from the Holy Sepulcher on the way to the Temple. Liturgical processions from the Holy Sepulcher to the Temple were not uncommon during the year, occurring also on Palm Sunday, on Purification, on Christmas Eve, during the Major and Minor

158. Pringle, *The Churches of the Crusader Kingdom*, 3:401–402.
159. The items do not appear in O¹.
160. On the competition: Heribert Busse, "Vom Felsendom zum Templum Domini," in *Das Heilige Land im Mittelalter: Begegnungsraum zwischen Orient und Okzident: Referate des 5. interdisziplinären Colloquiums des Zentralinstituts*, ed. Wolfdietrich Fischer and Jürgen Schneider (Degener: 1982), 19–32.
161. On the procession, see Amnon Linder, "The Liturgy of the Latin Kingdom of Jerusalem," in *Knights of the Holy Land: The Crusader Kingdom of Jerusalem*, ed. Silvia Rozenberg (Jerusalem: 1999), 97–98; Adrian Boas, *Jerusalem in the Time of the Crusades—Society, Landscape, and Art in the Holy City under Frankish Rule* (New York: 2001), 31–32. John, "The 'Feast of the Liberation,'" 422–430.
162. Linder, "'Like Purest Gold Resplendent'" 46–47.

Rogations, and on May 2.[163] As they processed to the Temple, the clergy offered praises to God. When they arrived at its entrance, they sang prayers taken from the office of the Dedication of the Church which spoke of "Your house, O Lord" and "this Temple." "Eternal peace from the eternal Father in this house."[164] And "Holiness becomes Your house, O Lord, for the length of days."[165]

Having finished this station, the ordinal explains, "we then proceed to the southern doorway, and turning around there, we turn toward that place where the city was captured."[166] Understanding the rubric properly depends on the translation of "meridianam portam," which has caused some confusion since it has been assumed that this referred to one of the gates in the city walls, and thus led the procession outside of the city. But other references in the ordinal make clear that the "meridianam portam" was the southern entrance to the Temple itself, which means there is no reason to think that the procession exited the confines of the city.[167] This was the more normal practice, in any event. Since the "meridianam portam" referred to the southern entrance to the Dome of the Rock (*Templum domini*), the procession most likely went back into the city through the "beautiful doorway," and then turned north into the Syrian quarter to go to the place at the north of the city where, in 1099, the wall had been breached. Simon John has argued that the procession, by connecting the Templum Domini (Old Testament), the Holy Sepulcher (New Testament), and the place where the crusaders breached the city wall (Crusader time), sought to frame crusader Jerusalem with its biblical forebear.[168] There, another station was performed, a sermon preached, and a blessing given. One can imagine a preacher here giving some version of the sermon discussed above that has survived under the putative authorship of Fulcher of Chartres. At this point, the cantor intoned a thanksgiving prayer to God taken from the Trinity liturgy, and the procession started back toward the Holy Sepulcher. Back at the mother church, if it was Sunday, the canons moved toward the Tomb itself, singing "I am the alpha and the omega." Then the canons picked up the regular office again, with dedicated services at terce, sext, none, and second vespers.

---

163. Salvadó, "The Liturgy of the Holy Sepulchre," 218–259.

164. CAO 4252, *Pax eterna.*

165. CAO 6235b, *Dominum tuum.* A common refrain throughout the day's liturgy.

166. See Appendix 1. Vat Barb Lat. 659, 101v; Salvadó, 630." Cf. Barletta 120r, Kohler, "Un rituel et un bréviaire," 429 reads *convertimur* instead of *convertimus.*

167. Examples are taken from Salavado's edition of Vat Barb Lat. 659. See, for Purification, 50v, and for Palm Sunday, 65r.

168. John, "The 'Feast of the Liberation,'" 409–431.

In 1149, at the Holy Sepulcher, the revised Jerusalem liturgy was combined with and subordinated to the liturgical celebration of the rededication of the Holy Sepulcher. The two ordinals describe an elaborate rite for
15 July that now involved an office and mass for the *Liberatio* that included
the procession, and an office and mass for the *Dedicatio*, but the celebration of the liberation was reduced to just the celebration of the Morrow (not
High) mass. One imagines that an office for the Liberation of Jerusalem
continued to be celebrated at other churches in the Holy City, although we
do not have the books to confirm this. But at the Holy Sepulcher, the day
now commemorated primarily the Dedication. The canons at the Holy Sepulcher adopted, with only a few changes, the rite for the Dedication of the
Church from the use of Chartres.[169] The chant was focused on place, full of
praises lauding the house of prayer, the house of the lord, the house of God.
The two more frequently repeated refrains were typical: "Sacredness becomes Your house, O Lord, for the length of days"[170] (cf. Psalms 95:2), and
"This is the house of the Lord, stoutly built, and founded solidly upon a
sturdy rock"[171] (cf. Matt 7:24–25). The theme throughout was of the Church
as the gateway to heaven. The office evoked Jacob's dream, climbing on his
ladder to the heavens to see the angels of God: "This is none other than the
house of God, and this is the gate of heaven" (cf. Genesis 28:17), an emphasis on house and place.[172] And it evoked Revelation chapter 14 and 21, exalting the Tabernacle of God, the walls made of precious stones, and angels
flying through the skies.[173] These were themes developed in the West to
emphasize the role of the Church in an individual's salvation that were easily transposed to the Holy Sepulcher and would have, one imagines, only
had added resonance when celebrated in Jerusalem, at the place of Christ's
resurrection.

All in all, then, 15 July came to celebrate, at least at the Holy Sepulcher,
less the eschatological importance of the holy city of Jerusalem and the role
of its capture by the Franks in 1099 within the larger scope of salvation
history, as the importance of the Holy Sepulcher—the new Temple, the
house of God, the center of the Christian world—in the ritual and devotional life of the Christian community. This may reflect a muting of the
eschatological enthusiasms that characterized the early years of the twelfth
century.[174] Or a theological revision that was appropriate specifically to the

---

169. Dondi 126–127.

170. CAO 6235b. Sung during the procession and then repeatedly in the Dedication office.

171. CAO 7595b.

172. CAO 7286. Dedicatio Ecclesie MA4, MR6, MR10.

173. CAO 7073. Dedicatio Ecclesie MR5, MRV8, LA3.

174. On the diminution of eschatological hopes, see Flori, *L'Islam et la fin des temps*, 272–
281; Jay Rubenstein, "Crusade and Apocalypse."

Holy Sepulcher. It may also reflect the institutionalization of the Church, the role of the Holy Sepulcher in the life of the Latin Church in the East, and the general normalizing of administration, life, and ritual in the East that took place over the course of a half-century.

After 1187

What did 1099 mean after 1187? The loss of Jerusalem to Saladin, of course, changed everything. After the settlement of the Third Crusade (1192), Saladin had permitted Western clergy to remain attached to the Holy Sepulcher in order to perform the Latin rite for pilgrims. But the city and the church were no longer "liberated" and the celebration of military and eschatological victory would have been either farcical or even painful. Even during the fifteen year "reprieve" negotiated by Frederick II when the Franks regained access to the city, the Holy Sepulcher was never secure. What then, can we tell about the celebration from the manuscripts that followed Holy Sepulcher use written after the passage of control of Jerusalem to the Ayyubids and beyond?

We probably do not have quite enough surviving evidence to be categorical, but we are helped by the catalog of Christina Dondi. Dondi has identified eighteen liturgical manuscripts that represent the "use of the Holy Sepulcher," meaning that they represent the liturgy established at the Holy Sepulcher and used throughout the patriarchate.[175] These range from sacramentaries, missals, breviaries, ordinals, pontificals, and psalters, and thus do not all give evidence of the Sanctorale. Of these eighteen manuscripts, only five date to the period before 1187. To these we can add Barletta, which preserves pre-1187 use. This said, of the thirteen that remain, ten *do* treat the Sanctorale and thus give us information about the 15 July rite, either minimally in the form of a calendar, or more expansively with proper prayers.

Of these ten, only two manuscripts include information about a proper celebration for 15 July. Someone copied out a version of the revised Jerusalem office on an empty page in the Lucca breviary after Jerusalem fell to Saladin.[176] Yet in only one manuscript copied after 1187 (London BL Egerton 2902, a missal dating to the second quarter of the thirteenth century) is the office included integrally in the Sanctorale.[177] The mass is titled

---

175. For this paragraph, see information in Dondi.

176. Aspesi, "The Contribution of the Cantors."

177. Dondi HS[13]. Buchthal dated the manuscript from 1228–1244. Dondi 85–86, dated the manuscript on the basis of Gerard's accession to the patriarchate in 1225 and the death of Queen Isabelle II in 1228 (because of the inclusion of a *missa pro regina*) to between those two dates. Dondi. See: *Missa pro libertate Ierusalem de manu paganorum* at 118v.

Missa pro liberate ierusalem de manu paganorum, and Aspesi has suggested that the traditional Liberation mass thus became, after the loss of Jerusalem, now a commemorative mass imploring God *for* the recapture of Jerusalem.[178] The prayers for the mass for the Liberatio feast replicate the rite that was performed at the Holy Sepulcher before 1187 and, indeed, before 1149, with the exception that it has replaced the Gospel reading (Matt 21:10) with Luke 19:41 in which Jesus weeps for Jerusalem. Four other manuscripts that were copied between 1187 and ca. 1225—two missals, a breviary, and a psalter—include no mention of the Liberation feast in either the calendar or the Sanctorale, although one—the psalter—lists the "Dedicatio ecclesie s. Sepulchri" in the calendar on 15 July. Five manuscripts—three breviaries, a missal, and a sacramentary—put together after the midcentury loss of Jerusalem include no proper items at all (although two do record the Liberatio in the calendar).[179] The notations in the calendar that are not matched with a listing in the Sanctorale or any proper items for the feast probably indicate—as we will see occurred at times in the West—a kind of annalistic notation, to record the event as part of sacred time. But the Liberation of Jerusalem was not itself celebrated.

Overall, given the spotty nature of the surviving manuscript record, the evidence points to an initial effort to preserve the celebration, and then its abandonment. Notwithstanding examples of the feast that were imported to the West by canons of the Holy Sepulcher or Hospitallers, the feast was largely muted in the Holy Land after 1187. After the fall of Jerusalem to Saladin in 1187 and the move of the kingdom in exile to Acre, although the Holy Sepulcher use was maintained, the liturgical celebration of the Liberation of Jerusalem (and the Dedication of the Holy Sepulcher) was apparently abandoned. When the Franks returned to Jerusalem, the feast was reestablished (as represented in Egerton 2902), but then quickly, again, after 1244, obviated when Jerusalem fell again to the Khwarazmian Turks.

Liturgy was both about memory and about commemoration. In 1244, in contrast to 1192, the Latin clergy lost all access to the shrine. In theory, the Latins might have continued to commemorate the capture of Jerusalem as a sacred event, but subsequent history had belied the interpretation that the liturgy advanced; it had denied that God had returned Jerusalem to His people and would remain with them there, secure and at peace. No longer could it be said that "to Sion I will give my salvation and to Jerusalem my glory."[180]

---

178. Aspesi, "The *libelli* of Lucca."

179. The five manuscripts are Dondi HS[13–18]. The two that include mention in the calendar are HS[15] and HS[16].

180. O[1] MV8 and O[2] MV4.

Or, "And the gates thereof shall not be shut."[181] Or "Rejoice Jerusalem, with great joy, for a Savior shall come to you."[182] Even during the fifteen-year reprieve negotiated by Frederick II (1229–1244), its celebration must have felt dissonant since ownership, as it were, had been negotiated rather than achieved through conquest and might. Chant such as: "Sion is the city of our fortitude, the Savior will be stationed on its wall and fortifications; Open the gates, for God is with us,"[183] may have hit the wrong note. But after 1244, there was no sense at all in it. The Savior, it seemed, was no longer with them. And thus the liturgy could not be sung. The theology on the matter was clear, both from the Old Testament examples and from twelfth-century thinkers. The loss of Jerusalem and God's abandonment of the Latin Kingdom was caused by sin. The Franks could hardly celebrate a triumphalist interpretation of history when the only appropriate mode was penitence. As will be discussed in chapter 6, after 1187, Christendom turned instead to penitential liturgy to beg God for forgiveness for the sins that had lost them Jerusalem, and to plead with him that the Holy City be returned.

181. O¹ MV3 and O² MV7.
182. O¹ MA8 or O² LA3.
183. O¹ LA2 and O² LA4.

5

Echoes of Victory in the West

Sometime around 1130, a monastic annalist from the monastery of Saint-André du Cateau (just east of Cambrai, on the border of France and the Empire), writing in an older style, wrote up a (very) short account of the First Crusade:

> On the *via Hierusalem*. In the year 1096, at the urging of the often mentioned Pope Urban, those who dwelt in the land began to strike out on the pilgrim's path to Jerusalem and the sound and love of going (there) spread to the ends of the earth. Counts, princes, nobles, and even common people of both sexes strove to go; many claimed that they saw portents and signs in the sky. It is not for me to describe how many dangers, how many bodily injuries, how great the famines, how many were the battles they undertook, especially in Antioch, in this journey, by what effort, by what pressures, they arrived at Jerusalem, by what skill, by what effort during the forty-day siege, with many thousands of Saracens slaughtered, and with what zeal they purified the Lord's Sepulcher and holy places, especially since they are described in hymns [*cantica*] and songs [*carmina*] distributed everywhere.[1]

The monk of Saint-André was recounting events that by his time were widely known. The news of victory in the Levant had immediately engendered an entirely new genre of writing—the Latin historiography of a single military campaign. Accounts of the events had been composed during or shortly after the events by Peter Tudebode, Raymond of Aguilers, Fulcher of Chartres, and above all, the anonymous *Gesta Francorum*.[2] In France, these "eyewitness" accounts were quickly rewritten and reimagined by Benedictine monks,

---

1. "Chronicon S. Andreae Castri Cameracensii" MGH SS 7:544–545. For the date, see p. 526.

2. For reaction in the West, see Tyerman, *God's War: A New History of the Crusades*, 244–247. The classic treatment of the early monastic authors is Riley-Smith, *The First Crusade*, 135–152. For the monastic treatment of the fall of Jerusalem specifically, see Jay Rubenstein, "Miracles and the Crusading Mind: Monastic Meditations on Jerusalem's Conquest," in *Prayer*

imbued with monastic learning and a monastic understanding of history, sitting in their monasteries and thinking through the meaning of the First Crusade in sacred history. Authors such as Baldric of Bourgueil (or of Dol), Guibert of Nogent, Robert ("the Monk") of Reims, Lambert of Liege, the anonymous author of the *Hystoria de via* (also known as the Montecassino chronicler), and a series of others, in an effort to understand the role of these extraordinary events in the scope of providential history, immediately rewrote these accounts into new, theologically sophisticated narratives. The most popular of these—an account that survives in well over one hundred manuscript copies—was the *Historia Iherosolimitana* of Robert of Reims. In his prologue, Robert said that, next to Christ's salvation on the cross, the crusade was the most extraordinary event since Creation itself.[3] The monk at Saint-André may well have known one of these early Benedictine narratives, as they circulated among monastic houses in the area. But he doesn't mention them. What he did say was that the events of the First Crusades were recounted (*descripta*) in hymns and song being recited everywhere.

Hymns and songs. *Cantica* and *carmina*. Both words can apply equally to sacred and secular song. To hymns and canticles. To songs and verse. In Latin and the vernacular. The First Crusade was celebrated in both. Yet in the Latin West, the liturgical commemoration of the great victory of 15 July 1099 was never formally instituted or universal. Rather it bubbled up from local devotion and enthusiasm, fanned by stories of the crusader successes in Antioch and the capture of Jerusalem. These local liturgical commemorations of 15 July were another sign of the enthusiasm that greeted the news. As with the theologizing narratives, the liturgy was a mechanism by which to conceptualize the transcendental, theological, and teleological meaning of the success of the First Crusade, symbolized first and foremost by the capture of the Holy City. This chapter is about the hymns and sacred songs that celebrated the fall of Jerusalem in the West, about the liturgies that inscribed it into formal devotions, and the broadly liturgical context to which they pertained. The incorporation of the memory of the First Crusade into the liturgical sphere occurred on a variety of registers, from simple, annalistic entries in liturgical calendars, to the composition of sacred songs to be sung on 15 July, to the incorporation of a formal liturgical rite to be performed on the feast day. Their variety is evidence of the local responses to the news of the victory, of the impulse to praise God through prayer and song for the miracle of the success of the First Crusade, and to the different ways in which ecclesiastical communities embraced the memory of 1099

and Thought in Monastic Tradition: Essays in Honour of Benedicta Ward SLG, ed. Santha Bhattacharji, Dominic Mattos, and Rowan Williams (New York: 2014), 197–210.
   3. RR 4 (tr. 77).

and encoded it into their liturgical life. They shared less in the typological and providential narrative of scripture (viz. chapter 4) as they represented and sacralized the historic events of the crusade, and in particular the role of the Franks, in ways that echoed the early historiographical writing in the region. In turn, however, the sacredness of the liturgical form and the ability to participate in a liturgical discourse permitted these hymns and songs to consecrate the event that they celebrated. Because this chapter draws on both strictly liturgical, and paraliturgical material, this material also shows that the liturgical commemoration of 15 July was not an exclusively clerical discourse. In these liturgical and quasi-liturgical forms, we see the ways in which the different spheres—liturgy, narrative, local memory—could intertwine and mutually reinforce.

Liturgical Commemoration and Calendars

Unlike in the Kingdom of Jerusalem, where a feast in honor of the capture of Jerusalem was formally established by the ecclesiastical authorities and adopted throughout the patriarchate, liturgical celebration and commemoration in the West was always ad hoc, the product of local enthusiasm and local identity. It was thus never that widespread. Yet especially in France, the wellspring of crusade enthusiasm and recruitment, a number of ecclesiastical houses memorialized the victory of the First Crusade, and specifically the capture of Jerusalem, by including it in the liturgical calendars that were usually copied out at the beginnings of service books. These were historiographical entries much like an obit designed to remember the day of someone's death. Calendars listed the *captio, liberatio*, or just *Sepulcrum domini*, on the Ides of July (15 July), which was the day the Franks finally succeeded in taking Jerusalem, situating the culminating event of the First Crusade squarely within liturgical time and thus sacred history. (To my knowledge, the victory of Antioch was never inscribed into the calendar, suggesting that, despite the central importance of Antioch in the narratives received from the East, in the West it was the capture of Jerusalem alone that represented the sacral triumph of the First Crusade.)

As a genre, simple annalistic records were rare. Calendars, usually found at the beginning of liturgical books, listed the fixed dates in the life of Christ and the Virgin (Christmas, Assumption) along with the feasts of the saints that any given church celebrated during the liturgical year.[4] (Moveable feasts, such as Easter, or Ascension, had to be calculated.) The liturgical calendar

---

4. Ray Clemens and Timothy Graham, *Introduction to Manuscript Studies* (Ithaca: 2007), 192–202. Jacques Dubois and Jean-Loup LeMaitre, *Sources et méthodes de l'hagiographie médiévale* (Paris: 1993), 135–160.

was thus the record of sacred people and events in historic time. It was also the tool used for structuring the ritualized, iterative commemoration and praise of the sacred people and events that the church (whether local or universal) wanted remembered. One of the most minor commemorations a saint could be given in a calendar was called simply a *memoria*.[5] The listing of the capture of Jerusalem on 15 July in this context thus elevated the event by contextualizing it within the scope of sacred time as framed by salvific history.

The same type of mostly Benedictine houses that produced or preserved copies of the accounts of the First Crusade recorded the capture of Jerusalem in their liturgical calendars. The fifteenth of July was identified in volumes associated with the church at Saint Omer ("Hierusalem franci capiunt, virtute potenti, die xx viiii anno mxc, viiii"),[6] a Benedictine monastery near Beauvais ("Capitur Iherusalem"),[7] the Benedictine monasteries of Saint Martin de Tours ("Liberatio Ierusalem"),[8] Saint Martial of Limoges ("Liberacio sancte civitatis Hiersualem),[9] Saint Corneille at Compiègne ("Divisio apostolorum et captio Ierusalem"),[10] Saint Emilion near Bourdeaux ("liberatio sancti sepulchri"),[11] the Priory of Foisy, a dependent priory of Fontevraux near Troyes ("Iherusalem nostris cesserunt menia francis"),[12] Fontevrault itself ("Sepulchri domini"),[13] Saint Martin-au-Val in Chartres ("Anno Domini MCC minus anno, Iherusalem capitur iulii cum dantur idus"),[14] Notre Dame of Laon ("Divisio apostolorum et captio Iherusalem a

5. M. Cecilia Gaposchkin, *The Making of Saint Louis: Kingship, Sanctity, and Crusade in the Later Middle Ages* (Ithaca: 2008), 15; Clemens and Graham, *Introduction to Manuscript Studies*, 198.

6. The Liber Floridus. Ghent University Library 92, 29v. My thanks to Jay Rubenstein for this information. On Lambert, see Jay Rubenstein, "Lambert of Saint-Omer and the Apocalyptic First Crusade," in *Remembering the Crusades: Myth, Image, and Identity*, ed. Nicholas Paul and Suzanne Yeager (Baltimore: 2012), 69–95.

7. Paris Bibliothèque St. Genevieve 95, 4r. Leroquais, *Sacr.* 1:197 (see 3:286 for date correction). This use might have been related to the celebration of the Feast of the Holy Sepulcher on 15 July at the monastery of Villers-Saint-Sepulchre, founded in the Beauvaisis and patronized by crusaders; see discussion below.

8. Tours BM 193, 5r, apparently added in a different but contemporary hand. Fernand Cabrol and Henri Leclercq, *Dictionnaire d'archéologie chrétienne et de liturgie* (Paris: 1855–1937), v.15.2, col. 2671, where the manuscript is dated to 1175–1180.

9. Paris BNF Lat. 822, 5r, in calendar. With thanks to Amnon Linder.

10. Paris BNF Lat. 17318, 15r, dating to the first half of the twelfth century.

11. A. Chauliac, "Un martyrologue du XIIe siècle de l'Abbaye de Saint-Émilion," *Revue Mabillon* (1914): 14.

12. Paris BNF Lat. 9437, 4r. No proper prayers in the Sanctorale.

13. Alençon BM 131, 4r. Leroquais, *Brév.* 1:7.

14. Paris Arsenal 103. Leroquais, *Brév.* 2:307.

christianis"),[15] and later, at churches in Paris,[16] Bourges,[17] Orleans,[18] and Valenciennes.[19] The calendrical notations shared language with other literary forms circulating in these houses. An entry in the annals of the Benedictine Trinity Abbey in Vendôme, for the year 1099, recorded "Anno milleno Centeno minus uno / Hierusalem capitur Iulii cum dicitur idus / Anno milleno Centeno quo minus uno / Hierusalem Franci capiunt virtute potenti,"[20] and verses included in a copy of Gautier of Compiègne's (a monk at Tours) *Otia de Machomete* (written 1137–1155), recorded "Jerusalem nostris cesserunt menia Francis."[21] The liturgical notations were participating here in a broader language. The nomenclature is worth noting both in that there was no standard name for the commemoration, and also because the earliest examples tend to speak of the event more often as the "captio" than as the "liberatio." This is consistent with the early accounts and may have been engendered by communication directly from Jerusalem. In the letter that Daimbert of Pisa wrote to the pope and "all the Christian faithful" in September 1099, he explained that "Jerusalem was captured by the Christians in the year of the Lord 1099, on the Ides of July, the sixth ferial in the seventh indiction, in the third year of their expedition." It took some time for the event to come to be known as the "liberation of Jerusalem," a formulation that did not appear in the early narratives and seems to have developed around the idea of the feast itself. A few examples of calendrical notation survive from outside France. One from

15. Laon, BM 262 *bis*. Leroquais, *Brév.* 2:156.

16. Mazarine 1165 A (a printed volume from 1505, Paris usage, which lists 15 July in calendar as *Anno m.c. minus uno hierusalem capitur iulii cum dr. idus*); Paris Arsenal 623, D: *capta est iherusalem*. With thanks to Amnon Linder.

17. Paris BNF nal 195, Hours of Bourges; in calendar: "Liberatio Iherusalem," see Victor Leroquais, *Les livres d'heures manuscrits de la Bibliothèque nationale* (Paris: 1927), 2:237; London BL Add. 39761, French, probably following the use of Bourges, see E. S. Dewick, "On a MS. Book of Hours Written in France for the Use of a Scottish Lady," *Transactions of the St. Paul's Ecclesiological Society*, n.s. 7 (1915): 112.

18. Paris BNF Lat. 14827, Hours of Orleans, in Calendar "Sepulchri sancti—Divisio apostolorum." Leroquais, *Les Livres d'heures*, 2:161.

19. Eugese Misset and W. H. I. Weale, *Analecta Liturgica*, 2 vols., Thesauris Hymnologicis (Lille: 1888–1892), 3:260.

20. Rose Graham, "The Annals of the Monastery of the Holy Trinity at Vendôme," *English Historical Review* 13 (1898): 696.

21. Paris BNF Lat. 11332, 28r. Hans Pruz, "Über des Gautier von Compiègne 'Otia de Machomete': Ein Beitrag zur Geschichte der Mohammedfabeln im Mittelalter und zur Kulturgeschichte der Kreuzzüge," *Sitzungsberichte der philosophische-philologischen und der historischen Klasse der K.B. Akademie der Wissenschaften zu München* (1904), 115. R. B. C. Huygens, "Otia de Machomete: Gedicht von Walter von Compiègne," *Sacris Erudiri* 8 (1956): 289.

Naples; one from a Benedictine abbey in Kempten.[22] I know of none in England. The great majority are found in France, in the heartland of both recruitment and of the celebratory memorialization that occurred in the first decades of the twelfth century. As with the evidence of the calendars, most of the historiography engendered by 1099 came from "the northern French speaking world,"[23] largely from Benedictine monastic centers. It turns out, these are also the same centers in which these narratives were circulated, copied, and preserved.

It is possible that in certain cases inclusion in the liturgical calendar indicated a celebration of a more elaborate liturgical ritual. At Laon for instance, a late twelfth-century breviary lists for 15 July *Divisio apostolorum et captio Iherusalem a christianis* in the calendar, although the breviary itself includes no indication of proper liturgical items in the Sanctorale for the Jerusalem feast.[24] But we know from two entirely different manuscripts that a feast on 15 July was celebrated well into the thirteenth century.[25] Likewise, an entry in a calendar at Tours for the *Liberatio Jerusalem* on 15 July in one manuscript was probably associated with the office for the Holy Sepulcher adopted at the cathedral in another.[26] Calendrical commemorations of the fall of Jerusalem in manuscripts from Saint Martial should probably be associated with liturgical celebrations found elsewhere in their repertory (on which, see below). In Nevers, a chapter book from the twelfth century included proper readings for the feast *"in liberacione civitatis ierusalem* in both the martyrology and in the capitulary."[27] The Gospel reading for the mass was Matthew 21:10, the same text used at the Holy Sepulcher, suggesting otherwise lost lines of transmission from the Latin East. Finally, in the calendar of a thirteenth-century breviary from Soissons, the feast of the *Divisio Apostolorum* was joined with the memorial of the capture of Jerusalem: *Divisio apostolorum. Ierusalem capta est a*

---

22. Naples, Cod. 452 (VIII.C.15), of Franciscan origin, end of 13th c, 71r–78r, *Inc. Idibus Iulii. Eodem die dedicatio ecclesie S. Sepulcri* (From Linder, personal communication 1.15.14, with my thanks to him) Zürich Zentralbibliothek, Rhenaugiensis 83, 6v, "Eo die hierusalem destructae." Arno Borst, *Der karolingische Reichskalender und seine Überlieferung bis ins 12. Jahrhundert*, 3 vols., MGH Libri Memoriales (Hannover: 1:231–232 and 2:1093 and 95, n. 18. For an eastern European example, see Ant. Kubiek, "Opavsky zaltar," *Casopis Matice moravské* 23 (1899): 309–325, at 315. The manuscript dates to ca. 1365.

23. Marcus Bull, "Robert the Monk and his Source(s)," in *Writing the Early Crusades: Text, Transmission, and Memory*, ed. Marcus Bull and Damien Kempf (Woodbridge, Suffolk: 2014), 128.

24. Laon, BM 262 *bis*.

25. Laon BM 263, 124r; Laon BM 244, 6r.

26. Tours BM 193, 5r; Loches BM 5, 383v–390.

27. Vat Lat. Reg 249, 108v, 160v.

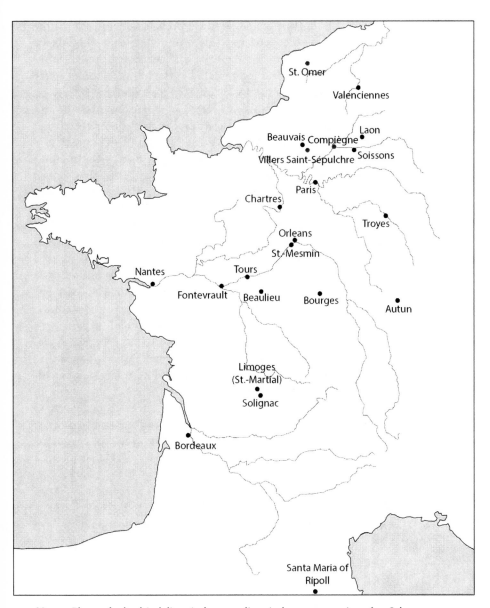

Map 1. Places of calendrical, liturgical, or paraliturgical commemoration of 15 July

Christianis.[28] Another breviary from Soissons includes a special ceremonial honoring the Holy Sepulcher in its rite for the Divisio apostolorum.[29]

The capture of Jerusalem on 15 July coincided with the existing Divisio feast commemorating the institution of the evangelizing mission of the twelve apostles and their dispersal into the world to preach the gospel. Contemporary authors certainly noticed this and drew conclusions. Daimbert's September letter to the West explained that the Franks' humble entry into Jerusalem on 15 July (humbly following the procession of 8 July) reversed the day on which the "primitive Church was expelled from Jerusalem."[30] Albert of Aachen explained that Jerusalem was "restored to her sons in great victory, on the solemn day of the division of the apostles."[31] Contemporaries saw the Frankish victory as the just revenge on the Jews for the expulsion of the evangelists from the Holy City. The Divisio feast was not widespread in the West before the First Crusade but gained ground in the high and later Middle Ages. Guy Philippart has even argued that the previously rare feast of the Divisio apostolorum was introduced to the West on the heels of the Frankish victory in 1099, although the feast of the Divisio was in the end celebrated far more frequently than that of the Liberatio, widely adopted and surviving into the later Middle Ages.[32] But in traditions that did associate the two events, like at Laon, Soissons, and Orleans, the association was one more way in which capture of the city was tied to salvific history through layers of historical typology fostered by liturgy.

Other ecclesiastical houses—mostly, but not only, monasteries—celebrated more formal rites. Two Benedictine monasteries—Beaulieu lès Loches and Villers Saint-Sépulcre—which both possessed relics of the Holy Sepulcher before 1099, celebrated, sometime after 1099, a feast on 15 July in honor of the Holy Sepulcher. Beaulieu was founded just outside Tours, in the heartland of crusading France, in the first decade of the eleventh century by Fulk III Nerra (d. 1040), the Count of Anjou.[33] Upon returning from one of his four (!) pilgrimages to the Holy Land, he gave a relic (which he

---

28. BNF Lat. 1259, 16r.

29. Paris Bibliothèque de l'Arsenal 102, 315r.

30. *Epistulae* no. XVIII (lat. 171, tr. *Letters* 35). EA *Hier.* 23; *Chr.* 152.

31. AA vi.28 (438–439). See also RA 151 (tr. 128).

32. Guy Philippart, "Le partage du monde entre les apotres. Les aléas d'une légende paléochrétienne dans la tradition occidentale," *Slovo: Časopis Staroslavenskog instituta* 60 (2010): 620–621.

33. Louis Halphen and Renée Poupardin, eds., *Chroniques des comtes d'Anjou et des seigneurs d'Amboise* (Paris: 1913), 50–51; Alexandre de Salies, *Histoire de Foulques-Nerra, comte d'Anjou d'après les chartes contemporaines et les anciennes chroniques—suivie de l'office du Saint-Sépulchre de l'abbaye de Beaulieu dont les leçons forment une chronique inédite* (Paris: 1874), 114–119; Bernard S. Bachrach, "The Pilgrimages of Fulk Nerra, Count of the Angevins," in *Religion, Culture and Society in the Early Middle Ages: Studies in Honour of R.E. Sullivan*, ed. Thoms F. X Noble and John J. Contreni (Kalamazoo, MI: 1987), 205–217.

had torn from the tomb with his teeth) to the monastery.[34] At Villers, just southeast of Beauvais, a Benedictine monastery was founded in 1060 in honor of a relic of the Holy Sepulcher that was brought back by a local knight (named Lancelin) from the Holy Land, and was subsequently named "Villers Saint-Sépulcre."[35] It is impossible to know whether these monastic houses celebrated a feast in honor of the relic before the First Crusade and then moved that celebration to 15 July after the news of the capture made its way back to France, or whether it was the news itself that prompted creation of a feast. Our evidence for the liturgical celebration of the relics on 15 July at both foundations postdates the First Crusade—in the case of Beaulieu from a fifteenth-century manuscript that earlier historians have assumed represents an office composed in either the eleventh or the twelfth century,[36] and for Villers a seventeenth-century manuscript that copied the liturgical office from what its nineteenth-century historian presumed was a thirteenth-century manuscript.[37] Neither mentions the crusade specifically or frames the office in terms of the narrative events of 1096 or 1097. The Villers office drew its chant from existing liturgies honoring the cycle of Christ's life (Advent, Easter), although it added some new hymns that praised the Sepulcher specifically.[38] At Beaulieu, the monks celebrated a proper office that also centered on the Passion and Resurrection, those events of Christ's life centered on the Holy Sepulcher. The abbey's eighteenth-century historian, Dom Martial Galand, supposed that some sort of feast had been originally celebrated on Easter Sunday, but that after 1099 the celebration was moved to 15 July to commemorate the victory. There is actually no evidence for this. The other possibility, of course, is that the relic was only given an exalted celebration once the news of the victory reached west. The liturgy itself appears to have been composed sometime in the twelfth century, probably, according to Hardion, around

---

34. Bachrach, "The Pilgrimages of Fulk Nerra," 205–217.

35. M. Renet, "Prieuré de Villers Saint-Sépulcre," *Mémoires de la Société académique d'archéologie, sciences et arts du département de l'Oise* 10 (1877): 496–504.

36. Salies, *Histoire de Foulques-Nerra*: 496. The citation here is imprecise. Salies refers to D. Galand throughout his book as the "moine de l'abbaye de Beaulieu," and of the office, Salies wrote "Le moine de Beaulieu nous dit, en effet, que la fête du Saint-Sépulcre fut d'abord célébrée dans l'abbaye 'avec celle de la résurrection de N. Saveur' mais qu'elle fut transportée au 15 juillet, 'à cause que l'armée chrétienne avait pris, ce jour-là, de l'an 1099, sur les infidèles, toute la Terre-Sainte, sous le commandement de Godefroy de Bouillon.'" Salies cites throughout an unedited manuscript of Galand's written in 1748 entitled *Mémoires pour servir à l'histoire de l'abbaye de la Très-Sainte-Trinité de Beaulieu Les Loches*. See Salies, xlvi. This manuscript is now Paris BNF naf 6652.

37. Renet, "Prieuré de Villers Saint-Sépulcre," 552–559. I have not been able to locate even the seventeenth-century manuscript.

38. Renet, "Prieuré de Villers Saint-Sépulcre," 553–554, and see at 554.

1130.[39] This date is significant since Fulk V of Anjou, descendant of Fulk Nerra, actually became king of Jerusalem in 1131, and because the Angevins counts had a tradition of promoting crusading memory in the ecclesiastical houses of their county.[40] These ties offer the context for upgrading the relic and promoting its genealogy and its local association with the Holy Land and the Frankish victory of 1099. As would the fact that the 15 July feast for the Holy Sepulcher was then adopted throughout the Limousin, at Tours,[41] Nantes,[42] and probably Saint Mesmin (a monastery near Orleans).[43] This certainly suggests a dedicated and coordinated promotion of the memory of the First Crusade, and the region's involvement in its glory, around the time that Fulk became Jerusalem's king. Either way, the July 15 feast demonstrates a repositioning of the relic in terms of the memory of the First Crusade. It tied the Holy Land relic to the victorious memory of the First Crusade, and in turn the memory of the First Crusade to the victory of Christ's resurrection at the Holy Sepulcher.

Other houses celebrated 15 July more specifically in terms of the historical events of 1099. This put the focus squarely on the success of the earthly events of the crusade, rather than the Christic event of the Resurrection. The clearest examples are found at Laon, Autun, and Bourges. A missal used by the Hospitaller priory of Autun preserves a mass for the feast of the liberation of Jerusalem (*In festo deliberacionis Iherusalem*) that was clearly related to (but not identical to) the liberation liturgy of the Holy Sepulcher.[44] In theory the Hospitallers, no matter where they were located,

39. Salies, *Histoire de Foulques-Nerra*: 487–488; Jean Hardion and L. Bosseboeuf, *L'abbaye de Beaulieu-lès-Loches et quelques monuments de sa dépendance* (Tours: 1904), 124–138; Halphen and Poupardin, *Chroniques des comtes d'Anjou et des seigneurs d'Amboise*, xi. Alexandre de Salies believed the surviving office dated to shortly after 1111, the date of a miracle that the lections describe as recent (*nuper*). But because the lections were taken from an earlier chronicle, as the lections themselves admit, Louis Halphen challenged this conclusion, since the confection of the liturgy could have been many years later. Jean Hardion split the difference, suggesting the office dated to after 1099, but underwent changes in the course of the twelfth century, probably around the 1130s. If a feast *was* originally celebrated on Easter Sunday, as Galand proposed, then it is unlikely that the proper liturgy was used, since it would have competed with the most important holy day of the year; and in any event, the early eleventh century would have been extremely early for a rhymed, versified office of this sort.

40. Nicholas Paul, *To Follow in Their Footsteps: The Crusades and Family Memory in the High Middle Ages* (Ithaca, NY: 2012), 215–219.

41. Loches BM 5, 383v–390; Tours BM 193, 5r.

42. Nantes BM 26, 225, "Festum Sancti Sepulchri Domini," for which see Leroquais *Brév.* 2:282. Nantes BM 25, a fifteenth-century breviary in which the calendar reads "S. Sepulcri, IX lect." Leroquais, *Brév.* 2:279.

43. Orleans BM 130. 'S Sepulchri.' Leroquais *Brév.* 2:295–296. Loches, BM 5, 383v–390. Note that Orleans, Tours, and Nantes all fell within the same ecclesiastical province. DuCange lists a "Festum S. Sepulcri" at Saint Mesmin in a cartulary for the year 1179; Charles Du Fresne DuCange, *Glossarium ad scriptores mediae et infimae Latinitatis*, 10 vols. (Paris: 1883–1887), 3:460b.

44. Paris BNF nal 1689, 231–231v.

were supposed to follow the rite of the Holy Sepulcher, but this does not seem to have been the case of the Liberatio service. The only other evidence we have for Hospitaller celebration of 15 July outside of Jerusalem are instructions in a Hospitaller constitution from southern France,[45] and a copy of the rite used in Jerusalem in a fourteenth-century Hospitaller breviary now in Germany.[46] That said, at Autun at least, the celebration naturally valorized Hospitaller ties to the Holy Land and their institutional mission to protect and defend the Holy Land, and thus their very identity.

An affinity with the Holy Sepulcher liturgy is also a characteristic of the feast of the liberatio that was celebrated in the diocese of Bourges, in the crusading heartland. Here, we have evidence that a full office "In Liberatione Ierusalem" was celebrated in the diocese and at the cathedral through the fifteenth century.[47] It is worth noting here that the two instances of celebration in the West that show demonstrable lines of transmission from the Holy Sepulcher's rite (Autun and Bourges) called the feast the "*liberation* of Jerusalem." At Bourges, the rite simply wedded the Easter Resurrection Office with the hymn "Urbs beata," which, from the Office of the Dedication of a Church, was also used for 15 July at the Holy Sepulcher. The hymn, we saw, celebrated the Church itself as an image of and gateway to the heavenly Jerusalem.[48] As in Jerusalem, "Urbs beata" affirmed the sacrality of the earthly city and the relationship of its possession to the heavenly city. In turn, the use at Bourges of the Easter liturgy for 15 July, to celebrate the liberation of the Holy City, modeled the military triumph of the Franks in 1099 in terms of the victory of Christ's Resurrection, as a salvific act of providential scale. It also echoes the earliest phase of liturgical victory at the Holy Sepulcher itself. Centered, obviously, on the Holy Sepulcher as the site of Christ's Resurrection, the use of the Easter liturgy affirmed the sacrality of the city and posited the liberation as a sacred act, a historic punctuation in the divine plan, of which the Resurrection was the anchor. It further equated the liberation with Easter itself, emphasizing the notion of salvific victory following on sacrifice, another early theme in the complex ideas animating crusading spirituality.

Notre Dame of Laon, the cathedral, also celebrated 15 July as the feast *De captione Ierusalem*. The evidence of the liturgy and of its performance at Laon is scattered among volumes, suggesting that the feast was adopted and

---

45. Santos García Larragueta, "Libro de los Estatutos Antiguos de la Orden de San Juan," *Príncipe de Viana* 226 (2002): 385.

46. Vienna ÖNB cod. 1928, 78v–79r.

47. Paris BNF Lat. 1255, 296r–v; Chateauroux BM 3, 305v–306r; Bourges BM 23, 329v–330r. The office is also attested at Le Bouveret, the Monastery of St.-Benoît de Port-Valais, 1, 341va (after 1428), see Josef Leisibach and François Huot, *Die liturgischen Handschriften des Kantons Wallis (ohne Kapitelsarchiv Sitten)*, Spicilegium Friburgense 18; Iter Helveticum 4 (Freiburg: 1984), 135. For books of hours, see Paris BNF nal. 195 and London BL 39761.

48. AH 51:110–112, no. 102.

special texts were appropriated or composed, but that, for whatever reason, it was never permanently inscribed into the rite. A missal includes the collect "Omnipotens deus qui virtute" (discussed below) that was written in Jerusalem and celebrated at the Holy Sepulcher by at least ca. 1130.[49] The most interesting text, the new sequence *Exultent agmina* is actually preserved in a kind of liturgical miscellany that was mostly a sequentiary but also included liturgical plays and other paraliturgical materials.[50] This is a theme that we will pick up below, as much of the evidence for the local production of liturgical and quasi-liturgical texts in honor of the capture of Jerusalem survives in nontraditional formats, not in sacramentaries, sequentiaries, or hymnals, but rather in various forms of liturgical and paraliturgical catchalls, suggesting moments of spontaneous composition and performance that failed to be codified. This, in any event, seems to be the case for Laon. By the thirteenth century, the evidence of breviaries and missals from Laon bear no indication that the feast was being celebrated. The sequence survives in only one copy. It praised rejoicing for Jerusalem's feast, extolled that Jerusalem was freed from subjugation to the Saracens, and praised the courageous deeds of the Franks by whom she was returned to the Christians.[51]

Exultent agmina	Let the entire crowd
fidelium cuncta	of the faithful rejoice,
laudes Deo canentia	singing praises to God.
Cuius sunt opera	Whose works
Semper mirificia[52]	are always wondrous,
Per ampla mundi spatia	through the vast expanse of the world.
Voce celsa,	With exalted voice,
mente simul defecata,	likewise with weary mind,
recolamus gaudia,	let us remember the joys,
que nobis anni orbita	which the most celebrated cycle of the year,
reducit celeberrima	brings back to us.
Cum civitas	Since the glorious
Jerusalem gloriosa	city of Jerusalem
effecta est libera	was made free,
que Sarracenis fuerat	which had for a long time
tamdiu tributaria	been subject to the Saracens.
Hinc Francorum	Henceforth let us sing
pangamus gesta fortia,	of the brave deeds of the Franks,

---

49. Collect: Laon BM 244, 5v–6.
50. Laon BM 263.
51. Cited hereafter as "Exultent agmina." AH 10:59–60, no. 73, from Laon 263, 124r. Discussed in Goswin Spreckelmeyer, *Das Kreuzzugslied des lateinischen Mittelalters*, Münstersche Mittelalter-Schriften. Bd. 21 (Munich: 1974), 214–219 (KL 4).
52. AH 10, no. 73, reads magnifica.

quorum probitate	by whose courage
sic est liberate	she was liberated,
sub Domini potentia.	underneath the power of the Lord.
Letetur ergo	Let [Jerusalem] rejoice,
Christianis reddita,	having been returned to the Christians,
quibus congaudet,	for whom she rejoices,
residens sede sua	sitting in her seat,
iam imperat ut domina.	now ruling as Queen.
Cui tota Francia	To whom all France,
iam flectit genua	now bows down on bent knee,
nec non Italia	and Italy as well.
Iamiamque Graecia	And now Greece,
fert ei munera	offers tributes,
nec non Arabia.	and also Arabia.
Mesopotamia,	Mesopotamia,
Eegyptus, Affrica	Egypt, Africa,
regnaque cetera	and the other kingdoms,
transeunt sub ea.	cross under her
Damascus, Ascalon,	Damascus, Ascalon,
Iope cum Acaron,	Joppa and Akkon,
Tirus atque Sidon	Tyre and Sidon,
mittunt ei dona.	send gifts to her.
Cuius agentes festa	Celebrating her feast,
Jerusalem in superna	let us enjoy Jerusalem
perfruamur gloria.	in her heavenly glory.

The use of the term *Sarracenis*, rather than *gentes* or *nationes*, is atypical of most of the early propaganda.[53] Yet it is not atypical of these hymns. The focus on earthly events, the geography of the Levant, and above all the praise of the deeds of the Franks in freeing "the glorious city of Jerusalem" from subjugation to the Saracens suggest a link to the narrative accounts of the First Crusade that were circulating in northern France by at latest 1110. One of the principle monastic historians of the First Crusade, Guibert of Nogent, lived just a few miles away from the cathedral and was intimately involved in its politics in precisely these years. He too composed a hymnlike paean to the capture of Jerusalem, in which he foretells a future where nations recognize Jerusalem's right to reign.[54]

---

53. Nicholas Morton, "Encountering the Turks: The First Crusaders Foreknowledge of their Enemy, Some Preliminary Findings," in *Crusading and Warfare in the Middle Ages: Realities and Representations. Essays in Honour of John France*, ed. Simon John and Nicholas Morton (Farnham, UK: 2014), 47–68.

54. GN vii.14 (lat. 289–290, tr. 135).

This dynamism, this individual, spontaneous liturgical response to historical events, is exemplified by the evolving practice of the Jerusalem commemoration. In the Laon missal, a prayer copied on the facing folio in a thirteenth-century hand shows how the performance of these celebrations could be adapted as historical events overtook things. One hundred and fifty years later, in the middle of Louis IX's first crusade (1248–1254)—probably in 1249 or early 1250, upon learning that their king, Louis IX, had successfully captured the city of Damietta in the early stages of his first crusade, but before they learned of the catastrophe of the Battle of Mansurah (April 5) and Louis's own capture (May 5)—someone at the cathedral took out the old missal that contained the standard collect for the 15 July mass, and adapted the collect to thank God for the capture of the city of Damietta. The original for the capture of Jerusalem, found in a twelfth century hand in the cathedral's missal, was:

Omnipotens deus qui virtute tua mirabili **iherusalem** civitatem tuam de manu paganorum, **eruisti**, et christinais reddisti, adesto quesumus nobis propicius, et concede ut qui hanc **sollempnitatem annua** devotione recolimus, ad superne **iherusalem** gaudia, pervenire mereamur. Per.[55]	Almighty God, who by Your wondrous power **snatched** Your city **Jerusalem** from the hands of pagans, and returned it to the Christians, be favorable, we beseech You, and grant that we who remember this **solemnity** in **annual** devotion should merit to arrive at the joy of the heavenly **Jerusalem**.

As said, this was the collect for the mass for the 15 July feast used in Jerusalem.[56] In a later, mid-thirteenth-century hand, copied on an empty folio facing the collect, was a new prayer, an adaptation of the standard *Omnipotens sempiterne*:

Omnipotens **sempiterne** deus qui virtute tua mirabili **damietam** civitatem **fortissimam ad instanciam christinissimi regis nostri ludovici** de manu paganorum **liberasti** et christianis **secondo** reddidisti, adesto quesumus nobis propitius & concede, ut qui hanc **liberationem pia** devotione recolimus, ad superne **felicitatis** gaudia pervenire mereamur. Per."[57]	Almighty, everlasting God, who by Your wondrous power **liberated the very strong city of Damietta through the effort of our most Christian king Louis** from the hands of pagans and then returned it **a second time** to the Christians, we beseech You, to look kindly on us and grant to us that we, who gained this **liberation** from **pious** devotion, might merit to arrive at the joy of eternal happiness.

55. Laon BM 244, 6r.
56. Rome Angelica 477, 159.
57. Laon BM 244, 5v.

Whether the canons at Laon anticipated establishing a new feast on the model of the 15 July feast to honor the capture of Damietta, or if they were simply composing a votive prayer in thanksgiving for the Damietta capture based on the collect for 15 July is not clear from the evidence. What is clear, despite the fact that no rubric introduces the prayer, is its specific devotional function. One way or another, the text demonstrates the extent to which these forms of liturgical invocation were a dynamic part of the ongoing conversation with God about the state of the Holy Land, the crusades, and the Christian people's role in providence.

Liturgy and Sacred Song

The example of the liturgy at Laon, both its thematic kinship to the heroic narrative traditions circulating in northern France and in the provisional and ad hoc way in which the evidence is now extant, is characteristic of another strain of liturgical devotion and memorialization in the West. These are three hymns exhorting crusade and commemorating the fall of Jerusalem that do not appear to ever have been formally integrated into the liturgy, but all assumed the context of liturgical commemoration of 15 July.[58] *Ierusalem mirabilis* and *Nomen a solemnibus* were both preserved in the chant repertory of the Abbey Church of Saint Martial, the venerable Benedictine monastery in the Limoges, in the heartland of crusading France. *Ierusalem letare* is preserved in materials from the Benedictine monastery of Santa Maria of Ripoll, the Catalan foundation nestled at the foot of the Pyrenees with close ties to the counts of Aragon and heavily involved in preserving the memory of the First Crusade. The texts themselves are preserved in various collections of liturgical and musical miscellany, suggesting a performance that was not subsequently codified. In the past, these have been categorized and discussed as songs (*Kreuzzugslied*),[59] and they are in one sense related to the vernacular genre of crusade songs that also reflected crusading enthusiasm and devotion.[60] But they belong, like the Laon sequence (which has in

58. For the structural and metrical characteristics of hymns, see Joseph Szövérffy, *Latin Hymns*, Typologie des sources su Moyen Age occidental, 55 (Turnhout: 1989); Susan Boynton, "Hymn, Monophonic Latin," *Grove Music Online. Oxford Music Online*, http://www.oxford musiconline.com/subscriber/article/grove/music/13648.

59. Goswin Spreckelmeyer, *Das Kreuzzugslied des lateinischen Mittelalters*; Goswin Spreckelmeyer, *Mittellateinische Kreuzzugslieder: Texte und Melodien*, Göppinger Arbeiten zur Germanistik 216 (Göppinger 1987); Anton Schmuck, "Mittellateinische Kreuzlieder: Poetische Werbung zum Kreuzzug" (1954). Many of the texts are also discussed in Joseph Szövérffy, *Secular Latin Lyrics and Minor Poetic Forms of the Middle Ages: A Historical Survey and Literary Repertory from the Tenth to the Late Fifteenth Century*, 3 vols. (Concord, NH: 1992).

60. The classic study is Jospeh Bédier and Pierre Aubry, *Les chansons de croisade, avec leurs mélodies* (1909; reprint Geneva: 1974).

fact been grouped with these in catalogues of Kreuzzugslied), to the liturgical realm, either as part of liturgical celebrations, as a paraliturgical text used in processions or special thanksgiving services, or as extraliturgical commemorations. Written in Latin, they were sacred in tone and content, either explicitly liturgical, or shading into the category of monophonic prayer known now as *cantiones*, that is, sacred songs that drew on the themes and formal musical and metrical characteristics of liturgy, but were performed, or "prayed," outside of the strict ritual categories of the mass and office.[61] They all took standard liturgical forms (in that they were strophic, and could include a refrain).[62] Cantiones could be derived from hymns, attesting to an adaption of a purely liturgical form to a paraliturgical but still sacred, clerical, and devotional context. A hymn used in a procession outside the church, for instance, was paraliturgical in the sense that it was not formally associated with the celebration of the mass or office but participated in the larger liturgical context of sacral celebration. It can be difficult to pin down the use of such compositions or the dividing line between "liturgical" and merely "sacred." Yet even if or when not directly liturgical, the surviving examples show that their music and their formal rhyme schemes borrowed sacred legitimacy from liturgical practice. They also may have had a wider audience than the texts reserved for the mass. And they may have been intended to reach beyond the confines of the church. They echo, in great measure, not the sublime language of liturgical chant, but a gritty, triumphant, historicized interpretation of the capture of Jerusalem that exulted in the Frankish victory. In this sense, they were akin in spirit to the *Manu plaudant* sequence composed in Jerusalem after 1099. They can thus be understood in relationship to the monastic narratives written in the same flush of exultant jubilation at the victory of 1099.

The institutional and codicological contexts for the production and performance of these hymns indicate the local and monastic context for production. We have already seen that the capture was recorded in at least two liturgical calendars associated with Saint Martial.[63] Saint Martial was one of the monastic centers and pilgrimage sites at the center of the devotional network that enveloped men who went on the First Crusade. The monastery was an active literary center. Her library preserved copies of the *Gesta*

---

61. On the form of the *cantio*, see usefully John Caldwell, "Cantio," in *Grove Music Online. Oxford Music Online,* and the bibliography listed there.

62. I make the argument for their liturgical form at greater length in an earlier form of this chapter, published as M. Cecilia Gaposchkin, "The Echoes of Victory: Liturgical and Para-liturgical Commemorations of the Capture of Jerusalem in the West," *Journal of Medieval History* 40 (2014): 237–259.

63. BNF Lat. 822. Calendar, 15 July "*Liberacio sancte civitatis Hierusalem,*" Amnon Linder discovered this reference. BNF Lat. 1341, 3v, an Ordinary from Saint Martial, includes *Festivitas Iherusalem quando capta fuit a christianis.*

Francorum and Raymond of Aguilers, and the monks were clearly interested in the historiographical reception of the First Crusade.[64] The abbey was also a center of and repository for liturgical and musical innovations of the eleventh and twelfth centuries, and her library comprised a treasure of manuscripts that preserved the creative liturgical culture that thrived at this time in the Limousin.[65] Among its books are preserved two cantica that participated in the discourse of these narratives. The first, *Ierusalem mirabilis*, survives in BNF Lat. 1139.[66] In the manuscript, the text is introduced by the liturgical rubric *versus*, a term that often designated a processional hymn. The second text, *Nomen a solemnibus*, was also preserved in two manuscripts of the Saint-Martial repertory (BNF Lat. mss 3549 and 3719) but may have been written at the nearby monastery of Solignac.[67] It is a strange text, with an odd opening stanza (that no one has been able to really figure out), but it was clearly intended for recitation on the feast day, since the refrain made its mention.

The most extraordinary of the surviving examples is *Hierusalem letare*, the long hymn preserved in a manuscript (Paris BNF Lat. 5132) associated with Ripoll.[68] John France proposed that it was "written in the scriptorium at Ripoll for the use of the monks in the celebration of the

---

64. Jean-Loup LeMaître, "Le combat pour dieu et les croisades dans les notes de Bernard Itier, moine de St. Martial de Limoges (1163–115)," in *"Militia Christi" e crociata nei secoli XI-XIII; atti della undecima Settimana internazionale di studio: Mendola, 28 agosto–1 settembre 1989* (Milan:1992), 733.

65. Janet Knapp, "Conductus," *Grove Music Online. Oxford Music Online*, http://www.oxfordmusiconline.com/subscriber/article/grove/music/06268. See subsection "Aquitaine and Related Areas." On Bernard Itier, see LeMaître, "Let combat pour Dieu," 730n.2.

66. BNF Lat. 1139, 50r. For text see: AH 45b:78, no 96. For discussion see Spreckelmeyer, *Kreuzzugslied*, 85–91 (KL2). Szövérffy, *Secular Latin Lyrics*. On liturgical qualities, see Nicole Sevestre, "Jérusalem Mirabilis," in *Jerusalem, Rome, Constantinople: L'image et le mythe de la ville au Moyen Age: Colloque du Département d'Etudes Médiévales de l'université de Paris-Sorbonne (Paris IV)* (Paris: 1987), 4–7.

67. Paris BNF Lat. 3549, 164r–164v. Paris BNF Lat. 3719, 41r–42r. For text of *Nomen a solemnibus*, see AH 21:163–164, no. 233. Discussion in Spreckelmeyer, *Kreuzzugslied*, 184–192 (KL5). Spreckelmeyer, *Mittellateinische Kreuzzugslieder*, 67–68; Szövérffy, *Secular Latin Lyrics*, 1:372.

68. Cited hereafter as *Hierusalem letare*. Found in Paris BNF Lat. 5132, 21r–v. Published in AH 45b:76–77, no. 95, France, "Text of the Account of the Capture of Jerusalem," 654–657. Discussed in Spreckelmeyer, *Kreuzzugslied*, 204–219 (KL 3); and Szövérffy, *Secular Latin Lyrics*, 1:370. For the suggestion that it may or may not have been in use at Ripoll, see Szövérffy, *Secular Latin Lyrics*, 3:76. For contents see further Jay Rubenstein, "Putting History to Use: Three Crusade Chronicles in Context," *Viator* 35 (2004): 131–168; Paul, *To Follow in Their Footsteps*, 304–307. Nicholas Paul, "The Fruits of Penitence and the Laurel of the Cross: the Poetics of Crusade and Conquest in the Memorials of Santa Maria de Ripoll," in *A Storm Against the Infidel: Crusading in the Iberian Peninsula and in the Baltic Region in the Central Middle Ages*, ed. Torben K. Nielsen and Iben Fonnesberg-Schmidt, *Outremer- Studies in the Crusades and the Latin East* (Turnhout: 2016), 245–273.

Feast of the Liberation of Jerusalem."[69] As with the liturgy surviving at the back of BL Add. 8927 (discussed in the last chapter and which, in a sense, should be added to the evidence of this list, since it may have been intended for performance in the West), it survives not in a liturgical volume but rather a memorial compendia that included, among other things, a fragment of the account of Raymond of Aguilers, a separate account of the taking of Jerusalem that speaks of it clearly as a "liberatio," and a series of sermons designed to accompany a liturgical feast. This suggests the various ways in which liturgy was memorializing, since its inscription in this nonliturgical volume was clearly intended to be part of a variety of crusade related memorabilia. France proposed that the narrative account of the liberation, which begins with Raymond of Aguilers and then veers off into a different, otherwise unknown account of the siege and capture, was written to be used as lections for the office. It is possible, given the context, but there is no indication in the manuscript itself that it was divided up for liturgical recitation, and the transition from Raymond's account in the transcription is seamless. But what is clear is that the entire program—the account of the siege, the sermon, and the hymn itself were part of an integrated program tagged to liturgical celebration. The text-possible-lections spoke of "Liberatio"—a title developing for the feast but not a formulation used in the narrative accounts informed by eyewitness and participants, and thus was probably a term that circulated with the idea of the liturgy itself. There is no doubt, though, that the context for all the texts was the liturgical feast of 15 July. For one, the hymn draws on the liturgical language of Letare Sunday. And more important, it too speaks specifically of the new feast.[70]

The sermon offers important clues about its intended audience.[71] The sermon, or "exhortation," is copied in the manuscript between the narrative account and the hymn, employs the phrase *Letare Iherusalem*, and like the hymn itself, refers to "this" feast day. It is addressed to soldiers—indeed, to the "best of soldiers" (*militum flores*)—and praises the works of the soldiers who participated in the First Crusade and who took Jerusalem. It

69. John France, "An Unknown Account of the Capture of Jerusalem," *English Historical Review* 87, no. 345 (1972): 783.

70. "Hierusalem letare," stanza 22: *Letare novis festis, Iherusalem exulta*. The plural is dictated by the rhyme scheme.

71. The sermon is transcribed France, "Text of the Account of the Capture of Jerusalem," 651–654; and in Amnon Linder, "A New Day, New Joy: The Liberation of Jerusalem on 15 July 1099," in *L'idea di Gerusalemme nella spiritualità cristiana del Medioevo: atti del Convegno internazionale in collaborazione con l'Instituto della Görres-Gesellschaft di Gerusalemme: Gerusalemme, Notre Dame of Jerusalem Center, 31 agosto—6 settembre 1999* (Vatican: 2003), 58–63. I follow France's edition below.

speaks of those who went to wage war in far-off lands and endured such a difficult pilgrimage.[72] It is full of anti-Jewish invective designed to highlight the errors of nonbelief, exemplifying the dangerous relationship between Holy Land crusade and anti-Jewish polemic. The sermon asks the Jews whether they really carry a vain hope of recuperating the city that was destroyed on their account, a reference to Titus and Vespasian's siege of Jerusalem and the destruction of the Temple in AD 70. And it asks whether it doesn't make sense for Jerusalem to be under the dominion of the "true Israelites" (that is, the Franks) rather than "foreigners" (i.e., Muslims).[73] And then the sermon turns to the soldiers "who avenged Your King who had suffered on Your account." In a fine echo of the vivid imagery of the early chronicles, the sermon says that indeed, the King could have produced "twelve legions of angels to avenge Himself" but did not wish to do so, in order, anticipating Bernard of Clairvaux, to give crusaders the fruits of penance.[74] Crusade is a spiritual opportunity. Like the 15 July sermon attributed to Fulcher of Chartres discussed in the last chapter, the sermon recalls the hunger and labor endured in order to get to Jerusalem. Now, the gate of Jerusalem is open, "through your labor." No enemy guards it. Now, no one asks for any tribute other than faith in order to enter the city. The tone is celebratory and triumphant. The sermon then exhorts its listeners to commemorate the feast day. "Blessed is the month of July, and the Friday on which the entrance to the city was given over to the sons of light, as a result of which the sun of justice shone everywhere and the power of the shadows fled."[75] And then the next and final line of the sermon, copied immediately before the transcription of the hymn, enjoins the audience: "So, again and again, and over and over, as we rejoice for Jerusalem, let us sing in her praise this melodious hymn, written by an unknown teacher."[76] The sermon is explicitly designed to introduce the hymn. Almost certainly composed by the same person, the sermon and the hymn share language and images[77] and assume a secular audience—a secular crusading audience no less. Here, we are in the fluid world of sacred and sacralizing song. Liturgical or paraliturgical. Encompassing clergy and probably laymen. Evoking sacred themes but aimed toward a secularized audience. Recalling the events of the First Crusade, drawing on the spirit of the early narratives, in the language of liturgy.

72. BNF Lat. 5132, 19v, *bellum gerendum* . . . (France, p. 651).

73. BNF Lat. 5132, 20v: *Quam melius habere* . . . (France, p. 653).

74. BNF Lat. 5132, 20v: *Vos, inquam, milites, ymo militum flores* . . . (France, p. 653).

75. BNF Lat. 5132, 21r: *Felix mensis ille quintilis* . . . (France, p. 653).

76. BNF Lat. 5132, 21r. *Item itemque etiam* . . . (France, p. 654).

77. BNF Lat. 5132, *Felix est ille mensis* (hymn, France, p. 656, Hierusalem Letare, stanza 23); *Felix mensis ille quintillis* (sermon, France, p. 653).

As a group, these hymns celebrated the specific history of the crusade and capture of Jerusalem as a sacred event within the larger providential scheme. *Ierusalem mirabilis*, for instance, recounted the Passion, Crucifixion, and burial "in the tomb, guarded by soldiers," before exhorting crusaders to "take back the temple of God."[78] The Ripoll hymn recalled the progression of the First Crusade. It bemoaned that Jerusalem had been so subjugated to the Turks.[79] It celebrated the discovery of the Holy Lance in Antioch:

Lancea regis caeli	The Lance of the king of heaven
genti datur fideli,	is given to the faithful people
ut sit mors infideli.	so that death might come to the infidel.
Iherusalem, exulta!	Jerusalem, exult!

And the siege of Jerusalem:

Felix est ille mensis,	Happy is this month
quo te tuorum ensis	in which the sword of your men
eruit ab infensis!	Plucked you from hostile [hands].
Iherusalem, exulta!	Jerusalem, exult!
Junius obsidendi	June is for besieging,
Iulius capiendi	July is for capturing.
ius dedit et gaudendi.	and the fruits of victory.
Iherusalem, exulta!	Jerusalem, exult!
Ab ortu redemptoris	From the birth of the Redeemer,
ad hoc tempus honoris	to the time of this honor,
certis maturis horis,	of this very hour.
Iherusalem, exulta!	Jerusalem, exult!
Anni centeni fructus,	The fruits of a hundred years,
undecies reductus,	eleven times over
diluit omnis luctus.	all grief washed away,
Iherusalem, exulta!	Jerusalem exult!

And it said that the city was taken at the very hour—noon—that Christ died on the Cross.[80]

Rex precipit ut gentes,	The King orders that the pagans,
gladiis renitentes,	opposing us with their swords,
te visitent gaudentes.	visit you rejoicing.
Iherusalem, exulta![81]	Jerusalem, exult!

78. "Ierusalem mirabilis," stanza 7.
79. "Hierusalem letare," stanza 2.
80. "Hierusalem letare," stanzas 27–28.
81. *Praecipit* in AH.

Above all, the texts celebrated the capture of the city from the infidel, adopting a triumphant tone around the concept of victory. At Laon, we saw, the victory was a kind of miracle, effected by God, which everyone ought praise and celebrate. In the Saint Martial repertory, *Nomen a solemnibus* cried out:

Exultemus et laetemur,	Let us exalt, and let us rejoice
canticum laetitiae	a canticle of joy.
ac reddamus, quas debemus,	and let us render, as we must,
laudes regi gloriae	the praises due to the glory of God,
qui salvavit urbem David	who today did save
a paganis hodie[82]	the city of David from the pagans

The hymn also exhorted that they should "celebrate this feast day . . . on which Jerusalem is rescued, returned to the Christians."[83] The refrain for the Ripoll hymn was "Jerusalem Exult"' (*Iherusalem exulta!*) and proclaimed that the pagans (*gentes*) resisted with their swords.[84] Likewise, the Laon sequence exhorted that the crowds rejoice and that the glorious city of Jerusalem has been freed, which had for such a long time been subjected to the Saracens.

It is Jerusalem, not the Holy Sepulcher, that is the focus of praise. This corresponds with Schein's observation that the devotional focus of crusade widened from the tomb specifically to the city more broadly in the immediate aftermath of the capture, a move which fostered a cult of the city of Jerusalem.[85] Jerusalem is on the one hand "the place of [Jesus'] death,"[86] but also "David's city,"[87] the "royal city,"[88] "the most noble city," and "this greatest city," "the city sacralized from heaven,"[89] "wondrous Jerusalem, more beautiful than all the others."[90] She is the site "of the Temple of God."[91] In *Ierusalem mirabilis* Jerusalem is:

Ierusalem mirabilis	O wondrous Jerusalem,
urbs beatior aliis	city more beautiful than others,
quam permanens optabilis	forever desirable,
gaudentibus te angelis.	with angels rejoicing with you.

82. "Nomen a solemnibus," stanza 1.
83. "Nomen a solemnibus," stanza 1 refrain.
84. "Hierusalem letare," stanza 14.
85. Schein, *Gateway to the Heavenly City*, 13–15.
86. "Hierusalem letare," stanza 6.
87. "Nomen a solemnibus," stanza 1.
88. "Hierualsem letare," stanza 13.
89. "Nomen a solemnibus," stanzas 2 and 3.
90. "Ierusalem mirabilis," stanza 1.
91. "Ierusalem mirabilis," stanza 7.

In "Nomen a solemnibus," Jerusalem is the noblest city:

Hec urbs nobilissima	This most noble city
prima regem habuit,	first had a King
in hac urbe maxima	in this greatest city,
domino complacuit,	[this King] was pleasing to the Lord;
in hac propter hominem	in this [city] He wished to be crucified
crucifigi voluit,	on account of man,
hic super apostolos	[and] here the [Holy] Spirit
spiritus intonuit	thundered down on the apostles.

and

Urbs sacrata celitus,	The city made sacred from Heaven,
adamata superis,	coveted from the heavens above,
regis tabernaculum,	the tabernacle of the King,
templum arce federis	the Temple of the Ark of the Covenant
hospitale pauperum	the hospital of the poor,
et asylum miseris,	the sanctuary for the wretched.
non timebis aliquid,	You will not fear anything,
dum in ea manseris.	so long as you remain here.

The stanza reaches backward to the Old Testament, evokes Jerusalem as a sanctuary in the present and the future of heavenly salvation. Elsewhere Jerusalem is the city vast and great, where the King (Christ) wished to be crucified, and where the Holy Spirit descended on the Apostles (a reference to Pentecost).[92] The bulk of *Ierusalem mirabilis* recalls the city as the place of Christ's Passion, death, and Resurrection. And Jerusalem reigns above all other cities. At Saint Martial, Jerusalem is described, "By the splendor of the light she surpasses the moon; with her sanctity, this city conquers all other cities."[93] The sequence from Laon describes Jerusalem as queen, with all of France, Greece, Arabia, Mesopotamia, Egypt, Africa, Damascus, Ascalon, Joppa, Acre, Tyre, and Sidon paying tribute to her.[94] At Ripoll, Christ is King and Father, where Jerusalem is mother.[95]

The songs absorbed the precepts of crusade ideology also evinced in the new narratives. The Ripoll hymn spoke of how Jerusalem had for a long time been in the service of the Turks, who were described as tyrants.[96] The chant

---

92. "Nomen a solemnibus," stanza 2a.
93. "Nomen a solemnibus," stanza 3r.
94. "Exultent agmina," stanza 4–5.
95. "Hierusalem letare," stanza 11.
96. "Hierusalem letare," stanzas 2, 5.

recalled the peoples of the West who partook in the crusade. For most, the crusaders were just "we," or the "Christians," but their leader was "Christ" or "God," who was "Father" or "King" and who led them into battle. In *Hierusalem letare* the Frankish army is described as the troops of heaven.[97] Those "signed with the cross" follow the King of heaven.[98] *Exultent agmina* praised in particular the Franks with brave deeds and great courage liberated Jerusalem.[99] The enemy was variously described as pagans,[100] the "infidel," "Turks," "Saracens,"[101] "evil people,"[102] and "tyrants,"[103] and a "race not devoted to God."[104]

The chant was martial in theme and belligerent in tone. *Hierusalem letare* juxtaposed "the group of faithful" who armed themselves so that they might "kill the tyrants who have been for so many years a plague to the Christians,"[105] with "the Turks . . . under whom you [Jerusalem] have been subjugated since the death of Jesus Christ." The hymn later exhorts the "faithful" that "death might come to the infidel,"[106] and spoke in turn of wiping out the enemy (*hostes delentur*) and snatching Jerusalem from the hostile people.[107] *Ierusalem mirabilis* spoke of having to destroy Saracens (*Sarcenos destruere*).[108] *Hierusalem letare* exhorted the faithful that if it "wishes to capture the heavens, [is should] undertake to gird itself with arrows."[109] *Hierusalem letare* asserted that "the King fights, and goes before [us]."[110] It exclaimed that "June was for besieging, and July for capturing." In celebrating the capture of the city, the hymn echoed some of the bloodiest descriptions of the early narrative accounts:

Rivi fluunt cruoris	Rivers of blood flow,
ierusalem in moris,	at that hour, in Jerusalem,
dum perit gens erroris	as the race of error dies,
Iherusalem, exulta!	Jerusalem, exult!

97. "Hierusalem letare," stanza 17.
98. "Hierusalem letare," stanza 15.
99. "Exultent agmina," stanza 3a.
100. "Nomen a solemnibus," stanza 1r.
101. "Exultent agmina," stanza 2b.
102. "Hierusalem letare," stanza 32.
103. "Hierusalem letare," stanza 5.
104. "Hierusalem letare," stanza 7.
105. "Hierusalem letare," stanza 5.
106. "Hierusalem letare," stanza 16.
107. "Hierusalem letare," stanza 23.
108. "Ierusalem mirabilis," stanza 7.
109. "Hierusalem letare," stanza 4.
110. "Hierusalem letare," stanza 20.

Et templi pavimentum	And the pavement of the Temple
efficitur cruentum	is made bloody
cruore morientum	with the blood of those who are dying.
Iherusalem, exulta!	Jerusalem exult!

Ipsi tradunt igni,	They handed them over to the fire,
vos gaudete, benigni,	you rejoice, O good ones,
nam pereunt maligni.	for the evils ones die.
Iherusalem, exulta!	Jerusalem exult!

In its description of the purifying slaughter, the hymn here reflected, for instance, the imagery of Raymond of Aguilers: "In the Temple of Solomon and the portico crusaders rode in blood to the knees and bridles of their horses."[111] Robert of Reims, in describing a battle of 1099 wrote, "But the military might of Christ inflicts a terrible death on them; the earth is crimson with blood, every fold of the mountain is red, and the river is swollen with flowing blood."[112] The cantica as a group thus tended to participate in the exultant triumphalism that placed the vivid history of the events of 1099 within its violent and apocalyptic scheme.

One of the tropes of this triumphalism was the idea that Saracens were Old Testament pagans. *Nomen a solemnibus* embraced the tradition of equating Mohammad with the pagan gods as part of the binary of Christian/non-Christian established early on in the development of crusade ideology. It made reference to the toppling of the pagan gods of the Old Testament in typological parallel to the Christian victory in Jerusalem:

Festum agitur,	The feast day is celebrated,
dies recolitur,	so as to remember the day on which
in qua Dagon frangitur	Dagon has been destroyed,
et Amalec vincitur,	and Amalec conquered;
natus Agar pellitur	The one born of Hagar is banished,
Jerusalem eripitur,	Jerusalem is rescued, and
Christianis redditur,	returned to the Christians;
diem colamus igitur.	let us thus celebrate this day.[113]

Dagon (Joshua 19:27; Judges 16:23; 1 Chronicles 10:8–10) was routinely evoked in the typology of pagan idolatry that was a precursor of crusade. The Amalechites, the descendants of Amalec, were one of the pagan tribes

---

111. RA 150–151 (tr. 127–128).
112. RR 27 (tr. 111).
113. "Nomen a solemnibus" refrain.

the Israelites were charged with annihilating. Muslims were the "sons of Hagar," here, banished from the Holy City. The entire refrain calls to mind the Song of Roland, of the overturning of Old Testament idols (in this case, Dagon) as the sign of Christian victory, conquering the progenitor of the Amalechites, the great enemy of the Israelites, as well as banishing the sons of Hagar (that is, Muslims) from Jerusalem.[114] Baldric of Bourgueil, writing during this same period of memorialization, called the Muslims both Hagarene and Amalechites (and pagans). He imagined a preacher saying to the Christian army as they charged the walls of Jerusalem that "it is your task to fight against the Amalechites . . . you fearless warriors, thrust and brandish your sword into Amalec."[115]

The promise of salvation—of the heavenly Jerusalem—as the reward for the earthly capture of the city was also present in these texts, and these celebrations could be mixed with a message of recruitment and reward. A number make explicit exhortations to crusaders or potential crusaders. *Hierusalem letare*, the narrative Ripoll hymn, recalls that the King (God) is the one who ordered the people to move on the Holy City, and thus "let them advance safely, clothed with the sign of the cross, following the King of Heaven."[116] The one who "wishes to capture the heavens" should arm himself.[117] And then the hymn assures that "the King fights and he goes before us; and death injures no one, who dies while he kills."[118] Anticipating Bernard of Clairvaux, who said that killing Muslims was not homicide but malicide, *Hierusalem letare* promised that killing ("Turks") is the route to salvation, and that death is not an injury but the heavenly reward. The vocabulary of martyrdom is not explicitly used but the idea that death was salvific and would end in heaven permeated these texts. "The King will give His rewards, which He Himself makes evident, to that one who will fight well. So why then, creature, do you not fight untroubled, since this [reward] you will indeed obtain?"[119] At Laon, the sequence

---

114. On the use of Old Testament typology in crusade ideology and propaganda, see Paul Alphandéry, "Les citations bibliques chez les historiens de la première croisade," *Revue de l'histoire des religions* 99 (1929): 139–157; Paul Rousset, "L'idée de croisade chez les chroniqueurs d'Occident," in *Storia del medioevo, Relazioni del X congresso internazionale di scienze storiche iii* (Florence: 1955), 556–559; Riley-Smith, *The First Crusade*, 140–143. For pagans idolaters as precursors for Muslims, see Strickland, *Saracens, Demons, and Jews*; Tolan, *Saracens*, 105–134.

115. BB 10. See also 62, 91, 99, 107 for references to Hagarenes.

116. "Hierusalem letare," stanzas 14–15.

117. "Hierusalem letare," stanza 4.

118. "Hierusalem letare," stanza 20.

119. "Hierusalem letare," stanza 9.

associated the capture of the earthly Jerusalem with the reward of the heavenly: "Celebrating her feast, let us enjoy Jerusalem in her heavenly glory."[120] In a stronger vein, the hymn *Ierusalem mirabilis* preserved in the Saint-Martial repertory, told of Christ's Passion and Resurrection, before exhorting

Illic[121] debemus pergere,	And to there, we must proceed.
nostros honores vendere,	We must sell our honors [i.e., properties].
templum dei acquirere,	We must conquer the Temple of God.
Saracenos destruere	We must destroy the Saracens.
Quid prodest nobis omnibus	What is the profit to any of us
honores acquirentibus	in acquiring honors,
animam dare penitus	and thus to give our souls to those
infernis tribulantibus	who deep in hell travail?
Illuc quicumque tenderit	Whomever should reach toward that place,
mortuus ibi fuerit	and should die there,
celi bona deceperit [ed. reads receperit]	he will receive the goods of heaven,
& cum sanctis permanserit.	and will reside forever with the saints.[122]

By adopting the liturgical form—by wedding the themes and motifs of the narrative accounts to the formal characteristics of liturgical prayer and celebratory praise of the divine—these sequences, hymns, and sacred songs sanctified and thus further legitimized the memory of 1099. As a whole, be they hymns, canticles, or sacred songs, they imbibed and thus participated in the priorities and ideologies of the early crusade narratives. In this sense the monk from Saint André de Cateau seems to have been right: the stories of the First Crusade that were written down in books like those of Baldric of Dol, Robert of Reims, and Guibert of Nogent, were being sung and sacralized in *carmina et cantica*. The reach suggests dispersion outside of the cloister, and perhaps even to nonelites. Precisely because of this, the evidence must represent only a slice of what once existed, of what was once sung in celebration and praise. By appropriating the liturgical form these hymns and poems further sacralized the events told in narrative. And

120. "Exultent agmina," stanza 6.
121. AH 45b:78, no. 96, reads illuc.
122. "Ierusalem mirabilis," stanzas 7–9.

existing in the fuzzy space between formal liturgical devotion and spontaneous devotion, they embraced a wider audience. And they confirmed, by
the sacrality of their liturgical ethos, the sacredness of the capture of Jerusalem, and its place in the divine plan. In this way, in the West as well, the
First Crusade was collapsed into salvific history.

6

Clamoring to God:
Liturgy as a Weapon of War

On 4 July 1187, eighty-eight years after the triumphant capture of Jerusalem, the combined Christian forces of the Latin Kingdom of Jerusalem were wiped out by Saladin's army. Two months later, Jerusalem itself fell. In the West, the devotion and liturgical response was to beg forgiveness, and then to raise a clamor, a call to God to exact His vengeance on the enemy. The entire spiritual forces of Christendom were to be marshaled to fight for Jerusalem. Invisible weapons, in the words of Honorius III (d. 1227), were deployed to fight visible armies.[1] These were only effective so long as those who wielded them were virtuous. And so eventually measures were taken to promote virtue and the display of humility. And wield these weapons they did. Over the course the next century, the aims of crusading would penetrate the very heart of the liturgy, and crusading itself would become inextricably linked with Christian religious identity.

By 1187, the Latin Kingdom was almost nine decades old, with an established political and military class of Frankish origin working to safeguard it in the face of revivified Islamic power in the region. Within a decade of the capture of Jerusalem in 1099, the Franks had established four Latin principalities (Edessa, Antioch, Jerusalem, Tyre). The first few decades saw the slow consolidation of territory under Frankish control. At the same time, however, fractured Islamic powers (whose divisions and infighting had allowed for the crusaders' success) began to regroup. The Second Crusade (1147–1149) was launched after Turkish forces under the leadership of a warlord named Zenghi recaptured the County of Edessa. In the event, the Second Crusade, aimed at Damascus, ended in failure. The campaign,

---

1. RHF 19:639.

led by the French king Louis VII and the German emperor Conrad III, collapsed after a four-day siege and was promptly aborted. In the years that followed, Muslim powers, first under Zenghi's son Nur-al-Din, and then under his successor, Saladin, gained increasing purpose and momentum. The Latin Kingdom suffered a succession of military and territorial losses throughout the 1160s, 1170s, and 1180s that slowly corroded the frontier of the Latin principalities. The Kingdom of Jerusalem in particular was slowly reduced, losing important outposts to the east and south of the city. And because the Holy City was also of central religious meaning in Islam, Saladin, who presented himself as a religious leader as much as a military one, set his sights on the Latin Kingdom of Jerusalem.

In the major battle that took place to the north of Jerusalem, at a twin peaked mountain known as the Horns of Hattin, Saladin's forces inflicted a catastrophic defeat on the army of the Latin Kingdom. The king of Jerusalem, Guy of Lusignan, was taken captive. Members of the military orders were all executed. The True Cross, which had represented Christ's presence on the battlefield, was seized by Saladin's army. The pope, Urban III, reportedly died on hearing the news.[2] In England, it was said that Henry II did not speak for days.[3] In Paris, Phillip the Chancellor composed a sacred lament, decrying that there was no one left to attend the solemnities of the Holy Sepulcher and asking the Lord to be the God of vengeance.[4]

Gregory VIII was elected on 21 October 1187, the day after Urban III's death. On becoming pope, Gregory knew about Hattin, but had not yet learned of the fall of Jerusalem which had happened only on 4 October. Even so, his first act as pope was to call the new crusade. The lyrical bull he issued on 29 October, *Audita tremendi* ("O, we have heard the terrible judgment!") advanced a theology of crusade and crusading failure predicated on human sin.[5] If the capture of Jerusalem in 1099 had been a providential event and the will of God, how, then, to explain its loss? Contemporary preachers blamed the Christians of the West, asking "whether there could be any greater sign of Christ's withdrawal than that He allowed the loss of the relic of the Lord's Passion."[6] "We ought not to believe," wrote Gregory,

2. WT Cont. ch. 74 (lat. 83–84, tr. 75). More broadly, Schein, *Gateway to the Heavenly City*, 159–187.

3. Schein, *Gateway to the Heavenly City*, 162.

4. Gordon A. Anderson, *Notre-Dame and Related Conductus: Opera Omnia*, 10 vols., Gesamtausgaben 10 (Henryville, PA: 1979–), 6:25–27, no. XLI. Wentzlaff-Eggbert, *Kreuzzugsdichung des Mittelalters: Studien zu ihrer geschichtlichen und dichterischen Wirklichkeit*, 168–172.

5. There are three surviving versions of *Audita tremendi*. Schein, *Gateway to the Heavenly City*, 164n19.

6. Matthew Phillips, "The Thief's Cross: Crusade and Penance in Alan of Lille's *Sermo de cruce domini*," *Crusades* 5 (2006): 147.

"that these things have happened through the injustice of a violent judge, but rather through the iniquity of a delinquent people."[7]

This was hardly a new explanation. During the First Crusade, it was the crusaders themselves whose sins were blamed for military failures and stresses. This is why men like Adhémar of LePuy and Peter the Hermit had instituted expiatory processions that the entire army was to partake in. Bernard of Clairvaux argued a half a century later, after the failure of the Second Crusade, that sins caused setbacks on the crusade, although Bernard's emphasis was more the sin and salvation of the individual than it was the social order. But as the catastrophes magnified, so surely must be their cause. For Gregory, Christendom as a whole was at fault. "Faced by such great distress concerning the land," he wrote, "we ought to consider not only the sins of its inhabitants, but also our own and those of the whole Christian people."[8] Gregory explained that it was the responsibility of Christendom as a whole, and particularly the Christians of the West, to repent, and to demonstrate humility and penitence and the cognizance of human sin: "It is therefore incumbent upon all of us to consider and to choose to amend our sins by voluntary chastisement and to turn to the Lord our God with penance and works of piety; and we should first amend in ourselves what we have done wrong and then turn our attention to treachery and malice of the enemy."[9]

The notion of sincere, widespread social reform was central to the liturgical program in the West and its efficacy in the Latin East. In *Nunquam melius*, issued on the same day as *Audita tremendi*, Gregory instituted a series of penitential measures and fasting (lasting five years), and a special mass to be chanted at nones from Advent through Christmas.[10] A chronicler reported that kings Philip II, Henry II, and Count Philip of Flanders all took the cross at the urging of the cardinal bishop and papal legate Henry of Albano, and that the bishop exhorted that the public prayers instituted by Pope Gregory be observed throughout the universal Church in order to avenge the destruction of Jerusalem.[11]

This chapter is about the institutional organization of liturgical penitence and supplication in the call for victory and vengeance that began in the wake of Hattin. Starting with Gregory, popes and other ecclesiastical authorities sought to mobilize the collective spiritual resources of Christendom to pray to God to beseech aid in prosecuting holy war.[12] Every major

---

7. RH *Chron.* 2:327 (tr. 2:71); HdE 8 (tr. 38–39).
8. RH *Chron.* 2:327–328 (tr. 2:72); HdE 8 (tr. 39).
9. RH *Chron.* 2:328 (tr. 2:72); HdE 8–9 (tr. 39).
10. PL 202:1539. See also RH *Chron*, 2:329–330.
11. MGH SS 24:719, for the year 1188. Linder RA 1–2.
12. Linder RA 1–3.

crusading initiative after was supported by a program liturgical supplication. This was a devotional response. And it was part of a larger program of social reform and pastoral organization that sought to widen spiritual and material support for the crusades and for Christian virtue in general. And most consequentially, it was part of the way in which the crusades were iteratively sacralized and brought into the very heart of Christian identity. Over the course of the thirteenth century, the program to call on God to support the crusade was embedded into the cursus of liturgical life. It also embedded the aims of crusading into the defining rituals of Christianity.

Begging Forgiveness and Clamoring for Help

The year after Gregory issued *Audita tremendi*, his successor, Clement III (1187–1191), ordered that all churches throughout Christendom perform special prayers during the mass beseeching God to help Christians retake Jerusalem. Clement declared fasting and instructed all churches, monasteries, and parishes to recite Psalm 78, *Deus venerunt gentes*, after the Lord's Prayer, to free Jerusalem, and liberate Christian prisoners taken by the enemy.[13] Arnold of Lübeck, recording the event in his chronicle, explained that Clement wrote "to all churches about the impious surrender and slaughter of the servants of God and about certain abominations perpetrated by the Saracens in the Holy Land, inciting all to zeal against the impious and toward vengeance for the Holy Blood."[14] What Clement was instituting was the regular and wide-scale performance of something called a clamor. The practice of the clamor—the insertion into the regular daily mass of special supplicatory prayers—had emerged around the year 1000, within the context of the breakdown of secular authority and the emergence of the Peace of God movement. Spurred by endemic local violence, the Frankish liturgy developed this peculiar form of liturgical supplication in which monks beseeched God for help against the rabid enemies of church properties.[15] The term *clamor* in the ancient world could indicate the bringing of a legal suit, a claim. In the eleventh and twelfth century, it could also indicate the juridical

13. The encyclical does not survive but was reported by contemporary chroniclers. RH *Gesta*, 2:53–54; RH *Chron.*, 2:359–360 (tr. 2:103–104). Both chronicles are now attributed to Roger of Howden; Doris M. Stenton, "Roger of Howden and Benedict," *The English Historical Review* 68, no. 269 (1953): 574–582. See also Conrad of Scheyer, "Chounradi Schirensis annales a. 1077–1226" MGH SS 17:630, for the year 1188.

14. Arnold of Lübeck, "Chronica Slavorum" MGH SS 21:169–170.

15. On the clamor, see Edmond Martène, *De antiquis ecclesiae ritibus libri*, 4 vols. (Antwerp: 1736–1738), 1:420–421 (I.IV.IX.V); Patrick J. Geary, "Humiliation of Saints," in *Living with the Dead in the Middle Ages* (Ithaca, NY: 1994), 95–115; Little, *Benedictine Maledictions*. Linder argued that the Holy Land clamor grew out of the Great Litany; Linder RA 5–6.

complaint brought to a lord who had the power to redress an injustice.[16] One *made* a clamor against someone. It also indicated, of course, a shout, a cry, a distressed plaint. In individual monastic houses (where monks also practiced judicial clamors), at moments of crisis or need, a (liturgical) clamor might be inserted into the conventual (main) mass, in which monks cried out to God for help and vengeance against invaders and persecutors—that is, probably, castellans and other arms-bearers who pillaged the church and damaged church properties. The purpose was analogous to the juridical clamor—to ask the juridical authority to correct a wrong. The clamor was inserted in the canon right before the elevation and communion, a moment at which celebrants were often prostrate before the altar. Sometimes relics would be laid out before the altar. A variety of formulas were known. The most common, probably composed by the canonist Fulbert of Chartres (d. 1028), began *In spiritu humilitatis,* and was to be said while prostrate, during the communal mass at the moment when the host is elevated and the priest asks for forgiveness of sins.[17] Because it was the sins of the beseechers that had caused spoliations by the enemy, the clamor asked God to forgive these sins and punish the enemy for their offenses. The clamor explicitly acknowledged sin as the cause of the abuses suffered, and then asked God to "rise up in support of us, comfort us and help us. Attack those who are attacking us, and break the pride of those who afflict Your place and us."[18] In this, the themes echoed the tradition of votive masses in times of war, calling on God to be an active agent of destruction in response to wrongdoing. But it was important that it involved the community—the people—before God.[19] Patrick Geary has emphasized the theme of humility among the beseechers against the pride of the attackers as the core virtue inscribed in the clamor, and of course it was precisely in humility that sin was acknowledged and thus vengeance was appropriate, since the invaders and despoilers were acting as much in their own interests as they were as agents of God to punish the monks.[20]

The clamor instituted by Clement on behalf of the Third Crusade was centered on the recitation in the middle of the mass of the whole of Psalm 78. Psalm 78 was originally one of the "exile" Psalms, written during the

16. Richard E. Barton, "Making a Clamor to the Lord: Noise, Justice, and Power in Eleventh- and Twelfth-Century France," in *Feud, Violence, and Practice: Essays in Medieval Studies in Honor of Stephen D. White* (Burlington, VT: 2010), 213–235.

17. Little, *Benedictine Maledictions*, 261–262 (with translation at 25), and for discussion of Fulbert's authorship, see 268–270. For the practice at Farfa, see Josef A. Jungmann, *The Mass of the Roman Rite: Its Origins and Development (Missarum sollemnia)*, trans. Francis A. Brunner, 2 vols. (New York: 1951–1955), 2:292. Yves Delaporte, *L'Ordinaire chartrain du XIIIe siècle*, Société Archéologique d'Eure-et-Loir, Mémoires, vol. 19 (Chartres: 1953), 196–197.

18. Little, *Benedictine Maledictions*, 25.

19. Little, *Benedictine Maledictions*, 20–21.

20. Geary, "Humiliation of Saints."

(original) Babylonian captivity to lament the Jewish displacement from the Temple and Jerusalem.[21] Its opening cried out for vengeance on the heathen (Latin: *gentes*): "O God, the heathens have come into Your inheritance, they have defiled Your holy temple, they have made Jerusalem as a place to keep fruit." It had been evoked in crusade discourse since the beginning, as a way of emphasizing Muslim pollution of the Holy Land and thus the justice of the crusade.[22] Urban II had purportedly evoked Psalm 78 in his famous sermon in 1095.[23] Following Hattin, the tone and theme of Psalm 78 was keyed perfectly to the outrage, lament, and dismay felt in the West.[24] It asked, "How long, O Lord, will You be angry forever [v. 5]. . . . Pour out Your wrath upon the nations [gentes] that have not known You, and upon the Kingdoms that have not called upon Your name [v.6]." "Remember not our former iniquities [v.8]." "Help us, O God, Our Savior; and for the glory of Your name, O Lord, deliver us, and forgive us our sins for the sake of Your name [v.9]."

Psalm 78 became the rallying cry for the crusade effort and the penitential preparation it required. In 1187, Gregory VIII had opened *Audita tremendi* by evoking Psalm 78. He had explained to Christendom that God's anger does not come suddenly, but "He puts off revenge and gives men time to do penance." And he had begged Christians to show repentance so that God might "pour out Your wrath upon the nations." The outrage expressed in the clamor was pinned to the sins that had caused them. Arnold of Lübeck's interpretation of Psalm 78 emphasized Christian responsibility for the loss of Jerusalem. Psalm 78 "prophetically commemorates all the misery perpetrated in the Holy Land, just as the sins by which we deserve this ire."[25] In Assisi, upon hearing of Jerusalem's fall, the city turned out wearing sack cloths, and the town's priests repeated Psalm 78 in procession day and night.[26] The author of an account of Frederick's expedition wrote that in Germany the "knights of Christ fixed the sign of the Lord's cross on themselves and prepared for the campaigns against the ancient enemy and his members, who '*had come into the inheritance of the Lord and had defiled*

---

21. *The New Interpreter's Bible: General Articles and Introduction, Commentary, and Reflections for Each Book of the Bible, Including the Apocryphal Deuterocanonical Books*, ed. Abingdon Press (Nashville: 1994), 4:994–997.

22. Penny Cole, "'O God, the Heathen Have Come into Your Inheritance' (Ps. 78.1): The Theme of Religious Pollution in Crusade Documents, 1095–1188," in *Crusaders and Muslims in Twelfth-Century Syria*, ed. Maya Shatzmiller, *The Medieval Mediterranean* (Leiden: 1993), 95–97.

23. BB 8; WT i.15 (lat. 133, tr. 91).

24. Cole, "'O God, the Heathen Have Come'"; Schein, *Gateway to the Heavenly City*, 159–187.

25. Arnold of Lübeck, "Chronica Slavorum," MGH SS 21:170.

26. Pazzelli, *Saint Francis and the Third Order: The Franciscans and the Pre-Franciscan Movement* (Chicago: 1982), 73.

his holy temple'" (Ps. 78:1).[27] In the Holy Land, the clamor was immediately added to one of the Holy Sepulcher's liturgical books.[28]

We do not know precisely what Clement prescribed in 1188, but echoes survive. Roger of Hoveden (d. 1201), the English chronicler who followed the reign of Henry II and went on crusade with Richard Lionheart, twice described the intercessory supplications practiced in London in the year 1188, so that, it was said, God might turn His anger and ire away from the Christian people (see appendix 2, col. 1).[29] "In the same year, it was enacted by our lord the pope and the cardinals that prayers should be put up to the Lord by the Church Universal, without intermission, for the peace and deliverance of the land of Jerusalem and of the Christian captives who were confined in chains by the Saracens."[30] Roger may have borrowed language from the original encyclical. These rites included an antiphon, a Psalm (different for each day of the week), and a special collect. The opening antiphon, "Yours is the power, Yours is the kingdom. O Lord, You who are above all nations, grant us peace" (*Tua est potentia, tuum regnum. Domine, tu es super omnes gentes. Da pacem, Domine, in diebus nostris*) was known from the common for the first Friday in October, following a lesson drawn from First Maccabees (3:25–28), in which the king "sent word to mobilize the troops of his whole kingdom, a very powerful army."[31] Each day, in addition, the antiphon was followed by the singing of a full psalm. A series of versicles (short, introductory prayers) preceded the collect—that is, the main prayer—which called on God to bring aid: "Almighty and everlasting God [*Omnipotens sempitere deus*], in whose hands are the power and rule of all kingdoms, in Your mercy look upon the Christian armies, that the heathen who put trust in their own ferocity may be vanquished by the power of Your right hand."[32]

Omnipotens sempiterne Deus would become one of the most important prayers in the history of crusade liturgy. The prayer called on the power of God's universalizing authority to vanquish the heathen enemy. It was an adaptation of a quite ancient prayer, dating back to the Old Gelasian, and found in both the Gregorian and the Gellone Sacramentary as part of the Temporale (used for the sixth day following Easter).[33] The prayer had sometimes been used as part of clamor rites for ad hoc situations in preceding centuries;[34] by the eleventh century, owing to its themes, it had been adopted in some manuscripts for masses against pagans and it was from there appropriated into

---

27. HdE 14 (tr. 44).
28. Lucca Bibliotecha Arcivescovile 5, 56r. Aspesi, "The *libelli* of Lucca."
29. RH *Gesta*, 2:53–54 (53 for quote); RH *Chron.*, 2:359–360 (tr. 2:103–104).
30. RH *Chron.*, 2:359 (tr. 2:103); RH *Gesta*, 2:53.
31. Highly attested in the Middle Ages (Cantus database).
32. RH *Chron.*, 2:360 (tr. 2:104); RH *Gesta*, 2:54.
33. CO 3846. Gregorian Scr. 345 (1:177); Gellone Scr. 653; Gelasian Scr. 407.
34. Little, *Benedictine Maledictions*, 26.

crusading liturgy.[35] It had been used at the Holy Sepulcher since at least ca. 1130 for a votive mass *contra paganos*.[36] In earlier forms, the prayer asked God to look kindly upon, not the army, but the emperor, or the Frankish kingdoms. "Auxilium" was replaced with "exercitum."[37] In 1188, it emphasized that military success was in God's power, that all lands and kingdoms came under God's dominion, alluded to the pride of the heathens (gentes), and begged for mercy for the Christian armies. The point of course was that military success depended not on military might or valor (and this was the mistake of the heathens) but God's power alone. It was also a clear statement of a desire for vengeance on the heathens, in line with the development of a clear ideology of crusade as vengeance as it had developed in the latter part of the twelfth century.[38]

Three years later, in France, while Philip Augustus was in Acre during the Third Crusade, the archbishop of Reims (William Whitehands, the king's uncle) and the queen (Adele of Champagne) organized an elaborate spectacle at St.-Denis to pray for the liberation of Jerusalem and the health of the king and his army. Rigord reports that on Friday, 23 August 1191, they had the relics of Denis, Rusticus, and Eleutherius brought out and placed on the altar with the other saints of the Church.

> All the faithful gathered together for such a holy spectacle, and, with tears and sighs, raising their pure hands to the Lord, with Moses, they poured out prayers for the liberation of the Holy Land and for the king of the French and all of his army; because Christians rely not on the power [*potentia*] of the army, but upon the power [*virtus*] and compassion of Christ, nor [do they rely] on themselves, but rather they place the power in God that they might overpower infidel people and reduce the enemies of the cross of Christ to nothing.[39]

Rigord here evoked the Moses trope, praying to God to defeat the Amalechites. Victory in the Levant depended on the power of God, not Philip's army.

Cistercian statutes for the years 1194 and 1196 prescribe the specific form that the clamor should take among the order, which appear to reflect more closely Clement's prescriptions (appendix 2, col. 2). Starting in 1194, possibly in response to the inconclusive end of the Third Crusade and despite earlier bans on additional formularies, the Cistercians instituted a *pro pace* collect, *pro terra ierosolimitana*, to be said along with Psalm 78.[40]

---

35. CO 3846B.
36. BNF Lat. 12056, 268r.
37. In the earlier version, the word *auxilium* is preserved. RH *Gesta*, 2:54.
38. Throop, *Crusading as an Act of Vengeance*, 73–116.
39. Rigord, *Histoire de Philippe Auguste*, ed. Élisabeth Carpentier, Georges Pon, Yves Chauvin, Sources d'histoire médiévale 33 (Paris 2006), 300–303.
40. Chrysogonus Waddell, *Twelfth-Century Statutes from the Cistercian General Chapter: Latin Text with English Notes and Commentary*, Studia et Documenta 12 (Brecht, Belgium: 2002), 286–287; and Joseph Canivez, *Statuta Capitulorum Generalium Ordinis Cisterciensis*

The clamor was to be said during conventual mass, probably after the Lord's Prayer, and with a collect from the votive Mass for the Holy Spirit, except for during the Mass for the Dead, in which case the collect was from the votive Mass for Peace.[41] The following year, the general statutes substantially expanded their instructions to address both the Holy Land situation and the invasions of the Saracens in Spain, joining here the two theaters of crusade.[42] It asked for peace for the Pope, the Lord Emperor, and the kings of France and England (and in one manuscript tradition, Spain). Individually, monks were to engage in weekly disciplines, and if traveling, should recite the seven penitential psalms, linking again virtue with liturgical warfare. Each Friday, the community as a whole, was to go in procession barefoot from the chapter room into the church, and there, prostrate, was to say the seven penitential psalms, the litany, the Lord's Prayer, a series of versicles and responses, and a prayer taken from the Gregorian Sacramentary's votive mass *contra iudices male agentes*.[43] The statute then prescribed Psalm 78 and *Omnipotens sempiterne Deus*.[44] It appears this continued through 1231 when the general council ordered that the practice be discontinued (although new prayers were instituted a few years later during Louis IX's preparations for his first crusade).[45]

Several manuscripts from the last two decades of the twelfth century preserve a clamor that that forwent *Omnipotens* in favor of a prayer specifically composed for Holy Land liberation (appendix 2, cols. 3 and 4). This new prayer, *Deus qui ad nostre redemptionis*, ran:

> O God, who, in order to show of the mystery of our redemption [*Deus qui ad nostre redemptionis*], singled out the promised land, free it, we beg, from the threat of the pagans, so that by the troubled disbelief of the heathens [*gentes*] the people believing in You might glory from the power [*potentia*] of Your strength [*virtutis*].[46]

The collect was probably the first overtly new prayer written for Holy Land restoration and seems to have been composed during the preparation for and prosecution of the Third Crusade. It was paired at some point with a series of versicles, including the opening line of Psalm 67 ("May God rise up and scatter His enemies; and let them that hate Him flee from before His

---

ab anno 1116 ad annum 1786, 8 vols., Bibliothéque de la revue d'histoire ecclésiastique (Louvain: 1935), 1:172.

41. Waddell, *Twelfth-Century Statutes*, 286–287.
42. Waddell, *Twelfth-Century Statutes*, 306–307.
43. Gregorian Scr. 1357 (1:447).
44. Waddell, *Twelfth-Century Statutes*, 307.
45. Canivez, *Statuta*, 2:94 (for 1231).
46. See appendix 2.

face"), and a prayer for "afflicted, captives, and pilgrims." It stressed the value of the Holy Land in eschatological terms (in referring to the mystery of our redemption and its relationship to the Promised Land), specified a dichotomy between believers and unbelievers, and emphasized above all God's ultimate power. It entreats not just victory against enemies but the liberation of the Promised Land itself from the threat of pagans. The collect seems to have had its origins in the years around 1180 in the Ile de France or northern French region, with instances from Sens, Arles, Arras, Fecamp, Saint Amand, Dijon, Paris, Reims, and Saint Denis.[47] It survives in other manuscripts of about 1200 in services *Contra paganorum incursiones*[48] and *Pro adversitate terre ierosolimitane.*[49] It was incorporated into different forms of the clamor, with various other traditional prayers. The Carthusian Order adopted it by 1223, perhaps earlier.[50] Additions *pro tribulationibus Iherusalem* found in one German manuscript of the late twelfth century include it in an early complete mass, along with *Omnipotens sempiterne* and another older *contra paganos* prayer, *Deus qui ad hoc irasceris.*[51] Finally, this new prayer was the basis of an elaborate clamor found in an early thirteenth-century ordinal from Chartres Cathedral (appendix 2, col. 5).[52] As part of the mass, following the *Pater noster*, the celebrant was to prostrate himself before the altar and recite Psalm 78 (*Deus venerunt gentes*), the seven penitential psalms, a special litany, and a series of supplicatory versicles (short, preliminary invocations) and prayers, including *Hostium nostrorum*, an *in tempore belli* prayer that asked the Lord to "destroy the pride of our enemies with the power of Your right hand."[53]

Innocent III

Heeding Gregory's call, the Western powers mounted the Third Crusade. Two kings and an emperor—Philip Augustus of France, Richard the Lionheart

---

47. Linder RA 35, with variants given on 36 and 37. The collect was in use in Bamberg and Trier, and by the later thirteenth century, in Catalonia (Gerona). Linder RA 35–37, 71–72. For Reims, see Reims BM 224, 258v.

48. Dartmstadt Hessische Landes und Hockschulbibliothek ms 3183, 188; Valenciennes BM ms 121, 88v.

49. Valenciennes BM 121, 88v; Linder RA 72. See also Paris BNF Lat. 9440, 14r (no rubric). Bamberg Staatsbibliothek ms msc Lit 11, 335v.

50. Carolo LeCouteulx, *Annales ordinis Cartusiensis ab anno 1084 ad annum 1429*, 6 vols. (Monstroli: 1887–1891), 3:392. For the Carthusians of Trier, François Huot O.S.B., *Les manuscrits liturgiques du canton de Genève*, Iter Helveticum 19 (Fribourg: 1990), 276. See Linder RA 71 for a French example.

51. London BL 17355, 194v–195r. CO 2304b. *Deus qui ad hoc irasceris . . .*

52. Delaporte, *L'Ordinaire chartrain du XIIIe siècle*, 197–199.

53. CO 3007, *Hostium nostrorum . . .*

of England, and Frederick Barbarossa of Germany—all took the cross. Frederick died on his journey East, probably of a heart attack while fording the Saleph River. Philip participated in the first stage of the crusade, which involved the (eventually successful) siege of Acre, the coastal city that served as the Latin Kingdom's principal entrepôt. Upon its recapture, Acre became the de facto capital of the Kingdom of Jerusalem, intended only as long as the Holy City itself was out of Christian control. Richard was the one who stayed on the longest and made the most gains. A natural military leader, he faced off against Saladin in 1191 and 1192, recaptured key territory (including Jaffa), and restored a modicum of security and control over the lands still in Christian possession. He could not stay long enough, however, to make a go at retaking Jerusalem, and in the end, the Third Crusade was concluded in 1192 in an uneasy three-year truce between Richard the Lionheart and Saladin.

It was following the end of that truce that the next Pope, Innocent III, mounted the Fourth Crusade. Innocent was probably the most powerful of medieval popes and the pope who did more than anyone to centralize, institutionalize, and ideologically focus the business of crusade. One of the first things Innocent III did upon his election to the papal throne was turn his attention to the uneasy settlement in the Levant. The call for the new crusade went out in 1198 in the papal bull, *Post miserabile*.[54] The clamor had probably been performed intermittently and locally since 1188, but Innocent at this stage made new efforts to institute widespread liturgical supplication. In 1199 he wrote to French bishops—a letter that has all the hallmarks of a general encyclical—asking them to recite Psalm 78 along "with the usual prayer."[55] That same year he asked a Sicilian bishop to perform a *pro tribulatione* votive mass for crusaders.[56] And in December of that year he wrote to clergy throughout Christendom instructing special masses to be said weekly for the remission of the sins of those Christians who made offerings to crusaders.[57]

In the event, the crusader forces that departed on the Fourth Crusade from the eastern coast of Italy in 1202 never made it to the Levant. Due to financial troubles, mismanagement, and divisions among the army's elite,

---

54. PL 214:308B (tr. C&C 28–37).

55. PL 214:34. Augustus Potthast, ed. *Regesta Pontificum Romanorum inde ab a. Post Christum natum MCXCVIII ad A. MCCCIV*, 2 vols. (London: 1875), no. 1045 (1:97). Presumably, the "usual prayer" was *Omnipotens sempiterne deus*.

56. Othmar Hageneder et al., eds., *Das Register Innocenz' III*, 11 vols., Publikationen des Österreichischen Kulturinstituts in Rom. Reihe 1, vols. 1–2, 5–10 (Graz: 1964–), no. 508 (1:742–743). PL 214:470.

57. Hageneder et al., *Das Register Innocenz' III*, nos. 258 (2:495) and 259 (2:270), p. 500. The prescriptions were repeated verbatim. Tr. Andrea *Sources*, 30.

the crusade was diverted first to Zara (on the Dalmatian coast), and then, famously, to Constantinople, where the forces got sucked into a dynastic dispute, ending up, first, as kingmakers, and then ultimately conquerors. Innocent was initially beside himself, and then tried to make the best of the situation by sanctioning the establishment of the new Latin Empire of Constantinople. But he was also dismayed at how radically the crusade had diverted from its primary purpose—the reclamation of Jerusalem, to which Innocent remained devoted. The worry was that Christendom simply did not deserve to hold Jerusalem, that Christendom remained so mired in vice and spiritual pollution that God could not grant the Holy City into its custody. The launching of the Albigensian crusade to wipe out heresy in southern France in 1209—another of Innocent's projects—was part of the effort to purify Christian society at home. So was the Fourth Lateran Council.

Innocent III called Lateran IV in April 1213 with the bull *Vineam Domini*. The aim was wide-scale reform of lay and clerical society and the planning of a new crusade.[58] Lateran IV and the organization of the Fifth Crusade were part of a massive overhaul and reconceptualization by the curia of the recruitment, spiritual privileges, and financing of the crusades. It also involved an ambitious program of pastoral reform that was to be promulgated within Christendom by the very same preachers who were to preach the crusade, since internal reform and social virtue was one side of the coin of crusading victory.[59] That same month, Innocent issued *Quia Maior*, the encyclical that called for a Fifth Crusade. As part of the long document, he reinstituted the clamor, promulgated a special collect, *Deus qui admirabili*, and ordered all Christians to come out for supplicatory processions to demonstrate piety and penance and beg God to help defeat the enemy (appendix 2, col. 6).

In one sense, the liturgical prescriptions in *Quia Maior* were not that dramatic, since popes, churchmen, and even kings had asked for special prayers for crusading since the late 1180s.[60] But Innocent made liturgical supplication a keystone in the new strategy. The expansion of liturgical

---

58. James M. Powell, *Anatomy of a Crusade: 1213–1221* (Philadelphia: 1986).

59. Jessalynn Bird, "The Religious' Role in a Post-Fourth Lateran World," in *Medieval Monastic Preaching*, ed. Carolyn Muessig (Leiden: 1998), 209–229; Jessalynn Bird, "Innocent III, Peter the Chanter's Circle, and the Crusade Indulgence: Theory, Implementation, and Aftermath," in *Innocenzo III: Urbs et Orbis*, ed. Andrea Sommerlechner (Rome: 2003), 502–525; Jessalynn Bird, "The Victorines, Peter the Chanter's Circle, and the Crusade: Two Unpublished Crusading Appeals in Paris, Bibliothèque Nationale, MS Latin 14470," *Medieval Sermon Studies* 48 (2004): 5–28; Jessalynn Bird, "Paris Masters and the Justification of the Albigensian Crusade," *Crusades* 6 (2007): 117–155.

60. For example, Celestine III in 1195. Ralph of Diceto, *opera historica*: 2:134. Note that Celestine cited Psalm 78 and also Psalm 68, which was (and would be) employed as a versicle in expanded clamors.

supplication for the means of war seems to have been motivated by the success of a liturgical supplication a year earlier. On 16 May 1212, in the lead up to the Spanish offensive against the Almohads that would culminate in the victory at Las Navas de Tolosa, Innocent had staged an expiatory procession (*supplicatio generalis*) in Rome and personally presided over the ceremony "for peace of the entire church and the Christian people, and so that God might be favorably inclined toward those in the war which is engaged between them and the Saracens in the place called Spain, and so that [God] might not hand over His inheritance in shame, with nations [i.e., nonbelievers] ruling over them."[61] The language itself evoked Psalm 78's plea for God's inheritance. Men, women, clergy, and nuns, stripped of jewelry or finery, fasting and barefoot, were choreographed in an elaborate penitential procession, marching through various routes, from Santa Maria Maggiore to the Lateran and Saint Peter's, and then Santa Croce.[62] Rome's Santa Croce was actually called "Santa Croce in Jerusalem," making the procession into a symbolic pilgrimage.[63] The pope, with the relic of the True Cross taken from the Sancta Sanctorum (the pope's private chapel in the Lateran, and the location of an enormous stash of Holy Land relics),[64] preached a public sermon in open air before the Lateran, after which the pope himself performed mass in the basilica. The collect he used was the *Omnipotens sempiterne Deus*.[65] The rite was modeled on the Roman feast of the Exaltation of the Holy Cross. The relic was displayed to the faithful before the basilica and then paraded to the Lateran for the performance of a votive mass.[66] The showcasing of the relic only underscored the loss of the cross at Hattin, a fact which was now a stock element of crusade propaganda.

Innocent asked other churches to perform analogous supplications. As early as 31 January (1212), he had written to French bishops asking them to promote prayers throughout their districts for the upcoming Iberian confrontation and the pilgrims who would faithfully pursue it.[67] The Cistercian

61. PL 216:698.

62. Susan Twyman, "The *Roman Fraternitas* and Urban Processions at Rome in the Twelfth and Thirteenth Centuries," in *Pope, Church, and City: Essays in Honour of Brenda M. Boulton*, ed. Frances Andrews, Christoph Egger, and Constance Rosseau (Leiden: 2004), 205–221, particularly at pp. 217–219; Christoph T. Maier, "Mass, the Eucharist and the Cross: Innocent III and the Relocation of the Crusade," in *Pope Innocent III and His World*, ed. John Moore (Brookfield VT: 1999), 352–354; Cabrere, *Las Navas de Tolosa*: 142–153; C&C 82–85.

63. Cabrere, *Las Navas de Tolosa*, 147–148.

64. H. E. J. Cowdrey, "Pope Urban II and the idea of Crusade," *Studi Medievali* 3rd s. 36 (1995): 733–739.

65. PL 216:699.

66. Twyman, "The *Roman Fraternitas*," 219.

67. PL 216:513–514 (nos. CLIV and CLV).

chronicler Alberic of Trois Fontaines (d. >1252) spoke of how in May litanies and prayers were performed in France "for the Christians who were about to fight in Spain," probably in consort with Innocent's initial processions preceding La Navas.[68] And over a century later, another writer, also talking about 1212, spoke of how "at that time processions were being made throughout France to plead for God's grace against the infidels."[69] Gary Dickson has argued that the public, penitential processions in 1212 that were mounted in Chartres spurred the mobilization of the *pueri* that instigated the fated movement known as the Children's crusade.[70] During these processions, in which participants carried candles, banners, censers, and crosses, the pueri chanted (in French) not only for victory in Spain but also in the Holy Land: "O Lord God, exalt Christendom; O Lord God, return to us the True Cross."[71] Another chronicler reported that they acclaimed, "Towards Jerusalem; strive towards the Holy Land."[72]

Two months later (16 July 1212), the Christian forces won an extraordinary victory against the Almohads at Las Navas de Tolosa. This seems to have convinced Innocent of the efficacy of such supplication. Innocent wrote to King Alphonso VIII of Castile to remind him that the victory was the work of God and the papacy, which had organized the liturgical supplication that had been so decisive.[73] Then, in April of the following year, Innocent issued *Quia Maior*. The bull included wide-scale prescriptions for liturgical and processional intercessions. Innocent explained that such prayers could be militarily effective, saying that divine clemency was more powerful than human might, and that Christians should be fighting with spiritual weapons as much as corporeal ones.[74] In the bull itself, Innocent ordered a general procession every month, everywhere, with, when possible, men separated from women. The form of the procession would have been guided by whatever was the local rite for the Rogation processions—the general supplicatory processions done before Ascension. At the end of the procession, a sermon on the "work of the salvation bearing cross" should be

68. Alberic of Trois Fontaines, *Chronica*, MGH SS 23:894.

69. Jean d'Ypres, author of the *Chronica monasterii sancti Bertini*. Quote from Gary Dickson, "Stephen of Cloyes, Philip Augustus, and the Children's Crusade of 1212," in *Journeys Toward God: Pilgrimage and Crusade*, ed. Barbara N. Sargent-Baur (Kalamazoo, MI: 1992), 88. Original text in MGH SS 25:828.

70. RHF 18:603. Gary Dickson, *The Children's Crusade: Medieval History, Modern Mythistory* (New York: 2008).

71. RHF 18:355.

72. Gary Dickson, "La Genèse de la Croisade des Enfants," *Bibliothèque de l'École des chartres* 153 (1995): 99.

73. Cabrere, *Las Navas de Tolosa*, 153.

74. PL 216:820.

preached, a special mass said, and then a trunk for collections for the crusade be placed in the church, secured with keys entrusted each to an honest prelate, a devout layman, and another faithful churchman (*regularem*).

> And thus we institute and order that each month there be a general procession, with men separate, and women, where possible, also separate, in humility of mind and body, with a devout urgency in the beseechers' prayers that the merciful God should spare us from the disgrace of this confusion by liberating from the hands of pagans that land where He instituted all the sacraments of our redemption, by restoring [that land] to the Christian people for the praise and glory of His name; [and] by prudently providing that as part of this procession a sermon be preached on the salvation-bearing cross through diligent exhortation to the people. These prayers ought be done together with fasting and alms, so that by means of these things, as with the others, this prayer might more easily and more quickly fly up to those most pious ears of God, who clemently heeds us at this suitable time.[75]

Processions, prayers, alms, and a salvific sermon on the cross came as a package. This was part of the financing effort. But it was above all a part of the broader penitential program for the whole of Christendom that would be promulgated at the general council in 1215. It was a mechanism of having the entire community perform their commitment to the crusade, and to perform the penance that was understood to be critical to its success. As part of this overhaul, Innocent extended the indulgence and the status of *crucesignatus* to anyone who supported the crusade effort financially, meaning that being crucesignatus—being a crusader—was no longer about taking up arms. Likewise, liturgical prescriptions enveloped the Christian people as a whole into the crusading (and fundraising) effort. The instructions were of a piece with Innocent's program to enlarge the community of Christians who could, in different ways, be crucesignatus.

The encyclical specified that the clamor should be inserted into the mass each day, thus renewing the practice that Clement III had instituted twenty-five years earlier. Everybody should humble themselves before the altar as the clerics intone the plaintive, vengeful Psalm 78.

> Each day, too, as part of the solemn mass, after the kiss of peace, just before the offering for the sins of the world is performed, and just before the host of salvation is taken up, both men and women should humbly prostrate themselves on the ground. Then, this Psalm should be sung by the clerics aloud [alta voce]: *Deus venerunt gentes in hereditatem tuam* [Psalm 78]. And when this is devoutly completed, [sing] the verse *Exsurgat Deus, et dissipentur inimici ejus, et fugiant a facie ejus qui oderunt eam* (Ps. 67:2).[76]

75. PL 216:820 (see C&C 111–112, for a different translation).
76. PL 216:821.

Psalm 78 remained at the heart of the ideological message of crusade. It was central to a series of crusade appeals that were promulgated in the years following *Quia Maior* and was explicated in sermons on the cross.[77] A versicle was added from the equally militant Psalm 67: "Let God rise up, and may His enemies be scattered; and let them that hate Him flee before His face" (*Exsurgat Deus . . .*). Psalm 67, originally a song of victory and thanksgiving, portraying God as a divine warrior and celebrating God's reign, echoed the theme of the larger rite, which entrusted victory in the Holy Land to God's power.[78] The versicle was already being used for the clamor, notably by the Cistercians.[79] All were to prostrate themselves in humility before the altar and to recite the entirety of Psalm 78.[80] One manuscript instructed the priest, after the collect, to recite the antiphon: "Give peace to us, O Lord, in our days, because there is none other who fights for us except You, our Lord."[81]

Notably, Innocent replaced *Deus omnipotens sempiterne* with a new collect explicitly focused on the Holy Land. *Quia Maior* instructed that "then, the celebrating priest should sing this prayer above the altar": God, You who arranges all with astonishing providence (*Deus qui admirabili providencia*), we suppliantly beg You to restore to Christian worship that land, which Your own begotten son consecrated with His own blood, snatching it from the hands of the enemies of the cross, by mercifully directing the vows of the faithful pressing hard for its liberation, into the way of eternal salvation."[82] The collect echoed basic war prayers, but the aim here was specifically the liberation of the Holy Land and the restoration of the Christian worship, elemental aspects of crusading rhetoric since the time of Urban II. Muslims were identified as the "enemies of the cross"—a standard of crusading discourse derived ultimately from Philippians 3.18.[83] The Christians in prayer are eager for the work of this liberation, but any success is ultimately in God's hands. A number of manuscripts included an amplified version (originating in some versions of the original encyclical), which included an additional phrase: the supplicants were asking God to snatch the Holy Land from the hand (now singular) of the enemies of the

---

77. Jessalynn Bird, "Rogations, Litanies and Crusade Preaching: The Liturgical Front in the Early Thirteenth Century," in *The Papacy, Peace, the Crusade and Christian-Muslim Relations: Essays in Memory of James M. Powell*, ed. Jessalynn Bird (Routledge, forthcoming).

78. *The New Interpreter's Bible*, 4:944–978.

79. Waddell 2002, 286–287, 306–307. See appendix 2, col. 2.

80. Albi BM 5, 161r: *Oratione dominica completa, omnes humiliter se prosternant, et dicant psalmus totus.* Delaporte, *L'Ordinaire chartrain du XIIIe siècle*, 197.

81. London BL Add. 26655, 103r (Evreux missal, 13c): *Da pacem domine in diebus nostris quia non est alius qui pugnet pro nobis, nisi tu deus noster* (CAO 2090).

82. PL 216:821.

83. Kienzle, "Preaching the Cross," 13–14.

cross who "has odiously occupied [the land], not so much from the strength of his own power than from our own iniquities," before asking that God restore the land to Christian worship.[84] This version denied Muslim ethical or military superiority. It also amplified Christian culpability and sin. Innocent also spoke of "the Land which Your only begotten son our Lord consecrated with His own blood," emphasizing instead the increasingly important crusading theme of the Passion and the Christic. Christoph Maier has highlighted the sharply Eucharistic evocations, emphasizing Christ's sacrifice and thus Christic piety, as part of Innocent's largely devotional theology, as applied to crusading, which emphasized taking the cross as penance in imitation of Christ's own sacrifice.[85] As such, the deliberate shift under Innocent from *Omnipotens* to *admirabili* is emblematic of the themes of Christ's humanity and Passion that we have come to appreciate as a fundamental facet of crusading ideology in the thirteenth century.[86]

The Theology of Failure and the Power of Prayer

The liturgical project may have been part of a larger pastoral regime, but it was also designed to help the actual prosecution of war. Gregory VIII had established special supplicatory rites after Hattin so that God might "pardon us and leave His blessing behind Him."[87] This was in keeping with the theology of God's aid embedded in the earlier war rites, which assumed that military setbacks were caused by pride and sin, not by military deficiency or martial inferiority; that inner (or spiritual) purity was a prerequisite for outer (or material) victory. It was also in keeping with the pastoral and theological focus on sin and penance that preoccupied reforming thinkers coming out of Paris who influenced crusade thinking in the years around 1200, and the pastoral outreach embedded in the reform program inaugurated by Innocent III in the Fourth Lateran Council.[88] The earthly and salvific economy that balanced sin and defeat on the one hand, and purity, penance, and earthly victory on the other, was at the heart of the liturgical program operative throughout the thirteenth century.

The model was found in the stories of sin, defeat, purity, and military victory found throughout the Old Testament. The Old Testament, we have

84. Linder RA 40. Linder traced this variant to a different form of the text that was disseminated in copies of the original bull, *Quia Maior*.

85. Maier, "Crisis," 638–639.

86. Penny Cole, *The Preaching of the Crusades to the Holy Land, 1095–1270* (Cambridge, MA: 1991); Maier, *Crusade Propaganda*.

87. PL 202:1539.

88. Jessalynn Bird, "Heresy, Crusade and Reform in the Circle of Peter the Chanter, c.1187–c.1240" (University of Oxford, 2001); Bird, "Paris Masters"; Jean Flori, *Prêcher la croisade: XIᵉ–XIIIᵉ siècle, Communication et propagande* (Paris: 2012).

seen, offered many examples of prayer and penitence in the face of military losses. Two were particularly important in the thirteenth century. The first— the model for the function of the priest and his role as intermediary—was of Moses, holding his hands aloft in prayer allowing Joshua and the Israelites to defeat the Amalechites (Exodus 17). "When the law-giver [Moses] fought with prayers," said Innocent IV to the French clergy requesting the organization of liturgical intercession after the capture of Louis IX, "Israel quickly conquered in battle, and by means of his secret combat [that is, prayer] he returned a clear victory."[89] The second was the Ninevites—the model for communal repentance in the face of defeat and loss in order to showcase collective responsibility and collective penitential worthiness (Jonah 3:5–6). In 1217, during the prosecution of the Fifth Crusade, Honorius III, calling for special liturgical services for the Fifth Crusade, reminded his audience that God had spared the Ninevites only after they had repented, worn sack cloths and ashes, marched in procession, and beseeched forgiveness.[90]

Starting in the second decade of the thirteenth century with Innocent III, popes, preachers, and other churchmen repeatedly asserted the efficacy of faith and in particular prayer in promulgating requests for special prayers for Holy Land recovery.[91] Innocent himself had claimed that corporeal weapons should be matched by spiritual ones.[92] In a real sense then, the home front could fight the crusade through virtue, penitence, and above all through supplicatory prayer. Prayer was thus juxtaposed to swords as the means of victory. Philip the Chancellor, the Parisian clergyman who had called for vengeance on the Saracens in the aftermath of Hattin, preached a sermon in 1226 about the efficacy of intercessory prayers organized by the Church.[93] He explained that, in an effort to beg God to extend His

89. André Duchesne, *Historiae Francorum scriptores coaetanei . . . Quorum plurimi nunc primum ex variis codicibus mss. in lucem prodeunt: alij vero auctiores & emendatiores. Cvm epistolis regvm, reginarvm, pontificvm . . . et aliis veteribus rerum francicarum monumentis,* 5 vols. (Paris: 1636–1649), 5:417. Found also in Mansi 23:599, 24:402. See also *Regestum Clementis Papae V*: 4:312–313, no. 4769. Innocent III also evoked the Moses trope repeatedly in discussion Holy Land aid; see Hageneder et al., *Das Register Innocenz' III*, nos. 258 (2:495) and 259 (2:500).

90. RHF 19:639–640.

91. Jessalynn Bird, "Crusade and Reform: The Sermons of Bibliothèque Nationale, MS nouv. Acq. Lat. 999," in *The Fifth Crusade in Context: The Crusading Movement in the Early Thirteenth Century*, ed. Jan Vandeburie, Elizabeth Mylod, and Guy Perry (New York: Routledge: 2017).

92. PL 216:820.

93. Nicole Bériou, "La prédication de croisade de Philippe le Chancelier et d'Eudes de Châteauroux en 1226," *Cahiers de Fanjeaux* 32 (1997): 94. Maier, "Crisis," 646n98. I am enormously grateful to Christoph Maier and Nicole Bériou for sharing with me their not-yet-published editions of these sermons and permitting me to use the materials here.

hand to help in the crusade, "we do not cease to recite, on bent knee, the *Deus venerunt gentes*."[94] Nothing, he explained, would help in the Holy Land or in the South of France except recourse to divine aid and the suffrages of prayer, on the example of Esther.[95] The clergy's prayers are shields (*clipei*), just as soldiers fight with swords (*gladio*). "Clergy and other ecclesiastical people protect the body and the head of the church with the shield of prayer; however it is for the soldiers (*milites*) and laity to fight with the sword. In this way the sons of Israel conquered [the Amalechites] when Moses prayed and others fought."[96]

The Old Testament referent was of course in line with the larger framework encompassing sacred violence, providential meaning, and moral rectitude, which underlined crusade ideology and legitimization more broadly. Reform preachers active in the first two decades of the thirteenth century such as John of Abbeville, Philip the Chancellor, Jacques de Vitry, and Odo of Cheriton routinely evoked Old Testament models for the military efficacy of prayer. In addition to Moses in prayer against the Amalechites, and the Ninevites, examples include the wars of the Benjaminites (Judges 20)[97] and Joshua parading in supplication around the city of Ai.[98] In a sermon preached in Paris around the time of the Fifth Crusade, John of Abbeville called on the Benjaminites to explain how the outcome in war depends on the faith of the fighters.[99] The Israelites fasted and repented in the face of loss in the Benjaminite wars and God returned victory (Judg. 20). John was at pains to underscore the importance of penitence and penitential action in proving worthiness before the Lord. A few years later, during the Albigensian crusade, Odo of Chateauroux, the papal legate, in a sermon on the cross, alluded to the fact that the church had instituted special prayers and processions "in order to implore the saints for aid" and explained that the Israelites were only victorious after "they lamented before the Lord and fasted all day long until the evening and brought peace offerings and offerings of thanks."[100]

94. *Non cessamus multiplicare dicentes illud propter flexibus genibus: 'Deus venerunt gentes' etc.* Avranches BM 132, 248v–250r, and Troyes BM 1099, 15v–17r.

95. *Nichil igitur restat nobis, nisi recurrere ad auxilium divinum et ad suffragia oracionum et alia exemplo Ester.* Avranches 132, 248v–250r, and Troyes 1099, 15v–17r.

96. *Clerici quidem et ecclesiastice persone protegunt corpus ecclesie et caput, quod est fides, clipeo orationis; militum autem et laicorum est pugnare cum gladio; sic enim vincebant filii Israel cum Moyses orabat et alii pugnabant.* The sermon is found in Avranches 132, 248v–250r; and Troyes 1099, 15v–17r.

97. Ralph of Diceto, *Opera historica*: 2:133–134. Cole, *The Preaching of the Crusades*, 155, 225–226.

98. Jessalynn Bird, "Rogations, Litanies, and Crusade Preaching," discusses a series of preachers who use this trope.

99. Cole, *The Preaching of the Crusades*, 155, 225–226.

100. Maier, "Crisis," 640–641.

Preachers also insisted on the importance of these penitential and prayer exercises to help the work of crusaders in the Holy Land. Humbert of Romans OP, in a manual on preaching the cross, instructed preachers to explain that prayer could help fight wars, cited Judith who triumphed over Holophernes and his army by offering such prayers and Moses, whose prayers helped the Israelites conquer the infidel (*populum infidelem*); he hoped that "prayer might be useful against the infidels. And then he cited the special prayers said along with the *Deus venerunt gentes* Psalm."[101] An early thirteenth-century model sermon known as the *brevis ordinacio* explained,

> He who fights is in fear of death and ought not to be burdened, and the burden ought to be taken away from him, so that he might be agile. Rightly, thus, the church ought to unburden her warrior, who fights for her, and ought to sustain his burden. For this reason the Lord Pope justly remits to crusaders [*cruce signatis*] the penalty of sinners, and obliges the universal church to work on the behalf of those who are to be cleansed through their own contrition, devotion, confession, labours, and through the prayers and alms which are done by all Christians for pilgrims to the Holy Land.[102]

The sermon tied the success of the fighter to the contrition and penance of those praying on the home front. That was part of the point. Within the papal program, Christians throughout *Christianitas*—all Christians—bore a central function in waging war. This function was both liturgical and devotional. And this was in line with Innocent III's program of growing the social body invested in the fighting of the crusades.

That program was at heart one of social purity and reform. The *brevis ordinacio* called not only for prayers but also for devotion, contrition, and alms. One of the themes running throughout the sermons is the importance of fasting, charity, and almsgiving as a prerequisite for supplicatory prayer. These were the same qualities needed for a virtuous crusader (a temporary monk) to merit God's support in battle. But the point was that fighting against vice at home was the cognate of fighting the infidel abroad. The penitential disposition in the face of God's might was at the core of any earthly military success. The language understood penitential prayers explicitly in military terms. They also understood the penitential reform at home that was the key to success on the field as part of a larger eschatological war.

This idea was perhaps best visualized for the crusading kings of the French court in their exquisite series of moralized Bibles. The versions

---

101. Humbert of Romans, "Liber de predicatione."
102. QBS 8–9.

Figure 6.1 Moralization of Exodus 17.11. The top roundel shows Moses in prayer, supported by Aaron and Hur, allowing the Israelites to defeat the Amalechites. The lower roundel shows a priest at an altar fighting vices with prayer. Oxford Bodleian 270b, 51v. Ca. 1235, Image after Alexandre de Laborde, *La Bible moralisée illustrée conservée à Oxford, Paris et Londres*. Paris: 1911–1927.

Figure 6.2 Moralization of Exodus 17.8. The top roundel shows the Amalechites attacking the Israelites, after which the Israelites ask Moses for help. The bottom roundel shows good Christians clamoring to the Lord to defend them against the devil. Vienna ÖNB 1179, 34 Bb. Moralized Bible, ca. 1220.

finished in the 1220s and 1230s allegorized the episode of Moses praying and the Israelites achieving military victory (Exodus 17.8–11) as the fight against vice (Figs. 6.1 and 6.4). The gloss accompanying the picture that showed Moses in prayer read: "Moses who raises his hands in the air, which Ur and Aaron support while he prays, so that God might give them victory, signifies the prelate who extends hands on the sacrament of the altar and the Father and the Son sustain him and the Holy Spirit who sends to him the body of the Son whose presence gives victory to the people of God and expunges vices."[103] In the moralized Bible made for the crusading king Louis VIII, the imagery juxtaposed Moses in prayer with the priest at the altar (Fig. 6.3), and the Israelites (looking very much like crusaders) in battle against the Amalechites to three angels, beneath the hand of God, holding shields, swords, and spears, crushing vices (Fig. 6.4).[104] In Amalec's fight against the Israelites "the sons of Israel asking for help from Moses signify good Christians [who, in the top roundel, look like crusaders] who clamor [clamant] to the Lord so that He might defend them against the devil with His grace and excuse them (Fig. 6.2)."[105] The image done a decade later (Fig. 6.1), probably for the wife of another crusading king, Louis IX around 1235, shows clearly laymen and women of the community, barefoot, following the priest in prayer, and trampling vices underfoot.[106] Fighting against infidels and fighting against vices were the two poles of the same battle.

The Fifth Crusade would go to Egypt, with the aim of capturing Cairo and thus annihilating the center of Ayyubid power. Only then, the strategists argued, would the crusaders be able to take and keep Jerusalem.[107] As part of the vast spiritual and practical organization which Innocent instituted in preparation for the Fifth Crusade, Innocent deputized his army of crusade

---

103. Oxford, Bodleian 270b, 51v Aa, allegorizing Exodus 17.11: "Moyses qui tendit manus in altum quas ur & aaron sustinent dum orat ut deus det eis victoriam significat prelatum qui tendit manus sursum in sacramento altaris et pater & filius eum sustinent & spiritus sanctus qui ei mittit corpus filii cuius presentia populo dei victoria datur & vicia expugnantur."

104. Vienna ONB 1179, 34Dd. "Hoc significatur patrem qui mittit suo prelato corpus filii presentia cuius populo dei victoria datur & vicia expugnantur." The personified vices hold a scroll identifying them as vicia victa—conquered vices. The earliest of the moralized Bibles, Vienna ÖNB 2554 included the episode as well (23RCc). There, the old French moralization spoke of slaughtering miscreants and heretics (detrenchent les mescreanz et les populicanz). On dating, see John Lowden, The Making of the Bibles Moralisées (University Park, PA: 2000).

105. Vienna ÖNB 1179, 34. "Filii Israhel petentes auxilium a Moyse significant bonos christianos qui clamant ad dominum ut eos contra diabolum muniat sua gratia ad ipsum excusandum."

106. Oxford Bodleian 270b, 51v, Aa. That these figures are secular and not monks, priests, and nuns is clear from the iconography. The woman's hat is clearly secular. No one bears a tonsure. And the extra sleeves were signs of wealth, not used for habits.

107. Powell, Anatomy of a Crusade.

Figure 6.3 Moralization of Exodus 17.11. The top roundel shows Moses, supported by Aaron and Hur, in prayer to the Lord. The bottom roundel shows a priest performing mass, supported by the Father, the Son, and the Holy Spirit. Vienna ÖNB 1179, 34 Cc. Moralized Bible, ca. 1220.

oyfes tendes
manuf in
attum uincc
bat ist'. si autt
paululu remi
fiss supetabat
amaleth.

Be sigmsté.
patiem q
intttt suo p
letto torpuf tili
ptesenta auf
ppl'o den uicton
q datut.z uia
a expugnate.

Figure 6.4 Moralization of Exodus 17.11. The top roundel shows the Israelites defeating the Amalechites. The bottom roundel shows three angels defeating vices, identified by the scroll, which reads *vicia victa* (conquered vices). Vienna ÖNB 1179, 34 Dd. Moralized Bible, ca. 1220.

preachers and legates to institute and publicize the prescriptions for intercessory liturgical processions and prayers. He sent Oliver of Paderborn and Herman of Bonn to Liège to preach the cross, to organize monthly processions, and to make collections for the Jerusalem crusade.[108] William of London, Leo of Wells, and Philip of Oxford were sent to England to organize the local campaigns.[109] Liturgies were promulgated at local councils and synods designed to promote ecclesiastical and lay reform needed for successful crusade. Special prayers *pro terra Jersosolimitana et Constantinopolitana, [et] pro christianitate de Albigeis* to be offered in all the major churches in Paris were recorded in an early thirteenth-century copy of the "Constitutions of Eudes of Sully [Bishop of Paris]."[110]

The call for processions often went hand in hand with the renewal of the clamor and may have been assumed as part of the general liturgical crusading package that popes and their legates prescribed, following Innocent, throughout the thirteenth century. In 1217, with the crusaders on their way to Egypt, Honorius III repeated Innocent's Roman procession of 1212, and he then ordered the episcopacy in France and then Germany to organize processions and prayers throughout their dioceses on the first Friday of each month.[111] This was essentially the renewal of Innocent III's liturgical program. At one point, Honorius even spoke of "sticking to the footsteps of our predecessors."[112] In an encyclical that reinstituted monthly communal processions, he laid out his understanding of providential history and the devotional logic that underwrote the need for penitential processions.[113] He began by explaining that "old examples" (from the Old Testament) teach us to "fight against visible enemies with invisible weapons, that is, with prayers," as does, Honorius remembered, the recent example (of Las Navas of Tolosa) when "God delivered the multitude of the army of the infidel in the war in

108. RHF 18:630; MGH SS 16:671. See also details for Innocent sending preachers to England in 1212 or (more likely) 1213, in the *Annales de Dunstaplia*, in the *Annales Monastici*, ed. H. R. Luard (London: 1864–1869), RS 36, 3:40.

109. *Annales Monastici*, ed. H.R. Luard, 5 vols., RS 36, 3:40.

110. Odette Pontal, ed. *Les Statuts synodaux français du XIIIe siècle: précédés de l'historique du synode diocésain depuis ses origines*, Collection de documents inédits sur l'histoire de France. Série in-80, 9, 15, 19, 23, 29 (Paris: 1971-), 1:96.

111. RHF 19:639–640 (for 1217); Petrus Pressuti, ed. *Regesta Honorii Papae III*, 2 vols. (Rome: 1888, 1905), 149–150 (no. 885), to the bishop of Ariège (in the Garonne). For Germany, see letter contained in the Chronicle of Richard of Saint Germain, Augusto Gaudenzi, *Ignoti Monachi Cisterciensis S. Mariae de Ferraria Chronica et Ryccardi de Sancto Germano Chronica priora / repperit in codice ms. Bononiensi atque nunc primum edidit Augustus Gaudenzi; adiectis ejusdem Ryccardi chronicis posterioribus ex editione Georgii Pertzii* (Naples: 1888), 119–121.

112. Gaudenzi, *Ignoti Monachi Cisterciensis*, 120–121. RHF 19:639–640 (to French bishops). See also the Pressuti, *Registra Honorii Papae III*, Rome 1888, 149–150, no. 885.

113. He made at least two separate requests in 1217: Pressuti, *Regesta Honorii Papae III*, 1:149–150, no. 885; RHF 19:639–649.

Spain into the hands of the few faithful, and [delivered] glory."[114] And thus the entire faithful must undertake these things and sprinkle their heads with ashes.[115] "Now is the time when we ought to clamor [*exclamare*] to the heavens with our tears and with our prayers."[116] Victories in the East will be won not by the army, but by the power of God. Honorius wrote that those who had landed in the Levant, "knowing full well, since victory does not come from the size of the army but is ministered from heaven, that there is no difference in the sight of heaven's God between liberating by the many or by the few, they—indeed, few in number—entered the land of Babylon [i.e., Egypt] trusting greatly in aid from above."[117] Drawing on the corporate metaphor for the faithful—the Ecclesia whose head is Christ—Honorius explained that the members of the Church might more easily than "the few" (the fighting men) obtain the "mercy of divine power" through the entreaty of such prayer. They must clamor (*exclamare*) to God with the voices of their hearts and their mouths. Indeed, this work, he said, must be borne by "the entire Christian people," which is the *Ecclesia*, and which "must at this very hour begin a glorious battle for the faith in Christ."[118] Following *Quia Maior*, processions were ordered for the first Friday of every month in every city (or any place where there is a sufficient crowd of people), by everyone, barefoot, and wearing the cross (except those canonically cloistered "by which they are spared from the great tumults of the world"). Honorius then evoked the Ninevites dressing in sackcloths and performing processions, Moses praying and causing the Amalechites to turn in flight, and Joshua stilling the sun with his prayers. And thus, Honorius promised, God, assailed by the devout clamors (*clamoribus*) of so many of His faithful, "will incline His ears to hear the prayers of His servant, and *will pour out His ire on the heathen who do not know Him, and in the kingdoms where they do not invoke His name.* [Ps. 78:6] To His praise and Glory may He destroy the horns of sin."[119] The "horns of sin" was a reference to Ps. 74:11: "And I will break all the horns of the sinners; but the horns of the just shall be exalted." The line preceding it—that God will pour His Ire upon the infidel, from Psalm 78—was recited in full as part of the clamor that followed the processions. Men and women, remembering the Ninevites and in accordance with their example, were to be carefully reminded that they perform these rites "not in precious clothing or with other vain splendors" but should bear themselves in mutual devotion

114. RHF 19:639.
115. RHF 19:639.
116. RHF 19:639.
117. RHF 19:639.
118. RHF 19:639–640.
119. RHF 19:639–640.

and with internal and external humility.[120] In this way, the processions and zealous exhortations will aid the crusaders (crucesignatos) so that, led by God, those fortified by the sign of the cross might journey forward.[121]

Institutionalization and Response

Liturgical supplication and the crusade procession became a central feature of papal crusading policy in the thirteenth century. The progress of the Fifth Crusade, despite an initial success in taking the coastal city of Damietta, ended in defeat in 1221 when the crusaders undertook their march on Cairo. This only redoubled plans to undertake new ventures. There was always a trickle of men from the West who left to shore up the military defenses of Christians in the East. But the central campaigns after the failure of the march on Cairo were the crusade of Frederick II (considered by many a farce, but which did succeed in a negotiated return of Jerusalem to the Latin Kingdom), the Barons' Crusade (1239–1241), and especially, the two crusades of Louis IX. Louis left on his first crusade in 1248, headed, as during the Fifth Crusade, to Egypt. After a rapid conquest of Damietta (celebrated, we saw, liturgically at the Cathedral of Laon), the army headed for Cairo. A battle outside of the outpost at Mansurah resulted in heavily depleted forces. When the king finally ordered retreat, the result was catastrophic. The king and pretty much all the surviving soldiers were captured by the Egyptians. Louis and what remained of his army left Egypt only after a negotiated ransom. When he took up the cross again (1267), he headed for North Africa. But this, Louis's second crusade, largely dissipated after he died in 1270. His brother, Charles of Anjou, king of Sicily, and the future King Edward I, continued to the East. Edward made some gains against the Mamluk general Baybars in 1271 but ultimately was called home.

Alongside this constant concern and frequent project planning for crusade throughout the thirteenth century, prayers, clamors, and processions in aid of the Holy Land became utterly commonplace in Latin Christendom. They were frequently legislated at the top. Popes, legates, bishops, and other churchmen made repeated requests for these prayers (See appendix 3) of the churches in their ambit. After Innocent III (d. 1216) and Honorius III (d. 1227), requests for the clamors and processions were made by Popes Gregory IX (1227–1241),[122] Innocent IV (1243–1254),[123] Alexander IV

120. RHF 19:640.
121. RHF 19:640.
122. MP 4:111. Matthew Paris dates this to 1241.
123. Thomas Rymer, *Foedera: conventiones, litterae, et cujuscunque generis acta publica, inter reges Angliae et alios quosvis imperatores, reges, pontifices, principes, vel communitates, ab ingressu Gulielmi I in Angliam*, 4 in 7 vols. (London: 1641–1713), 1.i:286. Elie Berger, ed. *Les*

(1254–1261),[124] and Gregory X (1271–1276).[125] Orders were issued from the curia but circulated to the local level through encyclicals and through papal legates.[126] These could be intended for broad application throughout Christendom, but usually they were directed to a specific area, often in conjunction with a particular recruiting effort or to support a particular crusade. Supplications could then be promulgated at a more local level, by bishops,[127] at local councils and synods, usually, although not always, in response to the papal prescription.[128] They were generally instituted in support of specific military efforts. So, in the 1240s, following Mongol advances into Russia and Poland in 1240 and 1241, the German and English episcopacy instituted fasting, special prayers, and processions against the Mongols.[129] In the same period, while Louis IX was preparing for his first Crusade, the legate, Odo of Chateauroux, promulgated an expanded clamor that included not only Innocent III's *Deus qui admirabili* but also the prayer for the king, which was appropriate for the crusade being headed up by the king of France (see appendix 2, col. 9).[130] This may have originated with Innocent IV, though the evidence survives only in French manuscripts. A series of short versicles were added at this time, including one that prayed for "captives," a particularly important concern after the unsatisfactory conclusion of the Fifth Crusade. In France, the king and queen themselves seem to have made special requests for prayers for the success of the crusade.[131] There is plenty of evidence in the manuscripts that communities adopted and performed the rite. Salimbene reports that Louis himself asked the Franciscans to pray for crusade and that they recited Psalm 78 every day for

Registres d'Innocent IV, 3 vols., Bibliothèque des Écoles française d'Athènes et de Rome (Rome: 1884–1921), vol. 3, nos. 6035 and 6036; Duchesne, *Historiae francorum scriptores*: 5:417.

124. Mansi, 23:1045–1047; Eudes of Rouen, *Regestrum visitationum archiepiscopi rothomagensis; journal des visites pastorales d'Eude Rigaud, archevêque de Rouen, 1248–1269. Pub. pour la première fois, d'après le manuscrit de la Bibliothèque nationale*, ed. Th. Bonnin (Rouen: 1852), 389. Karl Joseph von Hefele, *Histoire des conciles d'apres les documents originaux*, trans. Henri Leclercq (Paris: 1907–), 6.1:99.

125. Canivez, *Statuta* 3:127; Tanner, *Decrees of the Ecumenical Councils*: 1.310–311.

126. Canivez, *Statuta* 2:289.

127. Bartholomew Cotton, *Historia anglicana (A.D. 449–1298.)*, RS 16 (London: 1859), 207.

128. Pontal, *Les Statuts synodaux français*, 5:60, no. 30. Mansi 23:798. Salimbene 1:580 (tr. 404). Gilles Gerard Meersseman, "Disciplinati e Penitenti nel Duecento," in *Il Movimento dei Disciplinati nel Settimo Centenario dal suo inizio (Perugia—1260)* (Perugia: 1962), 65.

129. Peter Jackson, "The Crusade against the Mongols (1241)," *Journal of Ecclesiastical History* 42 (1991): 1–18. Jean-Louis-Alphones Huillard-Bréholles, ed. *Historia diplomatica Friderici Secundi, sive constitutiones, privilegia, mandata, instrumenta quae supersunt istius Imperatoris et filiorum ejus*, 7 vols. (Paris: 1852–1860), 5.ii:1211; *Annales Monastici*: 3:157; F. M. Powicke and R.C. Cheney, *Councils and Synods, with Other Documents Relating to the English Church*, 2 in 4 vols. (Oxford: 1964–1981), 2.i:340.

130. Linder RA 44–45.

131. Salimbene 1:320, 323 (tr. 213); RHF 20:412–413.

a full year.[132] The Cistercians, who had begun praying for the Holy Land in 1188, reissued statutes repeatedly for the singing of Psalm 78 *pro negotio sancti*.[133] The Carthusians had adopted the practice by 1223.[134] The Dominicans performed the clamor for Louis both in 1248 and in advance of Louis IX's second crusade.[135] Again in the 1260s, after the fall of the Latin Empire of Constantinople, the papacy encouraged liturgical supplication.[136] By the time Acre fell to Al-Ashraf Khalil in 1291, the clamor was so ubiquitous that William Durandus included it in his new pontifical, and it was, through Durandus, disseminated widely through Latin Christendom in the fourteenth century.[137] Here it was titled the "Ordo for the Liberation of the Holy Land from the Enemies of the Faith."[138] Although most of these were keyed to the Holy Land, clamors, processions, and supplications on that model were also performed for the Albigensian crusade,[139] for crusading in Spain,[140] for the threat to the Kingdom of Constantinople,[141] and even for Innocent IV's crusade against his archenemy, Frederick II.[142]

The manuscript record shows the extent to which these prescriptions were adopted and enacted on the local level. Different versions of the clamor were copied into the margins, or the back, of manuscripts as churchmen received the instructions.[143] Linder was able to identify Innocent IV's expansion of the clamor in the 1240s not by the encyclical, which does not survive, but by the many on-the-ground examples of the manuscripts into which it had been copied. By the end of the century, clamors, votive masses, or other prayers were found in liturgical books across Christendom, from Catalonia, to England, to southern Italy, and Slovenia. These

---

132. Salimbene 1:320, 323, 340 (tr. 213, 214, 229).

133. See appendix 2 for summaries.

134. LeCouteulx, *Annales ordinis Cartusiensis*: 3:392. Their version was the *Deus qui ad nostre redemptionis* clamor.

135. Elie Berger, ed. *Layettes du Trésor des chartes*, 5 vols., vol. 4, Inventaires et documents (Paris: 1863), 3:33, no. 3674. Daniel Antonin Mortier, *Histoire des maître généraux de l'ordre des frères prêcheurs [par] R.P. Mortier des frères prêcheurs*, 8 vols. (Paris: 1904–1914), 2:78. For proper prayers, see Ansgarius Dirks, "De liturgiae dominicanae evolutione (continuatio)," *Archivum Fratrum Praedicatorum* 54 (1984): 43–44.

136. Mansi 23:1045–1047; Salimbene 1:580. Eudes of Rouen, *Regestrum visitationum*, 389.

137. Pierre-Marie Gy, "Guillaume Durand: 'Evêque de Mende (v. 1230–1296), canoniste, liturgiste et homme politique: actes de la table ronde du C.N.R.S., Mende 24–27 mai 1990" (Paris, 1992); Vogel, *Medieval Liturgy*, 253–255.

138. PWD III.XVI.1–3 (630–631).

139. Canivez, *Statuta* 2:219 (no. 18, for 1240).

140. Waddell, *Twelfth-Century Statutes*, 306–307.

141. Canivez, *Statuta* 2:69 (for 1228), 78 (for 1229), 128–129 (for 1234), 201 (1239), 219 (for 1240).

142. Matthew Paris 4:11.

143. Linder RA 72–73.

bore rubrics such as "prayers for the land of Jerusalem,"[144] to "against those who invade Jerusalem,"[145] to "for the Holy Land and for Christians; against pagans and those fighting in that place"[146] to "for the tribulations of the land of Jerusalem"[147] and "against the incursions of the pagans."[148] In contrast, the manuscript record also offers evidence of how local communities established their own liturgical practices, totally unrelated to the larger institutional effort. In Catalonia, for instance, the community adapted a standard *contra paganos* votive mass to be used in support of "the Holy Land and city of Jerusalem," that was used in Tortosa and Girona.[149] The English developed their own clamor that differed slightly from the papal prescription (appendix 2, col. 12).[150] A German mass from the late twelfth or early thirteenth century includes an entirely novel votive mass *pro tribulatione Ierusalem.*[151] Vernacular entreaties ("bidding prayers") directed at the parish were composed throughout this period in England, France, and Spain.[152] These translated the larger liturgical program and ideology into a vernacular pastoral program that could then be reinforced through preaching. In general, the bidding prayers asked the parish to pray for the Holy Land and for the Christian people and that it be delivered from Saracen hands.

"Whensoever It Might Happen that Someone Celebrates the Office of the Mass"

This is all to say that the practice of the clamor was widely established when Clement V (1305–1314) switched the liturgical form of the standard crusading supplication. The situation in the Latin East that Clement inherited when he acceded to the papacy had never been worse. Antioch had fallen to the Mamluks in 1268. Louis IX's last crusade never made it out of Tunis. Edward I's marginal gains were quickly wiped out by a steady onslaught of the Mamluks. Under Baybars (1260–1277), Kalavun (1279–1290), and then Khalil (1290–1293), the Mamluks steadily eroded the remaining Latin possessions in the Levant, taking Tripoli in 1289 and finally, Acre, always described as the last Latin outpost in the Levant, in

---

144. London BL Add. 15419, 60r: *Pro terra hierosolimitana Preces.*
145. Provins BM 11, 96v: *Contra invasores Iherusalem.*
146. Arras BM 49, 142r. *Pro terra sancta et pro christianis contra paganos et in ea certantibus.*
147. Valenciennes BM 108, 50v: *Pro tribulatione terre ierosolimitane.*
148. Dartmstadt Hessische Landes und Hockschulbibliothek ms 3183, 188r: *Contra paganorum incursiones.*
149. Linder RA 107–108, 150–151: *et super terram ac civitatem sanctam Hierusalem.*
150. Linder RA 55–67.
151. Linder DWM 21.
152. Linder RA 353–361.

1291. At the time, of course, the loss was not seen as permanent, and discussions continued about mounting a new crusade. But strategy was changing, and the first order of business was to shore up the security and military strength of what Christian forces remained in the region. For Clement, who became pope in 1305, this meant providing targeted aid to the Kingdom of Armenia against the Mongols. In 1308, less than a generation since the collapse of the Latin East to the Mamluks, Clement got news of the Mongol advances, and in response, he organized a circumscribed venture (*a passagium particulare*) in which the Hospitallers would go to the aid of the Christian kingdom in advance of a larger French expedition that he hoped King Philip IV ("the Fair") would mount.[153] This was one of three planned passages—the other two being in Aragon and against Venice—which Clement sponsored in these years, but the only one toward which he apparently marshaled spiritual defenses. It was to be the first expedition into the Mediterranean launched since the fall of Acre in 1291.

On 11 August 1308, Clement issued a series of bulls to organize the five-year venture designed to defend the Kingdom of Armenia and disrupt Mongol trade in the Mediterranean. One promoted preaching, raising funds, and promulgated special "orations ordained throughout the church against the perfidy of pagans" which were to be said for the five-year duration.[154] The bull opened with Psalm 67: *Exurgat Deus et inimici dissipentur ipsius* (Let God rise up and let his enemies be scattered), the verse that had been used as a versicle in Holy Land recovery liturgy since the early thirteenth century. He called for the collection of prorated indulgences, preaching and confession throughout the dioceses, and for special prayers to be said for the five-year period. And he specified the incipits of three standard *contra paganos* prayers from the Roman missal: *Omnipotens sempiterne deus*, *Sacrificium domine*, and *Protector noster*. A year later, on 11 July 1309, alarmed by the "widening seizures of the Holy Land by the impious hands of pagans," the pope issued a second encyclical again asking clergy—both secular and monastic—to insert the *contra paganos* prayers in masses for the Hospitallers who were fighting overseas.[155] He evoked Moses fighting through prayer[156] and gave the precise wording of the three central prayers.

---

153. Norman Housley, "Pope Clement V and the Crusades of 1309–10," *Journal of Medieval History* 8 (1982): 29–43; Norman Housley, *The Avignon Papacy and the Crusades, 1305–1378* (Oxford: 1986); Sylvia Schein, *Fideles Crucis: The Papacy, the West, and the Recovery of the Holy Land, 1274–1314* (Oxford and New York: 1991), 220–233.

154. *Regestum Clementis Papae V*: 3:161, no. 2989. 11 Aug. 1308.

155. *Regestum Clementis Papae V*: 4:312–313, no. 4769. 11 July 1309. Georgiou, "Propagating the Hospitallers' *Passagium*: Crusade Preaching and Liturgy in 1308–1309," 60–61. He also wrote Cistercians asking for specific prayers.

156. *Regestum Clementis Papae V*: 4:312–313, no. 4769.

For the collect:

Omnipotens sempiterne Deus: Almighty and everlasting God, in whose hands are the power and rule of all kingdoms, take care for the Christian armies [*or* look down in aid of the Christians; this issue is how one translates *auxilium*] such that the pagan people who put trust in their own valor may be vanquished by the power of Your right hand.

For the Secret:

Sacrificium Domine: Look upon, O Lord, the sacrifice that we offer up, so that You might release Your defenders [*propugnatores*] from all the evils of the pagans and that we might be placed in the security of Your protection.

And for the Postcommunion:

Protector noster. Look upon [us] O God, our protector, and defend Your defenders from the dangers of pagans, so that all perturbations having been warded off, they might serve You with unfettered souls.[157]

This sequence followed the standard *contra paganos* votive mass,[158] but Clement used an updated version to heighten the opposition between "Christian" and "the pagan peoples" and to emphasize the militant and oppositional context. God is asked to "look kindly on the Christian armies" (*auxilium christianorum*, instead of the Roman Empire, or the Frankish kingdom) so that the *gentes paganorum* (instead of just the *gentes*) might be wiped out. "We" became "Your defenders." The "dangers of wars" became "the dangers of pagans." And God is asked to defend us from "the pagans" rather than, simply, "the enemy." These prayers reflected the form of the *contra paganos* mass used in the Kingdom of Jerusalem since the early twelfth century.[159] The changes aligned the old votive mass more directly with the crusading project, and obviously, undergirded once again the old trope of Muslims as pagans.[160]

Clement, as Linder noted, was essentially turning every mass said in Christendom into a votive mass to "aid Christians" and "destroy the race of

---

157. *Regestum Clementis Papae V*: 2989. "Oratio: Omnipotens sempiterne Deus, in cuius manu sunt omnium potestates et omnia iura regnorum, respice in auxilium christianorum, ut gentes paganorum, que in sua feritate confidunt, dextere tue potentia conterantur. Secreta: Sacrificium Domine, quod immolamus intende, et propugnatores tuos ab omni exuas paganorum nequitia et in tue protectionis securitate constituas. Post communionem. Protector noster aspice Deus et propugnatores tuos a paganorum defende periculis ut ab omnibus perturbationibus summoti liberis tibi mentibus serviant." Cf. CO 3846 (with many variants), 5217a, and 4746 respectively.
158. SMRL 2:324.
159. From the evidence of BNF Lat. 12056, 268r; see chapter 4.
160. For examples, see Linder RA 151–154.

pagans" for the duration of the campaign.[161] Some localities had composed special votive masses in the late twelfth and thirteenth centuries, but up until 1308 liturgical warfare had generally come in the form of the clamor.[162] Gone, thus, was Psalm 78 and Innocent's *Deus qui admirabili*, both clearly centered on Jerusalem, perhaps because the immediate focus was the Kingdom of Armenia, not Jerusalem. Also gone was the call for processions—perhaps because the goal here was less recruitment than it was supplication, and thus the need to bring the Christian community into the ritual call to God was not as urgent. The point here was entreating God more than it was soliciting the penitential aid of the larger community.

Ideologically, this was a stunning development. The central ritual of the Christian faith, the ritual that defined God's community theologically and that expressed that community through ritual action, was being used to define the enemy both ideologically and militarily. Clement had specifically instructed that "whensoever it might happen that one celebrates the office of the mass," special prayers "against the perfidy of pagans" should be ordered throughout the Church, by anyone who has been ordained a priest.[163] Crusading had moved right to the very heart of the central ritual of the community, making crusading synonymous with being Christian, and in turn defining Christianity itself in relation to its military fight against pagans. Innocent had done a version of this in 1213 with the clamor, but the use of core prayers underscored that the essential function of the mass was now advocating to God for help in fighting the crusades. That is, the central ritual of personal and collective salvation was now intrinsically, essentially, and existentially connected not only to the definition of the religious community, but also its now inherent and belligerent stance against Islam. The mass itself was being co-opted for the very specific aim of achieving victory over the infidel. This only made sense because of the long liturgical tradition of associating the enemy of Christ with the enemies of the Cross. As we saw in the first chapter, the eternal, or otherworldly, enemy was increasingly transformed into the temporal and real-world military and religious enemies. The liturgy had actualized its spiritual belligerence. Christian salvific history was being ever more associated with victory and triumph—the victory and triumph of the cross—in this world. And crusading was now existentially related to the broad, providential, and eschatological battle between God and the devil.

161. Linder RA 120.
162. Linder RA 103–108.
163. *Regestum Clementis Papae V*: 3:161, no. 2989.

7

Praying against the Turks

Shortly after 29 May 1453, on learning the news of the fall of Constantinople to the young Mehmet the Conqueror, Bernard, the bishop of Cattaro (d. 1457), composed a special mass "asking for God's help against the imminent savagery of the perfidious Turks."[1] Bernard was a native of Padua but had been posted to Cattaro, on the Dalmatian coast, just a few months earlier. Cattaro (modern: Kotor, in Montenegro), was a Venetian colony, a Catholic see on the Dalmatian coast that belonged to the archdiocese of Bari; but, adjacent to Hungary, the city was nearer the immediate danger posed by the Ottoman advance. Bernard's mass was at once militant and full of despair. It asked the Lord "who has fought in wars from the very start, [to] raise up Your arm against the heathen," and "waste their strength, O Lord, and scatter them, so that they should know there is no one other who fights for us except You"; "Destroy the power [*potentiam*] of the Turks with Your power [*virtute*], and may their strength [*robur*] perish in Your wrath."[2] The secret compared the Ottoman threat to the Passion and God's aid to redemption. Addressing God, the sole conqueror who rules over all kingdoms and princes, the prayer begs: "Just as we are redeemed from servitude to the devil through the Passion of Our Lord Jesus Christ, so might we be free by Your help and protection from the threat of the Turks."[3] And it included a long and extraordinary rhyming sequence that crystallized the penitential reaction to the defeat, which began by reviewing the political and religious threat posed by the Ottomans.[4]

---

1. The texts for this mass are found in Linder RA DWM 37, 262–268. On Bernard of Venice, see Daniel Farlati, Filippo Riceputi, and Jacopo Coleti, *Illyrici sacri*, 8 vols. (Venice: 1751–1819), 6:466–468.
2. Linder RA DWM 37, p. 264, Graduale verses.
3. Linder RA DWM 37, p. 267.
4. Linder RA DWM 37, pp. 264–266, the Prosa.

They have gathered together, invading our land, in fury and with the
sword.
They then began to subjugate and they held Byzantium with great power.
They profaned sacred shrines, they plundered the temples of Christ, just like
rabid dogs.
They destroyed the priesthood; they pillaged sacred instruments without
reverence.
They dug up the saints of Christ, they dismembered the blessed bones by
throwing them to the dogs.
They killed or sold off those worshipping the faith of Christ, there they sent
them into exile.
They profaned the altars, and the chaste vestal virgins dear to God.
They destroyed unremittingly the walls on which Christ and His mother
were depicted.
They disfigured the saints; the pulpits and the bell towers remain silent.
They subverted the cult of God.

The sequence echoed the usual complaints about Turkish cruelty and barbarism that reflected the anti-Turkish propaganda circulating in the West in the mid-fifteenth century.[5] Then the sequence shifted to the present tense. The Turks are rising up again, threatening to dominate all of Greece. They invade, attack Christians, and force them to serve idolatry. They even threaten the Holy City (Rome), despising the seat of Saint Peter, the vicar of Christ. This too echoed a pervasive rumor that Mehmet had vowed to come next to Rome. The sequence then ordered, "Clamor now! Pray now!" It is time to supplicate the Redeemer, the One who redeemed our sins with His own blood; the One who broke through the gates of hell, and founded the Church; he who has struck down heretics and damned schismatics. It is He who makes your walls strong. But His force and power is dependent on your contrition, your penitential sincerity. "If you are faithful and doubt, and pray with your whole heart, Christ will hear you." Then the sequence calls on the power of Christ himself: "Oppose and crush those opposing us. The church will be profaned unless Your strong hand aids from above. Send down Your hand from on high, and put this rebel—this profane, Turkish dog—to flight. Since You, God, are the ruler of everything, and we are nothing without Your help. Please hear us in clemency, Jesus, loving and powerful, destroy the enemies." And then: "Give us help. Defend us. Give us victory."

Bernard's mass foreshadowed a flowering of liturgical supplication in support of crusading against the Ottomans in the fifteenth century.[6] It represents

5. Reviewed by Robert Schwoebel, *The Shadow of the Crescent: The Renaissance Image of the Turk (1453–1517)* (New York: 1967), 12–14; Margaret Meserve, *Empires of Islam in Renaissance Historical Thought* (Cambridge MA: 2008), 65–116; Nancy Bisaha, *Creating East and West: Renaissance Humanists and the Ottoman Turks* (Philadelphia: 2004).
6. Paul II confirmed the ceremony in 1470. It was included in a printed Teutonic missal in 1499: Adolph Franz, *Die Messe im deutschen Mittelalter: Beiträge zur Geschichte der Liturgie*

a genre, identified by Adolph Franz in 1902 and catalogued by Amnon Linder in 2003, of what Linder calls the "Dedicated War Mass"—long proper masses with a large number of proper readings—directed principally though not exclusively against the Turks that exploded in the second half of the fifteenth century, principally, although again not exclusively, in France, Germany, and in ecclesiastical centers along the Danube. Although examples of the genre date to the fourteenth century (and one to the thirteenth), the examples multiplied in the fifteenth in response to the Ottoman advance. The amplification of these forms of ceremonial supplication in the fifteenth century demonstrates the continued importance of holy war and crusading long after 1291.

The explosion of dedicated war masses in the fifteenth century attests to both continuities and innovation in the practice and devotional content of crusading liturgy. These continuities of form and content occurred against the broader backdrop of epochal changes in context: Arab Muslims ("Saracens") and (Seljuk) Turks of the Levant had been traded in for the Ottomans; early humanism and stirrings of Reformation thought had begun to transform the texture and priorities of medieval thought; a unified Christendom had begun to atomize in favor of states (epitomized by the Hundred Years War). Among the changes was a shift in crusading ideology and practice.[7]

In many ways, this last shift (in crusading ideology and practice) was actually a culmination of trends that, over three centuries, had transformed crusading from a movement to an institution. They included the routinization of crusade financing, the essentially diplomatic nature of crusade organization, and above all the professionalization of the military itself. When seen from the vantage of the Latin West, crusade had morphed from an overtly offensive effort to a defensive one. Indulgences were offered for financial support more frequently than for actual fighters. Appeal to divine aid, both through formal liturgical supplication and through private prayer, increasingly fell to Christians who might contribute to the war effort through proper piety and liturgical supplication.

In the ongoing debate about the vitality or decline of the later crusades, the explosion of liturgical forms argues for the richness with which the fifteenth century worked with the devotional ideology and vocabulary inherited from the Middle Ages. The ritual texts at the heart of this chapter give texture to the eschatological ideas animating the reaction to the Ottoman

---

und des religiösen Volkslebens (Freiburg: 1902), 209. Linder RA 262, 267. A variation of the mass was adopted in the Regensburg region in the second half of the fifteenth century: Franz, *Die Messe im deutschen mittelalter*, 209–211, citing Munich Clm 12262, 209r.

7. These changes are masterfully synthesized in the introductory section in James Hankins, "Renaissance Crusaders: Humanist Crusade Literature in the Age of Mehmed II," *Dumbarton Oaks Papers* 49 (1995): 111–207. See also Meserve, *Empires of Islam*; Bisaha, *Creating East and West*.

advance, revealing both spiritual/religious and material/practical anxieties. They bespeak men's (and women's) understanding of their relationship to God, offer an interpretation of current (that is, fifteenth-century) events, and reveal an apocalyptic anxiety pinned to the Ottoman specter (different in agency and reception from the apocalyptic expectations of the early crusaders). Above all, these texts suggest the extent to which the ideological constructs underlying the reaction to the Ottomans, which was itself a medieval inheritance, became an integral part of the fabric of early modern devotional life.

The Ottoman Advance

After 1291, the focus of crusading moved inexorably westward as the Mamluk Empire consolidated control over Syria in the first half of the fourteenth century and the Ottomans emerged as the powerhouse of Muslim strength in its second half. The Mamluks continued to make advances in the former Christian territories, but by the time, in 1375, that the Christian Kingdom of Armenia finally fell to the Mamluks, concern in the West had largely shifted to the new Satan, the Ottomans, and their astonishing march through the remnants of the Byzantine Empire and into Latin Europe. The papacy began to advocate crusading—that is, papally sponsored military expeditions that garnered spiritual rewards, in which fighters wore the cross, and that was understood as holy war in the name of God against the enemies of the Church—against the Turks as early as 1366, and Gregory XI asked for special masses to be said for the fight against the Turks in 1373.[8] Ottoman Turks were replacing Saracens as the principal military-religious threat to Christendom, and as the new Muslim enemy to the East, the fight against the Ottomans was grafted onto, mutatis mutandis, the established framework of Jerusalem crusade.[9]

Men and women in the Latin West continued to pray for Holy Land recovery long after 1291. Throughout the later period, and well through the end of the fifteenth century, a variety of prayer texts could be found in hundreds if not thousands of liturgical books throughout Christendom, any one of which could be deployed when the community felt endangered, or wanted to defend the idea and territory of Christianitas. Rites *Pro subsidio terre sancte* (or some variation of this) continued to be copied into, and later, printed into, missals well into the fifteenth and sixteenth centuries.[10] The Clementine prayers were still often labeled "For the aid of the Holy

8. *Annales Ecclesiastici* ad annum 1373, §5 (26:220–221).
9. Weber, *Lutter contre les Turcs*, 490–495.
10. I count at least sixty from the fifteenth and sixteenth centuries in my notes. Early printed missals routinely contained "Pro terra sancta" votive masses. Linder's repertory contain even more.

Land" in fifteenth-century and even sixteenth-century missals. Expanded forms of Innocent's clamor (focused on the Holy Land) continued to be copied into new missals well into the sixteenth century. William Durandus's pontifical[11] transmitted an evolved form of Innocent's clamor—titled *Ordo pro liberatione terre sancte a fiei ininimicis*—throughout continental Europe."[12] In England, the Sarum variant of the clamor was also routinely included in new missals.[13] The West thus continued to pray for Holy Land recovery long after 1291, long after specific military engagements had been immediately directed at Jerusalem. No longer targeted at specific campaigns, the ideal of Jerusalem recovery was instead encoded into the liturgical cursus.

As the Turks began to press in on the European imagination, many of these tools were refocused on them. Yet with the rise of the Ottomans as the key focus of crusade (while Jerusalem remained in Mamluk control) the ideology of holy war was no longer keyed to the Holy Sepulcher and was no longer understood as a pilgrimage.[14] Crusaders continued to take the cross. But, in the Roman rite in any event, they no longer took the scrip and staff.[15] In 1485, when Innocent VIII ordered a revised edition of the Roman Pontifical—the *Editio Princeps*—its editors mostly deferred to William Durandus. In their prologue they explained how they used the Pontifical of William Durandus as their base, remaining faithful to its structure and its contents, but also that they saw fit, at times, to correct it where corrupt and remove accreted or superfluous rites.[16] And thus, in the rite of departure, they did away entirely with the blessings of scrip and staff which had become superfluous. The rite kept the blessings for the "giving over of the cross to those setting out in aid of the Holy Land."[17] Both the rubrics and the prayer texts for the cross were taken over from the Pontifical of William Durandus, including the evocation of Matthew 16:24, *except* that the edition of 1485 elided the injunction that, in following Christ's words to

---

11. See, for instance, *Missale Parisiense* (Paris: 1481), ccxxix, "Pro terra sancta," copying an expanded form of the Innocentian clamor, followed by pro rege prayers, and then the departure rite for crusaders and pilgrims; *Missale ad usum insignis ecclesie Parisiensis* (Paris: 1497), xxxv(r), "Pro terra sancta," copying the expanded form of the Innocentian clamor.

12. PWD III:XVI. Its broad dissemination can be followed in Kay, *Pontificalia*.

13. Linder RA 52–64, 78–80.

14. Housley, *Crusading and the Ottoman Threat*, 26–28.

15. This was not true everywhere. For example, the Paris rite continued to include the traditional departure rite, *Missale Parisiense*: ccxxix(r–v). *Missale ad usum insignis ecclesie Parisiensis*, xxxv(v).

16. Vogel, *Medieval liturgy*, 255–256. Manlio Sodi, *Il "Pontificalis Liber" di Agostino Patrizi Piccolomini e Giovanni Burcardo (1485)*, Monumenta studia instrumenta liturgica (Vatican City: 2006). On the production of the *Editio Princeps*, see Mark Dykmans S.J., *Le pontifical romain révisé au XVe siècle*, Studi e testi 311 (Vatican City: 1985), 109–133.

17. Manlio Sodi, *Pontificalis Liber*, 485.

Figure 7.1 Blessing of the crusader's cross, from the first printed edition of the Roman Pontifical. *Pontificale Romanum Clementis VIII. Pont. Max. Iussi restitutum atque editum.* Rome: Apud Iacobus Lunam. Impensis Leonardi Parasoli & Sociorum, 1595, 534. Courtesy of the College of the Holy Cross Special Collections.

pick up the cross and follow Him, the cross wearer should "desire to hurry towards Your tomb," replacing it with the injunction that he "desire to hurry and fight against our enemies for the salvation of Your elect people."[18] In the next century, the illustration in the Roman Pontifical (fig. 7.1) was martial and military.

Crusade, divorced from Jerusalem, was now severed from pilgrimage, and from the devotional and penitential apparatus that had defined it in its infancy. The very idea of crusade as penitential pilgrimage was thus obsolete. It had been superseded by the waging of war in order to protect the people of *Christianitas*. And instead of being paired with the blessings of scrip and staff, which no longer played a part in the departure ceremony for crusaders, now the cross blessing was paired with blessings for the instruments of war. The blessing of the weapons, the blessing of the sword, and the blessing and handing over of the battle standard (*vexillum bellici*) were also taken over verbatim from Durandus, but in the thirteenth-century version of the text these had followed a series of unrelated blessings for a new well, a new field, and sick animals. In 1485, they were regrouped with

18. PWD 2.XXX.2 (p. 542): "desiderat et ad tuum properare sepulcrum." Manlio Sodi, *Pontificalis Liber*: 454: "ac contra inimicos nostros per salute populi tui electi properare et pugare desiderat."

the cross blessing for crusaders. These blessings for arms, the sword, and the standard asked that they might "assail all visible and invisible enemies," and be "terrible to the enemies of the Christian people."[19] This was the language of the early war rites, not of penitential pilgrimage, which now had no place in the ritual instantiation the increasingly professionalized crusader.[20] By the end of the fifteenth century, three decades after the fall of Constantinople, with Jerusalem long in Muslim hands, with the Ottomans pressing ever more forcefully at the eastern front of *Christianitas*, aiding the Holy Land no longer meant penitential pilgrimage. Taking the cross meant fighting to save Europe.

Institutional Considerations

These same years witnessed, alongside the evolution of the Roman departure rite, new trends in the pro-crusade, anti-Turk intercessions done during the mass. The updated language of the prayer sequence that Clement V instituted in 1308 and 1309 was promulgated through the Roman missal and disseminated in Christendom as part of the Roman liturgy's more general widening influence.[21] Despite the limited objective of the initial call—a five-year run during which time a small contingent fought in aid of the Kingdom of Armenia—the sequence became the standard *contra paganos* script. Linder has documented the dissemination of what he termed the "Clementine triple set" in hundreds of manuscripts.[22] The prayers were copied into missals of local use, often following the Roman missal's *contra paganos* title, but also increasingly under rubrics such as "For the aid of the Holy Land,"[23] "For the crusade [*passagio*] to the Holy Land,"[24] or "For victory against the infidels."[25] Also crucial to the use and

---

19. Manlio Sodi, *Pontificalis Liber*: 456: "contra invisbilium et visibilium hostium impugnationem," "Sitque inimicis christiani populi terribile."

20. For papal participation in these rituals, see Weber, *Lutter contre les Turcs*, 430.

21. *Missale Romanum* 473–474.

22. Linder RA 120. Linder writes that he stopped counting at 325.

23. *Pro subsidio terre sancte*: Auxerre BM 52, 314r (Auxerre Missal 15c); Le Mans Mediatheque Louis Aragon B. 243, 79r (Le Mans missal, 14c); Paris Arsenal 203, 29v–30 (Paris Missal, 14c); Paris BNF Lat. 17315, 357v (Paris missal, late 15c); Paris BNF Lat. 17316, 280 (Auxerre missal, 14c); Mazarine 410, 388r–v (Paris use, 15c); Mazarine 412, 404r–v (Paris missal); Pontarlier BM 12, 152v (Cistercian missal, 14c); Pontarlier BM 9, 170v (Cistercian missal, 14c); Reims BM 233, 336 (Paris missal, 15c). These citations are taken from Linder RA.

24. *Pro passagio sancte terre*: Paris BNF Lat.17316, 280 (Auxerre missal, 14c); Linder RA 151.

25. *Pro victoria contra infideles*: Toledo Bibliotheca del Cabildo ms 52–12, 140; Linder RA 156. Several indicated: *Iste sunt orationes quas dominus [noster, in Rouen only] papa Clemens precepit dicere pro terra sancta.* Rouen BM 279, 338r; Cambridge Fitzwilliam Museum, MS 84–1972, 230r.

adaptability of the liturgy was its retreat from a focus on the Holy Land to the broader categories of "pagan" and "enemy." Linder was exact on this point. Of the Clementine mass, he wrote:

> It underlies the apparently easy interchanging of policies towards Muslims, pagans, heretics, and Jews, and it is certainly essential for a correct understanding of the Crusade. For seen under this light the Crusade . . . emerges as a permanent struggle against the Infidel, and applicable, as such, to all Infidel species, wherever and whenever they are fought, rather than as a uniquely Holy Land institution dedicated to the establishment of Christian rule in Jerusalem, a goal that falls into its correct place among the other specific goals of the generic and ongoing struggle. The Clementine initiative merely translated this fundamental conception into liturgical action.[26]

Later in the century, and throughout the fifteenth and sixteenth centuries, these three prayers would constitute the architecture onto which longer, more replete, masses were built. Of the thirty-nine proper dedicated war masses that Linder documented, twenty-five were built around these three prayers.[27] Linder observed that their diffusion, rubrication, and promulgation reflects the ways in which the object of crusade and the idea of crusade shifted to the new challenges of the fifteenth and sixteenth centuries. Most of these were rubricated against pagans or against the Turks, but the form was also deployed for newer forms of Holy War, against heretics,[28] against Hussites,[29] Wyclifites, against infidels,[30] or simply, "against those who fight against Christians."[31] In the fourteenth century, as we saw, the rubrics still often included references to Holy Land recuperation or a particular expedition,[32] but by the fifteenth century the rubrics increasingly refer to the Turks: "Mass against Turks and pagans,"[33] "Mass for the faith and against the Turk and his army,"[34] and variations of these concepts. Around the same time, the papacy began asking for special clamors to be said for the good of the holy Church, which was being torn asunder by the "error of schisms," and in the middle of the Hundred Years War, "peace between kings."[35] Liturgical integration was one of the key ways in which these

26. Linder RA 121.
27. Linder RA DWM 1, 2, 3, 7, 9, 12, 14, 16, 17, 18, 19, 22, 23, 25, 26, 27, 28, 29, 30, 31, 32, 33, 34, 35, 39.
28. Linder RA DWM 5A, 19, 22, 23, 28D, 28E, 29, 32.
29. Linder RA DWM 5, 29.
30. Linder RA DWM 9, 12, 32.
31. Linder RA DWM 39.
32. Paris BNF Lat. 17316, 280 (Linder RA 151), *Pro passagio sancte terre.*
33. Reims BM 219, 160, *Missa contra turcos et paganos.*
34. New York Pierpont Morgan 48317 (print), CCCXIV(v)–CCCXV(v); Linder RA 167.
35. Canivez, *Statuta*, 3:378–379, 460–461, 465.

various initiatives were incorporated into the eschatology of holy war, pre-cisely because the liturgy ratified these *as* holy wars. In turn, a liturgical strategy was used increasingly in conflicts that were not, strictly speaking, crusades (in that they weren't called by the pope), but in which one side or another wished to claim the mantle of doing God's bidding. For historians who argue that crusading was not necessarily about Jerusalem (the "plural-ist" school), only now does the liturgy really fall into line.[36]

Papal institution of special prayers for the Holy Land and other targets of crusade were thus promulgated at key stages throughout the fourteenth century and the first half of the fifteenth century (see appendix 3). John XXII (1316–1334) issued new requests for prayers in 1322, 1328, 1331, and 1333 in relation to his efforts to continue the organization of the general passage that Clement had sought a decade earlier.[37] Urban V, in 1363 and 1364, issued new instructions as part of Peter I of Cyprus's designs on Mamluk Egypt.[38] In the course of the century, the popes began to ask for liturgical aid specifically against the Ottoman Turks.[39] Likewise, programs were increasingly promulgated in the early fifteenth century for newer ene-mies of the Church to which the papacy had granted crusade status through the application of the indulgence and the wearing of the cross (Hussites, Wyclifites, other heretics).[40] At this stage, indulgences could be acquired merely for participating in the liturgical effort. Praying was now rewarded as fighting.

The fifteenth-century evidence permits us, more closely than the thirteenth-century evidence allows, to trace how the liturgical efforts were disseminated socially and geographically. The promulgation of specific forms of the intercessions were handed over to legates who were dispatched to a particular region to preach the cross and organize liturgical activity.[41] In 1455, two years after the fall of Constantinople, Calixtus III dispatched special envoys throughout Christendom to organize preaching, alms col-

---

36. Constable, "The Historiography of the Crusades," 1–22.

37. *Annales Ecclesiastici* ad annum 1331 §20 (24:478–479); Auguste Coulon and Suzanne Clemencet, *Lettres secrètes et curiales du Pape Jean XXII 1316–1334, relatives á la France, extraites des registres du Vatican*, Bibliothèque des Écoles françaises d'Athènes et de Rome (ser. 3.1) (Paris: 1900–1972), no. 5210. On background, see Norman Housley, "The Franco-Papal Crusade Negotiations of 1322–3," *Papers of the British School at Rome* 48 (1980): 166–185; Housley, *The Avignon Papacy and the Crusades*, 20–24.

38. *Annales ecclesiastici* ad annum 1373 §18 (26:83); Housley, *The Avignon Papacy and the Crusades*, 41.

39. *Annales Ecclesiastici* ad annum 1373, §5 (26:220–221).

40. Frederick Heymann, "The Crusades against the Hussites," in *A History of the Crusades*, vol. 3, *The Fourteenth and Fifteenth Centuries*, ed. Kenneth M. Setton (Madison: 1975), 593; Palacký, *Urkundliche Beiträge*, 1:17–18, no. 12.

41. On this issue broadly, see Housley, *Crusading and the Ottoman Threat*, 135–167.

lecting, and liturgical interventions.[42] Many of these were from among the Observant Franciscans, who served as the principal arm of crusade preaching in this period.[43] Calixtus sent John Cajetan and John Capistrano out to Hungary to organize preaching, alms, and liturgies to prepare for John Hunyadi's meeting with Mehmet the Conqueror in advance of the Battle of Belgrade (1456). Cardinal Nicholas Cusa organized the liturgy in northern Germany, where he had been appointed bishop.[44] Our best evidence for the liturgical and homiletic aspects of this process comes from the written instructions sent out to Germany in 1421 by Cardinal Branda regarding plans for a crusade against the Hussites, to Canterbury in 1429 by Cardinal Beaufort (again, regarding the Hussites), and to preachers in Venice in 1463 by the Greek émigré and cardinal, John Bessarion, for preaching Pius's fatal crusade from Ancona. Bessarion's official letter, and Beaufort's before that, were directly modeled on Branda's (or on whoever's letter his was modeled on). This was a regular form. The letters outline precisely what preachers should be preaching in their sermons, how devotees should take up the cross, the prayers that ought be said during processions and mass, the details of the indulgence, and the rite of absolution. They give the liturgical blessing to be said on the red cross (made of either silk or cloth) sewn to someone taking the vow, the prayers of absolution, and the prayers for the liturgy. Everyone who supported the crusade, not just those who left to fight, could wear the cross. In the case of the English and German examples, the prayers were directed against "Wyclifites, Hussites, and other heretics."[45] In Cardinal Bessarion's letter to the Venetians, the specific homiletic and liturgical content was all specific to the "perfidious Turks."[46] Bessarion instructed preachers to explain the meaning of the cross worn by crusaders and the three "causes" for the crusade. First, they should "recall the capture of Constantinople" and the other territories, and describe the many outrages and atrocities committed by the Turks on the Christians in order to incite the people to desire revenge (*ac vindicite ardore populum commovere*) for the injuries done to Christ. The second *causa* was mercy for all the Christian captives in Turkish hands. And the third was the fact that the Turks were preparing "to subjugate the entire world." These were

---

42. Pastor, *The History of the Popes*, 2:351–354.

43. Pastor, *The History of the Popes*, 2:352. Housley, *Crusading and the Ottoman Threat*, 136–159.

44. Pastor, *The History of the Popes*, 2:401. G. Bickell, *Synodi Brixinenses Saeculi XV* (Oeniponte: 1880), 54. Nicholas of Cusa was actually a proponent of a peaceful solution with the Turks. Bisaha, *Creating East and West*, 144–145.

45. Swanson, "Preaching Crusade in Fifteenth-Century England," 194. Echoing the language of Palacký, *Urkundliche Beiträge*, 1:108–116, no. 10.

46. Mohler, "Bessarions Instruktion," 342.

the same themes inscribed in Bernard of Cattaros's special mass, showing the way in which the liturgical priorities of the mass were transmitted in the vernacular in preaching. Bessarion's preachers were to urge everyone to give alms and to explain that although "God sometimes allows His church and His people to be shaken about by various tribulations on account of their sins, He would never abandon us and in the end will help His people."[47]

Prayers and processions were then organized on a local level. Bishops and sometimes secular authorities could request the clergy in the diocese or kingdom to organize special liturgies. Church councils and synods sometimes recorded the promulgation of special prayers.[48] For example, in 1383, Henry the Despenser, in his capacity as the bishop of Norwich, instructed preachers to "beseech and advise the people to hold processions and make other prayers to God for the salvation of the Holy Church, of the realm, of the expedition, and of the pilgrims." Those who go on crusade should say prayers before they depart, and those who remain at home should "urgently pray for those who have gone on crusade."[49] A cluster of such local initiatives were organized in the immediate aftermath of 1453. In 1537, a German bishop asked for "processions, fastings, and prayers for . . . all those who are now setting out on the campaign against the Turk, so that the Almighty may grant success and victory."[50] In the remarkable sermon that accompanied this initiative, the preacher recalled the earlier history of both Innocent III and Clement V.

Throughout this long period laymen and women were often required to offer private prayers for the sake of Christian victory. Starting in the middle of the thirteenth century, church bells were rung during a mass that included crusading appeals so that those who were at home or at work could also offer prayers for victory.[51] Men and women who could not be in church were to say the *Pater noster* at the point where the church bells rang. In 1421, alongside the special prayers that were to be said during the mass, Cardinal Branda prescribed that literate laymen recite the seven penitential psalms and the litany, while everyone else was asked to recite fifty

---

47. Mohler, "Bessarions Instruktion," 341.

48. See appendix 3.

49. Henry Knighton, *Knighton's Chronicle: 1337–1396*, ed. G. H. Martin (Oxford: 1995), 331.

50. John Bohnstedt, "The Infidel Scourge of God: The Turkish Menace as Seen by German Pamphleteers of the Reformation Era," *Transactions of the American Philosophical Society* n.s. 58, no. 9 (1968): 41.

51. Maier, "Crisis," 635; Hefele, *Histoire des conciles*, 6.1:106 and 109 (for 1261). Powicke and Cheney, *Councils and Synods*: II.i.175 (for 1229). Rymer, *Foedera*, 1.i:286, for 1251. Robert Winchelsey, *Registrum Roberti Winchelsey Cantuariensis Archiepiscopi A.D. 1294–1313*, ed. Rose Graham (Oxford: 1952–1956), 26–30.

Pater Nosters and *Ave Marias*.[52] The same division of labor was made in 1427 in England for a Hussite campaign.[53] Robert Swanson remarked that, since more elaborate prayers garnered greater spiritual rewards (indulgences), the *illiteratus* remitted less time in purgatory.[54] Calixtus III made specifications for bell ringing in 1456.[55] When clergy gathered for the Fifth Lateran Council in 1512, they took up the issue of "an expedition against the enemies of the Christian faith" and reissued instructions for special collects and masses throughout Christendom "for the peace of Christians and the confounding of the infidels respectively," including the *Deus a quo sancta desideria*, and the *Deus in cuius manu sunt omnes potestates*. These were old prayers, respectively, a prayer for peace and a prayer for war.[56] But supplication and prayer "for the complete destruction of the infidel" was now the responsibility of every Christian and should extend into private homes throughout Christendom. Clergy and religious leaders:

> are no less to enjoin on members of their diocese and on any other person of either sex, whether ecclesiastical or secular, over whom they have authority by reason of a prelature or any other ecclesiastical position of authority . . . that they should pour forth in private devout prayers to God himself and to his most glorious mother, in the Pater Noster and the Ave Maria, for the peace of Christians (as mentioned above) and for the complete destruction of the infidel.[57]

Between Lateran IV and Lateran V, liturgical supplication to God for help in wars against the enemies of the Christian name had become a constant feature of Christian life.[58] Christians were individually and collectively responsible for participating in the prayer effort, to marshal the invisible weapons of the fight for God.

New Efforts

When, in 1453, Constantinople, the New Rome, finally fell to the Turks, Europeans reverted to the old traditions of Christian thought. The fall of

---

52. Palacký, *Urkundliche Beiträge*, 1:108–116, no. 10.

53. Robert Swanson, "Prayer and Participation in Late Medieval England," in *Elite and Popular Religion*, ed. Kate Cooper and Jeremy Gregory (Woodbridge, UK: 2006), 136.

54. Swanson, "Prayer and Participation," 130–139.

55. Lajos Vecsey, *Callixti III Bulla orationum: ex codice originali Reg. Vat. eruta atque cum introductione in relatione ad pulsationem meridianam instructa* (Appensell 1955), 48–52.

56. Tanner, *Decrees of the Ecumenical Councils*, 1:609, 611. Session 9, 5 May 1514.

57. Tanner, *Decrees of the Ecumenical Councils*, 1:611.

58. Ottavia Niccoli, *Prophecy and People in Renaissance Italy*, trans. Lydia G. Cochrane (Princeton: 1990), 80–81. Bohnstedt, "The Infidel Scourge of God," 41.

Constantinople, was the result of Christian sin.[59] The Ottomans were God's punishment, the scourge of Europe. They were also, in some quarters, thought to be a sign of the Apocalypse. This was particularly true in Germany and Hungary, the areas most immediately threatened by the Ottoman advance.[60] The loss of Constantinople ushered in a period of renewed apocalyptic speculation, but also, predictably, a critique of Rome and calls for internal reform.[61] These were interrelated insofar as the coming of the Apocalypse signaled a call for penance. The pope who received the news of the city's capture, Nicolas V (1447–1455), identified Mehmet II ("the Conqueror") with the Beast of the Apocalypse.[62] Aeneas Silvius Piccolomini, the future Pope Pius II and an important voice at the curia in these years, imagined the Emperor Constantine asking Jesus himself why he had let his city fall to the Turks, recalling that Christ had often punished the Jews when they had transgressed "but when they cried to heaven and begged forgiveness, a Savior straightway appeared who delivered them from the hand of iniquity . . . if You have no mind to aid Christians in war, at least don't favor the Turks."[63] Jesus responded to Constantine simply that "the successes of the Turks, too, We have ordained. The Turks have brought deserved punishment upon false Christian kin. For when were crimes more plentiful?"[64] Yet again, plans for holy war were paired with plans for Christian reform.

The fall of the ancient city to the Turks was the single greatest impetus both to renewed plans for crusade, and for the production of new, elaborate liturgical forms.[65] The very first reaction to the news, in many quarters, was to pray to God for deliverance. On Crete, a monk hearing the news observed that "nothing worse than this has or will happen." And then he added, "May the Lord God have mercy on us, and deliver us from His terrible menaces."[66] The authorities quickly sought to organize formal

59. Hankins, "Renaissance Crusaders," 134.

60. Sinan Akilli, "Apocalyptic Eschatology, Astrology, Prophecy, and the Image of the Turks in Seventeenth-Century England," *Edebiyat Fakültesi Dergisi / Journal of Faculty of Letters* 29 (2012): 34–35; Pál Fodor, "The View of the Turk in Hungary: The Apocalyptic Tradition and the Legend of the Red Apple in Ottoman-Hungarian Context," in *Les traditions apocalyptiques au tournant de la chute de Constantinople*, ed. Benjamin Lellouch (2000), 99–131.

61. Bernard McGinn, *Visions of the End: Apocalpytic Traditions in the Middle Ages* (New York: 1979), 270–272. Kenneth M. Setton, *Western Hostility to Islam and Prophecies of Turkish Doom* (Philadelphia: 1992), 15–27.

62. Hankins, "Renaissance Crusaders," 142.

63. Hankins, "Renaissance Crusaders," 134.

64. Hankins, "Renaissance Crusaders," 134.

65. For a recent narrative, see: Michael Angold, *The Fall of Constantinople to the Ottomas* (Harlow, UK: 2012), 84–119.

66. R. Browning, "A Note of the Capture of Constantinople in 1453," *Byzantion* 22 (1952): 381.

liturgical supplication. Initially, these were on an ad hoc basis by individuals or churches that sought God's aid. In England, the archbishop of Canterbury requested prayers and processions in all churches, parishes, and cities in the diocese of Canterbury for a full year, citing (predictably) the Ninevites, Judith against Holophernes, Moses against the Amalechites, and the Maccabees.[67] His call linked the taking of Jerusalem by "the damnable sect of Saracens" to the more recent losses in Greece and Constantinople, and warned of Turks making it all the way to Rome.[68] Once the new crusade was announced, the archbishop of York instituted propitiatory prayers for its success in his dioceses.[69] In Ireland, the archbishop of Dublin ordered a three-day fast and led a procession with his clergy clothed in sackcloth and ashes.[70] In Florence in 1455 the city turned out for a public procession to beg God for aid in the next crusade against the Ottomans.[71] And on the Dalmatian coast, the bishop of Cattaro, we saw, composed a plaintive votive mass begging God to "put the Turkish dog to flight."

Bernard of Cattaro's mass reflected the general mood of terror and despair. Preaching, orations, and propaganda plumbed the stories of the Turkish atrocities of 1453.[72] Ten years later, preachers were instructed specifically to describe how men were cut down, women raped, babies murdered, the bellies of pregnant mothers' pierced, churches and altars profaned, images of the saints, of the Virgin, and of the Lord disfigured or destroyed.[73] The response to the Turkish advance was understood in traditional crusading terms. Pope Nicholas V received the news of the fall in early July, and, on 30 September, in the bull *Etsi Ecclesia Christi* called a new crusade to recapture Constantinople.[74] The pope's primary aim was to establish peace among the warring Italian princes in order to mount a unified *negotium fidei et totius christiane religionis*, that is, a new holy war.[75] The bull revived all the classic tropes of crusade: the indulgence, ecclesiastical protections, the wearing of the cross. Nicholas called Mahomet (Muhammad) the son of Satan, evoked

67. David Wilkins, *Concilia Magnae Britanniae et Hiberniae, a Syndo Verolamiensi, A.D. CCCCXLVI. Londinensem A.D. MDCCXVII. Accedunt Constitutiones et alia ad historam Ecclesiae Anglicanae spectantia*, 4 vols. (1767), 3:563–564.

68. Wilkins, *Concilia Magnae Britanniae*, 3:564, "damnabilis Saracenorum secta."

69. Jonathan Harris, "Publicising the Crusade: English Bishops and the Jubilee Indulgence of 1455," *Journal of Ecclesiastical History* 50, no. 1 (1999): 30–31.

70. Harris, "Publicising the Crusade," 26.

71. Richard Trexler, *Public Life in Renaissance Florence* (Ithaca: 1980), 376–377.

72. Housley, *Crusading and the Ottoman Threat*, 153–154. Mohler, "Bessarions Instruktion," 339–340.

73. Mohler, "Bessarions Instruktion," 339–340.

74. *Annales ecclesiastici* ad annum 1453, §9–11 (28:599). L. M. Baath, *Diplomatarium svecanum Appendix. Acta pontificum svecia I. Acta cameralia*, 2 vols. (Stockholm: 1942–1957), 2:385–387, no. 1243.

75. Baath, *Acta Cameralia* no. 1243 (p. 385).

the Apocalypse, recalled the pollution of the holy city of Jerusalem and the injuries to the faithful in Christ, and called for a crusade on the model of those who had gone in aid of the Holy Land.[76]

Meanwhile, the Ottomans pressed onward against the eastern frontier of Christendom. After Constantinople, Mehmet II set his sights on Hungary, and in June 1456, the sultan began marching toward Belgrade. When Calixtus III (1455–1458), who had succeeded Nicholas V upon his death, learned that Mehmet was on the march, he sent his legate, the Spaniard John Carvajal, and called upon Christians to prevail on the power of prayer. In May 1455 Calixtus had renewed the indulgence that Nicholas V had issued in 1453 and had resumed preparations for the Turkish wars.[77] On 20 June 1456, the pope issued a bull, *Cum his superioribus*, in which, in addition to the regular list of requirements, protections, and indulgences, he promulgated new liturgical services for help against the Turks in the Balkans.[78] Special services were ordered throughout all of Italy, Germany, Hungary, Spain, and France such that prayers would be said continually throughout the Christian world "so that God himself would give success to our labors against the perfidious enemy of our religion."[79] In 1456, Calixtus explained that it was because of prayer, not weapons, that the Israelites defeated the Amalechites.[80] Samuel's prayer, he explained, helped beat the Philistines, because the Lord intervened. Ezekias's prayer helped defeat the 80,000 knights of Sennacherib, since angels came to the rescue.[81] In Mainz, no less than Johann Gutenberg printed the bull. The bull called for *contra paganos* masses in which *Omnipotens* was intoned, and for the daily ringing of bells, between noon and vespers, to remind people not in church to pray.[82] Calixtus also ordered processions on the first Sunday of every month, which ought include clergy, religious, and laymen, and after which a sermon ought be preached on the need for victory against the Turks.[83] Processions, which were to be done in all dioceses, rain or shine, were to include the singing of the litany and the seven penitential psalms (standard elements of the Rogation rites). Christians could earn indulgences by participating in the ritual supplications. Writing from Rome, Calixtus asked his legate to Eastern Europe to promulgate its orders "throughout the entire

76. *Annales ecclesiastici* ad annum 1453, §§9–10 (28:599–600).

77. Pastor, *The History of the Popes*, 2:349.

78. *Annales Ecclesiastici* ad annum 1456, §19 (29:67–70); Vecsey, *Callixti III Bulla orationum*. See discussion in Weber, *Lutter contre les Turcs*, 440–442.

79. Pastor, *The History of the Popes*, 2:401.

80. *Annales Ecclesiastici* ad annum 1456, §20 (29:68).

81. *Annales Ecclesiastici* ad annum 1456, §20 (29:68).

82. Vecsey, *Callixti III Bulla orationum*, 48–52. For the mass itself, see Linder RA 237–241, No. 28.

83. *Annales Ecclesiastici* ad annum 1456, §19 (29:68).

Christian world," and also ordered his envoy, Bishop Solerius, to Aragon to have masses and processions organized in Iberia.[84] Nicholas of Cusa promulgated the measures in Brixen.[85] Presumably other legates did so elsewhere as well.

Although the pope addressed the bull to all of Christendom, the manuscript record for the Calixtus mass is manifest primarily in Eastern Europe.[86] The bull itself identifies only the recitation of *Omnipotens*, so the mass must have been transmitted separately—presumably by Carvajal, who traveled there in 1455—but three separate manuscripts identify a mass as the one Calixtus promulgated in 1456. The mass was incorporated into the uses of dozens of churches and was then adopted by local versions of the Roman missal in use along the Danube.[87] The mass took several forms (Linder identified six variants). The dominant motif was beseeching God to hear their prayers and come to the rescue. It includes the standard Clementine prayers, *Omnipotens*, *Sacrificium domine*, and *Protector noster*. It reminded God that in the past He had responded to the power of petition, using both John 16:24 ("Ask and you will receive") and Luke 11:9–13 ("Seek and it shall be given to you"). And it begged, not for revenge, but merely for safety: "Make Your people safe, O Lord, and bless Your inheritance," "Deliver me from my enemies, O my God; and free me from them that rise against me," and reminded God "You will make safe the humble people, O Lord, and You will humble the eyes of the proud."[88] The Epistle reading underscores the theme of righteous prayer, beginning with a slight rewriting of II Maccabees 1:23: "The priests make a prayer while they offer the sacrifice for the people of Israel." The reading then begged God to hear the rightful prayers of its supplicants, to be reconciled to them, and to bring them peace (2 Macc.1:2–5).

John Hunyadi, Hungarian nobleman and a reputed military genius, and John Capistrano, charismatic crusade preacher and future saint, met the Ottomans on three occasions in 1456, decisively defeating them at the Battle of Belgrade in late July. Their unlikely victory was seen as a miracle on par with those of the First Crusade and those of the Old Testament.[89] When the news made it to the Italian Peninsula, celebrations and thanksgiving

84. Weber, *Lutter contre les Turcs*, 441; *Annales Ecclesiastici* ad annum 1456, §§19–20 (29:68).

85. Bickell, *Synodi Brixinenses Saeculi XV*, 54.

86. The basic formulary survives in dozens of manuscripts from Germany and Bavaria from the second half of the fifteenth century. Linder RA DWM 28 (with variants A-E), edited on pp. 237–246, discussed 186–187. For rubrics, see 237, not 361, and 238.

87. Linder RA 237–238.

88. Linder RA DWM 28.

89. Norman Housley, "Giovanni da Capistrano and the Crusade of 1456," in *Crusading in the Fifteenth Century*, ed. Norman Housley (New York: 2004), 106.

processions were organized in Florence, Venice, and Bologna.[90] Calixtus, like Innocent III two centuries earlier, credited the victory to the liturgical supplications.[91] In October of that year he said he believed that it was because of the prayers he had instituted throughout all of Christendom that God gave success to "our labors against the perfidy of the enemies of their religion."[92] In 1457, the prayers became a daily obligation.[93]

Despite Hunyadi's victory, the Turkish threat remained the driving force behind the papacy of Calixtus's successor. Pius II, the great humanist author Aeneas Silvius Piccolomini, was probably the most committed crusading pope of the Renaissance (1458–1464). Immediately upon his accession he called the Council of Mantua in an effort to rend cooperation from Christian powers. His opening oration at the council framed the challenge in apocalyptic terms. At the end of the Council, on 14 January 1460, he issued the bull *Ecclesiam Christi* in which for all intents and purposes he declared war on the Turks. The bull offered the usual indulgences and, recalling Moses, renewed the calls for a special mass every Sunday.[94] He linked the wars against the Turks with the historic wars to free the Holy Land. Prayers should be poured out "so that the Unconquered Fighter might help those who are fighting for Him."[95] Then again in 1463, responding to reports from Hungary, citing the need to try to avert imminent danger, and mounting his own (fateful) crusade, Pius II ordered weekly solemn processions by clergy and laity throughout all of Christendom, in every single church, monastery, and religious location.[96] In 1463 Pius II said simply that "temporal arms can accomplish nothing absent divine aid or without spiritual arms," that "human strength was nothing without divine power," and that, pleased by prayers, and the Christians having done penance for their pride, he hoped that God "might grant the hoped-for victory to the Christian faithful from the heavens."[97] Elsewhere Pius compared himself to Moses fighting the Amalechites with prayer.[98] He asked that the usual prayers be said. It is not clear whether or not the "usual prayers" were the Clementine triple set, but careful instructions to preachers in Venice from Bessarion

90. Franz Babinger, *Mehmed the Conqueror and His Time*, trans. Ralph Manheim (Princeton 1978), 144.

91. Pastor, *The History of the Popes*, 2:402. He also has in a note on 401 that the papal command was carried out in the papal states and in Brixen. *Annales Ecclesiastici* ad annum 1456, §§19–24 (29:67–70).

92. Pastor, *The History of the Popes*, 2:400–401, see footnote at bottom of 400.

93. Weber, *Lutter contre les Turcs*, 442.

94. *Annales Ecclesiastici* ad annum 1460, §3 (29:220).

95. *Annales Ecclesiastici* ad annum 1460, §3 (29:220).

96. *Annales Ecclesiastici* ad annum 1463, §13 (29:350).

97. *Annales Ecclesiastici* ad annum 1463, §13 (29:350).

98. Weber, *Lutter contre les Turcs*, 501. *Pugnantem contra Amalechi* remains unpublished.

included specific processional chant and proper prayers for the mass. Bessarion was following the model that had been promulgated in Germany forty years earlier by Cardinal Branda da Castiglione in support of Martin V's Hussite Crusade of 1421–1422.[99] Bessarion told his preachers to use Clement's *Omnipotens*, but then a collect for the enemies of the Church (*Ecclesie tue*, used elsewhere in crusading contexts),[100] standard suffrages to the Virgin Mary, and Psalm 128.[101] Psalm 128 wailed, "From my youth on, they have frequently fought me, but they could not prevail over me. . . . The Lord who is just will cut the necks of sinners; let them all be confounded and turned back that hate Sion."[102] While preachers were asking the faithful to support the crusade effort, priests were asking God to forgive us our sins, and "for the peace and unity of all Christians, grant us victory against the savagery of the pagans."[103]

By this point, spiritual measures as a feature of military strategy against the Ottoman Turks had become part of the punctuated reaction to individual crises and ongoing uncertainties, and they continued on, in one form or another, well into the sixteenth century. The appeals for special liturgical intercessions were routinely buttressed by reference to Moses fighting the Amalechites with prayers.[104] Pius died, having taken the cross, at Ancona in 1464. His successor was Pope Paul II (1464–1471). In July 1470, despite Venetian efforts, the Ottomans seized Negroponte in the Aegean. In Venice, the authorities organized expiatory processions when, on 30 July, they got the news.[105] That year, Paul II confirmed Bernard of Cattaro's vehement anti-Turkish mass.[106] The next year, 1471, in France, the archbishop of Tours instituted public processions and supplications to be held throughout France to beg God for help against the Turks and to entreat Louis XI to take the cross.[107] Dedicated war masses began to appear in French missals with greater frequency.[108] In 1480, after the Ottoman attack on Italian soil (Otranto, in Apulia), Sixtus IV began making plans for a new offensive. The Turkish seizure of the city was widely believed to be Mehmet's staging

---

99. Palacký, *Urkundliche Beiträge*, 111–112. Branda da Castiglione was Cardinal to John XXIII.

100. Cf. CO 2404. For examples of its use in crusade contexts, see examples listed on Linder RA 404.

101. Mohler, "Bessarions Instruktion," 344–345.

102. Psalm 128, 1, 2, 4–5.

103. Mohler, "Bessarions Instruktion," 344.

104. Calixtus III, *Annales Ecclesiastici* ad annum 1456 §20 (29:68); Pius II, *Annales Ecclesiastici* ad annum 1460, §3 (29:220); *Annales Ecclesiastici* ad annum 1500 §16 (30:315).

105. Babinger, *Mehmed the Conqueror*, 283.

106. Linder RA 186.

107. *Annales Ecclesiastiques* ad annum 1471, §§ 43–44 (29:508–509).

108. Linder RA DWM 1, 6, 16, 15, 30, 31.

ground for an advance onto mainland Italy. In addition to military preparation, Sixtus asked for special prayers to be said on All Saints' and promulgated a new *contra Turcum* mass.[109] A rubric in a monastic manuscript
from northern France identifies a version of a *contra Turcum* mass that was
adopted fairly widely in France in the last decades of the fifteenth century
as having been the one "ordered by our Lord, Pope Sixtus IV."[110] The mass
contained the usual mix of entreaties for mercy in the face of sin, calls for
deliverance, and pleas to crush the enemy. The Epistle, from I Maccabees,
asked God "How shall we be able to stand up before their face unless You,
O God, help us?"[111] A special mass commemorating peace in Italy, a precondition for taking up arms against the infidel, included a special sequence
begging for the forgiveness of sins, and to inspire the faithful to raise an
army against the Turks that Penny Cole has associated with 1480.[112] By the
1480s and 1490s, most of the new masses preserved are to be found in liturgical books from the East, particularly from churches and communities
along the Danube. Narrative evidence survives also of ad hoc supplications
in the face of particular episodes.[113] In 1500 Alexander VI prescribed
prayers and processions again for the province of Wallachia.[114] He too recalled that the Israelites maintained victory only so long as Moses remained
in prayer, and that the enemies conquered when he stopped.[115] The goal
remained, hopefully, those going in aid of the Holy Land.[116] In 1512, we
saw, the Fifth Lateran Council issued directions for special prayers to be
said during the mass throughout all of Christendom for the "suppression of
the haughty madness of the wicked enemies of the Christian name" and
"for the complete destruction of the infidels."[117]

The Argument of the Liturgy

These rituals were both entreaties *and* arguments to God for why He should
help His people achieve victory. In this sense, the liturgy was an important
mechanism for the influence or continuity of medieval ideas about Islam on

---

109. Babinger, *Mehmed the Conqueror*, 394. Linder RA 187.
110. Linder RA DWM 16. Douai BM 91, 142–143v.
111. I Maccabees 3:53.
112. Penny Cole, "Cambridge Fitzwilliam Museum Ms. McClean 51, Pope Sixtus IV, and
the Fall of Otranto," in *A Distinct Voice: Medieval Studies in honor of Leonard E. Boyle, O.P.*
(Notre Dame: 1997), 103–120.
113. *Annales Ecclesiastici* ad annum 1499, §7–8 (30: 296).
114. *Annales Ecclesiastici* ad annum 1500, §§15–16. (30:315).
115. *Annales Ecclesaistici* ad annum 1500, §16 (30:315).
116. *Annales Ecclesiastici* ad annum 1500, §§15–16 (30:315).
117. Tanner, *Decrees of the Ecumenical Councils*: 1:611.

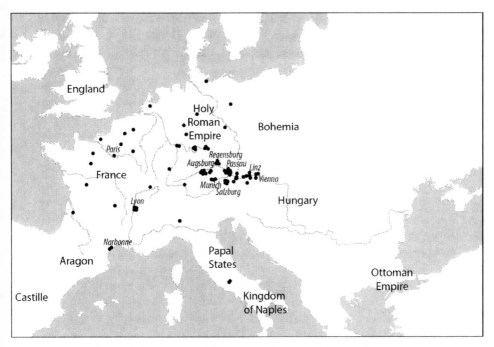

Map 2. Localizable dedicated war masses (fourteenth to sixteenth centuries)

early modern thought and as applied to the Ottomans.[118] But these ideas were more fully developed because the nature of the war rites meant that they could flesh out the ideas about sin, repentance, and election. Any number of proper prayers, verses, and readings, usually scriptural, were added to make what became a sophisticated appeal to God for His aid based on scriptural precedent. These could range anywhere from special verses for the Introit, the Alleluia, or the Tract, to proper sequences, to newly chosen readings for the Gospel or the Epistle. Carefully chosen, they together transmit a clear sense of the spiritual dimensions of the Ottoman threat and of the religious response to the Turkish specter. Following Linder, the bulk of the surviving examples of these special masses come from France and Germany. Oddly, not a single example survives from England, only one (late) example from Spain, and two (also late) from Italy. Several examples survive from the fourteenth century, but the production and creation of these special war masses really followed the Ottoman advance into Europe in the wake of the fall of Constantinople in 1453. One can even trace the Ottoman threat to Eastern Europe in the fifteenth century on a map plotting surviving examples of

118. The range of possibilities is outlined in Bisaha, *Creating East and West*. Bisaha discusses the transmission of medieval ideas through texts, preaching, and papal bulls at 136–143.

liturgical books that include dedicated *contra paganos* and *contra Turcos* masses (map 2). A concentration is found along the Danube, from Augsburg to Vienna. None survive to the east of Vienna, in lands ultimately conquered by the Ottomans.

Many of these were closely related, with many shared texts or uses, and a number of families, or affinities, between different traditions. The central themes and the core biblical and prayer texts chosen repeatedly to express them are variants of one another across the corpus. The themes elaborated were familiar from earlier calls—the persecution of the Christian community by the Turks, an admission of sin as the cause for military losses and subjugation, recognition of the justice of that persecution, expressions of sincere contrition, a call for mercy and deliverance, and also a call for revenge—but articulated in prayer to God with renewed vigor and urgency. These were expressed in a traditional language of liturgy, a language itself generally derived from scripture: current adversity and danger as the punishment for sin and God's judgment on His people for their disobedience, a plea for the deliverance of Israel (in this case, the Christian community) from danger and extinction, a call for the extension of God's name and glory into foreign kingdoms, the outpouring of God's wrath on the enemy of the people of Israel, and the manifestation of God's power through military action.

Pervading all of these was the ritual admission of sin that was understood to be the cause of what the liturgy termed "tribulations." This was a key element in the larger argument that the Ottomans were God's scourge for Christian sin. It was also a common theme in fifteenth-century sermons that tied the advance of the Turks to the need for internal reform and penance.[119] The earliest surviving of these masses adopted an old (non-Roman) *pro paganis* collect, begged God, who grows angry so that He might come to our aid, to spare us and relieve us from the pagans who oppress us because of our sins.[120] The sentiment in this prayer was standard: "God who severely pierces the filth of our sins with the sword of pagans hateful to the Christian name, taking pity receive the prayers of Your church, and concede that we, in serving You, might evade their power, they whose savageness we encounter in neglecting You."[121] The introit for Sixtus V's mass (after 1480) cried out that the Turks were pressing on "in true judgment, because we have sinned against You and we have not obeyed Your commands."[122] This theme was as old as the crusades themselves, but should also be seen as part of the sincere reaction to Turkish victories and advances, which fed both a broad program of ecclesiastical and social reform (itself part of the broader culture that would lead the Reformation) and an

---

119. Bisaha, *Creating East and West,* 156–157.
120. Linder RA DWM 13, and adopted also in 21. Cf. CO 2304b.
121. Linder RA DWM 10, 11: Collect.
122. Linder RA DWM 16.

apocalyptical interpretation of geopolitical events. The old prayers remained relevant, reanimated by the cloak of their new context.

In turn, celebrants professed true penitence and begged for mercy.[123] One grouping, for instance, asked, "All which You have done to us, O Lord, You have done in true judgment, because we have sinned against You and we have not obeyed Your commands, but give glory to Your name and deal with us according to the multitude of Your mercies."[124] By mercy was meant deliverance from persecution. Standard refrains included "Deliver me from my enemies, O Lord."[125] And "My Deliverer from the enraged heathens, and from those rising up against me, raise me up, and snatch me away from the unjust one, O Lord."[126] Some rites assert that the persecution is unjust. "In Your salvation in Your word my soul has hoped; when will You execute judgment on those that persecute me, they who have persecuted me unjustly? Help me, O Lord my God."[127]

The "enemy" was described simply as pagans (*paganos*) or pagan people (*gentes paganos*). Clement V, we saw, adapted some of this language to heighten the contrast between the Christian army and the "pagan" people. Liturgically and scripturally, the pagan people are those who do not recognize God's name (a formulation taken from the Psalms). Among many examples evoked in the liturgy is Psalm 78 (vv. 9–10), used frequently for the Alleluia verse, which asked, "O Lord, deliver us, and forgive us our sins for Your name's sake. Lest they should say among the gentiles [*gentibus*], 'where is their God?' and let Him be made known among the nations [*nationibus*] before our eyes, by revenging the blood of Your servants, which has been shed."[128] Other rites used Psalm 78:6: "Pour out Your anger against the nations [*gentes*] that have not known You, and against the kingdoms that have not called Your name."[129]

The militancy and belligerence of the earlier war-rites were amplified in these masses. The core prayer sequence included aggressive language, including the request that the heathens might be "vanquished by the power of Your right hand,"[130] and that God "suppress the enemies of the Christian name."

---

123. Linder RA DWM 15, 38.
124. Linder RA DWM 16, 17, 18: Introit. See also Linder RA DWM 6.
125. *Eripe me de inimicis meis, domine.* Very common.
126. Linder RA DWM 13, 14. Introit: *Liberator meus de gentibus iracundis, et ab insurgentibus in me exaltabis me, a viro iniquo eripies me, domine.* (cf. Psalm 17.48–49). See further Nos. 8, 9, 10, 11, 25 (all fifteenth-century German). A variant is found in 16, 17, 18 (French). Also, nos. 30, 28, 9, 10, 11, 26, 33.
127. Linder RA DWM 16, 17, 18, Communion.
128. Psalm 78:9–10. Linder RA DWM 21, 24, 32, 35, 38, 39. See also Psalm 82:19–20, in Linder RA DWM 30, 6, 14, 3, 7, 8 10, 11, 26.
129. Linder RA DWM 14, 24, 35. See also us of Psalm 82:19–20 in Linder RA DWM 15, 6, 14, 3, 21, 12, 7, 8, 9, 10, 11, 26.
130. CO 3846, *Omnipotens sempiterne deus . . .*

New prayers culled scripture relevant to the argument, with the Psalms naturally providing the bulk: "Take hold of arms and shield, and throw down those who oppress us, O Lord, and strike down those in defiance in their pride, God our Savior" (Ps. 34:2).[131] "Scatter them in Your power and destroy them, O Lord, our protector" (cf. Ps. 58:12).[132] "Please hear us in clemency, Jesus, loving and powerful; destroy our enemies."[133] "He has subjugated the peoples under us, and the heathen beneath our feet" (Ps. 46:4).[134] And, "Pour out Your wrath upon the heathens who have not known You and against the kingdoms that have not called Your name."[135] Yet another asked God to "subdue, we beg, the pagan people beneath our feet."[136] Some late rites begged for revenge. French and Italian masses entreated the Lord to "revenge the blood of Your servants that has been shed" (cf. Psalm 78:10–11).[137] Several masses drew the Gospel from Luke 18, the parable of the unjust judge.[138] The end reads: "And will not God vindicate His elect, who cry to Him day and night? Will He delay long over them? I tell you, He will vindicate them speedily. Nevertheless, when the Son of Man comes, will He find faith on earth?" (Luke 18:7–8). The passage had apocalyptic overtones (to which we will return), but the core purpose was clear: the prayer of the righteous will ultimately be rewarded by divine vindication.[139]

The Devotional Use of Old Testament Narrative

The expanded war masses chronicled here provided ample opportunity to cull evidence from scripture to ask God for help; in a sense, to remind God of His part in the covenant. This was particularly true of the longer scriptural passages read during the Gospel and especially the Epistle readings. In the Epistles, liturgists made pointed use of examples of Old Testament texts and narratives. Crusading had, of course, since the very start, drawn meaning from Old Testament narrative and the theology of sin and war embedded in it, and the Old Testament continued to serve as the model for holy war well into the fifteenth century.[140] Because of the form of the supplicatory prayers that constituted the basis of liturgical entreaty in the

---

131. Linder RA DWM 37, Alleluia verse.
132. Linder RA DWM 1, Introit Psalm.
133. Linder RA DWM 37: *Ergo exaudi nos* . . .
134. Linder RA DWM 18: Alleluia Verse tempore pasce: *Subiecit populos nobis, et gentes sub pedibus nostris* (cf. Psalm 46:4). See also examples in Linder RA DWM 30, 16, 17, 18.
135. Linder RA DWM 14, 24, 35, *Effunde iram tuam* . . .
136. Linder RA DWM 15: *Rex omnium seculorum* . . .
137. Linder RA DWM 14 and 6: *Ultio sanguinis servorum.* . . . See also no. 35.
138. Linder RA DWM 12, 8, 9, 25, 39, 24.
139. For vengeance, see also use of Romans 12:16 in Linder RA DWM 11, Epistle.
140. Weber, *Lutter contre les Turcs*, 501–502.

twelfth, thirteenth, and much of the fourteenth centuries, the themes (of sin, setback; prayer and penance; deliverance) were consonant with that theology, but not directly evoked in the liturgy. This changed with the expansion of the supplicatory masses in the later period, which fielded a much greater range of texts and allowed for the evocation of biblical narrative, particularly in the Epistle readings (the reading following the collect, which generally came from one of the Epistles, but it could also be drawn from Acts, Revelation, or, as in these cases, the Old Testament). One of the most powerful Old Testament Epistles was an extended prayer from Ecclesiasticus (Sirach) 36 (1–10, 1–13, or 1–18, depending) that was taken up in no less than ten of the surviving dedicated war masses and replicated in dozens of manuscripts.[141] It was utterly appropriate, calling on God to have mercy and to "send fear upon the nations that have not sought after You; that they may know that there is no God besides You" and to "renew Your signs and work new miracles. Glorify Your hand, and Your right arm. Raise up indignation, and pour out wrath; Take away the adversary, and crush the enemy." The scriptural passage was itself a prayer, and it evoked many of the themes found throughout the tradition, in particular the importance of extending God's name and glory over nonbelievers, the manifestation of His might through military action, and the protection of His people.

In other masses, the use of readings drew on applicable Old Testament narrative that presented desired parallels. A German mass from the second half of the fifteenth century (from the Bamberg and Regensburg regions), used for the Epistle Judith 7:18–8:27.[142] The passage was taken from the story of Judith, the young Israelite widow who rescued her people from foreign subjugation. The passage itself contained the admission that "we have sinned with our fathers, we have done unjustly, we have committed iniquity. Have mercy on us, because You are good, or punish our iniquities by chastising us Yourself, and do not deliver them that trust in You to a people that does not know You" (7:19–20). The reading included descriptions of Judith's own piety, and a lengthy prayer in which she asked the Lord for mercy and recalled the sins of their fathers who had turned against the Lord, thus recognizing that the community was being punished for disobedience. Judith's prayer also said, "But esteeming these very punishments to be less than our sins deserve, let us believe that these scourges of the Lord, which like servants we are chastised, have happened for our amendment, and not for our destruction" (v. 8:27). This echoed other prayers claiming that the extent of persecution was out of proportion and thus unjust. In the Ottoman context,

---

141. Linder RA DWM 8, 9, 12, 13, 14, 15, 21, 24, 26, 36.
142. Linder RA DWM 22.

it was a direct plea to stay the power of the Ottomans. As with Ecclesiasticus 36, the passage was also itself a prayer and was invoked as a prayer. But it was also an argument. It was an argument to God to be merciful and aid the Christians as He had aided the Jews in the time of old. To fulfill his part of His covenant with the chosen people.

The use of these narrative passages thus embraced the long tradition of Old Testament models for holy war and the eschatological meaning of defeat, here usually invoking instances of prayer and supplication to God within the context of warfare or violence. Other rites used the prayers for deliverance of the Jewish people from the Book of Esther. Three rites evoked Mordecai's exhortation to Esther: "O Lord, Lord, almighty king, for all things are in Your power, and there is none that can resist Your will, if You determined to save Israel" (Est. 13:9).[143] Others evoked Esther's own prayer,[144] which included her plea that

> I have heard from my father that You, O Lord, took Israel from among all nations, and our fathers from all their predecessors, to possess them as an everlasting inheritance, and You have done to them as You have promised. We have sinned in Your sight, and therefore You have delivered us into the hands of our enemies. For we have worshipped their gods. You are just, O Lord. And now they are not content to oppress us with most hard bondage, but attribute the strength of their hands to the power of their idols. They design to change Your promises and destroy Your inheritance, and shut the mouths of them that praise You, and extinguish the glory of Your temple and altar. (Est. 14: 3–9)[145]

As with the passages from Sirach, these embedded prayers evoked standard themes of God's might, the community's sin and loss of favor, and the plea for deliverance. But the passage also permitted invocation of the entire narrative, in which Mordecai's and Esther's pleas are heard, and Israel is saved. The prayer reminded God of how He repaid Esther's devotion, and thus her success in saving the Jewish people from violent extinction through an appeal to God for mercy and piety.

The other narrative evoked repeatedly was the story of Judas Maccabeus, the general who led the Israelite rebellion against the Seleucids under Antiochus and reestablished worship at the Temple. This Old Testament warrior was a model of military piety and had been routinely deployed in crusading rhetoric. A late mass "against those who attack Christians" used 1 Maccabees 3:13–22, which was at once a statement of defiance against

---

143. Linder RA DWM 7, 32, Epistle.
144. Linder RA DWM 32, 32A, 33, 36, 37.
145. Linder RA DWM 14, 28D, 33, 36, Epistle.

the enemy, and of faith in God's might.[146] The core trope is one common throughout the long tradition of the righteous few against the multitude. The passage comes early on in Judas Maccabeus's story, right before his first major confrontation with the Syrian army:

> It is an easy matter for many to be shut up in the hands of a few: and there is no difference in the sight of the God of heaven to deliver with a great multitude, or with a small company. For the success of war is not in the multitude of the army, but the strength comes from heaven. They come against us with an insolent multitude, and with pride, to destroy us, and our wives and our children and to take our spoils. But we will fight for our lives and our laws: And the Lord Himself will overthrow them before our face; but as for you, fear them not. (1 Macc. 3:18–22)[147]

The rhetoric of the many against the few is one we have seen repeatedly throughout the history of liturgical supplication. We know that the story of the Maccabees, and in particular this passage, featured in crusade preaching and other propaganda from the start. The famed Franciscan preacher, John of Capistrano, drew on 1 Maccabees 3:21 ("They come against us with an insolent multitude . . .") in his crusade sermons at the time of the siege of Belgrade in 1456.[148] Pius II had cited the ease with which God could allow the few to beat the multitude. "It is as easy for our God to conquer with a few than with a multitude. Ours is God's cause and we fight for God's law, and that God will expunge the enemy before our face."[149] It was a statement of the seeming outsized odds of beating the Ottomans on military power alone. Liturgically, this was a hopeful passage to proclaim up to God. That Judas Maccabeus ultimately won this battle and reestablished the cult at the Temple was vital to the liturgical argument. It also, of course, linked the effort broadly and rhetorically to the ideal of eventually reclaiming Jerusalem. Another family of rites, this one from France, used a passage from slightly later in the same chapter, from I Maccabees 3:43–53, which emphasized instead the penitential and liturgical aspects of successful warring.[150] The passage described how Judas Maccabeus's forces gathered together "that they might ready for battle; and that they might pray, and ask mercy and compassion" (v. 44), and the army

> fasted that day, and put on haircloth, and put ashes upon their heads, and they rent their garments. . . . And they cried with a loud voice toward heaven,

146. Linder RA DWM 39, *Missa contra oppugnatores Christianorum*.
147. Range depended; most quoted I Macc. 3:13–22.
148. Housley, *Crusading and the Ottoman Threat*, 154–155.
149. Weber, *Lutter contre les Turcs*, 502n313.
150. Linder RA DWM 16, 17, 18, Epistle.

saying: What shall we do with these, and whither shall we carry them? For Your holies are trodden down and are profaned, and Your priests are in mourning, and are brought low. And behold the nations are come together against us to destroy us; You know what they intend against us. How shall we be able to stand before the face, unless You, O God, help us. (vv. 47–53)

The use here of II Maccabees 3:43–53 presented the biblical model for precisely the type of liturgical supplication that the celebrants of this mass were themselves doing: penitential rituals preceding a loud cry toward heaven asking God for help against those pagans (*nationes*) that have come to destroy them. The framing narrative was critical to the entreaty, since the entire narrative of the battle involved reliance on God's might to render Jewish victory. "Thus, Israel had great deliverance that day" (4:25). Another tradition (French, fourteenth century) used I Maccabees 4:30–33, another prebattle prayer to the Lord to crush the enemy:

Blessed are You, O Savior of Israel, who broke the violence of the many by the hand of Your servant David, and delivered up the camp of the strangers into the hands of Jonathan, the son of Saul, and of his armor-bearer. Shut up this army in the hands of Your people Israel, and let them be confounded in their host and their horsemen. Strike them down with fear, and cause the boldness of their strength to languish, and let them quake at their own destruction. Cast them down with the sword of them that love You, and let all that know Your name, praise You with hymns. (1 Macc. 4:30–33)

Finally, the popular mass established by Calixtus IV before the Battle of Belgrade (1456) used a passage from II Maccabees 1. The passage was somewhat altered so as to set the opening invocation of the book (from 1:2–5) in the words of a collective prayer, led by the priest, described only at 1:23. The prayer from vv. 2–5 reminded God of his covenant with Abraham, Isaac, and Jacob, and asked that He hear our prayers, be reconciled to us, send peace, and "never forsake [us] in evil time." And as with the French example using I Maccabees 3:43–53, the internal framing of the scriptural texts provided the salutary model for the liturgical supplication that the mass itself represented.

The most remarkable element of the fifteenth-century masses was their palpable expression of apocalyptic anxiety. The passages from Ecclesiasticus 36 discussed above that were used in so many of the rites had strongly apocalyptic overtones, asking God to "rouse Your anger and pour out Your wrath, destroy the adversary and wipe out the enemy, and Hasten the day and remember the appointed time."[151] Luke 18, used in other masses,

---

151. Ecclesiasticus (Sirach) 36:7–8.

evoked "The Son of Man, when He comes" who will "avenge His elect who cry to Him day and night."[152] Apocalyptic prophecy was often evoked in the Gospel reading. The Synoptic Gospels each included a passage of Jesus foretelling the coming of the End: Matthew 24:4–36, Mark 13:3–37, and Luke 21, each of which was employed in one or another of the traditions. The Gospel reading, taken from Mark 13:1–12, that both foretold the destruction of Jerusalem and a day of future judgment was used in the early German *Missa pro tribulatione Ierusalem*.[153] The sole thirteenth-century dedicated war mass survives in a single example from an interpolation to an earlier missal and is truncated. The mass is paired with traditional prayers for Holy Land delivery, including *Omnipotens* and the Holy Land specific *Deus qui ad nostre redemptionis*, and is clearly focused on the Levant. In the reading, Jesus describes how "nation shall rise against nation and kingdom against kingdom" and other sorrows that foretell the end-times. And explains also that the gospel must be preached to all nations, and that ultimately the community would be saved.

The apocalyptic theme became dominant after the fall of Constantinople, both in early humanist crusading writings and the liturgies.[154] It was particularly felt in Hungary and Germany, where the Ottoman threat loomed most darkly. Bernard of Cattaro used Matthew 24 in the mass he wrote in 1454, along with a series of other imagery evoking the coming judgment. Several masses from Germany (Warzburg) and France (Cambria, Noyon, Reims, Besancon) employed Luke 21:9–19 for the Gospel reading.[155] This was the synoptic equivalent of the passage from Mark 13, as was also the passage from Matthew used in another dedicated rite in Würzburg. Here, the mass *contra hereticos aut thurcos* adopted the key apocalyptic text describing "the sign of Your coming and the consummation of the world."[156]

And Jesus answering, said to them: Take heed that no man seduce you. For many will come in My name saying, I am Christ. And they will seduce many. And you shall hear of wars and rumors of wars. See that ye not be troubled. For these things must come to pass: but the end is not yet. For nations shall rise against nation, and kingdom against kingdom: And there shall be pestilences and famines and earthquakes in places. Now all these are the beginnings of sorrows. Then shall they deliver you up to be afflicted and shall put you to death: and you shall be hated by all nations for my name's sake. And then

152. Luke 18:6, 8. See nos. 8, 9, 12, 24, 25, 39.
153. BL Add. 17355, 194v–195v. Linder RA DWM 21.
154. Hankins, "Renaissance Crusaders"; Bisaha, *Creating East and West*, 153–157.
155. Linder RA DWM 30, 15, 18, 26, and 14 (from Montecassino).
156. Linder RA DWM 19.

shall many be scandalized and betray one another and shall hate one another. And many false prophets shall rise and shall seduce many. (Matthew 24:3–11)

These were the key Gospel texts prophesying the Second Coming. Here, Mohammad, and Islam, and by extension the Ottomans, were written into salvation history. Mohammad had been routinely associated with one of the false prophets of verse 11 throughout the Middle Ages, and the fall of Constantinople was seen in some quarters as a sign of the end-times.[157]

Apocalypticism was hardly a new thread in crusade thinking, but its inflection feels here quite different. The apocalypticism associated with the elite discourse around the First Crusade was animated by an excited expectation of agency. (In this view, the crusaders themselves were moving history forward as the agents of apocalyptic violence toward the end-times.) The apocalypticism expressed in the fifteenth-century liturgical materials reflects rather an anxiety about annihilation and thus the need to repent in expectation of Judgment. This anxiety certainly reflected a strain of historical and providential interpretations that sought to incorporate the Turks and their military successes into a vision of history as the sign of end-times that would ultimately end with the triumph of the Church. Yet the emphasis was on the need for repentance and reform. That is, it was the Ottomans, not the Franks, "moving history forward."[158] The Turks were both the scourge of Europe, punishing Christians for their sins, *and* thus also the prelude to the eschatological battle that would usher in the triumph of the Church and ultimately the Second Coming.[159] This view of the role of the Turkish menace owed much to earlier frameworks of prophetic history, most crucially in the influence of the Pseudo-Methodius (who was the first to frame Islam as the coming of Gog and Magog, God's instrument in the eschatological struggle to punish Christians, but who would ultimately be vanquished by the Last Emperor) and its intermingling with late medieval Joachitism that was bequeathed to the fifteenth-century thinkers.[160] It was in German and Hungarian circles that these prophecies held most appeal, and with the advent of printing, gained widest popular circulation. The Last Emperor prophecy, which had placed such an important role in the apocalyptic concerns of the First Crusade, was immediately revived, and a number of tracts advancing

157. Setton, *Western Hostility*, 11.

158. I owe the idea of "moving history forward" to Buc, *Holy War, Martyrdom, and Terror*, 152–176.

159. For this as a recurrent theme, see Housley, *Religious Warfare in Europe, 1400–1536*, 20–25.

160. Setton, *Western Hostility*; Yoko Mikamoto, "The Influence of Medieval Prophecies on Views of the Turks: Islam and Apocalypticism in the Sixteenth Century," *Journal of Turkish Studies* 17 (1993); Fodor, "The View of the Turk in Hungary."

apocalyptic prophecies found their way into print in the last half of the fifteenth century.[161] The Prophecy of the Pseudo-Methodius was printed in Germany in 1475. And so were the prayers delivered up to God to honor Christian supplication and rescue the community from destruction.

Within this context, the clearly apocalyptic readings in many of the rites served to link the earthly battles against the Ottomans to the long-standing eschatological battle with the devil. This duality went back to the earliest of the war and cross rites, but the evocation of the apocalyptic texts made the battle more immediate, more present. And in a sense, reversed. Here is where we must recontextualize the meaning of the liturgical form in the context of palpable apocalyptic expectations. The anti-Turkish, antipagan, and antiheretical masses had grown out of the war rites of the earlier period, but by the fifteenth century they may not always have been keyed to specific military campaigns. That is, the devotional ideology of crusade and crusading had been embedded into the very fabric of devotional life in the Latin West. The rites expressed in a sense a crusading society constantly at battle, in preparation for the end-times, both against internal enemies (vices and heretics) and the scourges of their punishment (Turks). Certainly, as evidenced by the papal calls, the organization of new crusades was often supported by particular liturgical campaigns. But these rites, and the many others from earlier periods that continued to be copied or printed in new liturgical books throughout this period, could just as easily have been performed, not for a particular campaign, but as part of the greater earthly battle being constantly waged between the forces of God and the devil. The battle against the Ottomans had become, like the battle against the devil, an ongoing, daily, metaphysical endeavor.

161. Mikamoto, "The Influence of Medieval Prophecies," 144.

Conclusion

Between 1095 and the close of the Middle Ages, Latin Christians made recourse to the liturgy repeatedly as part of their fight against the "enemies of Christ" in the series of military engagements that have come to be known as the crusades. The rituals of consecration, supplication, and thanksgiving were perhaps the chief mechanisms through which the crusades and their offshoots were consecrated, constituted thus as holy wars, and given their transcendental meaning. The liturgy reified repeatedly the essential proposition of crusade as a holy war effecting God's will, incorporating any single campaign into the larger ideal and ideology of crusade as a sacred project. Through liturgical and paraliturgical ritual, the men and women of the church played their part in fighting the crusades, wielding the invisible weapons of prayer and supplication. And over the course of the twelfth and thirteenth centuries, laymen and women were also increasingly enveloped into the liturgical project of crusading through prayer, thus bringing them at once into the fold of the crusading enterprise and, more broadly, into the defining rites of Christianity. It has been one of the chief points of this book that the liturgy was understood as a component of the strategy of holy war and one of the weapons of crusading warfare. In this sense, the widening scope of crusade liturgy represents an important facet of how the devotional elements of crusading spirituality were enacted, both on the field and at home; and also how those devotional ideas inflected and were expressed through the liturgies that were performed in the service of crusading.

From the outset, liturgical consecration and supplications were used in underwriting the crusading effort and ultimately defining the project in essentially religious terms. In the years before the crusades had begun, the liturgy articulated an eschatological worldview in which Christ on the cross overcame the devil as part of larger narrative in which God would defeat Satan at the end of time. It was within the imagination carved out by the liturgy that the crusades were conceived and conducted, deeply influenced by the language and ideology embedded in the liturgy. Since the earliest historians of the crusades were themselves mostly monks and clergyment whose essential work was the performance of the liturgy, the ideology of the liturgy informed the earliest crusading narratives. It is also true that crusading itself grew out of and was dependent on a whole series of sacralized activities—waging holy war, doing penance, going on pilgrimage. As crusading took shape, it drew definition, meaning, and sacrality from the liturgical rites that defined its basic building blocks. Among the most important was the liturgy of the cross. The liturgy of the cross reflected the broader devotion to the cross that was enacted mostly in monasteries and other churches throughout the Latin West, and it was the liturgy of the cross that provided definition from an early stage to what it meant both to fight for the cross (that is, fighting against the devil and his minions, and the other enemies of the cross such as infidel Muslims and heretics). But these ideas, these dichotomies, and these values, were embedded in a whole range of liturgical practices that would come to play a part in the long history of crusading, including the liturgies of pilgrimage and the liturgies of warfare that were implicated from the start.

One of the ideas that the crusaders inherited from earlier practice was that military failure or enemy threat was a scourge inflicted by God on the community as a warning and a punishment for sin. This idea was embedded in a variety of earlier liturgical practices, and it was through liturgy and ritual prayer that the community sought to perform penance and demonstrate worthiness before God in the hopes of gaining his material support. These rituals were deployed repeatedly while on the crusades themselves. These did not so much sacralize any specific crusade as they recognized the eschatological framework within which any particular crusade was being fought, and sought to use the liturgy as the mechanism of formal communication with God about the state of the community, its desire to please God and be the agents of his will, and to perform acts of penance to demonstrate its worthiness.

The liturgy linked the temporal and historical to the providential and eschatological, since victory in war was understood not only as ratifying God's support, but also indicating that the community itself was both doing God's work and, as the New Israel, saved. This was one of the many ways that the liturgy articulated a binary (God:devil, Christians:Muslims/Saracens/Turks, army:enemy, Christ:enemies of Christ, Cross:enemies of the cross) that gave definition and eschatological meaning to crusading. And it was the liturgy that conferred redemptive power to the devotional activity of crusading—that made crusading warfare a sacramental act. The liturgy, because it was always operating on different registers at the same time, connected thus the specific event to the larger arc of providential history. A blessing for a departing crusader linked God's protection on the crusading journey to the crusader's salvation. A supplication to God before battle linked victory in that battle to the salvific state of the community. A liturgy of thanksgiving commemorated a particular event, but placed it within a providential framework. This had been true of warfare in general in the early medieval period, but because of the extraordinary nature of the victory of the First Crusade, the capture of Jerusalem, and the apocalyptic expectations that may have followed, the earliest historiography placed the events of 1095–1099 (and in particular 1098 and 1099) firmly within an interpretive eschatological framework. Episodes of liturgical supplication and appeal within those early accounts thus underscored this larger interpretation, serving to define the nature and expectations of subsequent ventures to be operating within a proxy eschatology. For this same reason, the climactic event of the First Crusade—the taking of Jerusalem on 15 July 1099—was placed in the liturgical calendar. The liturgy defined the precise place of the event within this eschatological frame as a fulfillment of prophecy and a promise of the Second Coming. The feast of the Liberation of Jerusalem, treated in chapters 4 and 5, belonged to the category of liturgy that was explicitly celebratory in recognition and thanksgiving to God for the extraordinary miracle of victory. Here again, the liturgy was the mechanism by which the project of the crusades were placed squarely within a salvific and eschatological framework, which tied victory to salvation, and the historical event to providential history.

When Jerusalem fell to Saladin in 1187, the crusading community again turned to the liturgy to communicate penance with God. This time, it was not to express thanksgiving, but rather to demonstrate repentance and plead for mercy. The rise of the Ayyubids and their subsequent conquests were understood, according to the old theology of failure, as punishment for sin. And the magnitude of the loss—in direct negation of the magnitude of the victory expressed in the 15 July liturgy—suggested that all of *christianitas* was at fault. The papacy thus turned to established forms of supplicatory liturgies and made these a component of papal policy in preparing, first for the Third Crusade, and then each of the major crusades and other individual crusading campaigns thereafter. The top-down nature of this effort, starting with Clement III (1188) in advance of the Third Crusade and cemented during Innocent III's preparations for the Fifth Crusade (starting in 1213), indicates that the liturgy had become part of the institutionalization and papal organization of crusading. Under Innocent, it was also a mechanism of augmenting the crusading base, through processions that were to be enacted monthly throughout Christendom by both clergy and laity. In this way, Innocent both widened the number of Christians supplicating God on behalf of the crusades, *and* involved these same Christians in penitential rigors that were themselves understood as central to the project of internal reform on which Eastern victories depended.

The widespread and regular involvement of the liturgy to beseech the crusading cause linked Christianity to crusading in a systemic and systematic way. Innocent and his successors took care in promulgating these regulations through legates and other intermediaries throughout Christendom, and crusading liturgy became a central feature of ecclesiastical ritual throughout the later medieval period. Amnon Linder has documented the widespread existence of various prayers for the Holy Land in the liturgical books of the later Middle Ages. These prayers were reinvigorated in the fifteenth century with the rise of the Ottoman threat. The extent to which they continued to be prescribed and performed, especially after the fall of Constantinople in 1453, gives strong evidence for the ideological continuity of the crusading venture into the Ottoman period; and also the tenor of its religious interpretation as part a providential history on the model of the Old Testament within an apocalyptic scenario. It also indicates the extent to which the goals of crusading had been fully integrated into Christian ideology.

In seeking to explore the intersections between liturgy and crusading I hope this book offers several broader contributions. The first is to give greater texture to the premise that the crusades were a religious enterprise, and that crusaders were participating in part for religious reasons, in ways partly governed by religious ideas. The extent to which the crusades were religiously motivated is of course a point of debate in the field, and the conservative articulation of this premise might acknowledge merely that the crusades took place within a religious framework, animated by religious beliefs, practices, and rituals. More boldly, we might suggest that the liturgical story helps us define crusading history as an integrated part of devotional and religious history in the period and demonstrates an important facet of how crusading was conceived of and enacted as a religious—even sacramental—act. It was through the liturgy that men and women, monks and other religious, and laity, priests, and parishioners, enacted, put into practice, and performed those religious ideas. It is through the story of the liturgy that we see how the religious ideals articulated by the liturgy shaped the understanding of crusading, how liturgical prayer was deployed as part of crusading, and ultimately how the project of crusade was incorporated into the larger religious practices and ideology of the Christian West. We see one of the mechanisms through which Benedictine spirituality was able to infuse early crusading and how then the devotional ideology of crusading as it developed was in turn absorbed by liturgical practices, which itself more broadly inflected contemporary historical and historiographical understanding of crusading. We can trace in the liturgy the transformation in devotional ideology more broadly from the remission of sin, to a suffering for Christ, and then ultimately to crusading warfare as separate from pilgrimage and connected to sacral violence. In the liturgy we can locate the mechanism by which the stories and images of the Old Testament infused the practice of crusade. We can trace a shift in the penitential ideals from pilgrimage to social reform. And we can register the extent to which the crusading vision was inflected with apocalyptic expectations and anxieties. And thus the story of the liturgy shows how the First Crusade was epiphenomenal, a sacramental act, which was then inscribed *into* the liturgy as an apocalyptic puncture in sacred history. And how, after subsequent crusades lost the charismatic aura of the First Crusade's heightened religiosity, it was the liturgy, through its subsequent incorporation of crusading goals, that maintained crusade's sacred character and import.

Second, the longer history reveals the extent to which the liturgy was understood as a weapon of warfare. This is consonant and sensible with the first premise about the religious texture of crusading because the liturgical evidence itself reveals how fully war—and in particular crusading war—had religious meaning and operated ideologically within the religious plane. Throughout the history of the crusades we see crusaders and their clerical and lay supporters initiating supplicatory rites as part of a war strategy. At first this was local, tactical, and directed to a specific moment or event at a time of crisis. But with the institutionalization of crusading, and the leadership of the papacy at the end of the twelfth century, the liturgical strategy was instituted "from the top" as part of a wholesale planning for the next campaign. Again, the fact that that strategy was linked to internal religious reform, and that both goals—external victory and internal reform—were affected strategically by the same set of liturgical appeals, demonstrates the extent to which the project of crusading was fundamentally grounded in a set of religious principles that was expressed and reified through the liturgy.

Finally, I hope this history reveals how much the liturgy, both its language and its rituals, was implicated in the evolving ideology of crusade, and in turn, the extent to which crusading, through the liturgy, was brought into the very heart and definition of Christianity. The point has been repeatedly made that it was the liturgy that both constituted crusading as holy war, and placed the acts of crusading and the events of crusading within a transcendental and eschatological framework, giving definition and legitimacy to the idea that crusading was a salvific enterprise. This became more frequent, and appeals for crusading were embedded ever more closely into the heart of the Eucharistic rite. The liturgy was always about the Christian community. The specific enemy was defined in rubrics and titles (*contra paganos*, *contra Turcos*), but the liturgy itself lumped these together into the category simply of *enemy*, that encompassed everything from the Canaanites of the Old Testament, to the Muslim opponent, to the devil himself. In this way, the liturgy imbibed the ideals of crusade such that crusade ideals and aspirations became part of Christian identity. The liturgical project was thus ultimately about the definition and identity of the Christian community and the central place that the larger goals of crusade held within it.

Appendix 1

The Liturgy of the 15 July Commemoration

Both offices are presented in the order they appear in the base manuscripts. The incipits offered in both sources have been expanded with a complete version of the (likely) chant. Text in **bold** represents the incipit as it appears in the base manuscript. Text in regular, nonbold type is the remainder of the chant item, reconstructed using Hesbert's CAO, the Cantus Database, the Cantus Index, or the *Corpus Orationum*. The chant texts have been punctuated and capitalized according to the CAO, although *ae, oe, and e* have all been rendered as *e*. The source feast is the one that the line of chant is primarily associated with. In some cases, the chant is associated with a variety of feasts, which has been indicated by "varia." More precise designations are not indicated, but can be easily tracked through the Cantus Database or the Cantus Index.

O¹ = The Office found in BL Additional ms. 8927
M¹ = The Mass found in BL Additional ms. 8927
O² = The Office found in Vatican Barberini 659 and the Barletta manuscript. An earlier version of this office, representing its state before it got tangled up with the *Dedicatio Ecclesiae* celebration in 1149, is preserved in Lucca Biblioteca Arcivescovile ms. 5 and is noted marginally.
M² = The Mass found in Vatican Barberini 659 and the Barletta manuscript.

BL Add. Ms. 8927 is the only witness to O¹ and M¹. I have used Vat. Barb Lat. Ms. 659 as the base manuscript for O² and M². The version of the feast in Barletta, although highly damaged and unreadable in parts, is consistent with the version of 659 in portions of the manuscript that can be made out, and I have noted only differences of substance, not differences in orthography, length of cues, order of items, and so forth. The version in

Lucca (57r) is shorter, and I have likewise noted only elements of substantive difference between the prescribed items.

Although I have consulted the manuscripts themselves either in reproduction or in the original, I have relied on previous editions. The presentation of O¹ and M¹ has been facilitated by Linder's 1990 edition in his "The Liturgy of the Liberation of Jerusalem," 113–121. The presentation of O² and M² has been facilitated by Kohler's transcription of the Barletta ordinal in "Un ritual et un bréviaire du Saint Sépulcre," 427–429, and by Salvadó's edition of Barbarini Lat. 659 in "The Liturgy of the Holy Sepulcher," 630–631. Salvadó is currently preparing an edition for the *Spicilegium Fribergense* series. Readers are also directed to Aspesi's forthcoming work on Lucca and the 15 July feast.

These two offices are presented in a side-by-side comparative format and their relationship discussed in *Mediaeval Studies*, vol. 77 (2015), pp. 170–181.

O¹

London British Library Add. ms. 8927, 134r–v.

In festivitate sancte hierusalem

Vespers

VA1   Ant. **Ecce nomen Domini** venit de longinquo, et claritas ejus replet orbem terrarum.
              Is. 30.27–28
              CAO 2527
              First Sunday of Advent
              =O² VA1

              Ps. **Letatus sum.** [Ps 121]
              ≠O² VA1

VA2   Ant. **Leva Ierusalem,** oculos et vide potentiam Regis ecce Salvator venit solvere te a vinculo.
              Is. 60.4
              CAO 3606
              Advent varia (First Sunday of Advent; and Monday, one week in Advent)
              =O² VA3

              Ps. **Qui confidunt** [Ps. 124]
              ≠O² VA3

VA3   Ant. **Levabit Dominus signum** in nationibus, et congregabit dispersos Israel.
              Is. 11.12
              CAO 3607
              Saturday, second week Advent
              =O² VA5
              Cf: William of Tyre 1.16

              Ps. **In convertendo** [Ps. 125]
              ≠O² VA5

VA4   Ant. **Elevare, elevare,** consurge Ierusalem; solve vincla colli tui, captiva filia Sion.
> Is. 51. 17
> CAO 2633
> Advent Varia
> No equivalent

Ps. **Super flumina** [Ps. 136.1]

VA5   Ant. **Letamini cum Ierusalem** et exsultate in ea, omnes qui diligitis eam in eternum.
> Is. 66.10
> CAO 3562
> Advent Varia (Third Sunday of Advent; Thursday, third week in Advent; and others),
> =O^2 LA2

Ps. **Lauda Ierusalem** [Ps 147.12]
> ≠O^2 LA2 Ps. =O^2 VA5 Ps.

Cap. **Surge illuminare** [Is. 60.1]
R. Benedictus [Ps. 60.1]
V. Replebitur [Ps. 71.19]

Hymnus
Urbs beata Ierusalem . . .
> Dedicatio Ecclesie
> CAO 8405
> AH 51:110
> =O^2 Hymn

v. **Omnes de Saba venient.**
> Is. 60.6
> CAO 8159.
> Epiphany
> Used once in O^2 and frequently in the MS's Dedication liturgy

Magnificat   Ant. **Venite, ascendamus** ad montem Domini, quia de Sion exivit
Antiphon   lex, et verbum Domini de Ierusalem.
> Is. 3.3
> CAO 5349
> Advent season varia
> No equivalent

Magnificat   Canticum: **Magnificat.**

     Oratio: **Deus qui nobis per singulos annos sancte civitatis tue Ierusalem acceptionis reparas diem; et sacris semper mysteriis representas incolumes, exaudi preces populi tui; et presta, ut, quisquis eam civitatem petiturus, ingreditur, cuncta se impetrasse letetur. Per.**
       Cf: CO 1825, *Missa in anniversario dedicationis basilicae*

Matins

Invititory	Invitatorium. **Filie sion currite, adsunt enim celebria matris vestre solempnia, iubilemus igitur Deo nostro unanimes, qui sibi eam gratuitam elegit ecclesiam.**

Cant 3.11, Zach 9.9ss, Ps. 147, Rev 21.
CAO 1079
Dedication of a church
=O^2 Invit.
NB: use of the word *ecclesiam* in the place of *clementia*.

First Nocturn

MA1   Ant. **Ierusalem respice** ad Orientem et vide, alleluia.
Is. 33.20
CAO 3481
Monday, first week of Advent
=O^2 VA2

Ps. **Domine Dominus noster.** [Ps. 8]
≠O^2 VA2 Ps

MA2   Ant. **De Syon exibit lex,** et verbum Domini de Ierusalem. Alleluia.
Is. 2.3
CAO 2119
Advent season varia
No equivalent

Ps. **Celi enarrant** [Ps. 18]

MA3   Ant. **Sion, noli timere:** ecce Deus tuus veniet, alleluia.
Is. 35.4
CAO 4969
Saturday, first week of Advent
No equivalent

Ps. **Domini est terra** [Ps. 23]

v. **Super te, Ierusalem.**
Is. 60.2
CAO 8210.
Sunday, first week of Advent
No equivalent

Lectiones   *Lectiones de historia ubi capta fuit Hierusalem, incipiuntur enim sic.*
Est enim civitas Ierusalem in montano loco sita.
Fulcher of Chartres, *Historia Hiersolymitana*, I.26 (Ed.
Hagenmeyer, Heidelberg: C Winter, 1913, p. 281)

MRV1

Resp. **Illuminare, illuminare,** Ierusalem: venit lux tua, et gloria Domini super te orta est.
>Is. 60.1
>CAO 6882
>Epiphany
>$=O^2$ MR6

v. **Et ambulabunt gentes** in lumine tuo, et reges in splendore ortus tui.
>Is. 60.3
>CAO 6882a
>Epiphany
>$=O^2$ MV6

MRV2

Resp. **Ierusalem cito veniet salus** tua. Quare merore consumeris? Numquid consiliarius non est tibi quia innovabit te dolor? Salvabo te et liberabo te: noli timere.
>Mich 4, 8–9
>CAO 7031
>Second Sunday of Advent
>$=O^2$ MR1

v. **Israhel si me audieris,** non erit in te Deus recens, neque adorabis deum alienum: ego enim Dominus.
>Ps. 80.9–11
>CAO 7031a
>Second Sunday of Advent
>$=O^2$ MV1

MRV3

Resp. **Hec est Ierusalem, civitas magna** celestis ornate, tamquam sponsam Agni quoniam tabernaculum facta est, alleluia.
>Rev. 21.2,3
>CAO 6803
>Easter varia
>$=O^2$ MR7

v. **Porte eius non claudentur** per diem, nox enim non erit in ea.
>Rev. 21.25
>CAO 6803b
>Easter varia
>$=O^2$ MV7

Second Nocturn

MA4

Ant. **Fluminis impetus** letificat, alleluia, civitatem Dei, alleluia.
>Ps. 45.5
>CAO 2886
>Epiphany
>$=O^2$ MA2

Ps. **Deus noster** [Ps. 45]
=O² MA2 Ps. 45

MA5   Ant. **Super te, Ierusalem,** orietur Dominus, et gloria ejus in te
videbitur.
Is 60.2
CAO 5065
Tuesday, second week of Advent
No equivalent

Ps. **Magnus Dominus** [Ps. 47]
=O² MA4 Ps. 47

MA6   Ant. **Dabo in Syon** salute, et in Ierusalem gloriam meam, alleluia.
Is 46.13
CAO 2094
Third Sunday of Advent
Cf: O² MV4, and O¹ MV8

Ps. **Te decet ymnus** [Ps. 64].

v. **Tu exurgens domine misereberis** Sion.
Ps. 101.14
CAO 7790
First Sunday of Advent
No equivalent

MRV4   Resp. **Civitas Ierusalem** noli flere, quoniam doluit Dominus super
te, et auferet a te omnem tribulationem.
Cf: Luke 23.28
CAO 6290
Second Sunday of Advent
=O² MR2

v. **Ecce in fortitudine** veniet, et bracchium ejus dominabitur.
Is 40.10
CAO 6290b
Second Sunday of Advent
=O² MV2

MRV5   Resp. **Ierusalem plantabis** vineam in montibus tuis, et exsultabis quia
dies Domini veniet. Surge Sion, convertere ad Deum tuum. Gaude et
letare Jacob, quia de medio gentium Salvator tuus veniet.
Jer. 31.5–7
CAO 7033
Second Sunday of Advent
No equivalent

v. **Exsulta satis** filia Sion, jubila filia Ierusalem.
Zach 9.9
CAO 7033
Second Sunday Advent
No equivalent

MRV6

Resp. **Lapides pretiosi** omnes muri tui, et turres Ierusalem gemmis edificabuntur.
Tob. 13.21, Rev. 21.11–12
CAO 7074
Dedication of a church
=MR5 of post 1149 dedication liturgy

v. **Cumque a ioanne** describerentur universa secreta celi, intuens civitatem sanctam dixit.
Rev. 21.2, 21.10
CAO 7074b
Dedication of the Church
No equivalent

Third Nocturn

MA7

Ant. **Syon renovaberis** et, videbis justum tuum qui venturus est in te.
Is. 62.2
CAO 4970
Wednesday, second week of Advent
No equivalent

Ps. **Quam dilecta** [Ps. 83]

MA8

Ant. **Iersualem gaude** gaudio magno, quia veniet tibi Salvator, Alleluia.
Zach 9.9
CAO 3478
Third Sunday of Advent
=O² LA3

Ps. **Fundamenta** [Ps. 86.1]
=O² LA3 Ps.

MA9

Ant. **Ierusalem civitas sancta, ornamentis martyrum decorata, cuius platee sonant laudes de die in diem. alleluia.**
Rev 19.1,3, Rev 21, Rev 22.2.
CAO 3477
Varia (Common Saints Eastertide, Common for martyrs, and other feasts)
No equivalent

Ps. **Cantate domino** canticum novum; laus eius ab [Ps. 149.1]
=O² MA9 Ps.

v. **Reges Tharsis et insule munera offerunt**
Ps. 71.10
CAO 8180
Epiphany
=O² Verse

MRV7

Resp. **Super muros tuos,** Ierusalem, constitui custodies: tota die et
nocte non tacebunt laudare nomen Domini.
Is 62.6
CAO 7723
Summer Histories, from the Prophets; Dedication of the Church
=O² MR5

v. **Predicabunt** populis fortitudinem meam, et annuntiabunt
gentibus gloriam meam.
Is. 66.19
CAO 7723b
Summer Histories, from the Prophets
No equivalent

MRV8

Resp. **Sicut mater** consolatur filios suos ita consolabor vos,
dicit Dominus; et de Ierusalem, civitate quam elegi, veniet vobis
auxilium: et videbitis, et gaudebit cor vestrum.
Is. 66.13–14
CAO 7660
Second Sunday of Advent
=O² MR4

v. **Dabo in Sion** salute, et in Ierusalem gloriam meam.
Is. 46.13
CAO 7660b
Second Sunday of Advent
=O² MV4

MRV9

Resp. **Platee tue Ierusalem,** sternentur auro mundo alleluia; et
cantabitur in te canticum letitie: Alleluia; et per omnes vicos tuos
ab universis dicetur: alleluia alleluia.
Tob 13.22, 13
CAO 7390
Second Sunday after Easter
No equivalent

v. **Luce splendida** fulgebis, et omnes fines terre adorabunt te.
Tob. 13.13
CAO 7390
Second Sunday after Easter
No equivalent

Lauds	**In Laudibus**[1]

LA1

Ant. **Jucundare, filia Sion;** exsulta satis, filia Ierusalem alleluia.
Zach 9.9
CAO 3509
First Sunday of Advent
=O² LA1

LA2

Ant. **Urbs fortitudinis** nostre Sion, Salvator ponetur in ea murus
et antemurale, aperite portas, quia Nobiscum Deus, alleluia.
Is. 26.1–2
CAO 5281
Second Sunday of Advent
=O² VA4

LA3

Ant. **Ierusalem, gaude** gaudio magno, quia veniet tibi Salvator, alleluia.
Zach 9.9
CAO 3478
Third Sunday of Advent
=O² LA3

LA4

Ant. **Omnes naciones venient a longe, portantes munera sua, alleluia.**
Is 60.6, Ps 71.10, Tob 13.14
CAO 4128
Epiphany octave
=O² LA4

LA5

Ant. **Leva, Ierusalem,** oculos, et vide potentiam Regis: ecce
Salvator veniet solvere te a vinculo.
Is 60.4
CAO 3606
First Sunday of Advent
=O² VA3 (and above, O¹ VE (Benedictus))

Hymnus: **Urbs beata Ierusalem** [ut supra]

v. **Venit lumen tuum, Ierusalem**
Is. 60.1
CAO 8234
Epiphany

Benedictus antiphon

In evangelium Ant. **Cum appropinquaret** Dominus Ierusalem,
videns civitatem flevit super illam, et dixit: Quia si cognovisses et
tu; quia venient dies in te, et circumdabunt te et coangustabunt
te undique, et ad terram prosternent te: eo quod non cognovisti
tempus visitationis, tue alleluia.

1. No Psalms are given in the manuscript for Lauds antiphons. They were probably taken
from the standard Sunday pattern which is most commonly 92, 99, 62, Benedicite, 148–150.

Matt 21.1
Eleventh Sunday After Pentecost
CAO 1975
=M¹ Gospel
Canticum. **Benedictus**. [Canticum Zacharie; Lk 1.68–79]

v. **Venit lumen tuum**

M¹   **Ad missam**

Introit   **Letare Ierusalem** et conventum facite omnes qui diligitis, eam,
                gaudet cum letitia, qui in tristitia fuistis, ut exsultetis, et satiemini
                ab uberibus consolationis vestre
                    Is. 66.10–11
                    Cantus Index g00776
                    Fourth Sunday in Lent

                Ps. Letatus sum [Ps. 121]

Collect   **Or. Deus qui nobis annos.** . . . Ut supra
                See office collect above.

Epistle   **Surge illuminare** . . .
                    Is. 60.1

Gradual   **Re. Omnes de Saba venient** aurem et thus deferentes, et laudem
                Domino annunutiantes.
                    Is. 60.6
                    Cantus Index: g00597
                    Epiphany

                Vers. Surge et illuminare Ierusalem; quia gloria Domini super te
                orta est.
                    Is. 60.1
                    Cantus Index: g00598
                    Epiphany

Alleluia   **Alleluia**
                Vers. Te decet hymnus Deus in Sion et tibi reddetur votum in
                Ierusalem.
                    Ps. 64.2
                    Cantus Index: g01181
                    Tenth Sunday after Pent.
                vel,
                Qui confidunt in Domino sicut mons Sion non commovebitur in
                eternum qui habitat in Ierusalem.
                    Ps. 124.1
                    Cantus Index: g02201
                    21st Sunday after Pent.

Sequence	**Prosa** **Manu plaudant omnes gentes ad nova miracula . . .**[2]
Gospel	**Cum approprinquaret ihesus Ierusalem misit duos discipulos . . .** Matt 21.1
Offertory	**Off. Dextera Domini fecit virtutem** dextera Domini exaltavit me non moriar sed vivam et narrabo opera Domini. Ps. 117. 16–17 Cantus Index: g00629 Third Sunday after Epiphany
Secret	**Secr.** Annue quesumus domine precibus nostris, ut quicumque fideles istam civitatem cuius anniversarium acceptionis diem celebramus ingrediuntur, plena tibi atque perfecta corporis et anime devocione placeant ut dum hec presentia vota reddunt, ad eterna premia te adiuvante pervenire mereantur. Per. Cf. CO 266c. *Missa in anniversario dedicationis basilicae*
Communion	**Comm. Iersualem surge** et sta in excelso et vide jucunditatem que veniet tibi a deo tuo. Bar.5.5, 4.36 Cantus Index: g00500 Second Sunday of Adventus
Postcommunion	**Or. [Post communio]: Deus qui ecclesiam tuam sponsam vocare** **dignatus es, ut que haberet gratiam per fidei devocionem, haberet** **etiam ex nomine pietatem; da ut omnis hec plebs nomini tuo** **serviens huius vocabuli consortio digna esse mereatur, et que** **sancte civitatis tue Ierusalem acceptionis celebrat diem, tibi** **collecta, te timeat, te diligat te sequatur, ut dum iugiter per vestigia** **tua graditur ad celestia promissa te ducente pervenire mereamur.** **Per.** Cf. CO 1576: *Missa in anniversario dedicatio basilicae*

Alleluia
Omnipotens sempiterne Deus qui angelum tuum de celo misisti
ab hostio monumenti saxum magnum sublevare, ut sedens
super illud testimonium dominice resurrectionis Ihesu Christi
Domini nostri blando sermone mulieribus nunciaret; prebe
nobis quesumus ut per venerabile atque gloriosum eiusdeom
redemptoris nostri sepulcrum, a viciorum sepulcris resuscitari
mereamur, et felicitatis eterne gaudia consequemur. Per eundem.
CO 3891. *Missa de sepulcro domini.*

---

2. Entire sequence given in manuscript is not included here. AH 40:71–72, no 60. Linder, "Feast of the Liberation," 119–120 and discussed in chapter 4, above.

O²

Vatican Barb. Lat. ms. 659, 101r–102r (Against Barletta, 109v–110v and Lucca Biblioteca Arcivescovile 5, 57r)

*In liberatione sancte civitatis iherusalem de manibus turchorum*³

Vespers	**Ad vesperas**

VA1

Ant. **Ecce nomen Domini** venit de longinquo, et claritas ejus replet orbem terrarum.
Is. 30.27–28
CAO 2527
First Sunday of Advent
=O¹ VA1

Ps. **Laudate pueri** [Ps. 112]
≠O¹ VA1

VA2

Ant. **Ierusalem respice** ad Orientem et vide, alleluia.
Is. 33.20
CAO 3481
Monday, first week in Advent
=O¹ MA1

Ps. **Laudate dominum omnes gentes**⁴ [Ps. 116]
≠O¹ MA1

VA3

Ant. **Leva Ierusalem**, oculos et vide potentiam Regis ecce Salvator veniet solvere te a vinculo.
Is 60.4
CAO 3606
First Sunday of Advent
=O¹ VA2 and VE (Benedictus)

Ps. **Lauda anima mea** [Ps. 145]
≠O¹ VA2

VA4

Ant. **Urbs fortitudinis** nostre Sion, Salvator ponetur in ea murus et antemurale, aperite portas, quia nobiscum Deus, alleluia.
Is. 26.1–2
CAO 5281
Second Sunday of Advent
=O¹ LA2

Ps. **Laudate dominum quoniam** [Ps. 146.1]

---

3. Lucca supplies no rubric or title. [de manibus turchorum] *om.* Barletta.
4. Omnes gentes] *om.* Lucca.

VA5   Ant. **Levabit Dominus** signum in nationibus, et congregabit
dispersos Israel.
    Is. 11.12
    CAO 3607
    Saturday, second week of Advent
    =O¹ VA3

    Ps. **Lauda Iherusalem** [Ps 147.12]
    ≠O¹ VA3 Ps.

    Capitulum. **Surge, illuminare Iherusalem.**
    Is. 60.1
    CAO 7729
    Epiphany
    =O¹ Epistola

    Resp. **Quis Deus magnus** sicut Deus noster? tu es Deus qui facis
mirabilia.
    Ps. 76.14–15
    CAO 7498a
    Trinity
    No equivalent

    v. **Notam fecisti** in populis virtutem tuam. redemisti in bracchio
tuo populum tuum.
    Ps. 76.15–16
    CAO 7498a
    Trinity
    No equivalent

    Hymnus
    Urbs beata iherusalem . . .
    Dedicatio Ecclesie
    CAP 8405
    AH 51:110
    =O¹ Hymn

    v. **Reges tharsis** et insule munera offerunt.
    Ps. 71.10
    CAO 8180
    Epiphany
    =O¹ after MA9

Magnificat   Ant. **Venit lumen tuum**, Ierusalem, et gloria Domini super te orta
Antiphon   est; et ambulabunt Gentes in lumine tuo, alleluia
    Is. 60.1
    CAO 5344
    Epiphany
    Cf: Lauds versicle

Collect	Oratio **Omnipotens sempiterne Deus qui dedisti** famulis tuis in confessione vere fidei eterne trinitatis gloriam agnoscere et in potentia maiestatis adorare unitatem, quesumus, ut eiusdem fidei firmitate ab omnibus semper muniamur adversis.[5]

        CO 3920
        Missa de sancta Trinitate, and others, used also after Pentecost.

Matins   **Ad Matutinas**[6]

Invitatory   Invitatorium **Filie Syon currite,** adsunt enim celebria matris vestre solemnia, jubilemus igitur Deo nostro unanimes, qui sibi eam gratuitam elegit clementia.[7]
        Cant 3.11, Zach 9.9ff, Ps. 147, Rev 21.
        CAO 1079
        Dedication of a church
        $=O^1$ Invitatory

        Hymnus : **Angulare fundamentum**
        Hymn for the Dedication of the Church (Originally part of *Beatus Urbs*)
        $=O^1$ and O^2 Vespers hymn.

First Nocturn   **In primo nocturno**[8]

MA1   Ant. **Afferte Domino,** filii Dei, adorate dominum in aula sancta ejus.
        Ps. 28.2
        CAO 1303
        Epiphany
        No equivalent

        Ps. **Ipsum** [i.e., Psalm 28]

MA2   Ant. **Fluminis impetus** letificat, alleluia, civitatem Dei, alleluia.
        Ps. 45.5
        CAO 2886
        Epiphany
        $=O^1$ MA4

        Ps. **Deus noster refugium** [Ps. 45]
        $=O^1$ MA4 Ps.

---

5. *om.* Lucca.
6. *om.* Lucca.
7. *add.* Lucca: Ps. Venite.
8. *om.* Lucca.

MA3   Ant. **Psallite deo nostro** psallite; psallite Regi nostro, psallite
           sapienter.
           > Ps. 46.7
           > CAO 4406
           > Epiphany
           > No equivalent

           Ps. **Omnes gentes** [Ps. 46]

           v. **Reges tharsis** et insule munera offerunt.
           > Ps. 71.10
           > CAO 8180
           > Epiphany
           > =O^1 after MA9, and O^2 after V Hymn

Lections   Lectio I: **Surge illuminare** [Is. 60.1–5]

           Lectio II: **Omne peccus** [Is. 60.6–12]

           Lectio III: **Gloria libani ad te**[9] [Is. 60.13–22]

MRV1   Resp. **Ierusalem cito veniet** salus tua. Quare merore consumeris?
           Numquid consiliarius non est tibi quia innovabit te dolor?
           Salvabo te et liberabo: te noli timere.
           > Mich 4, 8–9
           > CAO 7031
           > Second Sunday of Advent
           > =O^1 MR2

           v. **Israhel si me audieris**, non erit in te Deus recens, neque
           adorabis deum alienum: ego enim Dominus.
           > Ps. 80.9–11
           > CAO 7031a
           > Second Sunday of Advent
           > =O^1 MV2

MRV2   Resp. **Civitas Ierusalem**, noli flere, quoniam doluit Dominus
           super te, et auferet a te omnem tribulationem.
           > Is 35.4
           > CAO 6290
           > Second Sunday of Advent
           > =O^1 MR4

           v. **Ecce in fortitudine** veniet, et bracchium ejus dominabitur.
           > Is 40.10
           > CAO 6290b
           > Second Sunday of Advent
           > =O^1 MV4

---

9. Lucca omits the lections.

MRV3

Resp. **Vidi Ierusalem** descendentem de celo ornatam auro mundo, et lapidibus pretiosis intextam, alleluia.
Rev. 21.1
CAO 7876
Second Sunday after Easter
No equivalent

v. **Ab intus** in fimbriis aureis circumamicta varietate.
Psalms 44.14
CAO 7876a
Second Sunday after Easter
No equivalent

Second Nocturn

In secundo nocturno

MA4

Ant. **Suscepimus Deus** misericordiam tuam in medio templi tui secundum, nomen tuum.
Ps 47.10
CAO 5085
Epiphany
No equivalent

Ps. **Magnus** Dominus [Ps. 47]
=O¹ MA5 Ps. 47

MA5

Ant. **Omnis terra** adoret te et psallat tibi; psalmum dicat nomini tuo domine.
Ps 65.4
CAO 4155
Epiphany
No equivalent

Ps. **Jubilate deo** [Ps. 65]

MA6

Ant. **Omnes gentes quascumque** fecisti venient, et adorabunt coram te, Domine.
Ps. 85.9
CAO 4125
Epiphany
No equivalent

Ps. **Inclina domine** [Ps. 85]

v. **Omnes de Sabba venient.**
Is. 60.6
CAO 8159
Epiphany
=O¹ Magnificat antiphon

Lections	Lectio IIII: **Spiritus Domini super me** [Is. 61.1–9] Lectio V: **Gaudens gaudebo** [Is. 61.10–62.5] Lectio VI: **Super muros tuos**[10] [Is. 62.6–62.12(?)]
MRV4	Resp. **Sicut mater** consolatur filios suos ita consolabor vos, dicit Dominus; et de Ierusalem, civitate quam elegi, veniet vobis auxilium: et videbitis, et gaudebit cor vestrum. Is. 66.13–14 CAO 7660 Second Sunday of Advent =O¹ MR8
	v. **Dabo in Syon** salutem, et in Ierusalem gloriam meam. Is. 46.13 CAO 7660b Second Sunday of Advent =O¹ MV8
MRV5	Resp. **Super muros tuos**, Ierusalem, constitui custodies: tota die et nocte non tacebunt laudare nomen Domini. Is 62.6 CAO 7723 Summer Histories (from the Prophets) =O¹ MR7
	v. **Qui reminiscimini** Domini, ne taceatis et ne detis silentium ei.[11] Is. 62.6 (used in sixth lection) CAO 7723a Summer Histories (from the Prophets) No equivalent
MRV6	Resp. **Illuminare,** illuminare, Ierusalem: venit lux tua, et gloria Domini super te orta est. Is. 60.1 (N.B.: also used for the first lection) CAO 6882 Epiphany =O¹ MR1
	v. **Et ambulabunt** gentes in lumine tuo, et reges in splendore ortus tui. Is. 60.3 CAO 6882a Epiphany =O¹ MV1

10. Lucca omits the lections.

11. **Qui reminiscimini** Domini ne taceatis et ne detis silentium ei] **Predicabunt populis qui reminiscimini** Lucca.

Third Nocturn	**In tercio nocturno**

MA7

Ant. **Adorate Dominum, alleluia, in aula** sancta ejus, alleluia.
Ps. 95.9
CAO 1288
Epiphany
No equivalent

Ps. **Cantate [domino]. i. [Ps. 95]**

MA8

Ant. **Adorate Dominum,** alleluia, omnes angeli ejus, alleluia.
Ps. 96.7
CAO 1289
Epiphany
No equivalent in O¹

Ps. **Dominus regnavit exultet** [Ps. 96]

MA9

Ant. **Notum fecit** Dominus, alleluia, salutare suum, alleluia.
Ps. 97.2
CAO 3964
Christmas/Epiphany/Octave of Epiphany
No equivalent in O¹

Ps. **Cantate domino. ii. [Ps. 97]**

v. **Omnes gentes** quascumque fecisiti. R. Venient et adorabunt. [cf MA6]
CAO 8160.

Lectiones ii de evangelio. **Cum intrasset**[12] **Ihesu Iherosolimam**[13] [Matt 21.10]

IX lectio. **Credimus sanctam Trinitatem**[14]

MRV7

Resp. **Hec est Ierusalem,** civitas magna celestis, ornata tamquam sponsam Agni, quoniam tabernaculum facta est, alleluia.
Rev 21.2–3
CAO 6803
Easter varia
=O¹ MR3

---

12. Kohler reads "venisset" in Barletta, but it is almost entirely gone.
13. *om.* Lucca.
14. *om.* Lucca. For the lections in 659/Barletta, see Alcuin, *De fide Sanctae Trinitatis et de incarnatione Christi. Quaestiones de Sancta Trinitate,* edited by Eric Knibbs and E. Ann Matter (Turnhout: 2012), 144.

v. **Porte eius** non claudentur per diem, nox enim in ea.
Rev. 21.25
CAO 6803b
Easter varia
=O¹ MV3

MRV8   Resp. **Vidi civitatem** sanctam, Ierusalem novam descendentem de celo a Deo paratam, et audivi vocem de throno dicentem: Ecce tabernaculam Dei cum hominibus, et habitabit cum eis.
Rev 21.2–3
CAO 7871[15]
Dedication of a church
No equivalent

MRV9   v. **Vidi angelum Dei volantem** per medium celum voce magna clamantem et dicentem.
Rev. 14.6–7
CantusID 7871zc. CAO 7873v
Dedication of a church (and others, including Easter, Common Apostles, etc.)
No equivalent

Resp. **Summe Trinitati, simplici** Deo una divinitas, equalis Gloria, coeterna majestas Patri Prolique Sanctoque flamini, qui totum subdit suis orbem legibus.
CAO 7718
Trinity
No equivalent

v. **Prestet nobis** gratiam Deitas beata, Patris ac Nati pariterque Spiritus almi.
CAO 7718a
Trinity
No equivalent

Lauds   **In Laudibus**

LA1   Ant. **Jocundare, filia Sion;** exsulta satis, filia Ierusalem alleluia.
Zach 9.9
CAO 3509
First Sunday of Advent
=O¹ LA1

Ps. **Dominus regnat**[16] [Ps 92]

---

15. In theory, this could also be CAO 7872, but 7871 is more likely and more appropriate.
16. *om.* Lucca.

LA2   Ant. **Letamini cum Ierusalem** et exsultate in ea, omnes qui
             diligitis eam in eternum.
             Is. 66.10
             CAO 3562
             Advent Varia (Third Sunday in Advent; Thursday, third week
             in Advent; and others),
             =O¹ VA5

             Ps. **Iubilate**[17] [Ps. 99]

LA3   Ant. **Iersualem, gaude** gaudio magno, quia veniet tibi Salvator,
             Alleluia.
             Zach 9.9
             CAO 3478
             Third Sunday of Advent
             =O¹ MA8

             Ps. **Deus Deus meus**[18] [Ps. 62]

LA4   Ant. **Omnes nationes** venient a longe, portantes munera sua,
             alleluia.
             Is. 60.6, Ps 71.10, Tobit. 13.14
             CAO 4128
             Epiphany Octave
             =O¹ LA4

             Benedicite[19] [Dan 3.57–88, 56]

LA5   Ant. **Cantate domino canticum** novum.
             Ps. 149.1
             CAO 1762
             Ferial office for Thursday
             No equivalent

             Ps. **Laudate**[20] [Ps. 148–150]

             Capitulum[21] **Filii tui de longe** venient et filie tue de latere surgent
             [Isaiah 60.4][22]

17. *om.* Lucca.
18. *om.* Lucca.
19. om. Lucca.
20. *om.* Lucca.
21. Capitulum] Hymnus *in* Barletta.
22. Hymnus. Hoc in templo] *add. In* Lucca.

v. **Adorate dominum,** alleluia, in aula sancta ejus, alleluia.
Ps. 28.2
CAO 1288
Epiphany
No equivalent

Benedictus antiphon

In Evangelio Ant. **Benedicta sit** creatrix et gubernatrix omnium, sancta et individua trinitas et nunc et semper et per infinita seculorum secula.
CAO 1707
Trinity
No equivalent

Collect

Oratio **Omnipotens sempiterne Deus** [as above][23]

Prime

Ad I. Ant. **Iocundare**

Procession

Post primam cum sollempni processione procedimus ad Templum Domini laudantes et glorificantes.[24]
Hec cantando. Resp. **Benedictus Dominus** deus Israel qui facis mirabilia solus et benedictum nomen majestatis ejus in aeternum.
CAO 6249
Trinity

Resp. **Quis deus magnus** sicut deus noster tu es deus qui facis mirabilia.
CAO 7498
Trinity
et cetera, que ad que ad laudes pertinent.

In introitu templi, Ant. **Pax eterna** ab aeterno patre huic domui pax perennis verbum patris sit pax huic domui pacem pius consolator huic praestet domui.
CAO 4252
Dedication of a church

v. **domum tuam** domine decet sanctitudo in longitudinem dierum.
CAO 2425
Dedication of a church

Oratio. **Exaudi nos omnipotens Deus, et presta ut quisquis.**

Quibus expletis procedimus ad meridianam portam, et inde divertentes, convertimus contra illum locum ubi civitas capta fuit. Facta statione fit, sermo ad populum. Sermonem expleto, factaque benedictione, cantor incipit.

23. *om.* Lucca.
24. The entire section on the procession, starting with "post primam cum sollempni processione" and ending with the collect "Famulorum tuorum" right before the instructions for Terce, is absent in Lucca.

Ant. **Gratias tibi Deus** gratias tibi vera una trinitas una et trina veritas trina et una unitas.
CAO 2977
Trinity

Deinde[25] *revertunt ad dominicum sepulchrum, cantando, de prescriptis.*

Resp. In introitu ecclesie, si domenica fuerit, Ant. **Ego sum Alpha et Omega** primus et novissimus et stella matutina ego clavis David alleluia
CAO 2588 or 2589
Eastertide
et fit statio ante Sepulchrum.

v. **Surrexit Dominus de hoc** sepulcro qui pro nobis pependit in ligno.
CAO 7742. Note that this version change "de sepulcro" to "de hoc sepulcro."
Easter and varia

Oratio: **Deus qui hodierna die** pro incomparabilibus meritis gloriosissimam Mariam semper que virginem et matrem ad superna gaudia perduxisti, praesta illuc nos quoque tua pietate conscendere, quo ipsa meruit sublevari.
CO 1670
Assumption.

deinde[26] *de sancta Maria,* A. **Alma redemptoris m**ater quae pervia caeli porta manes et stella maris succurre cadenti surgere qui curat populo tu quae genuisti natura mirante tuum sanctum genitorem virgo prius ac posterius Gabrielis ab ore sumens illud ave peccatorum miserere.
CAO 1356
Suffrages of Virgin

De hac liberatione secundam novam institutionem nichil facimus propter processionem, et missa matutinalem post dedicationem ecclesie.[27]

v. **Post partum virgo** [inviolata]
CAO 6370ze
Nativity of the Virgin

Oratio. **Famulorum tuorum** domine, delictis ignosce, ut, qui placere de actibus nostris non valemus, genitricis filii tui domini dei nostri intercessione salvemur.[28]

---

25. Deinde] *Kohler has* Demum.
26. Deinde] *Kohler has* Demum.
27. This explanatory rubric is not included in Barletta.
28. Barletta *has*: Famulorum tuorum quesumus, Domine. . . .

CO 2649
Assumption of the Virgin, et alia.

Terce	Ad III. Hymnus. **Hoc in templo** [from *Urbs Beata*, as above] **vel Nunc sancte nobis**[29] spiritus unum patri cum filio dignare promptus ingeri nostro refusus pectori

> CAO 8354
> AH 50:19–20, no. 18.
> Standard hymn for terce

Ant. **Letamini cum Ierusalem** [as above]
Capitulum **Surge illuminare** [as above]
Resp. **Reges tharsis** [as above]
v. **Omnes de Sabba** venient[30] [as above]
Collecta ut [Fol. 102r] supra[31]

Sext	Ad VI: Hymnus **Hoc in templo** [From *Urbs Beata*, as above] **vel Rector potens,**[32] (verax Deus).[as above]

> CAO 8380
> AH 50:20, no. 19
> Standard hymn for sext

Ant. **Ierusalem gaude** [as above]
Capitulum **Filii tui de longe** [as above]
Resp. **Omnes de Sabba venient** [as above]
v. **Omnes gentes**[33] [as above]

Oratio **Omnipotens sempiterne Deus edificator** et custos Ierusalem civitatis superne, edifica et custodi locum istum cum habitatoribus suis, ut perpetuum sit in eo domicilium incolumitatis et pacis.

> CO 3787
> Pro custodia monasterii et habitorum eius, collecta

None	Ad IX Hymnus. **Hoc in templo** [as above] **vel Rerum Deus tenax**[34] vigor immotus in te permanens lucis diurne tempora successibus determinans

> CAO 8382
> AH 50:20, no. 20
> Standard hymn for none

---

29. vel Nunc sancta nobis] *om.* Lucca.
30. *om.* Lucca.
31. *om.* Lucca. In Barletta, the mass formulary is inserted here. In Barberini 659, it appears later in the Ordinal.
32. vel rector potens] *om.* Lucca.
33. Omnes gentes] *om.* Lucca.
34. vel Rerum Deus tenax] *om.* Lucca.

Ant. **Cantate domino** [as above]
Capitulum Leva **Ierusalem** [as above]
Resp. **Omnes gentes**[35] [as above]
Vers. **Adorate dominum**[36] [as above]

Oratio ut supra

2 Vespers   **Ad Vesperas,**

VA1   Ant. **Jocundare filia**[37] [as above]
Ps. **Dixit Dominus**[38] cetere ad ceteros.

Capitulum **Surge illuminare.** [as above]
Resp. **Summe Trinitati.**[39] [as above]
Hymnus **Urbs beata Iherusalem** [as above]

v. **Beati qui habitant** in domo tua, Domine. R. In secula
seculorum laudabunt te.
CAO 7960
Dedication of a church
No equivalent

Magnificat   Ant. **O Iherusalem civitas Dei summi,**[40] leva in circuitu oculos tuos
antiphon   et vide Dominum Deum tuum quia jam veniet solvere te a vinculis.
CAO 4034
One of the "O" antiphons
No equivalent

Collecta ut supra

M²   **In liberatione sancte civitatis iherusalem de manibus turchorum.**[41]
Ipso die dedicatione ecclesie dominici sepulcri.

Missa matutinalis.

Introit   **Officium: Letare Iherusalem** et conventum facite omnes qui
diligitis eam, gaudete cum letitia, qui in trititia fuistis, ut
exsultetis, et satiemini ab uberibus consolationis vestre.
Is. 66.10–11
Cantus Index g00776 (Fourth Sunday of Lent)

35. Omnes] gentes add. Lucca.
36. *om.* Lucca.
37. Filia] *om.* Lucca.
38. *om.* Lucca.
39. Prestet nobis *add.* Lucca.
40. Lucca supplies an entire, slight variant: O iherusalem civitas regis summi leva in circuitu
oculos tuos et vide dominum deum tuum quia modo veniet solver te a vinculo. Lectiones require in Epiphania.
41. The mass is found in Barberini 659 at 132r–v. In Barletta, it is found at 110v. The mass,
added in the lower margin on Lucca 5, p. 57, is almost illegible.

Ps. Letatus sum [Ps. 121]

Kyrie	Kyrie. Cunctipotens genitor.
Collect	Or. **Omnipotens sempiterne deus qui dedisti** famuli tuis in confessione vere fidei eterne trinitatis gloriam agnoscere et in potentia maiestatis adorare unitatem, quesumus, ut eiusdem fidei firmitate ab omnibus semper muniamur adversis. CO 3920 Missa de sancta Trinitate
Epistle	Epistola[42]: **Surge illuminare . . .** Is. 60.1
Gradual	Resp. **Omnes de Sabba** venient aurem et thus deferentes et laudem Domino annunutiantes.[43] Is. 60.6. Cantus Index g00568 (Epiphany)
Alleluia	**v. Dies sanctificatus** illuxit nobis venite gentes et adorate Dominum quia hodie descendit lux magna super terram. Cantus Index a00087 (Christmas)
Sequence	**Clara chorus . . .** AH 54: 138–140, no. 94. In dedicatione ecclesiae vel **Manu plaudant . . .** AH 40:71–72, no 60. Linder, "The Liturgy of the Liberation" (1990), 119–120.
Gospel	**Cum intrasset Ihesus Iherosolimam . . .** Matt. 21.10
Offertory	**Dextera domini** fecit virtutem dextera domini exaltavit me non moriar sed vivam et narrabo opera Domini. Ps. 117:16–17 Cantus Index g00629 (Third Sunday after Epiphany)
Communion	**Iherusalem surge** et sta in excelso et vide iucunditatem que veniet tibi a deo tuo. Bar 5:5, 4:36 Cantus Index g00500 (Advent)

---

42. Epistola] *Barletta reads* Epistola Ysaie prophete.
43. Barletta includes the verse here, *Surge et . . .* Is. 60:1; Cantus Index g00598 (Epiphany).

Appendix 2

Comparative Development
of the Clamor

Linder established the various forms of the clamor, including the *Omnip-otens* clamor (cols. 1 and 2), the *Deus qui ad redemptionis* clamor (cols 3–5), and the development of Innocent III's *Deus qui admirabili* clamor (col. 6). He showed that the clamor instituted in 1213 in *Quia Maior* (col. 6) quickly underwent elaboration (col. 7). A special form was probably promulgated in France in the 1240s when Louis IX was preparing for his first crusade (cols. 8 and 9), and this was later adopted in missals in Paris that related to the court (col. 10). William Durandus added the *Hostium nost-rorum* prayer to the clamor he included in his pontifical of 1293 (col. 11), and in England the Sarum tradition, growing out of this earlier form, added several prayers in the fifteenth century (col. 12). New traditions did not supplant earlier traditions, which continued to be copied into manuscripts throughout the thirteenth, fourteenth, and fifteenth centuries; and there are plenty of other local and individual variants. The collects and, especially, the preces have been presented so that adoption, exclusion, and comparisons can be observed. The texts listed here are taken from single manuscript representatives, representing the main categories and development, but many variations of each exist and can be traced through Linder's *Raising Arms*.

TABLE 1

1 London 1188	2 Cistercian use 1194–1195	3 *Deus qui ad* *nostre* (1) ca. 1180	4 *Deus qui ad* *nostre* (2) <1200	5 *Deus qui ad* *nostre* (3) ca. 1225	6 Innocent III's clamor (1213)
As reported by Roger of Hovendon (1869), ed. Stubbs, v. 2, 359–360.	Clamor prescribed in 1194 and updated in 1195, as reconstructed by Waddell (2002), 286–287, 306–307; and Linder RA, 26.	Transcribed from Darmstadt Hessische Landes-und Hochschulbibliothek ms. 3183, pp. 188–189 (Mainz, 1175–1185) See Linder RA, 71–72, for sources.	Transcribed from Valenciennes BM ms. 121, 88v (late 12c.). See Linder RA, 71–72, for sources.	Chartres Ordo. After Delaporte (1953), 197–198.	After *Quia Maior* [PL 216, col. 821] Confirmed broadly in the manuscript record; Linder RA, 72–73.

RUBRIC

Pro pace et liberatione terre ierusalem et christianorum captivorum qui in vinculis sarracenorum detinebantur.	Oratio pro terra Ierosolimitana	Contra paganorum incursiones.	Pro adversitate terre ierosolimam.	Hic est ordo quando oratur pro terra iherosolimitana. Finita dominica oratione ad missam fiat prostratio ante altare, nisi sit dies dominica vel festum ix. lect.	

7 Expansion of clamor (<1245)	8 Cistercian use in 1245	9 French clamor, ca. 1245	10 French royal examples, ca. 1300	11 Durandus Pontifical, ca. 1293	12 Sarum clamor, >1405
Transcribed from Reims BM ms. 216, fol. 7r–v. See Linder RA, 74–75 for sources.	As instituted in Council statutes. Canivez (1935), 2:289.	Special Version promulgated in French kingdom, ca. 1245, in advance of Louis IX's first crusade. Transcribed from Reims BM ms. 218, fol. 122v (interpolated mid-century into missal of early 12c). See Linder RA, 76 for sources.	Transcribed from Lyon BM ms. 5122 fol. 398r–v (1297–1306) Linder RA (2003), 76–77 for sources.	PWD III.XVI (p. 630–631).	London BL Add. 16998, 57v–58r (early 15c). See Linder RA (2003), 78–80, for sources
Oratio terra iherosolimitana	Pro domino papa, pro rege Franciae, qui signum sanctae crucis assump- sit, et pro terra sancta maxime ad petitionem venerabilis patris Thus- culani epis- copi legati Franciae.		Pro Terra Sancta.	Pro terre sancte liberatione dicitur in missa, statim post *Pater noster*.	Iste preces dicantur in ferialibus diebus pro pace univer- salis ecclesie et regni posquam sac- erdos dixit. Per omnia S. s. Antequam dicat: Pax domini.

(continued)

TABLE 1 (continued)

1 London 1188	2 Cistercian use 1194–1195	3 *Deus qui ad nostre* (1) ca. 1180	4 *Deus qui ad nostre* (2) <1200	5 *Deus qui ad nostre* (3) ca. 1225	6 Innocent III's clamor (1213)
PSALM					
Varied per day of the week, starting on Sunday: Ps. 2, 53, 59, 73, 78, 82, 93.	Deus venerunt gentes [Ps. 78]	Deus venerunt gentes in hereditatem tuam . . . in generatione et generationem annuntiabimus laudem tuam [Ps. 78] *Note that the manuscript copies out entire psalm.*	Deus venerunt gentes. [Ps. 78]	Et dicatur Ps. Deus venerunt [Ps. 78]	Deus venerunt gentes in hereditatem tuam [Ps. 78]

7 Expansion of clamor (<1245)	8 Cistercian use in 1245	9 French clamor, ca. 1245	10 French royal examples, ca. 1300	11 Durandus Pontifical, ca. 1293	12 Sarum clamor, >1405
Deus venerunt gentes. [Ps. 78]	Deus venerunt gentes [Ps. 78]	Deus venerunt gentes inhereditatem tuam . . . in generatione et generationem annuntiabimus laudem tuam [Ps. 78] *Note that the manuscript copies out entire psalm*	Deus venerunt gentes. [Ps. 78]	Deus venerunt gentes [Ps. 78]	Deus venerunt [Ps. 78]
					Ps. Deus misereatur [Ps. 66]
					Ps. Levavi [Ps. 120].
					(Ant) Tua est potencia tuum regnum domine tu est super omnes gentes da pacem domine in diebus nostris [CAO 5224, from Macchabees]

(continued)

TABLE 1 (continued)

1 London 1188	2 Cistercian use 1194–1195	3 *Deus qui ad nostre* (1) ca. 1180	4 *Deus qui ad nostre* (2) <1200	5 *Deus qui ad nostre* (3) ca. 1225	6 Innocent III's clamor (1213)
Kyrieleison, Christeleison, Kyrieleison.		Gloria patri. Sicut erat.	Gloria patri. Sicut erat.	*cum* Glo- ria, *post* Kyrieleison,	
		Kyrieleison, Christeleison, Kyrieleison.	Clementissime deus exaudi preces nostras.	Christeleison, Kyrieleison.	
			Kyrieleison, Christeleison, Kyrieleison.		
Pater noster. Et ne nos	Pater noster.	Pater noster	Pater noster. Et ne nos.	Pater noster. Et ne nos.	

PRECES (VERSICLES)

Ostende
nobis domine
misericordiam
tuam
[Ps. 84.8]

Fiat mi-
sericordia
tua domine
super nos [Ps.
32.22]

Domine non
secundum
peccata
nostra facias
nobis [cf: Ps.
102.10]

Ne memineris
iniquitatum
nostrarum
antiquarum
[Ps. 78.8]

Adjuva nos
deus salutaris
noster [Ps.
78.9]

7 Expansion of clamor (<1245)	8 Cistercian use in 1245	9 French clamor, ca. 1245	10 French royal examples, ca. 1300	11 Durandus Pontifical, ca. 1293	12 Sarum clamor, >1405
Kyrieleison.	Kyrieleison	Gloria patri, Sicut [erat]. Kyrieleison, Christeleison, Kyrieleison.	Kyrieleison, Christeleison.	Gloria Patri. Kyrieleison, Christeleison.	Kyrieleison, Christeleison, Kyrieleison.
Pater noster. Et ne nos	Pater noster. Et ne nos (etc.)	Pater noster. Et ne nos. Sed libera.	Pater noster. Et ne nos.		Pater noster. Et ne nos.

(continued)

TABLE 1 (continued)

1 London 1188	2 Cistercian use 1194–1195	3 *Deus qui ad* *nostre* (1) ca. 1180	4 *Deus qui ad* *nostre* (2) <1200	5 *Deus qui ad* *nostre* (3) ca. 1225	6 Innocent III's clamor (1213)
	Preces: Exurgat Deus. [Ps. 67.2]	Exsurgat deus et dissipentur inimici eius, et fugiant qui oderunt eum a facie eius. [Ps. 67:2]	Exurgat deus et dissipentur inimici eius, et fugiunt qui oderunt eum a facie eius. [Ps. 67:2]	Exurgat deus et dissipentur in eius, et fugiant. [Ps. 67:2]	Exurgat Deus, et dissipentur inimici eius, et fugiant a facie eius qui oderunt eum. [Ps. 67:2]
			Non nobis domine non nobis sed nomini tuo da gloriam. [Ps. 113.9]	Non nobis domine non nobis; sed nomini tuo. [Ps. 113:9]	
Salvum fac populum tuum domine [cf: Ps. 27:9]	Salvum fac populum tuum. Fiat pax. [cf: Ps. 27:9]		Salvum fac populum tuum domine et benedic hereditati tue, et rege. [cf: Ps. 27:9]	Salvum fac populum; et benedic hereditati. [cf: Ps. 27:9]	
			Oremus pro afflictis et captivis.	Oremus pro afflictis et captivis; libera deus.	
			Libera eos deus Israel ex omnibus [cf: Ps. 24:22]		

7 Expansion of clamor (<1245)	8 Cistercian use in 1245	9 French clamor, ca. 1245	10 French royal examples, ca. 1300	11 Durandus Pontifical, ca. 1293	12 Sarum clamor, >1405
Exsurgat deus; et fugiant. [Ps. 67:2]	Exurgat deus [Ps. 67:2]	Exurgat deus et dissipenter inimici eius; et fugiant. [Ps. 67:2]	Exurgat deus, et dissipentur inimici eius. [Ps. 67:2]	Exurgat Deus et dissipentur inimici eius. [Ps. 67:2]	Exurgat deus et discipentur inimici eius. Et fugiant qui oderunt. [Ps. 67:2]
					Non nobis domine non nobis. [Ps. 113:9]
		Domine sal- vum fac regem. Et exaudi. [Ps 19:10]			
Salvum fac populum tuum domine et benedic, etc. [cf: Ps. 27:9]		Salvum fac populum domine, et benedic heredi- tati tue. Et rege eos et. [cf: Ps. 27:9]	Salvum fac pop- ulum tuum do- mine, et benedic hereditati tue. [cf: Ps. 27:9]	Salvum fac populum tuum. [cf: Ps. 27:9]	
Oremus pro afflictis et captivis et peregrinis christianis		Oremus pro afflicitis et captivis et peregrinis christianis	Oremus pro af- flictis et captiv- is et peregrinis christianis.	Oremus pro afflictis et peregrinis chris- tianis.	Oremus pro afflictis et captivis.
		Libera eos deus israhel. [cf: Ps. 24:22]			Libera eos de tribulation- ibus eorum. [cf: Ps. 24:22]
		Salvos fac ser- vos tuos. Deus meus.			

(continued)

TABLE 1 (continued)

1 London 1188	2 Cistercian use 1194–1195	3 *Deus qui ad* *nostre* (1) ca. 1180	4 *Deus qui ad* *nostre* (2) <1200	5 *Deus qui ad* *nostre* (3) ca. 1225	6 Innocent III's clamor (1213)
			Mitte eis do- mine auxilium de sancto et de syon tuere eos. [cf: Ps. 19:3]	Mitte eis domine auxilium; et de syon tuere. [cf: Ps. 19:3]	
Esto eis domine turris fortitudinis [Ps. 60:4]			Esto eis domine turris fortitudinis a facie inimici. [cf: Ps. 60:4]	Esto eis do- mine turris; a facie inimici. [cf: Ps. 60:4]	
Nihil proficiat inimicus in eis [Ps. 88:23]					
Fiat pax in virtute tua [Ps. 121.7]					
Domine deus virtute con- verte nos [Ps. 79.20]					
Domine exau- di orationem meam [Ps 101.2]			Domine exau- di. [Ps 101.2]	Domine exaudi; [Ps. 101.2]	
Dominus vobiscum,			Dominus vo- biscum et cum spiritu tuo.	Dominus vobiscum.	

7 Expansion of clamor (<1245)	8 Cistercian use in 1245	9 French clamor, ca. 1245	10 French royal examples, ca. 1300	11 Durandus Pontifical, ca. 1293	12 Sarum clamor, >1405
	Mitte eis Domine auxilium de sancto. [cf: Ps. 19:3]	Mitte eis domine auxilium de sancto; et de syon. [cf: Ps. 19:3]	Mitte eius domine auxilium de sancto et syon tuere eos. [cf: Ps. 19:3]	Mitte eis, domine, auxilium de sancto. [cf: Ps. 19:3]	Mitte eis auxilium de sancto. Et de Syon tuere eos. [cf: Ps. 19:3]
				Esto eis, domine, turris fortitudinis [cf: Ps. 60:4]	Esto eis domine turris fortitudinis, et facie inimici. [cf: Ps. 60:4]
	Domine exaudi [Ps. 101.2]	Domine exaudi et clamour. [Ps. 101.2]	Domine exaudi orationem meam. Et clamour meus ad te, veniet. [Ps. 101.2]	Domine exaudi. [Ps. 101.2]	Domine exaudi orationem meam. [Ps 101.2]
Dominus vobiscum.	Domine vobiscum	Dominus vobiscum.	Dominus vobiscum.		Dominus vobiscum.
			Et cum spiritu tuo.		
			Oremus.		

(continued)

TABLE 1 (continued)

1 London 1188	2 Cistercian use 1194–1195	3 *Deus qui ad nostre* (1) ca. 1180	4 *Deus qui ad nostre* (2) <1200	5 *Deus qui ad nostre* (3) ca. 1225	6 Innocent III's clamor (1213)
COLLECT(S) (*OREMUS*)					
Omnipotens sempiterne Deus, in cujus manu sunt omnium potestates, et Omnia jura regnorum, respice ad christianum benignus exercitum [or *auxilium*] ut gentes, que in sua feritate confidunt, potentia	1194: Et collecta: Deus a quo sancta desideria; quae etiam in missis defunctorum dicatur, in aliis vero *deus qui corda* addatur. 1195:[1] Deus, in cujus manu sunt omnium potestates, et Omnia jura regnorum, respice ad	Deus qui ad nostre redemptionis exhibenda misteria terram repromissionis elegisti, libera eam quesumus ab instancia paganorum, ut gentium incredulitate confusa, populus in te confidens de tue virtutis potencia glorietur. Per eundem dominum.	Deus qui ad nostre redemptionis exhibenda misteria terram promissionis elegisti libera eam quesumus instantia paganorum, ut gentium incredulitate confuse populus in te confidens de tue virtutis potentia	Deus qui ad nostre redemptionis exhibenda mysteria terram promissionis elegisti, libera eam quesumus ab instantia paganorum, ut gentium incredulitate confuse populous in te confidens de tue virtutis	Deus qui admirabili providentia cuncta disponis, te suppliciter exoramus, ut terram, quam unigenitus filius tuus proprio sanguine consecravit, de manibus inimicorum crucis eripiens restituas cultui christiano, vota fidelium

7 Expansion of clamor (<1245)	8 Cistercian use in 1245	9 French clamor, ca. 1245	10 French royal examples, ca. 1300	11 Durandus Pontifical, ca. 1293	12 Sarum clamor, >1405
	Deus omnium fidelium pastor, etc. [CO 1287, *pro papa vel epicopo,* etc.]	Oremus: Famulum tuum regem nostrorum quesumus domine tua semper protectione custodi ut libera mente tibi deserviat et de protegente a malis omnibus sit securus. [cf: CO 2663, *oratio super populum,* adapted for a king]			
Deus qui admirabili potentia tua cuncta disponis te suppliciter exoramus ut terram quam unigentisu filius tuus deus noster proprio sanguine, consecravit de manibus inimicorum crucis eripias qui eam non tam ex sue virtutis ptentia quam ex nostre	Deus qui admirabili providentia cuncta disponis, te suppliter exoramus, ut terram quam Unigenitus Filius tuus proprio sanguine consecravit, de manibus inimicorum crucis eripiens, restituas cultui christiano, vota	Deus qui amirabili potentia cuncta disponis de suppliciter exoramus ut terram quam unigenitus filius tuus deus noster proprio sanguine consecravit de manibus inimicorum crucis eripias qui eam non tam liberationem	ex sue virtutis potencia quam ex nostre iniquitatis offensa detinent occupatam ipsam que restituas cultui christiano ad laudem et gloriam nominis tui sancti vota fidelium qui ad eius Deus qui admirabili providentia cuncta disponis, te supplices	Deus, qui admirabili providentia cuncta disponis, te suppiciter exoramus, ut terram, quam unigenitus filius tuus **dominus noster Iesus Christus** proprio sanguine consecrative, de manibus inimicorum crucis eiripiens, restituas	Deus qui admirabili providencia cuncta disponis, te supplices exoramus ut terram quam unigenitus filius tuus proprio sanguine consecravit de manibus inimicorum crucis christi eripiens

(continued)

TABLE 1 (continued)

1 London 1188	2 Cistercian use 1194–1195	3 *Deus qui ad nostre* (1) ca. 1180	4 *Deus qui ad nostre* (2) <1200	5 *Deus qui ad nostre* (3) ca. 1225	6 Innocent III's clamor (1213)
dextere tue comprimantur, per dominum nostrum jesum christum.	christianum benignus auxilium ut gentes, que in sua feritate confidunt, potentia dextere tue comprimantur, per dominum nostrum jesum christum. [NB: *Deus a quo sancta desideria* was the votive mass for peace. *Deus qui corda* was the votive mass for the Holy Spirit.]		glorietur. Qui vivis et regnas cum deo patre.	potentia glorietur,	ad eius liberationem instantium misericorditer dirigendo in viam salutis eterne. Per eum dominum nostrum, etc.[2]
				et oratio *Hostium* [nostrorum, quaesumus, domine, elide superbiam et dexterae tuae virtute prosterne; CO 3007, *contra paganos*]	

7 Expansion of clamor (<1245)	8 Cistercian use in 1245	9 French clamor, ca. 1245	10 French royal examples, ca. 1300	11 Durandus Pontifical, ca. 1293	12 Sarum clamor, >1405
iniquitatis offensa detinent occupatam, ipsam que restituas cultui christiano ad laudem et gloriam nominis tui sancti vota fidelium qui ad eius liberationem institerint misericorditer dirigendo in viam salutis eterne. Per eundem dominum nostrum. [*Note that this is the variant form of Innocent III's prayer*]	fidelium ad eius liberationem instantium misericorditer dirigendo in viam salutis aeternae. Per eumdem Christum Dominum nostrum.	institerint misericorditer dirigendo in viam salutis eterne. Per eundem dominum nostrum. [*Note that this is the variant form of Innocent III's prayer*]	exoramus, ut terram quam unigenitus filius tuis proprio sanguine consecravit, de manibus inimicorum crucis eripiens restituas cultui christiano vota fidelium ad eius liberationem instancium misericorditer dirigendo in viam salutis eterne. Per eundem, Christum.	cultui christiano, vota fidelium ad eius liberationem instantium misericorditer dirigendo in viam salutis eterne. Per Christum. Resp. Amen	retituas cultui christianorum vota fidelium ad eius liberationem et instantacionem misericorditer dirigendo, in viam pacis eterne, Per.
		Ecclesie domine quesumus preces placatus admitte ut destructis adversitatibus et erroribus universis ecclesia tua secura tibi serviat liberatate. Per.	*Pro rege nostro.* Ps. Exaudiat te dominus Kyrieleison. Christeleyson. Kyrieleison. Pater noster. Et ne nos. Sed libera nos. Domine salvum fac regem.	Oratio: Hostium nostrorum, quesumus, domine, elide superbiam et eorum contumaciam dexter tue virtute prosterne. [CO 3007, *contra paganos*]	

(continued)

TABLE 1 (continued)

1 London 1188	2 Cistercian use 1194–1195	3 *Deus qui ad nostre* (1) ca. 1180	4 *Deus qui ad nostre* (2) <1200	5 *Deus qui ad nostre* (3) ca. 1225	6 Innocent III's clamor (1213)
				Quando dicuntur septem psalmi post terciam dicatur hec letania [*Follows with the recitation of a long lit- any, the Kyrie and Pater, fur- ther vesicles, and a series of penitential collects* (CO 74, 3938c, 1494, 1898, 2210, and 1582)]	

7 Expansion of clamor (<1245)	8 Cistercian use in 1245	9 French clamor, ca. 1245	10 French royal examples, ca. 1300	11 Durandus Pontifical, ca. 1293	12 Sarum clamor, >1405
		[CO 2404b, *pro universali* *ecclesia; contra* *adversarious* *ecclesiae*, etc.]	Et exaudi nos in die qua invo- caverimus te. Salvos fac servos tuos. Deus meus sper- antes in te. Mitte eis do- mine auxilium de sancto. Et de Syon tuere eos. Domine exaudi orationem meam. Et clamor meus ad te venia. Dominus vo- biscum. Oremus.	Per. Resp. Amen.	
	In regno vero Franciae dicatur ver- sus: *Domine* *salvum fac* *regem* *Et secundo* *loco collecta*: Famulum tuum regem nostrum quaesumus, domine,		*Oratio*: Fam- ulum tuum regem nostrum et famulos tuos quesumus do- mine tua semper protectione cus- todi ut libera tibi mente deserviant et te protegente ab omnibus malis omnibus sint securi, per christum		

(continued)

TABLE 1 (continued)

1 London 1188	2 Cistercian use 1194–1195	3 *Deus qui ad nostre* (1) ca. 1180	4 *Deus qui ad nostre* (2) <1200	5 *Deus qui ad nostre* (3) ca. 1225	6 Innocent III's clamor (1213)

1. Note that the instructions for the service are as follows: "Collecta: Ecclesiae tuae Deus a quo. Singulis septim<an>is in unusquisque privatam Disciplinam recipiat, nisi nimis aegritudine praegavetur. Oratio solita ad missam, *Deus venerunt*, non intermittantur. Sed tantum *Respice ad christianorum benignus auxilium emendetur*." This means that the votive mass against evildoers (*Ecclesiae tuae*) was said during private masses, and the votive mass for war (*Omnipotens deus*) was said during the conventual mass. See Waddell (2002), 307.

2. A variant runs: Deus qui ammirabili providential cuncta dispones, te supplices exoramus, ut terram, quam unigenitus filius tuus dominus noster proprio sanguine consecravit, de manu hostium crucis eripias, **qui non tam ex sui virtutis potentia quam ex nostre iniquitatis offense eam detinent occupatam**, ipsamque restituas cultui christiano ad laudem et gloriam nominis tui sancti, vota fidelium qui ad eius liberationem institerint misericorditer dirigendo in viam salutis eterne. See Linder RA 40.

7 Expansion of clamor (<1245)	8 Cistercian use in 1245	9 French clamor, ca. 1245	10 French royal examples, ca. 1300	11 Durandus Pontifical, ca. 1293	12 Sarum clamor, >1405
	tua semper protectione custodi, ut libera tibi mente deserviat, et te protegente a malis omnibus sit securus. [cf: CO 2663, *oratio super populum*, adapted for a king] Orationes vero consuetae *Aspice domine*, et *Pater noster* et *Veni creator* omittentur.		dominum. [cf: CO 2663, *oratio super populum*, adapted for a king]		

Appendix 3

Timeline of Nonliturgical Evidence for Liturgical Supplications

The following is a summary of evidence that I know of from chronicles, letters, and other sources (but excluding the liturgical manuscripts themselves) showing requests or prescriptions for liturgical services to be said for crusades or crusaders. Although much of this was documented in footnotes in Christoph Maier's "Crisis, Liturgy, and the Crusade" and Amnon Linder's *Raising Arms*, I hope compiled in this way it tells its own story. This is surely far from exhaustive and more evidence is certain to be found.

1187, 29 October. Following the defeat at Hattin to Saladin, Pope Gregory VIII calls Third Crusade. Issuing *Audita tremendi*, centered on Psalm 78.
 PL 202:1539–1542. MGH SS rerum germanicarum ns. 5:6–10
1187. In *Nunquam melius superni*, Gregory VIII issues instructions for fasting and a special mass following the defeat at Hattin.
 Roger of Hovendon, *Chronica Magistri Rogeri de Houedene*, II:329–330.
 PL 202:1539.
1188. A chronicler reports that Henry of Albano, in order to avenge the destruction of Jerusalem, instituted that "public prayers ordered by Pope Gregory VIII be observed throughout the entire church."
 Chronica Andrensis. MGH SS 24:719.
1188. Clement III issues clamor, attached to *Deus venerunt gentes* (Ps. 78), known from London, and other chroniclers. Original instructions do not survive, but were linked by Roger of Hoveden to the *Omnipotens sempiterne Deus* collect (CO 3846, from the *contra paganos* mass).
 Roger of Hoveden, *Chronica Magistri Rogeri de Houedene*, II:359–360.
 Conrad of Scheyern, *Annales*, MGH SS 17:630.
 Arnold of Lübeck, *Chronica Slavorum*, MGH SS 21:169–170.

1189–1192: The Third Crusade.

1190. Cistercians institute the weekly recitation the mass for the Holy Spirit for the kings and princes and other crusaders (*cruce signatis*). Any pilgrim who dies on the crusade will be included in the daily mass for the dead.

Canivez, *Statuta Capitulorum Generalium Ordinis Cisterciensis*, 1:122 (no. 16)

1191. Guillaume of Reims, Queen Adela, and bishops order that the relics of Denis, Rusticus, and Eleutherius be placed on the altar in Saint Denis and prayers be said "for the deliverance of the Holy Land, for the health of the king of France and all his army."

Rigord, *Histoire de Philippe Auguste*, ch. 87 (pp. 300–303)

1194. Cistercian General Statutes issue *Oratio pro terra Ierosolimitana*, including the *Deus venerunt gentes* Psalm (Ps. 78), the collect *Deus a quo sancta desideria* (CO 1088, from *pro pace* rites), and for masses for the dead, the *Deus qui corda* collect (from mass for the Holy Spirit).

Waddell, *Twelfth-Century Statutes from the Cistercian General Chapter* (Brecht, Belgium: 2002), 286–287.

Canivez, *Statuta Capitulorum Generalium Ordinis Cisterciensis*, I:172 (item 10).

1195. Cistercians expand Holy Land prayers *Pro tribulatione terrae sanctae* and include also Saracen invasions in Spain, and prayers for peace, for the pope, and for the kings of France and England; prescribe a procession every Friday in which the community chants the seven penitential psalms with the litany, the Lord's Prayer, vesicles (*Exurgat Deus, Salvum fac populum, fiat pax*, etc) and response, and the collects *Ecclesie tue* (CO 2404b, from the mass *contra adversarios ecclesiae*) and *Deus a quo* (CO 1088). Monks are to take weekly discipline. Daily clamor of *Deus venerunt gentes* (Ps. 78) as before, but including the *Omnipotens sempiterne Deus* collect (CO 3846).

Waddell, *Twelfth-Century Statutes from the Cistercian General Chapter* (Brecht, Belgium: 2002), 306–307.

Canivez, *Statuta Capitulorum Generalium Ordinis Cisterciensis*, 1:181–182 (item 1)

1195, 25 July. Celestine III writes to clergy of Canterbury, asking for prayers.

Radulfus de Diceto, *Opera Historica*, ed. W. Stubbs, vol. 2 (RS 68), 134.

1196. Cistercians reissue the *pro terra Ierosolimitana* statutes.

Waddell, *Twelfth-Century Statutes from the Cistercian General Chapter* (Brecht, Belgium: 2002), 372–373.

Canivez, *Statuta Capitulorum Generalium Ordinis Cisterciensis*, 1:208 (no. 57).

1197. Cistercians reissue the *Pro terra Ierusalem* statutes.

Waddell, *Twelfth-Century Statutes from the Cistercian General Chapter* (Brecht, Belgium: 2002), 379.

Canivez, *Statuta Capitulorum Generalium Ordinis Cisterciensis*, 1:210 (item 2).

1199, 5 January. Innocent III asks the church in Sicily to perform *Pro tribulatione* votive masses for crusaders.

PL 214:470.

Hageneder et al., *Das Register Innocenz' III*, vol. 1, no. 508 (1:741–743).

1199, 31 December. Innocent III, in general letter, asks that "in all churches mass should be publicly celebrated once a week for the remission of sins, and especially for those making offerings."

Hageneder et al., *Das Register Innocenz' III*, vol. 2, no. 258 (490–497, at 495) and no. 259 (497–501, at p. 500).

1203. In England, mention of a statute indicating weekly processions and special prayers to be said in the daily mass, and fasting *Propterea pro terra Ierosolimitana*, for the peace of the kingdom and the church, and for good weather and the fecundity of the earth.

Durham, Cathedral Library MS C.iv. 24, fol. 191r, edited in C.R. Cheney, "Levies on the English Clergy for the Poor and for the King, 1203" in *English Historical Review* 96 (1981) 583–584.

~1204. Innocent III, in a letter to the bishops and archbishops of France, instructs that "Psalm 78 (*Deus venerunt gentes*), with the usual prayer, be said," along with the collection of alms.

Gesta Innocentii, PL 214:134.

1202–1204: The Fourth Crusade. Army diverted to Constantinople.

1209–1229: Albigensian Crusade.

1212, May. Innocent III calls *supplicatio generalis* and presides over a public procession in Rome in order to supplicate God on behalf of the Christian army in Spain. Included use of *Omnipotens sempiterne Deus* collect (CO 3846).

Innocentii III Romani Pontificis Regestorum, PL 216:698–699.

1212, July 16. Battle of Las Navas de Tolosa. Christian forces defeat the Almohads in Spain.

1212: Children's crusade.

1212. Innocent III sends Philip of Oxford, Leo of Wells, and William of London to preach the cross and collect money "per singulas ecclesias statuentes."

Annales prioratus de Dunstaplia. Henry Richards Luard, ed., *Annales Monastici* (RS 36) 3:40.

1212, spring. Processions and prayers done by Christians in France for those who are leaving to fight in Spain.

Alberic of Trois-Fontaines, *Chronica*, MGH SS 23:894.

1213. Innocent III issues *Quia Maior*, the bull calling the Fifth Crusade, instituting special services, *Deus venerunt gentes* Psalm (Ps. 78), the (new) *Deus admirabili* collect, a procession, a sermon, and collection. The promulgation of these supplications is recorded by a number of contemporary and latterly compiled chronicles.

PL 216:817–821.

Flores Temporum, MGH SS 24:240;

Die Chronik Johanns von Winterthur. MGH SS Rerum Germanicarum, ns. 3:2.

Monumenta Erphesfurtensia, MGH SS rerum Germanicarum 42:648–649.

Chronica Reinhardsbrunnenses, ed. Holder Egger, MGH SS 30.i:588.

~1213. A supplement to a copy of the synodal statutes of Eudes de Sully (d. 1208) includes a list of prayers, including *pro terra Jerosoli/mi/tana et Constanti/no/politanta, pro christianitate de Albigeis.*

Pontal, *Les statuts synodaux français du XIIIe siècle*, 1:96.

1214, after 12 February. Oliver of Paderborn preaches the cross in the region around Lieges and is directed to organize processions, masses, and alms for the aid of the Holy Land.

Reiner of Saint Jacob. *Ex reineri ad sanctum Jacobum monachi chronico Leodiensi*, RHF 18:630–632.

Reineri annales, MGH SS 16:671.

1215, 21 August. Frederick II, having taken the cross, writes to the Cistercian General Chapter requesting prayers be said on his behalf.

Canivez, *Statuta Capitulorum Generalium Ordinis Cisterciensis*, 1:432.

Eduoard Winkelmann, *Acta imperii inedita saeculi* XIII (Innsbruck: 1880), 110–111 (no. 131).

1217–1219: The Fifth Crusade.

1217, 24 November. Honorius III writes to Archbishop Aubrey of Reims asking for prayers and processions to aid Andrew of Hungary and Leopold of Austria in the Holy Land, offering explication of the efficacy of penitential processions, and participates in a supplicatory procession in Rome with the heads of Peter and Paul.

RHF v. 19:639–640.

Regestra Honorii Papae III, ed. Presutti (Rome: 1888), 149–150, no. 885.

1219, spring. Jacques de Vitry tells of the army outside Damietta doing processions, prayers, and litanies. The people are urged to clamor to God.

Lettres de Jacques de Vitry, ed. R. B. C. Huygens (Leiden: 1960), 117.

1223 (or a little after). Carthusian chapter statutes indicates the use of an expanded clamor. "Tres orationes cum psalmo *Deus venerunt gentes* dicantur [Ps. 78], scilicet: *Deus qui ad nostrae redemptionis exhibenda mysteria, Eccelsiae tuae* et *Deus a quo sancta desideria* [CO 1088]. Preces vero sunt: *Exurgat Deus, non nobis domine, exurge Domine, adjuva nos*, et *Domine exaudi*."

Carolo LeCouteulx, *Annales ordinis Cartusiensis ab anno 1084 ad annum 1429*, 6 vols., Monstroli Typis Cartusiae S. Mariae de Pratis, 1887–1891, 3:392.

1224, 7 March. Honorius III, in a letter sent to various bishops and abbots, orders monthly processions and reissues the daily *Deus venerunt gentes* (Ps. 78) clamor "for the aid of the Holy Land," in support of the crusade army arrived in Damietta.

Ex Honorii III Registro, in MGH *Epistolae saeculi XIII* I:173 (no. 244).

1225. Honorius III orders the *Deus venerunt gentes* (Ps. 78) clamor along with the usual prayers daily except Sunday and feast days, and a monthly procession of men and women, "so that Merciful God might deign to liberate the land in which He effected the universal sacrament of our redemption from the hands of pagans."

Chronicle of Richard of Saint Germano. In Augusto Gaudenzi, *Ignoti Monachi Cisterciensis* (Naples: 1888), 120–121.

1226, March. Chronicle reports that Honorius III sent out preachers "to all provinces" to preach the crusade, orders the *Deus venerunt gentes*

(Ps. 78) clamor to be said in all masses except solemn and Sunday masses, and orders general processions to be performed monthly.

> *Chronico sancti Martini Turonensi*, MGH Scriptores 26:472.
> Leroquais, *bréviaires*, 1:cxiv (for Rouen).

1226. Sermon preached by Philip the Chancellor in 1226 in Paris, given on the occasion of a "procession in support of Louis VIII and the crusaders, who were at that time besieging Avignon."

> Avranches BM ms. 132, fol. 243a. Cited in:
> Christoph Maier, "Crisis, Liturgy, and the Crusade," 652, citing Avranches BM ms. 132, fol. 243a.
> Nicole Bériou, Nicole. "La prédication de croisade de Philippe le Chancelier et d'Eudes de Châteauroux en 1226." *Cahiers de Fanjeaux* 32 (1997): 102.

1226. Odo of Chateauroux preaches a sermon for the Albigensian crusade, in which he alludes to special liturgy and processions.

> Arras BM ms 137, fols 88v–90r. Cited in:
> Christoph Maier, "Crisis, Liturgy, and the Crusades," 1997, 640n63.
> Nicole Bériou, "La prédication de croisade" (1997), 102–103.

1228. Cistercians, general council of 1228, institute prayers for the pope, the peace of the Roman church and empire, for the papal legate, and for the "negotio Albigensium," including the mass *Salus populi*.

> Canivez, *Statuta Capitulorum Generalium Ordinis Cisterciensis*, 2:69.

1228–1229: Crusade of Emperor Frederick II.

1229. Statutes from Worcester, prescribing the ringing of church bells so that those not at church might say the Pater Noster *pro succursu Terre Sancte*.

> F.M. Powicke and R.C. Cheney, *Councils and Synods, with Other Documents Relating to the English Church*, 2 in 4 vols. (Oxford: 1964–1981), II.i.175 (item 30).

1229. Cistercians general council for 1229 reinstitute prayers *pro omnibus certantibus et laborantibus pro fide christiana*, including *Aspice Domine*, the antiphon *Salve Regina*, the seven penitential psalms, the discipline, and the mass *Salus populi*.

> Canivez, *Statuta Capitulorum Generalium Ordinis Cisterciensis*, 2:78

1231. Cistercians end the *Deus venerunt gentes* (Ps. 78) clamor.

> Canivez, *Statuta Capitulorum Generalium Ordinis Cisterciensis*, 2:94

1234. Petition for masses made by the bishop of Agen for, among other things the "land of Albigensians."

> Canivez, *Statuta Capitulorum Generalium Ordinis Cisterciensis*, 2:129.

1239–1241: The Barons Crusade.

1239. Cistercians institute prayers in support of the Duke of Burgundy and all who are signed by the cross *pro negotio Constantinopolitano*.

> Canivez, *Statuta Capitulorum Generalium Ordinis Cisterciensis*, 2:201 Item 3).

1240. Cistercians at general council establish a votive mass for the Holy Spirit for the king of France, Louis IX, Blanche of Castille, the [royal] family, "and for the Albigensian work."

Canivez, *Statuta Capitulorum Generalium Ordinis Cisterciensis*, 2:219.

1241–1242: Gregory IX sanctions minor crusade indulgences for the defense of Hungary following Mongol advances in Russia and Poland.

1241. Councils at Mainz and Cologne institute throughout the diocese that at
every mass, immediately following the *Agnus dei*, Psalm 78 will be
recited, along with the *Deus a quo sacra desideria* (CO 1088), on behalf
of those who take the cross against the Mongols. In addition a weekly
procession on Saturdays with the *Salus populi* prayer (or on Thursday
with the *Nisi quod redemptor* if a feast falls on Saturday). Siegfried, the
Archbishop of Mainz, also orders the preaching of the cross.
Historia diplomatica Frederici Secundi, 5/2:1211.
Annales Wormatienses, MGH SS 17:46.

1241. A letter from Henry of Lorraine to Henry of Brabant indicates that
Franciscans and Dominicans have been instructed to preach the cross,
and prayers and fasting have been ordered "ad bellum Jesus Christi."
Matthew Paris, *Chronica Majorca*, ed. Luard (RS 57) 4:110.

1241, after 10 March. Prayers, fasting, and alms are instituted in diverse regions
"so that God, who, as magnificent victor over His enemy, fights the few
as well as the many, being appeased, might destroy the pride of the
Tartars."
Matthew Paris, *Chronica Majorca*, ed. Luard (RS 57) 4:111.

1241, 29 or 30 November (possible). Council of Oxford, prescribes supplications
against the "ferocity of the Mongols." The clamor is Psalm 69 and 78,
and then the old *Omnipotens sempiterne Deus in cuius manu* prayer
("as said at Easter," CO 3846). Also includes special instructions for
prayers to be said during the penitential processions, including the *Deus
tibi proprium, Ecclesie tue* (CO 2404b), and *Deus a quo sancta desideria* (CO 1088), along with the penitential psalms and the litany.
F. M. Powicke and R. C. Cheney, *Councils and Synods, with Other
Documents Relating to the English Church*, 2 in 4 vols. (Oxford:
1964–1981), II.i.339–340.
Translated C&C 325–327.
Note that there is some chance that these statutes were promulgated not
in 1241, but at the Council of Lambeth in 1261, or sometime else
entirely. See Discussion in Powicke and Cheney II.i, 338. The text is
found in a thirteenth-century manuscript.

1244: Louis IX takes the Cross.

1245: Instructed by Eudes of Chateauroux (papal legate), the Cistercians issue
new prayers for the pope, the French king who has taken the cross, and
for the Holy Land, including Psalm 78, a series of versicles, and an
expanded form of Innocent III's *Deus ammirabili*. For Cistercians in the
kingdom of France several *Pro rege* versicles are added. This appears to
follow the First Council at Lyon under Innocent IV.
Canivez, *Statuta Capitulorum Generalium Ordinis Cisterciensis*, 2:289
(item 2).

1247. Cistercian general council issues a series of prayers, including one *pro omnibus cruce signatis*. The collect *Ineffabilem* (CO 3129, mass *in tribulatione*) is added to the *Salus populi* mass.
Canivez, *Statuta Capitulorum Generalium Ordinis Cisterciensis*, 2:315–316 (item 4).

1248. Franciscan general chapter at Sens. Louis IX asks Franciscans to pray for crusade, with reference to Psalm 78. Salimbene also makes reference to the daily recitation at the conventual mass of Psalm 78 in France, for a year.
Salimbene de Adam, *Chronica*, ed. Scalia, 1: 317–327, 340.

1248 May. Dominican general chapter celebrated in Paris during Louis's preparations for his first crusade promises masses to the Holy Spirit, the Holy Cross, and the Blessed Virgin, as well as a weekly mass for the king.
Layettes du Trésor des Chartes, ed. Laborde, 3:33, no. 3674.

1248–1254: The first crusade of Louis IX. Louis IX is captured by Egyptian forces on 5 May 1250.

1249, 24 September. Innocent IV writes to Canterbury asking for monthly processions and preaching in the fight against the Tartars and the struggle against Frederick II.
Matthew Paris, *Chronica Majorca*, ed. Luard (RS 57) 6:174

1250, before 10 August. After his release from captivity in Egypt, writing from Acre, Louis IX writes a letter to the French asking for people to take the cross to come to his aid in Acre, and for prelates to offer prayers everywhere in their dioceses for the crusade effort.
Duchesne, *Historiae Francorum Scriptores*, 5:432.

1250, 12 August. Innocent IV, learning of Louis IX's capture, writes to Rouen, Normandy (Eudes Rigaud) asking for a general procession for Louis and the preaching of sermons.
Duchesne, *Historiae Francorum Scriptores*, 5:417.
Mansi, *Sacrorum Conciliorum*, 23:599.

1251. John Baucinus, at the council of Arles, decreed that psalms should be sung to ensure that the expedition Outremer receive divine support, including Psalm 78, and the *Deus qui admirabili* collect.
Mansi, *Sacrorum Conciliorum*, 23:798 (Canon 12).

1252, 29 September. Innocent IV to the bishops and archbishops of the kingdom of England, institutes prayers (including Psalm 78), solemn masses, general monthly processions, and preaching.
Thomas Rymer, *Foedera: conventiones, litterae*, 4 vols. (London: 1816–1830), 1641–1713, vol. 1, part 1, p. 286.

1252, 19 October. Innocent writes two letters to secular and regular ecclesiastics in England asking for processions, litanies, and preaching.
Elie Berger, ed., *Les Registres d'Innocent IV*, 3 vols., Bibliothèque des Écoles française d'Athènes et de Rome (Rome, 1884–1921), 3:120, nos. 6035 and 6036.

1255, April. At the council of Cognac, Archbishop Gerald of Bordegal includes prayers in aid of the Holy Land, the Lord King of France, and crusaders, to be said daily in every church "just as ordered by the Lord Legate"; and each week, a Mass for the Holy Spirit, or a Mass for the Blessed Virgin, should be celebrated.

Mansi, *Sacrorum Conciliorum*, 23:873 (Canon 30).

1257. Cistercians reinstitute prayers "that they were in the habit of doing for the Holy Land, for the good of the kingdom of France, and for the entire church in general," except for Psalm 78 and the collect, which should be omitted.

Canivez, *Statuta Capitulorum Generalium Ordinis Cisterciensis*, 2:425.

1258. Cistercian renew prayers for the pope, the Holy Land, the kingdom of France, and the entire church.

Canivez, *Statuta Capitulorum Generalium Ordinis Cisterciensis*, 2: 435 (item 1).

1260. After receiving a letter from Innocent IV about Mongol invasions in Armenia, Antioch, Damascus, and Aleppo, Louis IX calls a counsel of bishops and princes in Paris, whence was ordered "many orations, the doing of processions, and the punishing of blasphemy."

Guillaume de Nangis, *Vie de Saint Louis*, RHF 20:412 (for Latin) and 413 (for French).

1260, 25 January. Eudes Rigaud, archbishop of Rouen, orders a special mass *pro terra sancta* in the province of Rouen, for our brothers *in terra transmarina*, specifically in Constantinople and in Morea. Daily during High Mass, Psalm 78, with the Pater noster, versicles, and *orationibus consuetis pro terra sancta* should be sung before the *Pax domini*.

Regestrum visitationum archiepiscopi Rothomagensis, ed. T. Bonnin, 389

1260. Council of Bordeaux, in written address to Alexander IV, processions are prescribed on the first Friday of each month, along with prayers, fasting, and alms, in all provinces, and the special collect and mass with the Psalm *Deus venerunt gentes* (Ps. 78), for aid against the Tartars and "to remove the scourge of God."

Mansi, *Sacrorum Consiliorum*, 23:1048 (§4).

1261. Council of Ravenna. Alexander IV asks the church to offer prayers against Mongols.

Salimbene de Adam, *Chronica*, ed. Scalia, 1:580–581

1261. Cistercians institute clamors on account of the "cruelty of the Tartars [Mongols]," including the responsory *Aspice Domine*, the verse *non enim*, the versicle *Ostende nobis Domine*, and the collect *Ineffabilem* (CO 3129). At daily mass should be sung Psalm 78 (as was done formerly) and the collect *Omnipotens sempiterne Deus in cuius manu sunt omnium potestates* (CO 3846), where the old "ad romanorum benignus imperium" is replaced with "respice ad christianorum benignus auxilium."

Canivez, *Statuta Capitulorum Generalium Ordinis Cisterciensis*, 2:475–476.

1261. Innocent IV promulgates through two councils, one at Mainz and one at Magdeburg, the *Deus venerunt gentes* (Ps. 78), with a series of versicles and the collect *Deus a quo sancta desideria* (CO 1088). The priests should cry out in the vernacular "Repent" and prostrate themselves and say the Pater Noster. Bells are rung so that all not present can pray, and this gives ten days of indulgence. All cities should have processions. Priests should fast. Those who participate in the procession receive a forty-day indulgence.

Karl Joseph von Hefele, *Histoire des conciles d'apres les documents originaux*, trans. Henri Leclercq (Paris: 1907–), 6.1, pp. 106, 109.

Mansi *Sacrorum Conciliorum*, 23:1073 (Council at Mainz).

1262. Collapse of Latin Empire of Constantinople.

1262. Cistercians resume prayers instituted in 1261.
Canivez, *Statuta Capitulorum Generalium Ordinis Cisterciensis*, 3:3.

~1245–1267. Statutes for the Disciplinati del Borgo Porta Nova di Vicenza include prayers *pro fidelibus romane ecclesie, pro persecutoribus eiusdem, pro sepulcro D.N.J. Christi, quod restituatur christianis et quod semper in manibus christianorum maneat.*
Gilles Gerard Meersseman, *Ordo Fraternitatis: Confraternite e pieta' dei laici nel medioevo*, Italia sacra 24–26, 2 vols. (Rome: 1977), p. 490.

1263, 25 April. Urban requests preaching and processions in the kingdom of France as well as Metz, Toul, Verdun, Liege, and Cambrai, for the liberation of the Holy Land and aid against the Mongols.
Annales Ecclesiastici ad annum 1263, §13 (22:96–97).

1267: Louis IX takes the Cross a second time.

1268. Cardinal Ottobuono, the papal legate to England, instituted at the council of London yearly solemn and public processions as well as prayers "to bring back peace" on account of the subjugation of the Holy Land and war in England.
F.M. Powicke and R.C. Cheney, *Councils and Synods, with Other Documents Relating to the English Church*, 2 in 4 vols. (Oxford: 1964–1981), II.ii.781–782 (item 30).
Mansi, *Sacrorum Conciliorum*. 23:1248 (canon 35).

1268. Cistercians institute the *Salus populi* mass "pro bono statu Terrae sanctae et pro defensione sanctae romanae ecclessiae."
Canivez, *Statuta Capitulorum Generalium Ordinis Cisterciensis*, 3:61.

1269–1270: Louis IX's second crusade to Tunis. Edward I of England continues on to the Holy Land.

1269. At the general chapter held in Paris, the Dominicans, who are commissioned to preach the cross, institute special prayers, including Psalm 78 "with its versicles and prayers" be said at the conventual mass, to begin after Easter, in support of Louis IX's crusade.
Acta Capitulorum Generalium (Rome: 1898), 1:149 (in vol. 3 of the *Monumenta Ordinis Fratrum Praedicatorum Historica* series).

1270. Marguerite of Provence requests Cistercians to say prayers for Louis IX and others who have taken the cross. The first day of every month a procession ending in the chapter house, with the responsory *Aspice Domine*, and the versicle *Exurgat Deus*, the collect *Ineffabilem* (CO 3129). In the kingdom of France, the collect *Famulum tuum regem nostrorum*, Psalm 78, with a series of versicles, including *Exurgat Deus*, *Ineffabilem*, the seven penitential psalms, and the litany. Also a petition to say the mass of the Holy Cross for pilgrims in the Holy Land.

Canivez, *Statuta Capitulorum Generalium Ordinis Cisterciensis*, 3:90, 91–92 (items 54, 75).

~1270. The Council of Cognac (ca. 1270), reinstitutes prayers for the work of the Holy Land and for the crusader Lord [Louis IX] King of France. These prayers should be done in every church each week, including the Mass of the Holy Spirit and of the Blessed Virgin Mary.

Pontal, *Les statuts synodaux français du XIIIe siècle*, 5:61 (no. 30).

1272. Gregory X requests Cistercians for prayers *pro terra sancta*, including the *Aspice Domine* responsory, *Exurgat Deus*, versicle, and Innocent III's *Deus qui admirabili* collect.

Canivez, *Statuta Capitulorum Generalium Ordinis Cisterciensis*, 3:112 (item 42).

1274. At the Second Council of Lyon, Gregory X institutes Psalm 78, with the versicle *Exurgat Deus*, and the collect *Deus qui admirabili providentia*, to be said at the conventual mass. This is recorded in the statutes of the Cistercian order for the year 1274.

Canivez, *Statuta Capitulorum Generalium Ordinis Cisterciensis*, 3:126–127 (item 1).

1290. Cistercians order the *Deus venerunt gentes* (Ps. 78) clamor, along with the usual versicles and collects to be said for the Holy Land, "which our Lord God consecrated with his blood," at the conventual (not high) mass throughout the order.

Canivez, *Statuta Capitulorum Generalium Ordinis Cisterciensis*, 3:248 (item 20).

1291: The fall of Acre to Kavalun. The end of the Latin Kingdoms in Palestine.

1292. Synod in the Province of Canterbury, the New Temple, London, and Lambeth, enjoins that all clergy every Sunday offer the prayers for the recuperation of the Holy Land. Report specifies the *Deus venerunt gentes* Psalm (Ps. 78) with the other prayers, "as are customary," vigils, and fasts.

F. M. Powicke and R. C. Cheney, *Councils and Synods, with Other Documents Relating to the English Church*, 2 in 4 vols. (Oxford: 1964–1981), II.ii.1109–1110 (item 1).

Bartholomew Cotton, *Historia Anglicana*, ed. H. R. Luard (RS 185), 206–207.

1295, 4–7 May. Robert of Winchelsey, the archbishop of Canterbury, issued detailed liturgical instructions to the English clergy and laity. Called for the *Salus populi* mass, three Psalms (78, 66, 122), six versicles, and three dedicated orations (*Deus qui admirabili*, *Deus auctor pacis* [CO 1110, *pro pacis*], and *Quesumus omnipotens deus ut famulus tuus* [CO 4880a, *pro rege*]), as well as regular Friday processions. The laity unable to attend were at minimum to recite Pater Nosters and Ave Marias.

Registrum Roberti Winchelsey, Cantuariensis Archiepiscopi AD 1294–1313, ed. Rose Graham, 1:26–30.

Also recorded in:

Registrum Johannis de Pontissara, episcopi Wyntoniensis, ed. Cecil Deedes (London: 1915), 1:191–193.

1297. Crusading prayers and processions previously ordered for the Holy land to be said for Edward I's upcoming expedition against the Scots.

Mansi *Sacrorum Conciliorum* 24:1176.

1298, 15 July. Robert of Winchelsey, archbishop of Canterbury, at a Council of the Province of Canterbury at the New Temple (London), renews instructions for solemn processions and prayers done for the state of the Holy Land and the prosperity of the kingdom.

Registrum Roberti Winchelsey, Cantuariensis Archiepiscopi AD 1294–1313, ed. Rose Graham 1:271. Also printed in:

F. M. Powicke and R. C. Cheney, *Councils and Synods, with Other Documents Relating to the English Church*, 2 in 4 vols. (Oxford: 1964–1981), II.2.1195–1196

13th century (date uncertain). In the synodal statutes from Soissons, the bishop orders that the "regular prayers" be done in aid of the Holy Land.

Pontal, *Les statuts synodaux français du XIIIe siècle*, 4:300, item 78.

1306: Hospitallers capture Rhodes.

1307. Clement V asks Cistercians to recite Psalm 78 with the usual collect.

Canivez, *Statuta Capitulorum Generalium Ordinis Cisterciensis*, 3:318 (item 7).

J. Loserth, "Aus den Annales diffiniciones d. Generalkapitels d. Zisterzienser in den Jahren 1290–1330," *Neues Archiv der Gesellschaft für ältere deutsche Geschichtskunde* (1919): 625.

1308, 11 August. Clement V prescribes *orationes contra paganorum* (proper mass prayers) against the "perfidy of pagans" in support of his plans for a Hospitaller expedition to Armenia. The prayers are *Omnipotens sempiterne Deus* (3846), *Sacrificium domine* (5217), and *Protector noster aspice* (CO 4746).

Regestum Clementis Papae V, 3:161, no. 2987.

1309, 11 July. Clement V reissues, with greater precision and emphasis, the prescription of the previous August.

Regestum Clementis Papae V, 4:313, no. 4769.

1312. Carmelite Ordinal gives instruction for "when and how the *Deus venerunt gentes* [Ps. 78]" prayers should be said, including the preces, the *Exurgat Deus* versicle, and the *Deus qui admirabili* collect.

Zimmerman, Benedict. *Ordinaire de l'Ordre de Notre-Dame du Mont Carmel.* (Paris: 1910), 86.

1322, 20 December. John XXII, in a letter to the archbishop of Toulouse, issued instructions for a weekly public sermon, and a mass to the Holy Trinity, to the Virgin Mary, and to the Holy Angels, which should include the *Deus venerunt gentes* (Ps. 78) clamor, a series of versicles, as well as the

Omnipotens sempiterne Deus (CO 3846) and the *Hostium nostrorum* (CO 3007) prayers. In all other masses said during the week, the clamor should be Psalm 69, the versicles as for the weekly mass, and *Hostium nostorum.*

Lettres secrètes, ed. Coulon and Clemence, 2:204–205, no. 1571.

1331. John XXII, in a letter to Peter, the patriarch of Jerusalem, and to all the archbishops and bishops in the kingdom of France, asks for masses for the liberation of the Holy Land from the hands of the enemy during the course of the prescribed crusade, the Mass for the Trinity, the Mass for the Cross, and the Mass for the Blessed Virgin, and celebration should include the standard prayers: *Deus qui admirabili providentia, Sacrificium Domine quod immolamus* (CO 5217), and *Protector noster aspice deus* (CO 4746).

Annales Ecclesiastici ad annum 1331, §30 (24:479–480).

1333, 26 July. John XXII to the Archbishop of Reims and suffragens, issues instructions for a "mass for the liberty of the Holy Land from the hands of the enemy" during the duration of a limited campaign, including a Mass for the Trinity, for the Cross, and for the Virgin. Institutes the *Deus qui admirabili* collect, the collection, and the *Protector noster aspice* (CO 4746), all prescribed in full.

Lettres secrètes, ed. Coulon and Clemence, 10:78, no. 5210.

1340, August 25. Benedict XII (from Avignon) to Spanish clergy asking for prayers and processions against the enemies of the faith, especially the "rege Marochitano."

Annales Ecclesiastici ad annum 1340, §49 (25:209).

1344, February 1. Clement VI to Edward III of England, reporting thanksgiving prayers and processions performed to thank God for the 1344 victory in capturing the port at Smyrna.

Annales Ecclesiastici ad annum 1344 §6 (25:328).

1344, July. Clement VI to Alfonse XI of Castile, reporting a thanksgiving procession at the Roman curia to celebrate the conclusion of the long siege of Algeciras in 1344.

Annales Ecclesiastici ad annum 1344 §52 (25:347).

1361. Philippe of Mézières reports that he organized solemn masses in Cyprus to celebrate the victory *contra fidei Christiane hostes dedisset* in Cyprus.

Annales Ecclesiastici ad annum 1361 §9 (26:60).

Philippe de Mézières, *The Life of Saint Peter Thomas*, ed. Joachim Smet (Rome: 1954) p. 97.

1363. Urban V, to the archbishop of Reims and his suffragens requests a daily mass *pro liberatione dictae Terrae de manibus hostium praedicatorum*, for the prosecution of the Savoyard crusade. The liturgical prescriptions are identical to those issued by John XII in 1333.

Annales Ecclesiastici ad anum 1363, §18 (26:83–84).

1364, 1 April. Urban V writes to French and German bishops announcing King John I's leadership of the crusade and instructing them to preach the cross and that the clamor be inserted weekly in a mass for the liberation of the Holy Land.

Lettre secrètes et curiales du Pape Urbain V, ed. P Lecacheux and G. Mollat, no. 3267.

1373, 23 March. Gregory XI, as part of preparations for a new crusade against the Turks, asks for the performance of the Mass of the Trinity, of the Cross, and the Blessed virgin.

Annales Ecclesiastici ad annum 1373 §5 (26:220–221).

1383. Henry Dispenser's crusade. Bishop's ordinances published for the crusade instructs preachers to advise people to hold processions and perform prayers for the salvation of the church, the realm, and the expedition of pilgrims.

Henry Knighton, *Knighton's Chronicle: 1337–1396*, ed. G. H. Martin (Oxford: 1995), 331.

1419–ca. 1434: Hussite crusades.

1421. 5 June. Cardinal Branda da Castiglione prescribes liturgical instructions for campaigns against Wycliffites, Hussites, and other heretics.

František Palacký. *Urkundliche Beiträge zur Geschichte des Hussitenkrieges vom Jahre 1419* an, 2 vols. (Prague: 1873), 1:108–116. For mass prayers, see 111–112.

1427. Prayers and fasting enjoined for the anti-Hussite Crusade of 1427.

Robert Swanson, "Prayer and Participation in Late Medieval England," in *Elite and Popular Religion*, ed. Kate Cooper and Jeremy Gregory (Woodbridge, UK: 2006), 136, citing Oxford Bodleian Library, ms Tanner 165, fol. 91r–v (Register of William Molash, Prior of Christ Church, Canterbury).

1428, 18 January. Pope Martin V to the archbishop of Canterbury, Henry Chichele, for the aid of the Hussite crusade. He ordered general processions on the first Sunday of each month to be said before the mass, "with the litany, responsories, and prayers according to the customs of each church," and with special prayers designated.

The Register of Edmund Lacy Bishop of Exeter 1420–1453, ed. G.R. Dunstan (Torquay: 1963), 1:209–11.

1429, January. Cardinal Beaufort (papal legate), organizing the crusade against the Hussites (called by Martin V) in Canterbury, established general processions, and mass propers, including a series of versicles, the *Ecclesie tue* (CO 2404b), *Hostium nostrorum* (CO 3007), and the *Omnipotens et misericors deus*.

Robert Swanson, "Preaching Crusade in Fifteenth-Century England: Instructions for the Administration of the Anti-Hussite Crusade of 1429 in the Diocese of Canterbury," *Crusades* 12 (2013): 192.

1453: Fall of Constantinople to the Ottomans, under Mehmet II.

1454, March. John Kemp, archbishop of Canterbury, ordered solemn processions be held in parish churches to pray for the defeat and the fall of the Turks.

David Wilkins, *Concilia Magnae Britanniae et Hiberniae* (London, 1767), 3:563–564.

1455, May 15: Calixtus III proclaims crusade to recapture Constantinople.

1455. Nicolas V extends indulgences to clergy preaching or saying the mass for the Burgundian crusade. The entire populace was to participate in asking for victory. Calixtus III confirmed these the following year.

> Benjamin Weber, *Lutter contre les Turcs*, 440, citing Vatican Secret Archives, Reg. Vat. 456, 1r–3r (a later confirmation of the bull by Calixtus III).

1455, April. William Booth, archbishop of York, orders prayers be said for the success of Calixtus III's expedition.

> Jonathan Harris, "Publicising the Crusade: English Bishops and the Jubilee Indulgence of 1455," *Journal of Ecclesiastical History* 50 (1999): 30–31, citing York, Borthwick Institute of Historical Research, Reg. 20, fols. 177v–178v.

1456, 29 June. In preparation for the relief of Belgrade, Pope Calixtus III, in *Cum hiis superioribus*, to all of Christendom, called for prayer, fasting, and penance, and that processions be held on the first Sunday of every month in support of the relief of Belgrade; included *contra paganos* mass, prescribing *Omnipotens sempiterne Deus* (CO 3846), and a sermon.

> Lajos Vecsey, *Callixti III Bulla orationum*, 1955, 48–52.

1456. Calixtus III asks the legate John Solerius to institute monthly processions and regular prayers in Spain *pro victoria habenda contra Turcos* and also asks his legate to Hungary to promulgate *Cum hiis superioribus* throughout the Christian world.

> *Annales Ecclesiastici* ad annum 1456, §§18–19 (29:67).
> Benjamin Weber, *Lutter contre les Turcs*, 441, citing Vatican Secret Archives, Arm. XXXIX, vol. 7, 18v–19v.

1456, August: Relief of Belgrade, under John Hunyadi. Ottomans pushed back.

1460, 14 January. Pius II, in *Ecclesiam Christi*, which he issued at the end of the Council of Mantua, asks for prayers in every town and place on Sunday to help in the crusade.

> *Annales Ecclesiastici* ad annum 1460, §3 (29:220).

1460, March. Pius II asks the nuns of the monastery of Corpus Christi in Boulogne to say, daily, five Pater Nosters and five Ave Marias for the success of the expedition of the Duke of Burgundy.

> Weber, *Lutter contre les Turcs*, 442, citing Vatican Secret Archives, Reg. Vat, 512, 142v.

1463, 24 August–1 September. Cardinal John Bessarion issues instructions to preachers that includes the organization of prayers, processions, and litanies to be done in all churches; and prescribes special (nonstandard) prayers for the litany, and special collect for the mass, including *Omnipotens sempiterne Deus* (CO 3846), and *Ecclesie tue* (CO2404b).

> Mohler, "Bessarions Instruktion," 344–345.

1463. Pius II, in *Sane cum perfidissimus*, ordered that in all churches and monasteries processions should be done each Thursday with litanies and prayers, since "without spiritual arms temporal arms will accomplish nothing."

> *Annales Ecclesiastici* ad annum 1463 §13 (29:349–350)

1470: Battle of Negroponte. Negroponte captured from Venetians by the Ottomans.

1470. Pope Paul II confirms Bernard of Cattaro's anti-Turk mass.
> Linder RA 186, 267.

1470, 30 September. Solemn processions and prayers were organized in Venice at the news of the fall of Negroponte.
> Franz Babinger, *Mehmed the Conqueror and his Time* (Princeton: 1978), 283, with no further source citation.

1471, 18 January. Following the capture of Negroponte, Elie de Bourdeilles, archbishop of Tours, institutes prayers and processions throughout the land with the hope of getting the king to participate in a new crusade.
> *Annales Ecclesiastici* ad annum 1471, §§43–44 (29:508–509).
> Setton, *Papacy and the Levant* (Philadelphia: 1976), 2:308.

1480, 21 August. Ottomans occupy Otranto. May-August, Ottomans besiege Rhodes.

1480. Pope Sixtus IV promulgates *Missa contra Turcum* (*Omnia que fecisti*), and processions and masses *contra Turcum* are organized in Rome.
> Linder, *Raising Arms*, 187.
> Setton, *The Papacy and the Levant* (Philadelphia: 1976), 2:355.

1500, 26 September. Pope Alexander VI orders processions in the province of Walachia, and sends Bishop Gaspar Calliensis to promulgate the supplications.
> *Annales Ecclesiastici* ad annum 1500. §§15–16 (30:315)

1510. In Iberia, processions prescribed for all clergy for three days, as done on Corpus Christi, in the effort *contra infideles et regem Tripolitanum.* Special mass, including three specially prescribed collects.
> *Annales Ecclesiastici* ad annum 1510, §§31–32 (30:531).

1512–17. Fifth Lateran Council, issues instructions for masses "for the peace of Christians and for the confounding of the infidels respectively," including *Deus a quo sancta desideria* (CO 1088) and *Deus in cuius manu sunt omnes potestates et omnia iura regnorum, respice in auxilium christianorum* (a version of CO 3846).
> Norman P. Tanner, *Decrees of the Ecumenical Councils* (Washington, DC: 1990), 1:611.

Selected Bibliography

Items listed in the Abbreviations, or cited only once in the body of the text, are not included in the bibliography. Unedited or unpublished manuscripts or portions thereof are included in the bibliography if consulted either directly or in reproduction (and I have indicated parenthetically when relevant portions of the material exists in an edited form). Manuscripts in standard published editions (such as the Gellone Sacramentary, or the Nevers Sacramentary) are included in the section on printed sources.

Manuscripts Cited

Albi, Bibliothèque Municipale ms. 5.
Alençon, Bibliothèque Municipale ms. 131.
Arras, Bibliothèque Municipale ms. 49.
Avignon, Bibliothèque Municipale mss. 143, 178.
Bamberg, Staatliche Bibliothek mss. Lit. 56, 58, 60, ms. msc Lit 11.
Barcelona Archivo de la Corona de Aragón, San Cugat del Valles ms. 73.
Barletta, Archivio della Chiesa del Santo Sepolcro, ms. s.n. (ed. Kohler 1900–1901).
Bourges, Bibliothèque Municipale mss. 23.
Cambrai, Bibliothèque Municipale ms. 223 (ed. Pick, 1995).
Cambridge, Trinity College Library ms. B.XI.10; University Library mss. Ff.6.9, Li.2.10, Mm.3.21 (ed. Brundage 1966).
Chateauroux, Bibliothèque Municipale ms. 3.
Darmstadt, Hessische Landes-und Hochschulbibliothek ms. 3183.
Erfurt, Universitätsbibliothek Dep. Erf. CA. 8° 44.
Graz, Universitätsbibliothek mss. 186, 239 (ed. Pennington 1974).
Laon, Bibliothèque Municipale mss. 244, 262bis, 263.
The LePuy Sacramentary. In private hands.
Loches, Bibliothèque Municipale ms. 5.

London, British Library (BL) Additional mss. 8927, 26655, 15419; Cotton Tiberius B. VIII; Cotton Vitellius E XII; Egerton mss. 1139, 2902.
Lucca, Biblioteca Arcivescovile ms. 5.
Lyon, Bibliothèque Municipale ms. 570.
Milan, Biblioteca Ambrosiana ms. A92.
Munich, Bayerische Staatsbibliothek (Clm) ms. 29345(8.
Oxford, Magdalene College Library, ms. 226 (ed. Wilson, 1910).
Paris, Bibliothèque de l'Arsenal mss. 35, 95, 102, 135, 332, 623.
Paris, Bibliothèque de la Compagnie des prêtres de Saint-Sulpice, ms. R 4.
Paris, Bibliothèque Nationale de France (BNF) mss. Latin 195, 822, 824, 831, 861, 969, 1139, 1193, 1255, 1259, 1341, 2293, 3549, 3719, 3779, 5132, 8895, 9437, 9440, 12056, 14827, 17318, 17333; nal 195, 1689.
Paris, Bibliothèque Mazarine ms. 406.
Provins, Bibliothèque Municipale ms. 11.
Reims, Bibliothèque Municipale mss. 224, 341.
Rome, Biblioteca Angelica ms. 477.
Rome, Biblioteca Casanatense ms. 614 (ed. Rivard, 2001).
Troyes, Bibliothèque Municipale mss. 193, 2140.
Valenciennes, Bibliothèque Municipale mss. 108, 121.
Vatican Library (Biblioteca Apostolica Vaticana), Lat. Reg. mss. 249, 9340; Barberini Lat. ms. 659.
Vienna, Österreichische Nationalbibliothek (ÖNB) ms. 1928.
Wroclaw, Biblioteka Uniwersytecka ms. I Qu.175.

Printed Source Material

Annales Monastici. RS 36. Edited by Henry Richards Luard. 5 vols. London: Longman, Green, Longman, Roberts, and Green, 1864–1869.
Banting, H. M. J. *Two Anglo-Saxon Pontificals (the Egbert and Signey Sussex Pontificals).* London: Boydell Press, 1989.
Berger, Elie, ed. *Les Registres d'Innocent IV.* 4 vols. Bibliothèque des Écoles française d'Athènes et de Rome. Paris: E Thorin, 1884–1921.
Bickell, G. *Synodi Brixinenses Saeculi XV.* Innsbruck: Rauch, 1880.
Canivez, Joseph. *Statuta Capitulorum Generalium Ordinis Cisterciensis ab anno 1116 ad annum 1786.* Bibliothéque de la revue d'histoire ecclésiastique. 8 vols. Louvain: Bureau de la Revue, 1933–1941.
Cotton, Bartholomew. *Historia anglicana (A.D. 449–1298).* RS 16. London: Longman, Green, Longman, and Roberts, 1859.
Coulon, Auguste, and Suzanne Clemencet. *Lettres secrètes et curiales du Pape Jean XXII 1316–1334, relatives à la France, extraites des registres du Vatican.* Bibliothèque des Écoles françaises d'Athènes et de Rome (ser. 3.1) Paris: A. Fontemoing, 1900–1972.
David, Charles Wendell. *De expugnatione Lyxbonensi = The conquest of Lisbon.* Translated by Charles Wendell David. New York: Columbia University Press, 1936.
Delaporte, Yves. *L'Ordinaire chartrain du XIIIᵉ siècle.* Société Archéologique d'Eure-et-Loir. Mémoires, Vol. 19. Chartres: Société Archéologique d'Eure-et-Loir, 1953.

Dold, Alban, and Klaus Gamber, eds. *Das Sakramentar von Monza*, Texte und Arbeiten 3. Beiheft: Beuron, 1957.

Duchesne, André. *Historiae Francorum scriptores coaetanei . . . Quorum plurimi nunc primum ex variis codicibus mss. in lucem prodeunt: alij vero auctiores & emendatiores. Cvm epistolis regvm, reginarvm, pontificvm . . . et aliis veteribus rerum francicarum monumentis.* 5 vols. Paris: Sumptibus S. Cramoisy, 1636–1649.

Durandus, William. *Rationale divinorum officiorum.* CCCM 140–140b. Edited by D. A. Davril and T. M. Thibodeau. 3 vols. Turnhout: Brepols, 1995–2000.

Eudes of Rouen. *Regestrum visitationum archiepiscopi rothomagensis; journal des visites pastorales d'Eude Rigaud, archevêque de Rouen, 1248–1269. Pub. pour la première fois, d'après le manuscrit de la Bibliothèque nationale.* Edited by Th. Bonnin. Rouen: Auguste Le Brument, 1852.

Gilo of Paris, and a second anonymous author. *The Historia vie Hierosolimitane.* Translated by C. W. Grocock and J. E. Siberry. Oxford: Clarendon Press, 1997.

Heiming, O.S.B., Odilo, ed. *Das Sacramentarium triplex. Die Handschrift C 43 der Zentralbibliothek Zürich.* Corpus Ambrosiano-liturgicum 1, vol. Liturgiewissenschaftliche Quellen und Forschungen 49. Münster: Aschendorffsche Verlagsbuchhandlung, 1968.

Huillard-Bréholles, Jean-Louis-Alphones, ed. *Historia diplomatica Friderici Secundi, sive constitutiones, privilegia, mandata, instrumenta quae supersunt istius Imperatoris et filiorum ejus.* 7 vols. Paris: Henricus Pl, 1852–1860.

Humbert of Romans. "Liber de predicatione sct. Crucis, transcribed and edited by Kurt Villads Jensen." http://www.jggj.dk/saracenos.htm.

Huygens, R.B.C., ed. *Lettres de Jacques de Vitry—1160/1170–1240, évêque de Saint-Jean d'Acre* Leiden: Brill, 1960.

Jackson, Richard A., ed. *Ordines Coronationis Franciae: Texts and Ordines for the Coronation of Frankish and French Kings and Queens in the Middle Ages.* 2 vols. Philadelphia: University of Pennsylvania Press, 1995–2000.

Jacques de Vitry. "Epistolae." In *Serta Mediaevalia: Textus varii saeculorum X–XIII, in Unum Collecti,* edited by R.B.C. Huygens, CCCM 171. Turnhout: Brepols, 2000.

Jean Sarrasin. *Lettre à Nicolas Arrode (1249).* Lettres Françaises du XIIIᵉ siècle. Edited by Alfred Foulet. Paris: Champion, 1924.

John Beleth. *Summa de ecclesiasticis officiis.* CCCM 41–41a. Edited by H. Douteil. Turnhout: Brepols, 1976.

Knighton, Henry. *Knighton's Chronicle: 1337–1396.* Edited by G. H. Martin. Oxford: Clarendon Press, 1995.

LeCouteulx, Carolo. *Annales ordinis Cartusiensis ab anno 1084 ad annum 1429.* 6 vols. Monstroli: Typis Cartusiae S. Mariae de Pratis, 1887–1891.

Manlio Sodi. *Il "Pontificalis Liber" di Agostino Patrizi Piccolomini e Giovanni Burcardo (1485).* Monumenta studia instrumenta liturgica. Vatican City: Libreria Editrice Vaticana, 2006.

Mohler, Ludwig. "Bessarions Instruktion für die Kreuzzugspredigt in Venedig (1463)." *Römische Quartalschrift* 35 (1927): 337–349.

Odo of Deuil. *De Profectione Ludovici VII in Orientem; The Journey of Louis VII to the East.* Translated by Virginia Gingerick Berry. New York: Columbia, 1948.

Olivar, Alejandro, ed. *El Sacramentario de Vich.* Monumenta Hispaniae Sacra, Serie liturgica 4 Barcelona: Consejo Superior de Investigaciones Científicas, Instituto P. Enrique Flórez, 1953.

Pontal, Odette, ed. *Les Statuts synodaux français du XIIIe siècle : précédées de l'historique du synode diocésain depuis ses origines.* Collection de documents inédits sur l'histoire de France. Série in-80, 9, 15, 19, 23, 29. Paris: Bibliothèque nationale, 1971–.

Potthast, Augustus, ed. *Regesta Pontificum Romanorum inde ab a. Post Christum natum MCXCVIII ad A. MCCCIV.* 2 vols. Paris: Berolini, 1875.

Pressuti, Petrus, ed. *Regesta Honorii Papae III.* 2 vols. Rome: Typographia Vaticana, 1888–1895.

Ralph of Diceto. *Radulfi de Diceto decani Lundoniensis opera historica. The Historical Works of Master Ralph de Diceto, Dean of London.* RS 68. Edited by William Stubbs. London: Longman, 1876.

Regestum Clementis Papae V. 9 vols. Rome: Typographia Vaticana, 1888–1892.

Rigord. *Histoire de Philippe Auguste.* Sources d'histoire médiévale 33. Edited by Élisabeth Carpentier, Georges Pon, and Yves Chauvin. Paris: CNRS éd., 2006.

Rymer, Thomas. *Foedera: conventiones, litterae, et cujuscunque generis acta publica, inter reges Angliae et alios quosvis iperatores, reges, pontifices, principes, vel communitates, ab ingressu Gulielmi I in Angliam.* 4 in 7 vols. London: Printed by George Eyre and Andrew Strahan, Printers to the King's Most Excellent Majesty, 1816–1830, 1641–1713.

Salies, Alexandre de. *Histoire de Foulques-Nerra, comte d'Anjou d'après les chartes contemporaines et les anciennes chroniques—suivie de l'office du Saint-Sépulchre de l'abbaye de Beaulieu dont les leçons forment une chronique inédite.* Paris: Chez J.-B. Dumoulin, 1874.

Salimbene de Adam. *Chronica.* CCCM 125–125A. Edited by G. Scalia. Turnhout: Brepols, 1998–1999.

Tanner, Norman P. *Decrees of the Ecumenical Councils.* Washington, DC: Georgetown University Press, 1990.

Vecsey, Lajos. *Callixti III Bulla orationum: ex codice originali Reg. Vat. eruta atque cum introductione in relatione ad pulsationem meridianam instructa.* Appensell: Genossenschafts-Buchdruckerei, 1955.

Vogel, Cyrille, and Reinhard Elze, eds. *Le Pontifical romano-germanique du dixième siècle.* 2 vols, Studi e testi 226–227. Rome: Vatican City, 1963.

Wilson, Henry A., ed. *The Benedictional of Archbishop Robert.* London: Henry Bradshaw Society, 1903.

——. *The Pontifical of Magdalen College: With an Appendix of Extracts from Other English MSS. of the Twelfth Century.* London: Henry Bradshaw Society, 1910.

——. *The Missal of Robert of Jumièges.* London: Henry Bradshaw Society, 1896.

Würzburg, John of. "Descriptio Terrae Sanctae." In *Descriptiones Terrae Sanctae ex saeculo XIII. IX. XII. et XV,* edited by Titus Tobler, 108–192. Leipzig: J. C. Hinrichs'sche Buchhandlung, 1874.

Studies

Aphandéry, Paul, and Alphonse Dupront. *La Chrétienté et l'idée de croisade.* Bibliothèque de l'évolution de l'humanité 10. 1954; reprint Paris: Albin Michel, 1995.

Armitage, David. "What's the Big Idea? Intellectual History and the Longue Durée." *History of European Ideas* 38 (2012): 493–507.

Ashworth, H. "*Urbs beata Jerusalem:* Scriptural and Patristic Sources." *Ephemerides Liturgica* 70 (1956): 238–241.

Aspesi, Cara. "The Contribution of the Cantors of the Holy Sepulchre to Crusade History and Frankish Identity." In *Music, Liturgy, and the Shaping of History (800–1500),* edited by Margot Fassler and Katie Bugyis. Woodbridge: York Medieval Press, forthcoming 2016.

——. "The *libelli* of Lucca, Biblioteca Arcivescvile MS 5: The Liturgy of the Siege of Acre?" *Journal of Medieval History* (forthcoming in 2017).

——. "Lucca, Biblioteca Arcivescovile MS 5: A Window onto Liturgy and Life in the Latin Kingdom of Jerusalem in the Twelfth Century." Ph.D. Thesis, South Bend, IN: University of Notre Dame, forthcoming.

Babinger, Franz. *Mehmed the Conqueror and his Time*. Translated by Ralph Manheim. Princeton: Princeton Princeton University Press, 1978.

Bachrach, Bernard S. "The Pilgrimages of Fulk Nerra, Count of the Angevins." In *Religion, Culture and Society in the Early Middles Ages: Studies in Honour of R. E. Sullivan*, edited by Thomas F. X Noble and John J. Contreni, 205–217. Kalamazoo, MI: Medieval Institute Publications, 1987.

Bachrach, David. *Religion and the Conduct of War c. 300–c. 1215*. Woodbridge, Suffolk: Boydell and Brewer, 2003.

Becker, Alfons. *Papst Urban II (1088–1099)*. 3 vols. Schriften der Monumenta Germaniae Historica 19. Stuttgart: Anton Hiersemann, 1964–2012.

Bériou, Nicole. "La prédication de croisade de Philippe le Chancelier et d'Eudes de Châteauroux en 1226." *Cahiers de Fanjeaux* 32 (1997): 85–109.

Bird, Jessalynn. "Heresy, Crusade and Reform in the Circle of Peter the Chanter, c.1187–c.1240." Ph.D. Thesis. Oxford University, 2001.

——. "Innocent III, Peter the Chanter's Circle, and the Crusade Indulgence: Theory, Implementation, and Aftermath." In *Innocenzo III: Urbs et Orbis*, edited by Andrea Sommerlechner, 501–525. Rome: Società Romana di Storia Patria. Instituto Storico Italiano per il Medioevo, 2003.

——. "Paris Masters and the Justification of the Albigensian Crusade." *Crusades* 6 (2007): 117–155.

——. "Preaching the Crusade and the Liturgical Year: The Palm Sunday Sermons." In *Essays in Medieval Studies* 30 (2015): 11–36.

——. "Preaching the Fifth Crusade: The Sermons of BN nouv. acq. lat. 999." In *The Fifth Crusade in Context: The Crusading Movement in the Early Thirteenth Century*, edited by Jan Vandeburie, Elizabeth Mylod and Guy Perry. Farnham, New York: Routledge, 2017.

——. "The Religious's Role in a Post Fourth Lateran World." In *Medieval Monastic Preaching*, edited by Carolyn Muessig. 209–229. Leiden: Brill, 1998.

——. "Rogations, Litanies and Crusade Preaching: the Liturgical Front in the Late Twelfth and Early Thirteenth Centuries." In *The Papacy, Peace, the Crusade and Christian-Muslim Relations: Essays in Memory of James M. Powell*, edited by Jessalynn Bird. Routledge, 2017, forthcoming.

——. "The Victorines, Peter the Chanter's Circle, and the Crusade: Two Unpublished Crusading Appeals in Paris, Bibliothèque Nationale, MS Latin 14470." *Medieval Sermon Studies* 48 (2004): 5–28.

Bisaha, Nancy. *Creating East and West: Renaissance Humanists and the Ottoman Turks*. Philadelphia: University of Pennsylvania Press, 2004.

Björkvall, Gunilla. "'Expectantes dominum.' Advent, the time of expectation, as reflected in liturgical poetry from tenth and eleventh centuries." In *In Quest of the Kingdom: Ten Papers on Medieval Monastic Spirituality*, 109–133. Stockholm: Almquist & Wiksell, 1991.

Bohnstedt, John. "The Infidel Scourge of God: The Turkish Menace as Seen by German Pamphleteers of the Reformation Era." *Transactions of the American Philosophical Society* n.s. 58 (1968): 1–58.

Borgehammar, Stephan. "Heraclius Learns Humility: Two Early Latin Accounts Composed for the Celebration of Exaltatio Crucis." In *Millennium: Jahrbuch zu Kultur und Geschichte des ersten Jahrtausends n. Chr.—Yearbook on the Culture and History of the First Millennium C.E.*, 145–202. Berlin: Walter de Gruyter, 2009.

Bronisch, Alexander Pierre. *Reconquista und Heiliger Krieg: die Deutung des Krieges im christlichen Spanien von den Westgoten bis ins frühe 12. Jahrhundert.* Munster: Aschendorff, 1998.

Brundage, James A. "'Cruce signari': The Rite for Taking the Cross in England." *Traditio* 22 (1966): 289–310.

——. *Medieval Canon Law and the Crusader.* Madison: University of Wisconsin Press, 1969.

Buc, Philippe. *The Dangers of Ritual: Between Early Medieval Texts and Social Scientific Theory.* Princeton: Princeton University Press, 2001.

——. *Holy War, Martyrdom, and Terror. Christianity, Violence, and the West* Philadelphia: University of Pennsylvania Press, 2015.

——. "Some Thoughts on the Christian Theology of Violence, Medieval and Modern, from the Middle Ages to the French Revolution." *Rivista di Storia del Cristianesimo* 5 (2008): 9–28.

Buchthal, Hugo. *Miniature Painting in the Latin Kingdom of Jerusalem: With Liturgical and Palaeographical Chapters by Francis Wormald.* Oxford: Clarendon Press, 1957.

Bull, Marcus. *Knightly Piety and the Lay Response to the First Crusade: The Limousin and Gascony, c. 970–c. 1130.* Oxford: Clarendon Press, 1993.

——. "The Relationship between the *Gesta Francorum* and Peter Tudebode's *Historia de Hierosolymitano Itinere*: The evidence of a Hitherto Unexamined Manuscirpt (St. Catharine's College, Cambridge, 3)." *Crusades* 11 (2012): 1–17.

——. "Robert the Monk and his Source(s)." In *Writing the Early Crusades: Text, Transmission and Memory*, edited by Marcus Bull and Damien Kempf, 127–139. Woodbridge, Suffolk: Boydell Press, 2014.

Cabrere, Martín Alvira. *Las Navas de Tolosa 1212: Idea, liturgia y memoria de la batalla.* Madrid: Silex, 2012.

Cattaneo, Enrico. "La partecipazione dei laici alla liturgia." In *I Laici nella "Societas Christiana" dei secoli XI e XII. (Atti della terza Settimana internazionale di studio, Mendola, 21–27 Agosto 1965*, 386–427. Milan: Società editrice vita e pensiero, 1968.

Chydenius, Johan. *Medieval Institutions and the Old Testament.* Helsinki: Societas Scientiarum Fennica, 1965.

Cole, Penny. "'O God, the heathen have come into your inheritance' (Ps. 78.1): The Theme of Religious Pollution in Crusade Documents, 1095–1188." In *Crusaders and Muslims in Twelfth-century Syria*, edited by Maya Shatzmiller. *The Medieval Mediterranean*, 1:84–111. Leiden: Brill, 1993.

——. *The Preaching of the Crusades to the Holy Land, 1095–1270.* Cambridge, MA: Medieval Academy of America, 1991.

Constable, Giles. "The Cross of the Crusaders." In *Crusaders and Crusading the Twelfth Century*, 45–91. Farnham, UK: Ashgate, 2008.

——. *Crusaders and Crusading in the Twelfth Century.* Farnham, UK: Ashgate, 2008.

——. "The Historiography of the Crusades." In *The Crusades from the Perspective of Byzantium and the Muslim World*, edited by Angeliki Laiou and Roy Parviz Mottahedeh, 1–22. Washington DC: Dumbarton Oaks Research Library and Collection, 2001.

——. "The Ideal of the Imitation of Christ." In *Three Studies in Medieval Religious and Social Thought*, 143–248. Cambridge: Cambridge University Press, 1995.

———. "Jerusalem and the Sign of the Cross (with Particular Reference to the Cross of Pilgrimage and Crusading in the Twelfth Century)." In *Jerusalem: Its Sanctity and Centrality to Judaism, Christianity, and Islam,* edited by Lee I. Levine, 371–381, 1999.

———. "Opposition to Pilgrimage in the Middle Ages." *Studia Gratiana* 29 (1947): 123–146.

———. "Second Crusade as Seen by Contemporaries." *Traditio* (1953): 213–279.

Delaruelle, Etienne. *L'idée de croisade au moyen âge.* Turin: Bottega d'Erasmo, 1980.

Dondi, Cristina. *The Liturgy of the Canons Regular of the Holy Sepulchre of Jerusalem: A Study and Catalogue of the Manuscript Sources.* Bibliotheca Victorina XVI. Turnhout: Brepols, 2004.

Driscoll, Michael. "Penance in Transition: Popular Piety and Practice." In *Medieval Liturgy: A Book of Essays,* edited by L. Larson-Miller, 121–163. New York: Garland, 1997.

Ellard, Gerald. "Devotion to the Holy Cross and a Dislocated Mass-Text." *Theological Studies* 11 (1950): 333–355.

Erdmann, Carl. *The Origin of the Idea of Crusade.* Translated by Marshall W. Baldwin and Walter Goffart. Princeton: Princeton University Press, 1977.

Fassler, Margot. *The Virgin of Chartres: Making History through Liturgy and the Arts.* New Haven: Yale University Press, 2010.

Flori, Jean. "Chevalerie et liturgie." *Le Moyen Age* 84 (1978): 266–278, 409–442.

———. *L'Essor de la chevalerie, XIe–XIIe siècles.* Geneva: Droz, 1986.

———. *L'idéologie du glaive: préhistoire de la chevalerie.* Geneva: Librairie Droz, 1983.

———. *L'Islam et la fin des temps: L'interprétation prophétiques des invasions musulmanes dans la chrétienté médiévale.* Paris: Éditions du Seuil, 2007.

———. *La guerre sainte—la formation de l'idée de croisade dans l'Occident chrétien.* Paris: Aubier, 2001.

———. "Les origines de l'abouement chevaleresque: étude des remise d'armes et du vocabulaire qui les exprime." *Traditio* 35 (1979): 209–272.

———. *Prêcher la croisade: XIe–XIIIe siècle, Communication et propagande.* Paris: Perrin, 2012.

Fodor, Pál. "The View of the Turk in Hungary: The Apocalyptic Tradition and the Legend of the Red Apple in Ottoman-Hungarian Context." In *Les traditions apocalyptiques au tournant de la chute de Constantinople,* edited by Benjamin Lellouch, 99–131. Paris: Harmattan, 2000.

Folda, Jaroslav. *The art of the crusaders in the Holy Land, 1098–1187.* Cambridge. Cambridge University Press, 1995.

France, John. "The Text of the Account of the Capture of Jerusalem in the Ripoll Manuscript, Bibliothèque Nationale (Latin) 5132." *English Historical Review* 103 (1988): 640–657.

———. "Two Types of Visions on the First Crusade: Stephen of Valence and Peter Bartholomew." *Crusades* 5 (2006): 1–20.

———. "An Unknown Account of the Capture of Jerusalem." *English Historical Review* 87 (1972): 771–783.

Franz, Adolph. *Die kirchlichen Benediktionen im Mittelalter.* 2 vols. 1909; reprint. Bonn: Verlag nova & vetera, 2006.

Gabriele, Matthew. "From Prophecy to Apocalypse: The Verb Tenses of Jerusalem in Robert the Monk's Historia of the First Crusade." *Journal of Medieval History* 42 (2016): 304–316.

Gaposchkin, M. Cecilia. "The Echoes of Victory: Liturgical and Para-liturgical Commemorations of the Capture of Jerusalem in the West." *Journal of Medieval History* 40 (2014): 237–259.

——. "The Feast of the Liberation of Jerusalem in British Library Additional MS 8927 Reconsidered." *Mediaeval Studies* 77 (2015) 127–181.

——. "The Liturgical Memory of 15 July 1099: Between History, Memory, and Eschatology." In *Remembering Crusades and Crusaders*, edited by Megan Cassidy-Welch. London: Routledge (2017) 34–48.

——. "Origins and Development of the Pilgrimage and Cross Blessings in the Roman Pontificals of the Twelfth and Thirteenth Centuries (RP12 and RP13)." *Mediaeval Studies* 73 (2011): 261–286.

——. "From Pilgrimage to Crusade: The Liturgy of Departure." *Speculum* 88 (2013): 44–91.

——. "The Role of Jerusalem in Western Crusading Rites of Departure (1095–1300)." *Catholic Historical Review* 99 (2013): 1–28.

Garrisson, Francis. "A propos des pèlerins et de leur condition juridique." In *Études d'histoire du droit canonique dediées à Gabriel Le Bras*, 2:1165–1189. Paris: Sirey, 1965.

Gaudenzi, Augusto. *Ignoti Monachi Cisterciensis S. Mariae de Ferraria Chronica et Ryccardi de Sancto Germano Chronica priora / repperit in codice ms. Bononiensi atque nunc primum edidit Augustus Gaudenzi; adiectis ejusdem Ryccardi chronicis posterioribus ex editione Georgii Pertzii.* Naples: F. Giannini, 1888.

Geary, Patrick J. "Humiliation of Saints." In *Living with the Dead in the Middle Ages*, 95–115. Ithaca, NY: Cornell University Press, 1994.

Georgiou, Constantinos. "Propagating the Hospitallers' *Passagium*: Crusade Preaching and Liturgy in 1308–1309." In *Islands and Military Orders, c. 1291–c. 1798*, edited by Emanuel Buttigieg and Simon Phillips, 53–63. Farnham, UK: Ashgate, 2013.

Guard, Timothy. *Chivalry, Kingship, and Crusade: The English Experience in the Fourteenth Century.* Woodbridge, UK: Boydell Press, 2013.

Halphen, Louis, and Renée Poupardin, eds. *Chroniques des comtes d'Anjou et des seigneurs d'Amboise.* Paris: Auguste Picard, 1913.

Hamilton, Bernard. *The Latin Church in the Crusader States: The Secular Church.* London: Variorum, 1980.

Hamilton, Louis. *A Sacred City: Consecrating Churches and Reforming Society in Eleventh-Century Italy.* Manchester Medieval Studies. Manchester: Manchester University Press, 2010.

Hankins, James. "Renaissance Crusaders: Humanist Crusade Literature in the Age of Mehmed II." *Dumbarton Oaks Papers* 49 (1995): 111–207.

Harris, Jonathan. "Publicising the Crusade: English Bishops and the Jubilee Indulgence of 1455." *Journal of Ecclesiastical History* 50 (1999): 23–37.

Hefele, Karl Joseph von. *Histoire des conciles d'apres les documents originaux.* Translated by Henri Leclercq. Paris: Letouzey, 1907–1952.

Henriet, Patrick. "L'idéologie de guerre sainte dans le haut moyen âge hispanique." *Francia: Forschungen zur westeuropäischen Geschichte* 29 (2002): 171–220.

Housley, Norman. *The Avignon Papacy and the Crusades, 1305–1378.* Oxford: Clarendon Press, 1986.

——. *Crusading and the Ottoman Threat, 1453–1505.* Oxford: Oxford University Press, 2012.

——. *Documents on the Later Crusades, 1274–1580.* Houndmills, UK: MacMillan Press, 1996.

——. *Fighting for the Cross: Crusading to the Holy Land.* New Haven: Yale University Press, 2008.

———. *Religious Warfare in Europe, 1400–1536.* Oxford: Oxford University Press, 2002.

John, Simon. "The 'Feast of the Liberation of Jerusalem': Remembering and Reconstructing the First Crusade in the Holy City, 1099–1187." *Journal of Medieval History* 41 (2015): 409–431.

Jordan, William Chester. *Crusader Prologues: Preparing for War in the Gothic Age: A Lecture Presented at the Moreau Center for the Arts, Saint Mary's College, Notre Dame, Indiana, November 3, 2009.* Notre Dame, IN: Saint Mary's College, 2009.

———. "Perpetual Alleluia and Sacred Violence: An Afterword." *International History Review* 17 (1995): 744–752.

Kay, Richard. *Pontificalia: A Repertory of Latin Manuscript Pontificals and Benedictionals.* Lawrence: University of Kansas, 2007.

Keen, Maurice. *Chivalry.* New Haven: Yale University Press, 1984.

Kohler, Charles. "Un rituel et un bréviaire du Saint Sépulcre de Jérusalem (XIIe–XIIIe siècle)." *Revue de l'Orient Latin* 8 (1900–1901): 383–500.

———. "Un sermon commémoratif de la prise de Jérusalem par les Croisés attribué à Foucher de Chartres." *Revue de l'Orient Latin* 8 (1900–1901): 158–164.

Lapidge, Michael. *Anglo-Saxon Litanies of the Saints.* Henry Bradshaw Society 106. Woodbridge, UK: Boydell Press, 1991.

Lapina, Elizabeth. *Warfare and the Miraculous in the Chronicles of the First Crusade.* University Park: The Pennsylvania State University Press, 2015.

Leclercq, Jean. "La dévotion médiévale envers le crucifié." *La Maison Dieu* 75 (1963): 119–132.

LeMaître, Jean-Loup. "Le combat pour dieu et les croisades dans les notes de Bernard Itier, moine de St. Martial de Limoges (1163–115)." In *'Militia Christi' e crociata nei secoli XI-XIII; atti della undecima Settimana internazionale di studio: Mendola, 28 agosto–1 settembre 1989,* 729–751. Milan: Vita e pensiero, 1992.

Linder, Amnon. "'Like Purest Gold Resplendent' The Fiftieth Anniversary of the Liberation of Jerusalem." *Crusades* 8 (2009): 31–50.

———. "The Liturgy of the Liberation of Jerusalem." *Mediaeval Studies* 52 (1990): 110–131.

———. *Raising Arms: Liturgy in the Struggle to Liberate Jerusalem in the Late Middle Ages.* Cultural Encounters in Late Antiquity and the Middle Ages 2. Turnhout: Brepols, 2003.

Little, Lester. *Benedictine Maledictions: Liturgical Cursing in Romanesque France.* Ithaca, NY: Cornell University Press, 1993.

Lobrichon, Guy. *1099: Jérusalem conquise.* Paris: Éditions du Seuil, 1998.

Lowden, John. *The Making of the Bibles Moralisées.* University Park: Pennsylvania State University Press, 2000.

MacEvitt, Christopher. *The Crusades and the Christian World of the East: Rough Tolerance.* Philadelphia: University of Pennsylvania Press, 2008.

Maier, Christoph T. "Crisis, Liturgy, and the Crusade in the Twelfth and Thirteenth Centuries." *Journal of Ecclesiastical History* 48 (1997): 628–657.

———. *Crusade Propaganda and Ideology: Model Sermons for the Preaching of the Cross.* Cambridge: Cambridge University Press, 2000.

———. *Preaching the Crusades: Mendicant Friars and the Cross in the Thirteenth Century.* Cambridge Studies in Medieval Life and Thought, 4th ser., 28. Cambridge: Cambridge University Press, 1994.

Martimort, Aimé Georges, Pierre Marie Gy, Pierre Journel, and Irénée Henri Dalmais. *The Church at Prayer: An Introduction to the Liturgy.* 4 vols. Collegeville MN: Liturgical Press, 1985–1988.

Mayer, Hans Eberhard. *The Crusades.* Translated by John Gillingham. 2nd ed. Oxford: Clarendon Press, 1988.

McCormick, Michael. *Eternal Victory: Triumphal Rulership in Late Antiquity, Byzantium, and the Early Medieval West.* Cambridge UK: Cambridge University Press, 1986.

———. "Liturgie et guerre des Carolingiens à la première croisade." In *Militia Christi e crociata nei secoli XI–XII: atti della undecima settimana internazionale di studio: Mendola 28 agosto–1 settembre 1989,* 209–240. Milan, 1992.

McGinn, Bernard. "Iter Sancti Sepulchri: The Piety of the First Crusaders." In *Essays on Medieval Civilization,* edited by Bede Lackner and Kenneth Philp, 33–71. Austin: University of Texas Press, 1978.

Mégier, Elisabeth. "Christian Historical Fulfilments of Old Testament Prophecies in Latin Commentaries on the Book of Isaiah (ca. 400 to ca. 1150)." *Journal of Medieval Latin* 17 (2007): 87–100.

Meserve, Margaret. *Empires of Islam in Renaissance Historical Thought.* Cambridge, MA: Harvard University Press, 2008.

Meyer, Ann R. *Medieval Allegory and the Building of the New Jerusalem.* Woodbridge, UK: D. S. Brewe, 2003.

Mikamoto, Yoko. "The Influence of Medieval Prophecies on Views of the Turks, Islam and Apocalypticism in the Sixteenth Century." *Journal of Turkish Studies* 17 (1993): 125–145.

Møller Jensen, Janus. *Denmark and the Crusades, 1400–1650.* Leiden: Brill, 2007.

Murray, Alan V. "'Mighty Against the Enemies of Christ': The Relic of the True Cross in the Armies of the Kingdom of Jerusalem." In *The Crusades and Their Sources: Essays Presented to Bernard Hamilton,* edited by John France and William G. Zajac, 217–238. Farnham, UK: Ashgate, 1998.

Nathan, Gregory. "Rogation Ceremonies in Late Antique Gaul." *Classica et Medievalia* 21 (1998): 276–303.

The New Interpreter's Bible: General Articles and Introduction, Commentary, and Reflections for Each Book of the Bible, Including the Apocryphal Deuterocanonical Books. edited by Abingdon Press. Nashville: Abingdon Press, 1994.

O'Callaghan, Joseph F. *The Last Crusade in the West: Castile and the Conquest of Granada.* Philadelphia: University of Pennsylvania Press, 2014.

———. *Reconquest and Crusade in Medieval Spain.* Philadelphia: University of Pennsylvania Press, 2003.

Palacký, František. *Urkundliche Beiträge zur Geschichte des Hussitenkrieges vom Jahre 1419 an.* 2 vols. Prague: Friedrich Tempsky, 1873.

Pastor, Ludwig. *The History of the Popes: From the Close of the Middle Ages. Drawn from the Secret Archives of the Vatican and Other Original Sources.* Translated by Frederick Ignatius Antrobus. London: Kegan Paul, Trench, Trümer, 1894–1899.

Paul, Nicholas. *To Follow in Their Footsteps: The Crusades and Family Memory in the High Middle Ages.* Ithaca, NY: Cornell University Press, 2012.

Paul, Nicholas, and Suzanne Yeager, eds. *Remembering the Crusades: Myth, Image, and Identity.* Baltimore: The Johns Hopkins University Press, 2012.

Pennington, Kenneth. "The Rite for Taking the Cross in the Twelfth Century." *Traditio* 30 (1974): 429–435.

Pick, Lucy. "*Signaculum Caritatis et Fortitudinis:* Blessing the Crusader's Cross in France." *Revue bénédictine* 105 (1995): 381–416.

Powell, James M. *Anatomy of a Crusade: 1213–1221.* Philadelphia: University of Pennsylvania Press, 1986.

Powicke, F. M., and R. C. Cheney. *Councils and Synods, with Other Documents Relating to the English Church.* 2 in 4 vols. Oxford: Clarendon Press, 1964–1981.

Pringle, Denys. *The Churches of the Crusader Kingdom of Jerusalem: A Corpus.* 4 vols. Cambridge: Cambridge University Press, 2007.

Purkis, William J. *Crusading Spirituality in the Holy Land and Iberia, c. 1095–1187.* Woodbridge, UK: Boydell Press, 2008.

Renet, M. "Prieuré de Villers Saint-Sépulcre." *Mémoires de la Société académique d'archéologie, sciences et arts du département de l'Oise* 10 (1877): 485–567.

Riley-Smith, Jonathan. *The Crusades, Christianity, and Islam.* New York: Columbia University Press, 2008.

——. *The First Crusade and the Idea of Crusading.* Philadelphia: University of Pennsylvania Press, 1986.

——. *The First Crusaders: 1095–1131.* New York: Cambridge University Press, 1997.

Riley-Smith, Jonathan, and Louise Riley-Smith. *The Crusades, Idea and Reality: 1095–1274.* London: E. Arnold, 1981.

Rose, André. "Jérusalem dans l'année liturgique." *La Vie Spirituelle* 86 (1952): 389–403.

Rubenstein, Jay. *Armies of Heaven: The First Crusade and the Quest for Apocalypse.* New York: Basic Books, 2011.

——. "Crusade and Apocalypse: History and the Last Days." *Questiones Medii Aevi Novae* 21 (2016).

——. "Guibert of Nogent, Albert of Aachen and Fulcher of Chartres: Three Crusade Chronicles Intersect." In *Writing the Early Crusades: Text, Transmission, and Memory,* edited by Marcus Bull and Damien Kempf, 24–37. Woodbridge, UK: Boydell Press, 2014.

——. "Lambert of Saint-Omer and the Apocalyptic First Crusade." In *Remembering the Crusades: Myth, Image, and Identity,* edited by Nicholas Paul and Suzanne Yeager, 69–95. Baltimore: The Johns Hopkins University Press, 2012.

——. "Miracles and the Crusading Mind: Monastic Meditations on Jerusalem's Conquest." In *Prayer and Thought in Monastic Tradition: Essays in Honour of Benedicta Ward SLG,* edited by Santha Bhattacharji, Roman Williams, and Dominic Mattos, 197–210. New York: Bloombury, 2014.

——. "Putting History to Use: Three Crusade Chronicles in Context." *Viator* 35 (2004): 131–168.

——. "What is the Gesta Francorum, and who was Peter Tudebode?" *Revue Mabillion* 16 (2005): 179–204.

Salvadó, Sebastián. "The Liturgy of the Holy Sepulchre and the Templar Rite: Edition and Analysis of the Jerusalem Ordinal (Rome, Bib. Vat., Barb. Lat. 659) with a Comparative Study of the Acre Breviary (Paris, Bib. Nat., Ms. Latin 10478)." Stanford, CA: Stanford University, 2011.

Schechner, Richard. *Performance Theory.* Rev. and expanded ed. New York: Routledge, 1988.

Schein, Sylvia. *Gateway to the Heavenly City: Crusader Jerusalem and the Catholic West (1099–1187).* Farnham, UK: Ashgate, 2005.

Setton, Kenneth M. *Western Hostility to Islam and Prophecies of Turkish Doom.* Philadelphia: American Philosophical Society, 1992.

——. *The Papacy and the Levant.* 4 vols. Philadelphia: American Philosophical Society, 1976–1984.

Shagrir, Iris. "The *Visitatio Sepulchri* in the Latin Church of the Holy Sepulchre in Jerusalem." *Al-Masaq: Islam and the Medieval Mediterranean* 22 (2010): 57–77.

Smith, Katherine Allen. "Glossing the Holy War: Constructions of the First Crusade, c. 1095–1146." *Studies in Medieval and Renaissance History* 10 (2013): 8–15.

——. *War and the Making of Medieval Monastic Culture.* Studies in the History of Medieval Religion. Woodbridge, UK: Boydell Press, 2011.

Spreckelmeyer, Goswin. *Das Kreuzzugslied des lateinischen Mittelalters.* Mèunstersche Mittelalter-Schriften. Bd. 21. Munich: W. Fink, 1974.

Strickland, Debra Higgs. *Saracens, Demons, and Jews: Making Monsters in Medieval Art.* Princeton: Princeton University Press, 2003.

Swanson, Robert. "Prayer and Participation in Late Medieval England." In *Elite and Popular Religion*, edited by Kate Cooper and Jeremy Gregory, 130–139. Woodbridge, UK: Boydell Press, for the Ecclesiastical History Society, 2006.

——. "Preaching Crusade in Fifteenth-Century England: Instructions for the Administraiton of the Anti-Hussite Crusade of 1429 in the Diocese of Canterbury." *Crusades* 12 (2013): 175–196.

Szövérffy, Joseph. " 'Crux fidelis . . .' Prologomena to a History of the Holy Cross Hymns." *Traditio* 22 (1966): 1–41.

——. *Secular Latin Lyrics and Minor Poetic Forms of the Middle Ages: A Historical Survey and Literary Repertory from the Tenth to the Late Fifteenth Century.* Concord, NH: Classical Folia Editions, 1992.

Tellenbach, Gerd, and Karl Hampe. *Römischer und christlicher Reichsgedanke in der Liturgie des frühen Mittelalters.* Sitzungsberichte der Heidelberger Akademie der Wissenschaften. Philosophisch-historische Klasse. (bd. 25) jahrg. 1934/35, 1. abh. Heidelberg: C. Winter, 1934.

Throop, Susannah. *Crusading as an Act of Vengeance, 1095–1216.* Farnham, UK: Ashgate, 2011.

Tolan, John Victor. *Saracens: Islam in the Medieval European Imagination.* New York: Columbia University Press, 2002.

Trexler, Richard. *Public Life in Renaissance Florence.* Ithaca, NY: Cornell University Press, 1980.

Turner, Victor and Edith Turner. *Image and Pilgrimage in Christian Culture: Anthropological Persepctives.* Lectures of the History of Religions, ns 11. New York: Columbia University Press, 1978.

Twyman, Susan. "The *Roman Fraternitas* and Urban Processions at Rome in the Twelfth and Thirteenth Centuries." In *Pope, Church, and City: Essays in Honour of Brenda M. Boulton*, edited by Frances Andrews, Christoph Egger, and Constance Rosseau, 205–221. Leiden: Brill, 2004.

Tyerman, Christopher. *The Debate on the Crusades.* Manchester: Manchester University Press, 2011.

——. *God's War: A New History of the Crusades.* Cambridge, MA: Belknap Press of Harvard University Press, 2006.

van Tongeren, Louis. *Exaltation of the Cross: Toward the Origins of the feast of the Cross and the Meaning of the Cross in Early Medieval Liturgy.* Liturgia Condenda 11. Leuven: Peeters, 2000.

——. "Imagining the Cross on Good Friday: Rubric, Ritual and Relic in Early Medieval Roman, Gallican and Hispanic Liturgical Traditions." In *Envisioning Christ on the Cross, Ireland and the Early Medieval West*, edited by Juliet Mullins, Jenifer Ní Ghrádaigh, and Richard Hawtree, 34–51. Dublin: Four Courts Press, 2013.

Vogel, Cyrille. *Medieval Liturgy: An Introduction to the Sources.* Translated by William G. Storey, Niels Krogh Rasmussen O.P., and John K. Brooks-Leonard. NPM Studies in Church Music and Liturgy. Washington, DC: Pastoral Press, 1986.

——. *Le pécheur et la pénitence au Moyen Age.* Paris: Éditions du Cerf, 1969.

——. "Le pèlerinage pénitenciel." In *Pellegrinaggi e culto dei Santi in Europa fino alla 1 Crociata*, 37–94. Todi: Convegni del Centro di Studi sulla Spiritualità Medievale, 1963.

Waddell, Chrysogonus. *Twelfth-Century Statutes from the Cistercian General Chapter: Latin Text with English Notes and Commentary*. Studia et Documenta 12. Brecht, Belgium: Citeaux, Commentarii cistercienses, 2002.

Weber, Benjamin. *Lutter contre les Turcs: les formes nouvelles de la croisade pontificale au XVe siecle*. Collection de l'École française de Rome 472, 2013.

Wentzlaff-Eggbert, Friedrich Wilhelm. *Kreuzzugsdichung des Mittelalters: Studien zu ihrer geschichtlichen und dichterischen Wirklichkeit*. Berlin: De Gruyter, 1960.

Wilmart, André. "Prières médiévales pour l'adoration de la croix." *Ephemerides liturgicae* 46 (1932): 22–65.

Zoeller, Wolf. "The Regular Canons and the Liturgy of the Latin East." *Journal of Medieval History* 43 (2017), forthcoming.

Index

CPSIA information can be obtained
at www.ICGtesting.com
Printed in the USA
LVOW08*1414160217

524497LV00002B/4/P